Communications in Computer and Information Science   633

Commenced Publication in 2007
Founding and Former Series Editors:
Alfredo Cuzzocrea, Dominik Ślęzak, and Xiaokang Yang

Editorial Board

Simone Diniz Junqueira Barbosa
  Pontifical Catholic University of Rio de Janeiro (PUC-Rio),
  Rio de Janeiro, Brazil
Phoebe Chen
  La Trobe University, Melbourne, Australia
Xiaoyong Du
  Renmin University of China, Beijing, China
Joaquim Filipe
  Polytechnic Institute of Setúbal, Setúbal, Portugal
Orhun Kara
  TÜBİTAK BİLGEM and Middle East Technical University, Ankara, Turkey
Igor Kotenko
  St. Petersburg Institute for Informatics and Automation of the Russian
  Academy of Sciences, St. Petersburg, Russia
Ting Liu
  Harbin Institute of Technology (HIT), Harbin, China
Krishna M. Sivalingam
  Indian Institute of Technology Madras, Chennai, India
Takashi Washio
  Osaka University, Osaka, Japan

More information about this series at http://www.springer.com/series/7899

Christian Kreiner · Rory V. O'Connor
Alexander Poth · Richard Messnarz (Eds.)

Systems, Software and Services Process Improvement

23rd European Conference, EuroSPI 2016
Graz, Austria, September 14–16, 2016
Proceedings

Editors
Christian Kreiner
Graz University of Technology
Graz
Austria

Alexander Poth
Volkswagen AG
Wolfsburg
Germany

Rory V. O'Connor
Dublin City University
Dublin 9
Ireland

Richard Messnarz
I.S.C.N. GesmbH
Graz
Austria

ISSN 1865-0929   ISSN 1865-0937 (electronic)
Communications in Computer and Information Science
ISBN 978-3-319-44816-9   ISBN 978-3-319-44817-6 (eBook)
DOI 10.1007/978-3-319-44817-6

Library of Congress Control Number: 2016948222

© Springer International Publishing Switzerland 2016
This work is subject to copyright. All rights are reserved by the Publisher, whether the whole or part of the material is concerned, specifically the rights of translation, reprinting, reuse of illustrations, recitation, broadcasting, reproduction on microfilms or in any other physical way, and transmission or information storage and retrieval, electronic adaptation, computer software, or by similar or dissimilar methodology now known or hereafter developed.
The use of general descriptive names, registered names, trademarks, service marks, etc. in this publication does not imply, even in the absence of a specific statement, that such names are exempt from the relevant protective laws and regulations and therefore free for general use.
The publisher, the authors and the editors are safe to assume that the advice and information in this book are believed to be true and accurate at the date of publication. Neither the publisher nor the authors or the editors give a warranty, express or implied, with respect to the material contained herein or for any errors or omissions that may have been made.

Printed on acid-free paper

This Springer imprint is published by Springer Nature
The registered company is Springer International Publishing AG Switzerland

Preface

This book comprises the proceedings of the 23rd EuroSPI conference, held during September 14–16, in Graz, Austria.

Since EuroSPI 2010, we have extended the scope of the conference from software process improvement to systems, software, and service-based process improvement. EMIRAcle is the institution for research in manufacturing and innovation, which emerged as a result of the largest network of excellence for innovation in manufacturing in Europe. EMIRAcle key representatives joined the EuroSPI community, and papers as well as case studies for process improvement on systems and products will be included in future.

Since 2008, EuroSPI partners packaged SPI knowledge in job role training and established a European certification association (www.ecqa.org) to transport this knowledge Europe-wide using standardized certification and exam processes.

Conferences were held in Dublin (Ireland) in 1994, in Vienna (Austria) in 1995, in Budapest (Hungary) in 1997, in Gothenburg (Sweden) in 1998, in Pori (Finland) in 1999, in Copenhagen (Denmark) in 2000, in Limerick (Ireland) in 2001, in Nuremberg (Germany) in 2002, in Graz (Austria) in 2003, in Trondheim (Norway) in 2004, in Budapest (Hungary) in 2005, in Joensuu (Finland) in 2006, in Potsdam (Germany) in 2007, in Dublin (Ireland) in 2008, in Alcala (Spain) in 2009, in Grenoble (France) in 2010, in Roskilde (Denmark) in 2011, in Vienna (Austria) in 2012, in Dundalk (Ireland) in 2013, in Luxembourg in 2014, and in Ankara (Turkey) 2015.

EuroSPI is an initiative with the following major action lines http://www.eurospi.net:

- Establishing an annual EuroSPI conference supported by software process improvement networks from different EU countries
- Establishing an Internet-based knowledge library, newsletters, and a set of proceedings and recommended books
- Establishing an effective team of national representatives (from each EU- country) growing step by step into more countries of Europe
- Establishing a European Qualification Framework for a pool of professions related with SPI and management. This is supported by European certificates and examination systems.

EuroSPI has established a newsletter series (newsletter.eurospi.net), the SPI Manifesto (SPI = Systems, Software and Services Process Improvement), an experience library (library.eurospi.net) that is continuously extended over the years and is made available to all attendees, and a Europe-wide certification for qualifications in the SPI area (www.ecqa.org, European Certification and Qualification Association).

A typical characterization of EuroSPI is reflected in a statement made by a company: "… the biggest value of EuroSPI lies in its function as a European knowledge and experience exchange mechanism for SPI and innovation."

Since its beginning in 1994 in Dublin, the EuroSPI initiative has outlined that there is not a single silver bullet with which to solve SPI issues, but that you need to understand a combination of different SPI methods and approaches to achieve concrete benefits. Therefore, each proceedings volume covers a variety of different topics, and at the conference we discuss potential synergies and the combined use of such methods and approaches. These proceedings contain selected research papers under six headings:

- Section I: SPI and the ISO/IEC 29110 Standard
- Section II: Communication and Team Issues in SPI
- Section III: SPI and Assessment
- Section IV: SPI in Secure and Safety Critical Environments
- Section V: SPI Initiatives
- Section VI: Selected Key Notes and Workshop Papers

Section I presents three papers related to the new standard ISO/IEC 29110 for Very Small Entities. In the first paper Sanchez-Gordón et al. present educational issues with respect to ISO/IEC 29110. The second and third papers in this series present useful case studies on implementing ISO/IEC 29110 in industrial settings.

Section II presents three papers under the umbrella topic of "Communication and Team Issues in SPI". In the first paper Clarke et al. examine the linguistic and terminological challenges in the industry, whilst the second paper examines the specific case of natural language in requirements, and finally the third paper, by Munoz et al., models highly effective teams for software development.

Section III explores the theme of "SPI and Assessment", with Cortina et al. examining the area of IT service management and in particular ISO/IEC 15504-8, TIPA, and ITIL. In the second paper in this series, Biró et al. examine challenges of automating traceability assessment. In the final paper Picard et al. explore TIPA IT service management issues.

Section IV presents three papers dealing with associated issues surrounding the topic of Secure and Safety Critical Environments. In the first paper Rauter et al. examine processes for secure embedded control devices, whilst in paper 2 Nevalainen et al. explore Situational Factors in Safety Critical Software Development. In the final paper of this set, Macher et al. explore cyber-security challenges in an automotive context.

Section V discusses issues surrounding "SPI Initiatives" with the first paper discussing risk assessment in SPI. In the second paper Stolfa et al. present the area of automotive quality and education, whilst in the final paper Pekki studies critical success factors in SPI.

Section VI presents selected keynotes from EuroSPI workshops concerning the future of SPI. From 2010 onwards EuroSPI has invited recognized key researchers to present papers on the future directions of SPI. These key messages are discussed in interactive workshops and help to create SPI communities based on new topics. The first set of papers relates to the GamifySPI workshop and explores Gamification and Persuasive Games for Software Process Improvement, Information Technology, and Innovation Management.

The second collection of papers relates to the topic of Functional Safety and addresses a broad range of issues related to cyber security and functional safety. Rodic et al. describe the application of the AQUA (Automotive Quality Knowledge Alliance) at master level at different universities and explain the application of the quality principles based on an in-wheel electric motor design. Riel et al. describe the Automotive Engineer Project where young researchers get introduced to modern quality strategies in Automotive which will empower the motivation of young engineers to join this leading industry in Europe. Larrucea et al. discuss how the Goal Structured Notation (GSN) can be used to build a safety case based on the example of a hall sensor which is a most common sensor principle nowadays used in cars. In the final paper Mac Airchinnigh analyses the available information about functional safety and proposes to integrate the experiences with formal methods in Europe with this growing set of functional safety standards.

The final collection of papers addresses innovation strategies in Europe which will motivate researchers, engineers, and managers to build an environment which empowers creativity and innovation in Europe. Innovation is a core ability empowering new concepts for implementing SPI. Messnarz et al. provide an overview of different European innovation initiatives and create a vision of a European network for innovation integrating the different approaches into a European innovation knowledge cluster. Reiner et al. illustrate how innovation strategies can be supported at universities to empower spin offs of young entrepreneurs. Munoz et al. describe in their paper how improvement strategies depend on the organization's context and how to deal with that, and in the final paper Siakas et al. describe the concept of open innovation and customer integration and how this influences the success of and value creation of an organization.

September 2016

Christian Kreiner
Rory V. O'Connor
Alexander Poth
Richard Messnarz

Recommended Further Reading

In [1] the proceedings of three EuroSPI conferences were integrated into one book, which was edited by 30 experts in Europe. The proceedings of EuroSPI 2005 to 2015 inclusive have been published by Springer in [2–11], respectively.

References

1. Messnarz, R., Tully, C. (eds.): Better Software Practice for Business Benefit – Principles and Experience, 409 pages. IEEE Computer Society Press, Los Alamitos (1999)
2. Richardson, I., Abrahamsson, P., Messnarz, R. (eds.): Software Process Improvement. LNCS, vol. 3792, p. 213. Springer, Heidelberg (2005)
3. Richardson, I., Runeson, P., Messnarz, R. (eds.): Software Process Improvement. LNCS, vol. 4257, pp. 11–13. Springer, Heidelberg (2006)
4. Abrahamsson, P., Baddoo, N., Margaria, T., Messnarz, R. (eds.): Software Process Improvement. LNCS, vol. 4764, pp. 1–6. Springer, Heidelberg (2007)
5. O'Connor, R.V., Baddoo, N., Smolander, K., Messnarz, R. (eds): Software Process Improvement. CCIS, vol. 16, Springer, Heidelberg (2008).
6. O'Connor, R.V., Baddoo, N., Gallego C., Rejas Muslera R., Smolander, K., Messnarz, R. (eds): Software Process Improvement. CCIS, vol. 42, Springer, Heidelberg (2009).
7. Riel A., O'Connor, R.V. Tichkiewitch S., Messnarz, R. (eds): Software, System, and Service Process Improvement. CCIS, vol. 99, Springer, Heidelberg (2010).
8. O'Connor, R., Pries-Heje, J. and Messnarz R., Systems, Software and Services Process Improvement, CCIS Vol. 172, Springer-Verlag, (2011).
9. Winkler, D., O'Connor, R.V. and Messnarz R. (Eds), Systems, Software and Services Process Improvement, CCIS 301, Springer-Verlag, (2012).
10. McCaffery, F., O'Connor, R.V. and Messnarz R. (Eds), Systems, Software and Services Process Improvement, CCIS 364, Springer-Verlag, (2013).
11. Barafort, B., O'Connor, R.V. and Messnarz R. (Eds), Systems, Software and Services Process Improvement, CCIS 425, Springer-Verlag, (2014).
12. O'Connor, R.V. Akkaya, M., Kemaneci K., Yilmaz, M., Poth, A. and Messnarz R. (Eds), Systems, Software and Services Process Improvement, CCIS 543, Springer-Verlag, (2015).

Organization

General Chair

Richard Messnarz — ISCN GesmbH, Graz, Austria

Scientific Co-chairs

Rory V. O'Connor — Dublin City University, Ireland
Christian Kreiner — Graz University of Technology, Austria

Organization Chair

Adrienne Clarke — ISCN Ltd, Ireland

Local Organization Chair

Christian Kreiner — Graz University of Technology, Austria

GamifySPI Workshop Chair

Murat Yilmaz — Cankaya University, Turkey

Board Members

EuroSPI Board Members represent centers or networks of SPI excellence having extensive experience with SPI. The board members collaborate with different European SPINS (Software Process Improvement Networks). The following organizations have been members of the conference board for a significant period:

- ASQ, http://www.asq.org
- ASQF, http://www.asqf.de
- Whitebox, http://www.whitebox.dk
- ISCN, http://www.iscn.com
- SINTEF, http://www.sintef.no
- FiSMA, http://www.fisma.fi

EuroSPI Scientific Program Committee

EuroSPI established an international committee of selected well-known experts in SPI who are willing to be mentioned in the program and to review a set of papers each year. The list below represents the Research Program Committee members. EuroSPI also has a separate Industrial Program Committee responsible for the industry/experience contributions.

Miklós Biró	Software Competence Center Hagenberg GmbH, Austria
Luigi Buglione	Ingegneria Informatica S.p.A., Italy
Jose Antonio Calvo-Manzano	Universidad Politécnica de Madrid, Spain
Paul M. Clarke	Dublin City University, Ireland
Darren Dalcher	University of Hertfordshire, UK
Masud Fazal-Baqaie	S&N CQM, Germany
Elli Georgiadou	Middlesex University, UK
Christian Kreiner	Graz University of Technology, Austria
Dieter Landes	Fachhochschule Coburg, Germany
Micheal Mac An Airchinnigh	ISCN, Ireland
Georg Macher	AVL, Austria
Timo Mäkinen	Tampere University of Technology, Finland
Antonia Mas Pichacos	Universitat de les Illes Balears, Spain
Miranda Mejia	CIMAT-Zacatecas, Mexico
Antoni Mesquida	Universitat de les Illes Balears, Spain
Mirna Muñoz	CIMAT-Zacatecas, Mexico
Rory V. O'Connor	Dublin City University, Ireland
Markku Oivo	University of Oulu, Finland
Egemen Özalp	Tubitak Uzay, Turkey
Efi Papatheocharous	SICS Swedish ICT AB, Sweden
Keith Phalp	Bournemouth University, UK
Tomas San Feliu	Universidad Politécnica de Madrid, Spain
Jakub Stolfa	Technical University of Ostrava, Czech Republic
Svatopluk Stolfa	Technical University of Ostrava, Czech Republic
Timo Varko	Tampere University of Technology, Finland
Paula Ventura Martins	University of Algarve, Portugal
Murat Yilmaz	Cankaya University, Turkey

Acknowledgements

Some contributions published in this book have been funded with support from the European Commission. European projects (supporting ECQA and EuroSPI) contributed to this Springer book including AQU (Automotive Quality Universe), and AE (Automotive Engineer).

In this case the publications reflect the views only of the author(s), and the Commission cannot be held responsible for any use, which may be made of the information contained therein.

Contents

SPI and the ISO/IEC 29110 Standard

Bridging the Gap Between SPI and SMEs in Educational Settings:
A Learning Tool Supporting ISO/IEC 29110   3
   Mary-Luz Sanchez-Gordón, Rory V. O'Connor,
   Ricardo Colomo-Palacios, and Eduardo Herranz

Implementing the New ISO/IEC 29110 Systems Engineering Process
Standard in a Small Public Transportation Company   15
   Claude Y. Laporte, Nicolas Tremblay, Jamil Menaceur,
   and Denis Poliquin

A Multi-case Study Analysis of Software Process Improvement in Very
Small Companies Using ISO/IEC 29110   30
   Claude Y. Laporte and Rory V. O'Connor

Communication and Team Issues in SPI

Refactoring Software Development Process Terminology Through the Use
of Ontology   47
   Paul M. Clarke, Antoni Lluís Mesquida Calafat, Damjan Ekert,
   J.J. Ekstrom, Tatjana Gornostaja, Milos Jovanovic, Jørn Johansen,
   Antonia Mas, Richard Messnarz, Blanca Nájera Villar,
   Alexander O'Connor, Rory V. O'Connor, Michael Reiner,
   Gabriele Sauberer, Klaus-Dirk Schmitz, and Murat Yilmaz

Cardion.spec: An Approach to Improve the Requirements Specification
Written in the Natural Language Through the Formal Method   58
   Masao Ito

Establishing Effective Software Development Teams: An Exploratory
Model   70
   Mirna Muñoz, Jezreel Mejia, Adriana Peña, and Nora Rangel

SPI and Assessment

Using a Process Assessment Model to Prepare for an ISO/IEC 20000-1
Certification: ISO/IEC 15504-8 or TIPA for ITIL?   83
   Stéphane Cortina, Béatrix Barafort, Michel Picard, and Alain Renault

Towards Automated Traceability Assessment through Augmented
Lifecycle Space 94
  Miklós Biró, József Klespitz, Johannes Gmeiner, Christa Illibauer,
  and Levente Kovács

Measuring Readiness for Compliance: A Gap Analysis Tool to Complete
the TIPA Process Assessment Framework 106
  Michel Picard, Alain Renault, Béatrix Barafort, and Stéphane Cortina

SPI in Secure and Safety Critical Environments

Development and Production Processes for Secure Embedded Control
Devices 119
  Tobias Rauter, Andrea Höller, Johannes Iber, and Christian Kreiner

Situational Factors in Safety Critical Software Development 132
  Risto Nevalainen, Paul Clarke, Fergal McCaffery, Rory V. O'Connor,
  and Timo Varkoi

Supporting Cyber-Security Based on Hardware-Software Interface
Definition... 148
  Georg Macher, Harald Sporer, Eugen Brenner, and Christian Kreiner

SPI Initiatives

Collective Intelligence-Based Quality Assurance: Combining Inspection
and Risk Assessment to Support Process Improvement
in Multi-Disciplinary Engineering 163
  Dietmar Winkler, Juergen Musil, Angelika Musil, and Stefan Biffl

Automotive Quality Universities - AQUA Alliance Extension to Higher
Education... 176
  Jakub Stolfa, Svatopluk Stolfa, Andreas Riel, Serge Tichkiewitch,
  Christian Kreiner, Richard Messnarz, Miran Rodic, and Monika Gaisch

How the Company Manages Critical Success Factors in Software Process
Improvement Initiatives: Pilot Case-Study in Finnish Software Company 188
  Jaana Pekki

Selected Key Notes and Workshop Papers

GamifySPI

Software Developer's Journey: A Story-Driven Approach to Support
Software Practitioners 203
  Murat Yilmaz, Berke Atasoy, Rory V. O'Connor, Jean-Bernard Martens,
  and Paul Clarke

Gamification Proposal for Defect Tracking in Software Development
Process 212
    *Gloria Piedad Gasca-Hurtado, María Clara Gómez-Alvarez,
    Mirna Muñoz, and Jezreel Mejía*

Process Improving by Playing: Implementing Best Practices through
Business Games 225
    Antoni-Lluís Mesquida, Milos Jovanovic, and Antònia Mas

Gamification and Human Factors in Quality Management Systems:
Mapping from Octalysis Framework to ISO 10018 234
    *Mary-Luz Sanchez-Gordón, Ricardo Colomo-Palacios,
    and Eduardo Herranz*

Gamifying the Onboarding Process for Novice Software Practitioners 242
    Mehmet Kosa and Murat Yilmaz

Functional Safety

Functional Safety Considerations for an In-wheel Electric Motor
for Education 251
    *Miran Rodic, Andreas Riel, Richard Messnarz, Jakub Stolfa,
    and Svatopluk Stolfa*

A Compact Introduction to Automotive Engineering Knowledge 259
    *Andreas Riel, Monique Kollenhof, Sebastiaan Boersma, Ron Gommans,
    Damjan Ekert, and Richard Messnarz*

A GSN Approach to SEooC for an Automotive Hall Sensor 269
    Xabier Larrucea, Silvana Mergen, and Alastair Walker

Formal Methods and Functional Safety 281
    Micheal Mac an Airchinnigh

Supporting Innovation and Improvement

Forming a European Innovation Cluster as a Think Tank and Knowledge
Pool 293
    *Richard Messnarz, Andreas Riel, Gabriele Sauberer,
    and Michael Reiner*

Innovative Marketing in Low-Tech Micro Companies - Lessons Learned
from Study Projects... 302
    Michael Reiner, Christian Reimann, and Elena Vitkauskaite

Method to Establish Strategies for Implementing Process Improvement
According to the Organization's Context 312
  *Mirna Muñoz, Jezreel Mejia, Gloria P. Gasca Hurtado,
  Maria C. Gómez-Álvarez, and Brenda Durón*

User Orientation through Open Innovation and Customer Integration 325
  Dimitrios Siakas and Kerstin Siakas

Author Index 343

SPI and the ISO/IEC 29110 Standard

Bridging the Gap Between SPI and SMEs in Educational Settings: A Learning Tool Supporting ISO/IEC 29110

Mary-Luz Sanchez-Gordón[1(✉)], Rory V. O'Connor[2],
Ricardo Colomo-Palacios[3], and Eduardo Herranz[1]

[1] Computer Science Department, Universidad Carlos III de Madrid,
Av. Universidad 30, Leganés, 28911 Madrid, Spain
mary_sanchezg@hotmail.com, eduardo.herranz@uc3m.es
[2] School of Computing, Dublin City University, Glasnevin, Dublin 9, Ireland
rory.oconnor@dcu.ie
[3] Faculty of Computer Sciences, Østfold University College,
1783 Halden, Norway
ricardo.colomo-palacios@hiof.no

Abstract. The software development industry is dominated by a myriad of smaller organizations world-wide, including very small entities (VSEs), which have up to 25 people. Managing software process is a big challenge for practitioners. In 2011, due to the VSEs' increasing importance, a set of ISO/IEC 29110 standards and guides were released. Although other initiatives are devoted to small entities, ISO/IEC 29110 is becoming the widely adopted standard. But it is an emerging standard and practitioners need to be actively engaged in their learning. In this sense, serious games offer the potential to entertain and educate. This study shows empirical evidence to support the overall applicability of the game proposed as learning tool. Moreover, the results indicate that the learning tool creates a positive experience, and therefore could be used as a strategy to promote the standard.

Keywords: VSE · ISO/IEC 29110 · Very small entity · Project management · Game-based learning · Game-based training

1 Introduction

Typically project teams tend to be small, even in large companies. In 2011, driven by the increasing importance of *very small entities*' (VSEs) and the growing need for systems and software life cycle profiles and guidelines, the International Organization for Standardization (ISO) and the International Electro technical Commission jointly published a set of standards and guides ISO/IEC 29110 [1], which are targeted at meeting the specific needs of *"an enterprise, organization, department or project having up to 25 people"* [2, 3]. The software industry recognizes the value of VSEs in contributing valuable products and services [4, 5], where certain VSEs also provide software components that are being assembled in larger software companies in order to generate critical and intensive software configurations [6]. In fact, there are a myriad of small software companies. According [4], the OECD (Organization for Economic Co-operation and Development) SME and Entrepreneurship Outlook report (2005) *"SMEs constitute the dominant form of business organization in all countries worldwide, accounting for over 95 % and up to 99 % of the business population depending on country"*.

Previous experiences in software process improvement (SPI) in graduate software engineering programs [7] reveled that a large percentage of students attending the SPI course were working in small organizations. The emphasis on the use of the CMMI framework in that course was gradually reduced to switch to the ISO/IEC 29110. Besides, it may not be appropriate at the undergraduate level to dedicate significant time of a related course and provide details about process models such as CMMI [8]. Likewise, the acceptance level and priority of any type or model of software quality or lifecycle standard in VSEs is very low [9] but the level of awareness of standards and potential benefits are high. Software is a complex product, difficult to develop [10]. Accordingly to the Standish Group *"a low percentage of successful projects delivering software on time, on budget, and with required features and functions"*. VSEs deal with this fact every day therefore the implementation of controls and structures to properly manage their software development activities is necessary and challenging [11]. The knowledge and skills required to do that imply training. For instance, software engineering courses at the university usually consist of lectures along with a small software project [12], but software process is often treated as an additional module to the core curriculum. Trainings in an industry environment are, on the other hand, organized in a workshop style with theoretical and practical parts interwoven [13]. Although ISO/IEC 29110 is well-structured and described in great details in the guides, it is a technical text on complex subject. It is easier than the ISO/IEC 12207 but practitioners could find software development difficult to understand and deploy it [14]. Thus international software standards are considered important in improving the software process but teaching them remains a challenging issue [15, 16]. Therefore new tools to facilitate teaching and learning process can be useful. There is also a growing interest in games for purposes beyond entertainment [15, 17, 18] and a consensus that serious games have a significant potential as a tool for instruction [19]. Thus the goal of our study is to investigate the potential of a learning tool for the Project Management (PM) process of ISO/IEC 29110.

The remainder of this paper is structured as follows: Sect. 2 presents the background of this study. Section 3 outlines the learning tool. In Sect. 4 authors report on the results of the pilot study. Section 5 summarizes a conclusion as well as outlines future work plans.

2 Background

This section summarizes the ISO/IEC 29110 standard (Sect. 2.1) and related work on games in software engineering (Sect. 2.2).

2.1 ISO/IEC 29110

The ISO/IEC 29110 Software engineering — Lifecycle profiles for Very Small Entities standard is aimed to approach Software Engineering and Project Management good practices to VSEs. It is aimed at addressing the specific needs of VSEs [2, 20, 21] and to tackle the issues of low standards adoption by small companies [9, 22–24]. Although there is still much work to be completed, there is an increasing interest on the standard [25]. There are profile Groups which are a collection of profiles related either by composition of processes (i.e. activities, tasks), by capability level, or both. The "Generic" profile group has been defined [3] as applicable to a vast majority of VSEs that do not develop critical software and have typical situational factors. To date the Basic Profile [3] and Entry Profile [26] has been published. It is worth noting that the Entry profile is contained in the Basic Profile. The guides are based on subsets of appropriate standards elements, referred to as VSE Profiles (ISO/IEC 12207, ISO/IEC 15289, ISO/IEC 15504, ISO 9001) [4, 6]. The so-called guides are gathered into the ISO/IEC 29110 Software engineering — Lifecycle profiles for Very Small Entities standard, which describes processes for project management and software implementation [27] and pretends to facilitate access to, and utilization of, ISO software engineering standards in VSEs [5].

Additionally, the guides are available in several languages: English, French, Portuguese and Spanish. Moreover, there is a series of Deployment Packages (DPs) and Implementation Guides which are not prescriptive but outline guidelines and explain in detail the processes defined in the ISO/IEC 29110 profiles in order to assist with its deployment and to provide guidance on its actual implementation in VSEs [28]. DPs are freely available from http://29110.org.

2.2 Games in Software Engineering

Given that there are some concepts related to the term "game", this section include the following discussion which is based on [29, 30]. But it is not comprehensive and is only intended to avoid misconceptions. *Games* are played just for entertainment. They include game thinking, game elements and gameplay. Examples are poker, solitaire and monopoly (see Fig. 1).

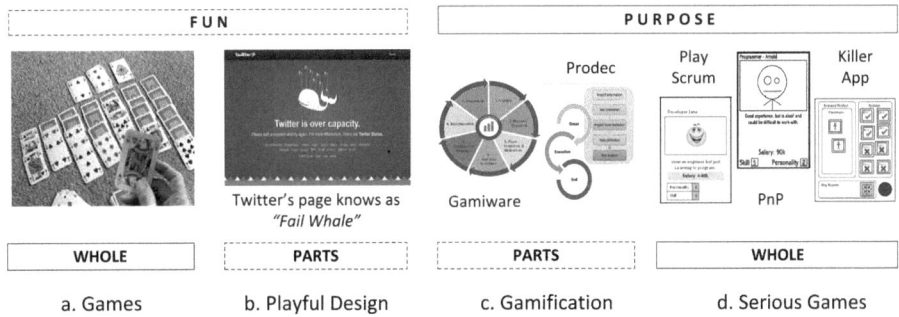

Fig. 1. Examples of games, playful design, gamification and serious game adapted from [29]

Playful design or *Gameful design* is using game-based aesthetics or limited usability based on game elements in non-game contexts with the purpose of drawing the user's attention. These elements are used to amuse users and cause an emotional response [29]. One successful example is the fail whale from Twitter. Rather than a boring old error when twitter is over capacity, they have the Fail Whale (Fig. 1-b).

Gamification is the use of game design elements in non-game contexts [30] (Fig. 1-c). In recent years, there is a growing interest in gamification [29, 31] as well as its applications and implications in the field of Education since it provides an alternative to engage and motivate students during the process of learning [29]. It proved to have potential to support education [32], although further research is needed. Moreover, there are few gamification approaches to improve the software development process [33, 34], and few experiences in education, for example project gamification of an introductory computer science class [35] and gamified Software Engineering courses [36, 37].

Serious games are games designed for non-recreational environments and for educational purposes. The term "serious" is employed because these games can focus on areas as diverse as economics, education, health, industry, military, engineering, and politics [29]. The main goal of this sort of training-environment is to convey information to the user. Seen from the perspective of the designer, serious games have all the elements of a real game (Fig. 1-d) — i.e. gameplay. Therefore, they are complete games whereas gamification is a way of designing products and services with the intention of a system that includes elements from games, not a full 'game proper' [30]. There are only several games related to software PM which have been used in educational area as a supplement to classroom-based teaching with some success [15, 38]. They fall into two broad groups: work based on computer games, and work based on non-computerized games. Authors focus on the last one because it is simple and fun to play, and also include relatively low development overhead, tactile immediacy, and direct face-to-face player interaction [39] — e.g. Problems and Programmers (PnP), SimulES, Killer App and PlayScrum. Moreover, the international initiative Semat (Software Engineering Methods and Theory) is aiming to collect the core elements essential to the development of software projects. It has games [40] such as SemCards, MetricC, Semat board-crossing and Semat game that are being used as a strategy to promote it. In relation to specialized decks of cards are not uncommon in the professional field [41–43]. They are used in poker planning, delegation poker, moving motivators, and so on. Moreover, some games have also been designed to teach the practices, values and concepts behind XP and object-oriented programming, one of the best known is XP War game.

Finally, as far as authors know, there are not any serious games in the state of the art for the ISO/IEC 29110 standard.

3 Learning Tool for Project Management Process of ISO/IEC 29110

This section describes different aspects of the learning tool (see our previous work [44] for details about its design). Regarding with the key requirement of the learning tool, our approach should be fast, painless and cost-effective because of VSEs having limited resources. That means it should not need software and hardware resources. Therefore, the learning tool for project management of ISO/IEC 29110 could be used by a wide audience of software engineers at different stage of their career – undergraduates, graduates or education for industry professionals - in order to promote and provoke awareness, and ultimately, understanding of the standard. Moreover, the game should be quick to play, and easy to learn and use in order to create a positive attitude towards their adoption and eventually promote the introduction of the standard beyond the academic and research areas. Thus, the idea behind non-computerized games was very attractive for us because they include relatively low development overhead, tactile immediacy, and direct face-to-face player interaction as they are simple and fun to play. If the game were complex, it would lose most of its effectiveness as a learning tool. And enjoyable is certainly important due to the players would want to play the game. Consequently, authors adopted a familiar and popular game concept: Card Game and authors created a specialized deck of cards.

In order to facilitate comprehension, learning, memory, communication and inference of the PM process, authors define a virtual board and color code based on the four activities in the PM process. Figure 2 shows as each activity is a suit: *Project Planning* (blue), *Project Plan Execution* (green), *Project Assessment and Control* (yellow), and *Project Closure* (red). The white color represents the input and the output of the PM process – «*Statement of Work*» and «*Software Configuration*». Each suit has two types of cards: an activity card and a state card. The first one depicts the work products and has a list of tasks related. The second one depicts the possible states of each work products.

The game can be played between 2 to 5 players, new or relatively new to project management process. They are the project team members and their mission is to complete the project management during which each player must develop a set of tasks. Thus, the relationships between the game's rules and best practices make the last one more intuitive and easy to remember. The Fig. 3 depicts the elements of the game: activity and state cards (mentioned before) and card reference guide.

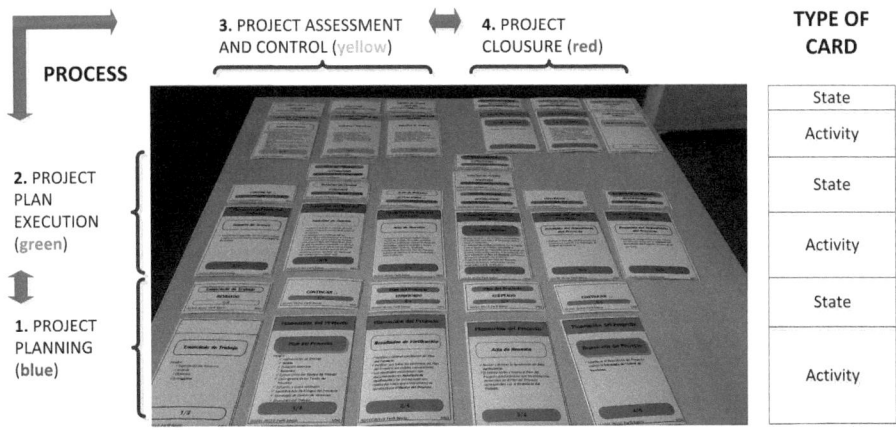

Fig. 2. An example of Virtual Board

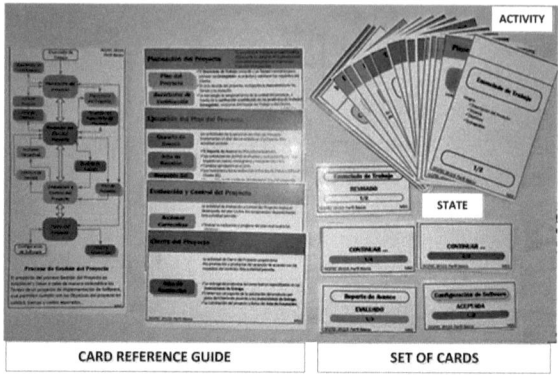

Fig. 3. Elements of the game

In this study, the proposed gameplay is a variation of our previous study [44]. The time activity was restricted up to 30 min, including a brief introduction of the game and the standard. Instead of the single elimination tournament, there are two leaderboards: one for teams and one for team members. Before starting the game, the participants are grouped in teams — every team has up to 5 members. Then, the cards are distributed among the team members. The first sub-mission starts with the player who holds the «*Statement of Work*» activity card. The player reads it and asks other players for the tasks, so they raise their hands to answer and he/she will add one point for each correct answer. The player who holds the activity card decides if the answer is valid and places it faces up on the table to make a first pile of the virtual board (see Fig. 2). After that, the state card should be played by the player who holds it. Play continues with the blue suit until the highest card of it is reached. Next, the second and third mission must be carried out in the same way. The fourth mission starts with the player who holds the «*Software Configuration*» card. Finally, the red suit is played. The game is over when players run out of cards or time is up. The winner of this game is the team that had more point.

The biggest challenge was the integration of learning content with core mechanic of the game in order to gain balance of fun and learning. The idea is to provide a participant engagement loop (i.e. the flow [45]), which helps player to learn and participate more frequently and ultimately create planned participant behavior. Therefore, the players interact with each other and the game. In addition, some degrees of accomplishment and whose outcomes can directly affect the session game were included in order to raise the player's experience. Also, some rewarding mechanisms were threaded throughout the game.

4 Pilot Project

Before launching the pilot project, the game was positively evaluated by an expert in the ISO/IEC 29110. The aim of this study is to provide empirical evidence in order to support the overall applicability of the game proposed as learning tool. The game was applied to three sub-groups: a 16-student sub-group (A) belonging of the course "*Software Engineering*" from the *National Polytechnic School of Ecuador* and 30-student group distributed in two sub-groups (B/C) belonging of the course "*Software development projects management*" from the *Carlos III University of Madrid*. The major difference between them is that participants in subgroup C were studying a dual degree in Computer Science Engineering and Business Administration. After the game, it was applied a 20-item survey with the aim of gathering information from the players. It is important to note that this survey has been used in our exploratory study about the design of this tool [44]. The results are summarized as follows.

Table 1 shows an overview of the background of the participants in this study. All the participants (39 men and 7 women) accepted voluntarily to take part in the study. Only three of them had previous Software Engineering experience in the industry. Three game sessions were held, one per sub-group, in two countries. Participants heard about the standard for the first time during the sessions. Two sessions lasted about 20–25 min. The other one lasted less (10–15 min). It was observed that participants in Ecuador overwhelmingly (100 %) agreed that would like to play again. Whilst 37 % of participants in Spain would not want to play again the reason behind could be that one of the sessions lasted less than 15 min such as one participant point out "*a short time to assimilate the rules and performance*" and other one claims "*more time is required to play*".

Table 1. Background

	Ecuador	Spain	
	A	B	C
Gender (Female/Male)	3/13	1/15	3/11
SE Experience (Industry)	0	2	1
SE Experience (Academic)	16	16	14
Semester	5	6	8
Group Size	16	16	14
Individuals per group	3-5	3-5	3-5
Game Length per round (minutes)	20-25	10-15	20-25
Would Play Again (YES/NO)	16/0	9/7	10/4

Table 2 summarizes the answers of all participants about the game in terms of arithmetic means and standard deviation. Responses were based on a five-point Likert scale ranging from "Strongly Disagree" (1) to "Strongly Agree" (5). Authors can see that two groups arose from the data. In the first group, the means vary between 4.04 and 3.70. 74 % of students stated that they were involved and engaged during the game while 78 % of participants pointed it was fun. It is worth noting that 30 % of out of the total strongly agreed with the last statement. In addition, 70 % of participants report that the game is an alternative to a traditional classroom activity. Although 63 % of the participants kept themselves interested during the game when authors analyzed the raw data, the remaining 35 % was neutral and 56 % of them are belonging to the sub-group C therefore the short playing time could be a disruptive factor as exemplified by the

Table 2. Frequencies, mean and standard deviation

	1	2	3	4	5	Mean	Standard Deviation
Participant Involvement	1	6	5	12	22	4.04	1.141252
Fun Factor			4	6	22	14	4.00	0.884651
Engaging	2		10	22	12	3.91	0.928441
Kept Me Interested	1		16	18	11	3.83	0.867388
Alternative to Classroom	4	3	7	15	17	3.83	1.238939
Design useful	4	4	7	18	13	3.70	1.213503
Knowledge acquisition			9	17	12	8	3.41	0.990741
Encourage to Knowledge	5	7	12	14	8	3.28	1.227635

next quotes from two of the participants "*It [the game] is not well understood it would be better if you will understand it*" and "*It [the game] may be interesting, but there was not time neither was clear what had to be done*". The rest (2 %) belongs to one individual. In this group, 67 % of the students also pointed that the game design is useful. They think that the game has a meaningful design because the cards include color coding and numbered linked with the processes flow. Once again, authors analyzed the raw data the 47 % of the remaining (33 %) are belonging to the sub-group C. In addition to the aforementioned quotes from this sub-group C another respondent stating that "*… It [the game] was explained too fast*".

In the second group, the means vary between 3.41 and 3.28. Authors note that 43 % of the students say that they improved their knowledge on the standard and 48 % of the respondents report that they are more encouraged to know more about the standard. Therefore, no indication for a significant difference on learning effectiveness could be shown. In order to understand the lowest scores, the data were analyzed by participant and by answers. 9 participants (20 % of the respondents) strongly disagree with some of the six issues studied - i.e. 100 % of these answers not included the issues: Fun Factor and Knowledge acquisition. However 4 of them (45 %) are belonging sub-group C. And another 12 participants (26 % of the respondents) disagree with some of the six issues studied - i.e. 100 % of these answers not included the issues: Engaging and Kept Me Interested. However 7 of them (58 %) are belonging sub-group C. Authors can see that a short playing time can affect perceptions of the players during the game and after.

Moreover, the lowest scores in each issue, excluding Encourage to Knowledge, appeared as outliers point when Pierces criterion were applied [46] (see Table 3). In order to do that, we obtained R from the table for one measured quantity assuming one doubtful observation and 46 measurements: R = 2.560. Then, authors calculated the maximum allowable deviation $|x_i - x_m|_{max} = R * SD = 2.92$ where x_i is a measured data value and x_m is the mean of the data set. Finally, authors obtained the actual deviations for the suspicious measurements $|x_i - x_m| = 3.04$ and authors eliminated the suspicious measurements if: $|x_i - x_m| > |x_i - x_m|_{max}$. As a result, there are 8 respondents (17 %) strongly disagree with five issues: Participant Involvement, Engaging, Kept Me Interested, Alternative to Classroom and Useful Design and disagree with the issue Fun Factor.

Table 3. Pierces criterion

	Mean	Standard Deviation	Pierce's Criterion	
			R * SD	$|x_i - x_m|$
Participant Involvement	4.04	1.141253	2.92	3.04
Fun Factor	4.00	0.884652	1.77	2.00
Engaging	3.91	0.928442	2.13	2.91
Kept Me Interested	3.83	0.867389	2.22	2.83
Alternative to Classroom	3.83	1.238940	2.47	2.83
Useful Design	3.70	1.213503	2.42	2.70
Encourage to Knowledge	3.28	1.227635	2.33	2.28

The two open questions shed light on the above results. Certainly, one important issue is that everyone has enough playing time as before mentioned. In general, the most respondents commented that the game was interesting, fun, didactic and intuitive as exemplified by one respondent *"I think it was an interesting and funny experience"* another participant stated *"Thus it is much easier to learn the ISO"*. Most players positively embraced the game as someone put it concisely *"It is a good experience…"* with another respondent confirming that *"It [game] has a great future"*. The gameplay environment forced participants become familiar with the ISO/IEC 29110 standard. Finally, the respondents suggested (i) make more iterations of the game, and (ii) create a game mechanics to link task.

5 Conclusions and Future Work

This paper describes the proposal of a learning tool, which is based on a serious game as a way to understand and support the project management process and activities of the ISO/IEC 291110 standard. The main limitation is the sample size of the study which was limited. Although it consisted of a pilot project carried out among students in two countries, Ecuador and Spain. The learning tool allows learners to gain an understanding of the standard quickly that might otherwise have been poorly understood or overlooked altogether. Indeed, the card game could be used as a checklist and support the project management in both academic and professional settings, but further study is needed. The present findings are consistent with the previous one [44], although there is a variation of gameplay, the game seems to be fun, immersive and certainly involve the participants. Nevertheless short playing time could be a disruption and the participants suggest "make more iterations of the game". Finally, the results give us confidence that this is a positive experience. Therefore, the game could be used as a strategy to promote the standard and show practitioners that learning a standard does not have to be boring and painful. In future work, authors propose to focus on improving the game mechanics in order to make the game as simple as possible, but no simpler. Moreover, authors are planning to increase the sample size and the learning tool could eventually become a software application.

Acknowledgments. The authors would like to thank Sandra Sanchez-Gordon, who is tutor of course *"Software Engineering"* of the *National Polytechnic School of Ecuador*. Also, a special thanks to all the students in Ecuador and Spain, who participated in the evaluation of the game.

References

1. Larrucea, X., O'Connor, R.V., Colomo-Palacios, R., Laporte, C.Y.: Software process improvement in very small organizations. IEEE Softw. **33**(2), 85–89 (2016)
2. O'Connor, R.V., Laporte, C.Y.: Deploying lifecycle profiles for very small entities: an early stage industry view. In: O'Connor, R.V., Rout, T., McCaffery, F., Dorling, A. (eds.) SPICE 2011. CCIS, vol. 155, pp. 227–230. Springer, Heidelberg (2011)
3. International Organization for Standardization (ISO): Software engineering – Lifecycle profiles for Very Small Entities (VSEs) Part 5-1-2: Management and engineering guide: Generic profile group: Basic Profile, Geneva (2011)
4. ISO/IEC: ISO/IEC TR 29110-5-1-1:2012 Software engineering – Lifecycle profiles for Very Small Entities (VSEs) – Part 5-1-1: Management and engineering guide: Generic profile group: Entry profile (2012)
5. Laporte, C.Y., April, A., Renault, A.: Applying ISO/IEC software engineering standards in small settings: historical perspectives and initial achievements. In: Proceedings of SPICE Conference, Luxembourg (2006)
6. Moreno-Campos, E.J., Sanchez-Gordón, M.-L., Colomo-Palacios, R.: ISO/IEC 29110: current overview of the standard. Rev. Procesos Métr. **10**, 24–40 (2013)
7. Laporte, C., O'Connor, R.: Software process improvement in graduate software engineering programs. Presented at the Proceedings of the 1st International Workshop on Software Process Education, Training and Professionalism, Sweden, June 2015
8. Biberoglu, E., Haddad, H.: A survey of industrial experiences with CMM and the teaching of CMM practices. J. Comput. Sci. Coll. **18**, 143–152 (2002)
9. Sanchez-Gordon, M.-L., O'Connor, R.V., Colomo-Palacios, R.: Evaluating VSEs viewpoint and sentiment towards the ISO/IEC 29110 standard: a two country grounded theory study. In: Rout, T., O'Connor, R.V., Dorling, A. (eds.) SPICE 2015. CCIS, vol. 526, pp. 114–127. Springer, Heidelberg (2015)
10. Fuggetta, A., Di Nitto, E.: Software process. In: Proceedings of the on Future of Software Engineering, pp. 1–12. ACM, New York (2014)
11. O'Connor, R.V., Laporte, C.Y.: An innovative approach to the development of an international software process lifecycle standard for very small entities. Int. J. Inf. Technol. Syst. Approach **7**, 1–22 (2014)
12. Baker, A., Oh Navarro, E., van der Hoek, A.: An experimental card game for teaching software engineering processes. J. Syst. Softw. **75**, 3–16 (2005)
13. Kuhrmann, M., Fernández, D.M., Münch, J.: Teaching software process modeling. In: Proceedings of the 2013 International Conference on Software Engineering, pp. 1138–1147. IEEE Press, Piscataway (2013)
14. Borstler, J., Carrington, D., Hislop, G.W., Lisack, S., Olson, K., Williams, L.: Teaching PSP: challenges and lessons learned. IEEE Softw. **19**, 42–48 (2002)
15. Aydan, U., Yilmaz, M., O'Connor, R.V.: Towards a serious game to teach ISO/IEC 12207 software lifecycle process: an interactive learning approach. In: Rout, T., O'Connor, R.V., Dorling, A. (eds.) SPICE 2015. CCIS, vol. 526, pp. 217–229. Springer, Heidelberg (2015)

16. Heredia, A., Colomo-Palacios, R., de Amescua-Seco, A.: A systematic mapping study on software process education. In: Proceedings of 1st International Workshop on Software Process Education, Training and Professionalism, pp. 7–17. Ceur Workshop Proceedings, Gothenburg, Sweden (2015)
17. Kosa, M., Yilmaz, M.: Designing Games for Improving the Software Development Process. In: O'Connor, R.V., Umay Akkaya, M., Kemaneci, K., Yilmaz, M., Poth, A., Messnarz, R. (eds.) EuroSPI 2015. CCIS, vol. 543, pp. 303–310. Springer, Heidelberg (2015). doi:10.1007/978-3-319-24647-5_25
18. Yilmaz, M., Saran, M., O'Connor, R.: Towards a quest-based contextualization process for game-based learning. In: Busch, C. (ed.) 8th European Conference on Games Based Learning, Academic Conferences and Publishing International Limited, pp. 645–651. Academic Conferences International Limited (2014)
19. Bellotti, F., Kapralos, B., Lee, K., Moreno-Ger, P., Berta, R.: Assessment in and of serious games: an overview. Adv. Hum. Comput. Interact. **2013**, 1–11 (2013)
20. O'Connor, R.V., Laporte, C.Y.: Towards the provision of assistance for very small entities in deploying software lifecycle standards. In: Proceedings of the 11th International Conference on Product Focused Software (PROFES 2010), pp. 4–7. ACM (2010)
21. O'Connor, R.V., Laporte, C.Y.: Using ISO/IEC 29110 to harness process improvement in very small entities. In: O'Connor, R.V., Pries-Heje, J., Messnarz, R. (eds.) EuroSPI 2011. CCIS, vol. 172, pp. 225–235. Springer, Heidelberg (2011)
22. Coleman, G., O'Connor, R.: Investigating software process in practice: a grounded theory perspective. J. Syst. Softw. **81**, 772–784 (2008)
23. O'Connor, R., Coleman, G.: Ignoring "best practice": why Irish software SMEs are rejecting CMMI and ISO 9000. Australas. J. Inf. Syst. **16** (2009)
24. Sánchez-Gordón, M.-L., O'Connor, R.V.: Understanding the gap between software process practices and actual practice in very small companies. Softw. Qual. J. **24**, 549–570 (2015)
25. Moreno-Campos, E., Sanchez-Gordón, M.-L., Colomo-Palacios, R., de Amescua Seco, A.: Towards measuring the impact of the ISO/IEC 29110 standard: a systematic review. In: Barafort, B., O'Connor, R.V., Poth, A., Messnarz, R. (eds.) EuroSPI 2014. CCIS, vol. 425, pp. 1–12. Springer, Heidelberg (2014)
26. International Organization for Standardization (ISO): Software engineering — Lifecycle profiles for Very Small Entities (VSEs) — Part 5-1-1: Management and engineering guide: Generic profile group: Entry profile, Geneva (2012)
27. Varkoi, T., Mäkinen, T.: A process assessment model for very small software entities. In: Rout, T., Lami, G., Fabbrini, F. (eds.) Process Improvement and Capability Determination in Software, Systems Engineering and Service Management. Proceedings of 10th International SPICE Conference 2010, Pisa, Italy (2010)
28. Laporte, C.Y., O'Connor, R.V., Paucar, L.H.G.: The implementation of ISO/IEC 29110 software engineering standards and guides in very small entities. In: Maciaszek, L.A., Filipe, J. (eds.) ENASE 2015. CCIS, vol. 599, pp. 162–179. Springer, Heidelberg (2016). doi:10.1007/978-3-319-30243-0_9
29. de Sousa Borges, S., Durelli, V.H.S., Reis, H.M., Isotani, S.: A systematic mapping on gamification applied to education. In: Proceedings of the 29th Annual ACM Symposium on Applied Computing, pp. 216–222. ACM, New York (2014)
30. Deterding, S., Dixon, D., Khaled, R., Nacke, L.: From game design elements to gamefulness: defining "gamification." In: Proceedings of the 15th International Academic MindTrek Conference: Envisioning Future Media Environments, pp. 9–15. ACM, New York (2011)
31. Pedreira, O., García, F., Brisaboa, N., Piattini, M.: Gamification in software engineering – a systematic mapping. Inf. Softw. Technol. **57**, 157–168 (2015)

32. von Wangenheim, C.G., Thiry, M., Kochanski, D.: Empirical evaluation of an educational game on software measurement. Empir. Softw. Eng. **14**, 418–452 (2008)
33. Herranz, E., Colomo-Palacios, R., de Amescua Seco, A., Yilmaz, M.: Gamification as a disruptive factor in software process improvement initiatives. J. Univers. Comput. Sci. **20**, 885–906 (2014)
34. Yilmaz, M., Yilmaz, M., O'Connor, R.V., Clarke, P.: A gamification approach to improve the software development process by exploring the personality of software practitioners. In: Clarke, P.M., O'Connor, R.V., Rout, T., Dorling, A. (eds.) SPICE 2016. CCIS, vol. 609, pp. 71–83. Springer, Heidelberg (2016). doi:10.1007/978-3-319-38980-6_6
35. Sheth, S., Bell, J., Kaiser, G.: A competitive-collaborative approach for introducing software engineering in a CS2 class. In: 2013 IEEE 26th Conference on Software Engineering Education and Training (CSEE&T), pp. 41–50 (2013)
36. Barata, G., Gama, S., Jorge, J., Goncalves, D.: engaging engineering students with gamification. In: 2013 5th International Conference on Games and Virtual Worlds for Serious Applications (VS-GAMES), pp. 1–8 (2013)
37. Thomas, C., Berkling, K.: Redesign of a gamified software engineering course. In: 2013 International Conference on Interactive Collaborative Learning, pp. 778–786 (2013)
38. Calderón, A., Ruiz, M.: Coverage of ISO/IEC 12207 software lifecycle process by a simulation-based serious game. In: Clarke, P.M., O'Connor, R.V., Rout, T., Dorling, A. (eds.) SPICE 2016. CCIS, vol. 609, pp. 59–70. Springer, Heidelberg (2016). doi:10.1007/978-3-319-38980-6_5
39. Jaramillo, C.M.Z., Alvarez, M.C.G.: Incorporating playful activities in the software engineering teaching. Dev. Bus. Simul. Exp. Learn. **41**, 248–255 (2014)
40. Zapata-Jaramillo, C.M., Lopez, M.D.R., Sanchez, R., Pinzon, L., Jimenez, D., Arango, E.: SEMAT GAME: applying a project management practice. Dev. Bus. Simul. Exp. Learn. **42**, 133–143 (2015)
41. Management 3.0. https://management30.com/product/card-games/
42. Industrial Logic. http://www.industriallogic.com/games
43. Dr.Dobb's. http://www.drdobbs.com/xp-war/184415908
44. Sánchez-Gordón, M.-L., O'Connor, R.V., Colomo-Palacios, R., Sanchez-Gordon, S.: A learning tool for the ISO/IEC 29110 standard: understanding the project management of basic profile. In: Clarke, P.M., O'Connor, R.V., Rout, T., Dorling, A. (eds.) SPICE 2016. CCIS, vol. 609, pp. 270–283. Springer, Heidelberg (2016). doi:10.1007/978-3-319-38980-6_20
45. Abuhamdeh, S., Csikszentmihalyi, M.: The importance of challenge for the enjoyment of intrinsically motivated. Goal-Directed Activities Pers. Soc. Psychol. Bull. **38**, 317–330 (2012)
46. Ross, S.M.: Peirce's criterion for the elimination of suspect experimental data. J. Eng. Technol. **20**, 38–41 (2003)

Implementing the New ISO/IEC 29110 Systems Engineering Process Standard in a Small Public Transportation Company

Claude Y. Laporte[1(✉)], Nicolas Tremblay[1], Jamil Menaceur[2], and Denis Poliquin[2]

[1] École de technologie supérieure, Montréal, Canada
`Claude.Y.Laporte@etsmtl.ca`,
`nicolas.tremblay.9@ens.etsmtl.ca`
[2] CSiT, Montréal, Canada
`{jamil.menaceur,den-is.poliquin}@csintrans.com`

Abstract. The recently published ISO/IEC 29110 for systems engineering has been used as the main framework for the development of the management and systems engineering processes at CSinTrans Inc. (CSiT), a Canadian company, founded in 2011. CSiT specializes in the integration of communication and security systems in transit industry such as trains, subways and buses as well as railway stations, subway stations and bus stops. CSiT approved an internal project to define and implement project management and systems engineering processes. The project's history, purpose and rationale that prompted CSiT to adopt the new systems engineering process standard are presented. The implementation of the ISO/IEC 29110 is described. The reflections and decisions made during the implementation are presented. Recommendations and advice for organizations wanting to implement ISO/IEC 29110 are described. ISO/IEC 29110 has helped raise the maturity of the young organization by implementing proven practices and developing consistent work products from one project to another. ISO/IEC 29110 was a good starting point to align processes of CSiT with practices of CMMI®. ISO/IEC 29110 has helped CSiT with developing light processes as well as remaining flexible and quick in its ability to respond to its customers.

Keywords: Very small entities · VSEs · ISO/IEC 29110 · Systems engineering · Process · Standards

1 Introduction

CSiT is a Canadian company, established in 2011 in Montreal, specializing in the integration of interactive systems, communication and security in the domain of public transport such as trains, subways and buses and railway stations, stations and stops Bus. In transit industry, customers often require a CMMI® [1] maturity level from suppliers such as CSiT. An independent evaluation confirming a CMMI® maturity level 2 increases the opportunity of winning contracts. Similarly, to ensure better work coordination and reduce risks, customers in this industry prefer working with mature suppliers in order to get timely quality products and within the agreed budget.

2 ISO/IEC 29110 Software and Systems Engineering Standards and Guides

As defined in ISO/IEC 29110 (ISO 29110 hereon), a Very Small Entity (VSE) is a company, an organization (e.g. government, not-for profit), a department or a project having up to 25 people [2]. VSEs can play different roles in systems engineering: either as suppliers or integrators, and sometimes both. Since most large organizations are structured in a way to be more manageable (e.g. project, department), VSEs are present at all stages of a product manufacturing chain.

A four-stage roadmap, called ISO 29110 profiles, has been developed for VSEs that do not develop critical systems or critical software: Entry, Basic, Intermediate and Advanced profiles. VSEs targeted by the Entry profile are those working on small projects (e.g., at most six person-months of effort) and for start-ups. The Basic profile describes the development practices of a single application by a single project team. The Intermediate profile is targeted at VSEs developing multiple projects with more than one team. The Advanced profile is targeted at VSEs wishing to sustain and grow as independent competitive businesses.

ISO 29110 has been successfully implemented in VSEs developing software (SW) in many countries [3]. ISO 29110 has been implemented, amongst others, in IT start-ups in Canada [4], in Peru [5] and in a VSE co-located in Tunisia and in Canada [6], in a large financial institution [7] and in a large utility provider [8]. VSEs that have implemented ISO 29110 management and engineering guides have improved one or more aspects of competitiveness (e.g. quality, cost, schedule). As an example, projects using ISO 29110 for the first time had only 10 % to 18 % of rework. A Canadian division of a large American engineering company has developed and implemented project management processes for their small-scale and medium-scale projects. The engineering organization used the Entry and Basic profiles of ISO 29110 for the development of their small and medium scale project management processes. An analysis of the cost and the benefits of the implementation of their small and medium scale project management processes was performed using an ISO economic benefits of standard methodology. The engineering enterprise estimated that, over a three-year timeframe, savings of about 780,000CA$ would be realized due to the implementation of project management processes using ISO 29110 [9, 10].

Systems, in the context of ISO/IEC 29110, are typically composed of hardware and software components. The systems engineering (SE) ISO 29110 has been developed using, as its main frameworks, the SW ISO 29110 [11] and ISO/IEC/IEEE 15288 [12]. With some exceptions, document descriptions are based on ISO/IEC/IEEE 15289 [13]. The SE Basic profile, as illustrated in Fig. 1, is composed of two processes: Project Management (PM) and System Definition and Realization (SR) [14]. An acquirer (i.e. a customer) provides a Statement of Work as an input to the PM process and receives a product as a result of SR process execution.

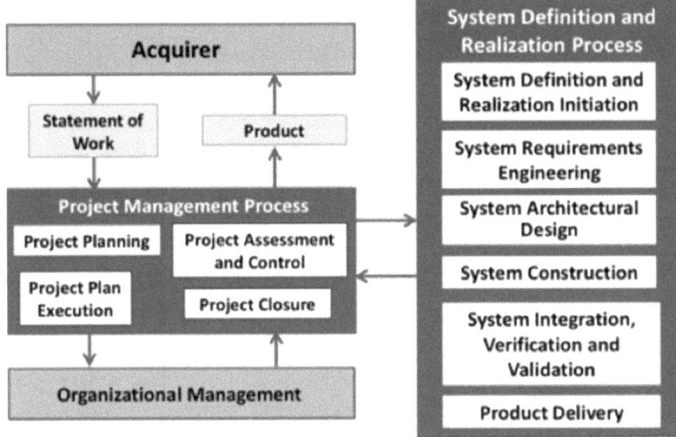

Fig. 1. Processes and activities of the ISO 29110 systems engineering Basic profile [14]

The SE ISO 29110 standard and guides are designed to work hand-in-hand with the SW ISO 29110 guides. ISO 29110 does not impose a specific life cycle model, therefore leaving VSEs free to choose the model that best suits their needs among the cascade, iterative, incremental, evolutionary and agile models. Similarly, ISO 29110 does not impose a specific method to its users [15].

Beside the published SW Entry and Basic profiles, the SE Entry profile [16] and the SE Basic profile [14] have been published. The SE Intermediate profile development should be completed in 2016 and published in 2017. The SE Advanced profile development should start in 2017 and should be published in 2018. The SE Basic profile guide is freely available in English and French from ISO. The German chapter of INCOSE (International Council on Systems Engineering), GfSE (Gesellschaft für Systems Engineering e.V.), has sponsored the translation of the systems engineering Basic profile. The German standard organization DIN (Deutsches Institut für Normung) should publish in 2017 the Basic profile in its catalogue. Finally, a translation in Arabic is led by a member of (International Council on Systems Engineering) INCOSE.

3 Motivations and Objectives of the Implementation of ISO 29110 at CSiT

Shortly after its creation in 2011, CSiT learned that an event in Montréal would be held on the new ISO 29110 management and engineering guide for systems engineering. This standard was seen as a good starting point towards implementing CMMI level 2. Thus, CSiT has undertaken a new project to implement the ISO 29110 standard to guide the project management and system development activities. The Intermediate profile was targeted as it applies to VSEs that conduct several projects simultaneously with more than one team. However, the Basic profile was selected since the Intermediate profile was not published when the project was initiated at CSiT.

3.1 Motivations for the Implementation of Project Management and Engineering Processes

Several factors prompted CSiT to develop and document their processes. Their first projects were based on employees' experience as well as recognized practices. This approach was effective and agile, but it was not possible to produce consistent deliverables from one project to another and be able to demonstrate that the work could be done over again since these practices were not documented into company's processes. Also, since there were no templates or checklists, project management and product development activities were done rather informally. Finally, considering business and nature of projects of CSiT, customers often require proof demonstrating rigorous work and a level of maturity.

The company considered the development and implementation of processes as a need, in other words the situation could become problematic if no action was taken. Specifically, the lack of a CMMI maturity level or compliance with international standards, such as ISO 29110, was not an option. CSiT wanted to ensure the company's growth and show its expertise and organizational maturity to its customers.

Guidance for the implementation project. To avoid making the process cumbersome and producing too many documents, participants gave themselves 2 sets of guidelines:

- For processes, the guideline was to add tasks not described in the SE Basic profile only if they bring value to the context and projects of the company or provide an alignment with CMMI level 2.
- For document templates, the guidelines were:
  - Group different documents into one where possible;
  - Each template's section must be relevant and applicable. If a section does not provide added value, it should not be included.

4 Approach to the Implementation of the SE ISO 29110 at CSiT

The first phase of the improvement project was to determine the set of documents to be produced during a typical project and how they should be organized in the document structure of the company. The five types of documents (i.e. policy, process, procedure, standard, support material) at the foundation of the company's quality system are illustrated in Fig. 2.

For the moment, CSiT decided to leave aside the creation of training material because this material can take time to develop and does not really bring value at this time. The company prefers to promote interactive training in person rather than the reading of a document or the viewing of a presentation. Documented processes of the company can be used as training material for new employees.

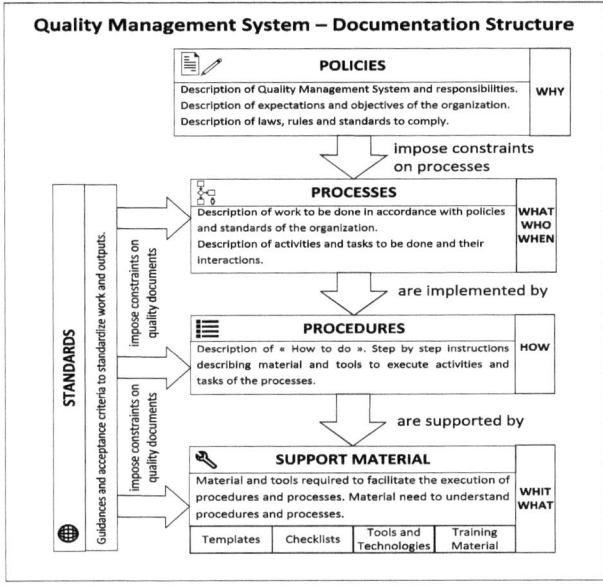

Fig. 2. Identification of documents and their relationships

4.1 Processes and Procedures Description

To better respond to different types of projects, CSiT decided to develop three process groups (i.e. light, standard, full), each being adapted to meet the attributes of projects such as the size and nature. Table 1 shows the three process groups and the frameworks to be used as reference.

Table 1. Classification of CSiT processes

	Light process	Standard process	Full process
Type of project	Proof of Concept, Prototype	Typical Project	Project when CMMI level 2 is required by a Customer
	Concept validation or Product Deployment at Customer Site	Product intended to be installed at Customer Site	Product intended to be installed at Customer site
	Small Project	Medium Project	Large Project
Framework to be used	ISO/IEC TR 29110-5-6-1 - Entry profile + CMMI - Supplier Agreement Management	ISO/IEC TR 29110-5-6-2 - Basic profile + CMMI - Supplier Agreement Management	CMMI (Level 2)

4.2 Using the Management and Engineering Guide of ISO 29110

To document CSiT processes, the management and engineering guide of ISO 29110 SE Basic profile was used as the main reference. The SW management and engineering guide of ISO 29110 Basic profile was also used as a reference to complement the SE guide. The SW guide was used to document processes involving the development of SW elements of a system. It is during the execution of the System Construction activity of the SE Basic profile that software components are developed. Then, in the next activity, as illustrated in Fig. 1, hardware and software components are integrated.

4.3 Using Deployment Packages

Members of the INCOSE VSE working group have created Deployment Packages (DPs) to facilitate the adoption and implementation of ISO 29110 [17]. These free resources, available on Internet, have been used to support the documentation of CSiT processes. Figure 3 shows the SE set of DPs.

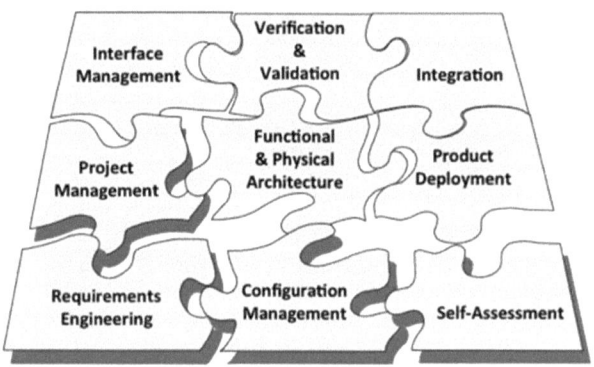

Fig. 3. Deployment packages to support the SE Basic profile

4.4 Process Documentation

For the description of processes, CSiT decided to break down processes into activities and tasks. There are two reasons for this representation. First, this representation is simple and it is commonly used in industry and literature. Second, it is consistent with ISO 29110, which is structured the same way.

It was decided that documentation of CSiT processes would consist of two parts: a graphical part and a textual part. Each of these parts has different but complementary goals. The graphical part is primarily targeted at "experts", while the textual part is targeted mainly at "beginners" (e.g. a new employee) or an intermediate user (e.g. an employee who has participated to an engineering project) [18, 19].

The ETVX notation (i.e. Entry-Task-Validation-eXit) was developed in the 80s by IBM [20]. Given its simplicity of use, this notation has been adopted by many organizations. The template for the graphical description of the activities and tasks is shown in Fig. 4. The textual part is a detailed description of activities, tasks and interactions between the activities of a process. The textual part describes the tasks, i.e. what to do, and the roles associated with each task.

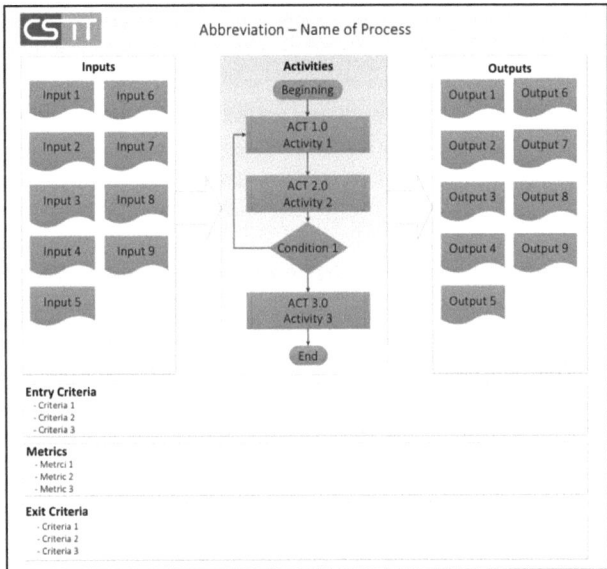

Fig. 4. Template for the graphical part of an activity

At CSiT, the format used to describe the activities is the notation used in the DPs of ISO 29110. Some adjustments were made to add a few attributes, such as measures to collect, entry criteria and exit criteria.

4.5 Techniques Used to Help Defining and Implementing ISO 29110

The Basic profile presents the project management and development processes using a waterfall lifecycle to simplify its understanding. However, the ISO 29110 guide indicates that it does not require the waterfall lifecycle, leaving VSEs to use the lifecycle that best suits their needs. Thus, CSiT decided to develop their own lifecycle models: a project lifecycle and a system development lifecycle. The definition of these lifecycle models have facilitated the description of the processes because they provided a clear understanding of when the processes need to be executed. In addition, the lifecycles have shown the importance of some processes that are not mentioned in the standard, but that must be used during the execution of projects. For example, it is possible that the company has to perform validation tests on the customer' site, to get the final acceptance of the system. For CSiT, this type of work is essential and was documented as a separate process.

4.6 Identification of Verification, Validation and Acceptance Activities Applicable to Work Products

An important decision, made during the development of CSiT's processes, was to determine the types of peer review activities to be applied to the various work products of a project. ISO 29110 states that verifications of work products must be made, but without specifying the type. This leaves VSEs free to decide what best verification method applies to their context. For each deliverable, a decision was made for the adequacy or the need to perform at least one type of peer review. Four types of reviews were selected: personal review, desk-check, walkthrough and inspection.

For each review, the output documents have been defined. The four types of document are: a document review report, an annotated document, minutes of meeting and a completed checklist. Table 2 illustrates an example of the type of verification, validation and acceptance activities selected for the System Requirement Specification.

ISO 29110 defines the roles needed to produce and review the project deliverables (documentation and product components), but it does not define the roles of the people who must approve and/or sign deliverables before they are sent to a customer, a supplier or other external stakeholders. The right side of Table 2 indicates, for each deliverable, whether or not an internal approval is needed, whether or not it should be sent to the customer and whether or not a customer approval is required. If needed, the table could easily be tailored to meet the needs of a specific project.

Table 2. Subset of the verification, validation and acceptance activities

Deliverables and Internal Work Products	VERIFICATION					VALIDATION		ACCEPTANCE AND SIGNATURE		
	Peer Review			Tests		Tests		Acceptance		
	Peer Review? (Y=Yes, N=No)	Type of Review (P=Personnal, D=DeskB Check)	Output Documents ANN=Annotations RR=Review Report MoM=Minutes of Meeting	Type of Test U=Unit I=Integration	Output Document UTR=Unit Test Report ITR=Integration Test Report	Type of Test F=Factory S=On Site	Output Document FTR=Factory Test Report STR=Site Test Report	Internal Approval (signature) (Y=Yes, N=No)	Delivered to Customer? (Y=Yes, N=No)	Acceptance required form (Y=Yes, N=No)
Description										
Technical (-) System Requirement Specification	Y	D,W	RR then MoM	N/A	N/A	N/A	N/A	Y	Y	O

4.7 Selection of Measures

The ISO 29110 management and engineering guide lists the tasks associated to the collection and use of measures (e.g. resource, cost, time). The Basic profile does not detail how to collect and analyze the measures. The Intermediate and Advanced profiles will provide more details about the collection, analysis and utilisation of measures. The selection of measures was based on two principles: (1) a measure must meet a company's needs for information and, (2) a measure must be easy to collect and analyze. A subset of the measures selected is described in Table 3.

An electronic time sheet has been established to record the number of hours worked on each work product of a project. The timesheet allows to classify efforts in 3 categories: (1) efforts spent on the initial production of a work product; (2) efforts spent on reviewing it; (3) efforts spent on correcting identified defects. This data provides valuable information when improving a process or a work product.

Table 3. Subset of process and product measures

Measure ID	Measures	Reasons
MET-01	Number of errors detected by document type and by phase of the development cycle	To know the overall quality of each work product
MET-02	Number of hours worked for each phase of the system development cycle	To be able to use the performance of past projects to estimate new projects
MET-03	The cost of each project	
MET-04	The attributes of each project: Number of change requests; Level of risk; Predominance hardware/software.	
MET-05	Distribution of effort related to the production, review and correction of deliverables	To be able to analyze the efficiency of processes on product quality
MET-06	Resources spent versus those that were planned in the project plan	To be able to analyze if the project is successful, to identify gaps and take the necessary remedial action

4.8 Traceability Between Work Products

ISO 29110 includes tasks to trace information between work products. Based on these tasks, a graphical representation was set up to show how traceability is generated between the various work products of CSiT. Only a few adjustments were made to the tasks of ISO 29110 to better reflect the context of CSiT:

- Traceability between unit tests and detailed design elements has been added.
- Traceability between the detailed design and architecture document has been defined as optional. This customization does not cause any problem for compliance with ISO 29110 since this type of traceability is not mentioned.
- Names of ISO 29110 documents have been adapted to fit documents' titles used by CSiT.

4.9 Definition of a Supplier Management Process

Since CSiT is a system integrator, the company uses suppliers for the purchase and development of components that will be used in a product. Therefore, it was imperative for CSiT to establish a supplier management process that defines how to work with them and to reduce project risks. The SE Basic profile has only a few tasks about the 'make or buy' decisions and follow-up actions (e.g. document, review and issue a purchase order). Unfortunately, the current version of the SE Basic profile does not describe a supplier management process. This process will be included in the Intermediate and Advanced profiles. The CMMI® for Development has been consulted, as well as ISO/IEC/IEEE 15288, the INCOSE SE Handbook [21] and the PMBOK® Guide [22]. The documentation of this process led to the creation of additional templates: request for proposal, supplier selection matrix, purchase order and purchase agreement. Also, three new sections have been added to the project plan of the SE ISO 29110 Basic profile: a list of acquisitions and potential suppliers, an acquisition plan/strategy, and a supplier management plan.

5 Coverage Between Frameworks

As mentioned earlier, the goal of the process project was to implement the SE Basic profile of the ISO 29110 and to complement it with CMMI level 2 requirements. In order to determine the achievement of this objective, an analysis of the coverage of CSiT processes was performed. This analysis was done in two stages. First, the correspondences between the CSiT processes with ISO 29110 have been defined. Then, connections between the processes of CSiT and those of CMMI were defined.

An analysis confirmed that the processes of CSiT fully cover the objectives and tasks of the processes defined in the Basic profile. During this analysis, mappings and tailoring have been documented. This documentation also explains the tailoring decisions of CSiT.

The mapping of CSiT processes with CMMI-DEV level 2 process areas, illustrated in Table 4, revealed that many of the generic practices and specific practices are covered. However, some practices still remain to be implemented or improved.

An analysis of the coverage of CSiT processes with CMMI-DEV level 3 process areas has also been completed.

Table 4. Approximate coverage of CSiT processes to CMMI-DEV

CMMI-DEV Level 2 – Process Areas	Percentage of Coverage
Configuration Management	50–70 %
Measurement and Analysis	20–40 %
Project Monitoring and Control	70–90 %
Project Planning	70–90 %
Process and Product Quality Assurance	45–65 %
Requirements Management	90–100 %
Supplier Agreement Management	70–90 %

6 Benefits for the VSE

Two categories of benefits were observed by CSiT: observable benefits in day-to-day project activities and benefits to the VSE as a business. The day-to-day benefits to the VSE are:

- Standardized work and consistent deliverables across projects
- Avoids reinventing the wheel for each project

- Work is done in a systematic and disciplined way
- Better quality of deliverables and products
- Better project management and project monitoring
- Reduction of project risks
- Better communication within the team because the semantic of communication is standardized

CSiT obtained the following business benefits as a result of the of their effort to define and improve their processes:

- Better credibility to bid on tenders
- Access to markets that require certification of a quality system in line with the business practices of the company
- Better recognition of the quality of work done and products developed
- Better trust from customers and business partners
- An important step towards a maturity level of the CMMI (a CMMI level is a requirement of some customers)

7 Implementation of ISO 29110 and Self-assessment and Audit

In 2012, CSiT started the development of a product suite called 'TRANSIS'. TRANSIS is a multimodal information data integration system with interactive extensions for operators and users of public transport. This project was intended to apply the processes and adjust them if necessary, ensuring a gradual adoption of the new work methods. CSiT has tested the degree of implementation of its processes in the TRANSIS project. To do this, the self-assessment score sheet of ISO 29110 was used. This score sheet was used to indicate the activities, tasks and documents produced during a project and determine the level of compliance with the standard. At the middle of the project, an assessment showed that most of the project management and system development tasks have been executed. The tasks that have not yet been covered will be executed in subsequent phases of the TRANSIS project. Recently, the processes of CSiT, based on the Basic Profile of the ISO 29110, have been successfully audited by a third-party audit composed of 2 independent auditors. One member of the audit team was a systems engineering domain expert.

8 Recommendations

Resulting from the development and implementation of project management and system engineering processes at CSiT, a set of recommendations was developed to help VSEs in implementing ISO 29110. Table 5 describes our mains recommendations.

Table 5. Main recommendations for VSEs

Recommendation	Description
Define the vision and objectives of a process improvement project	A clear definition of the business motivations and objectives of the initiative will help define the scope of the improvement project.
	With clear and ideally quantified objectives, it will be possible to determine whether the expected results have been met.
Choose a framework that meets the needs of the VSE	VSEs should take the time to choose the profile that best meets their organization. As described in Table 1, a VSE could implement the Entry profile for small projects and the Basic profile for its bigger projects.
Adapt the framework selected to the context of the VSE	ISO 29110 being a generic framework, it is important to do some adaptations (e.g. terminology), while remaining consistent with the selected framework.
Document all processes in a graphical notation first	This approach helps to get the big picture of the processes and their interactions. It enables the team to use and apply these processes faster in a pilot project. It also helps to determine whether the activities and tasks defined in the process are relevant and if some are missing.
Define the structure of the project directories or project repositories	A VSE should adopt a uniform directory structure from one project to another. In this way, it is easy to navigate and work more efficiently.
Define a generic template for documents	Having a generic template saves time when creating a template for a particular document or a project having specific needs.
Group documents as required	The SE Basic profile lists work products in a table for presentation purposes only. The work products may be combined by a VSE to meet the needs of a project.
	Grouping documents minimizes the number of manipulations (e.g. drafting, reviewing, approving) and the number of documents managed and stored.
Define the verification, validation and acceptance of documents and product elements	A good way to facilitate the documentation process is to define the verification, validation and acceptance criteria that applies to each output and each deliverable.
	Once completed, this table presents a clear picture of the quality control and acceptance activities that must be performed during a project.

(*Continued*)

Table 5. (*Continued*)

Recommendation	Description
Develop and use checklists	Checklists act as reminders to check items which are often the cause of defects in work products.
Define a minimal set of measures	A set of measures could be the budget spent, the number of hours spent, the number of days late or ahead of the original schedule, the number of defects found in a work product, the number of tasks performed compared to the number total of tasks defined in the project plan and, the risk level of the project.
Conduct a pilot project	New processes should be used first in a pilot project to test their effectiveness, to detect omissions, contradictions, errors and ambiguities. This allows a VSE to make adjustments smoothly before its deployment in all projects.

9 Conclusion

This article has presented the development and the implementation of management and engineering processes at CSiT using the recently published the ISO 29110 for systems engineering. The ISO 29110 has greatly facilitated this work because it describes in details the processes that must be documented and implemented. It was easy for CSiT to adapt the ISO 29110 to its business context. ISO 29110 helped implementing lightweight processes. This way CSiT remains a flexible organization. ISO 29110 helped raise the organization's maturity by using industry-recognized practices that are consistent from project to project. It can be said that ISO 29110 is simple to understand and use. It is a good starting point for a VSE that also wants to cover CMMI-DEV Level 2 and 3 practices. ISO 29110 enables VSEs, such as CSiT, to become more mature more rapidly by adopting systematic, disciplined and quantifiable methods of work, which are typical of engineering environments.

References

1. Software Engineering Institute, CMMI for Development, Version 1.3. Carnegie Mellon University, Pittsburgh. CMU/SEI-2010-TR-033 (2010)
2. ISO/IEC TR 29110-1:2016 - Systems and software engineering -Lifecycle profiles for Very Small Entities (VSES) - Part 1: Overview, ISO, Geneva, (2016). http://standards.iso.org/ittf/PubliclyAvailableStandards/index.html

3. Larrucea, X., O'Connor, R.V., Colomo-Palacios, R., Laporte, C.Y.: Software process improvement in very small organizations. IEEE Softw. **33**(2), 85–89 (2016)
4. Laporte, C.Y., Hébert, C., Mineau, C.: Development of a social network website using the new ISO/IEC 29110 standard developed specifically for very small entities. Softw. Qual. Prof. J. ASQ **16**(4), 4–25 (2014)
5. Garcia, L., Laporte, C.Y., Arteaga, J., Bruggmann, M.: Implementation and certification of ISO/IEC 29110 in an IT startup in Peru. Softw. Qual. Prof. J. ASQ **17**(2), 16–29 (2015)
6. Jeljeli, H., Laporte, C.Y.: Mise en oeuvre de processus logiciels à l'aide de la norme ISO/CEI 29110 dans une grande entreprise et dans un start-up. Génie logiciel Numéro **117** (2016) (in French)
7. Plante, F.: Développement et mise en oeuvre d'un processus de type agile au sein de la direction solution trésorerie du mouvement Desjardins, Rapport de projet de maitrise, École de technologie supérieure, April 2015 (in French)
8. Lebel, K.: Développement, en mode Agile, d'une application à l'aide de la norme ISO/CEI 29110 au sein du département solutions mobilité et géoréférencées d'Hydro-Québec, École de technologie supérieure 2016 (in French)
9. Laporte, C.Y., Chevalier, F.: An innovative approach to the development of project management processes for small-scale projects in a large engineering company. In: Jakobs, K. (ed.) Effective Standardization Management in Corporate Settings, Hershey (2016)
10. Laporte, C.Y., Chevalier, F.: An innovative approach to the development of project management processes for small-scale projects in a large engineering company. In: 25th Annual International Symposium of INCOSE, 13–16 July 2015, Seattle, USA (2015)
11. ISO/IEC TR 29110-5-1-2: 2011 - Software Engineering - Lifecycle profiles for Very Small Entities (VSES) - Part 5-1-2: Management and engineering guide: Generic profile group: Basic profile, ISO, Switzerland (2011). http://standards.iso.org/ittf/PubliclyAvailableStandards/index.html
12. ISO/IEC/IEEE 15288:2015: Systems and software engineering: system life cycle processes, 2nd ed. International Organization for Standardization, Geneva (2015)
13. ISO/IEC/IEEE 15289:2015: Systems and software engineering - Content of systems and software life cycle process information products (Documentation), ISO (2015)
14. ISO/IEC TR 29110-5-6-2:2014 - Systems and Software Engineering – Systems Engineering Lifecycle Profiles for Very Small Entities (VSEs) - Management and engineering guide: Generic profile group: Basic profile, ISO/IEC. Geneva, Switzerland. http://standards.iso.org/ittf/PubliclyAvailableStandards
15. Laporte, C.Y., O'Connor, R.V., Paucar, L.H.G.: The implementation of ISO/IEC 29110 software engineering standards and guides in very small entities. In: Maciaszek, L.A., Filipe, J. (eds.) ENASE 2015. CCIS, vol. 599, pp. 162–179. Springer, Heidelberg (2016). doi:10.1007/978-3-319-30243-0_9
16. ISO/IEC TR 29110-5-6-1:2015 - Systems and software engineering - Lifecycle profiles for Very Small Entities (VSES) - Part 5-6-1: Systems engineering - Management & engineering guide: Generic profile group: Entry Profile, ISO, Switzerland (2015). http://standards.iso.org/ittf/PubliclyAvailableStandards/index.html
17. ISO/IEC 29110 Public site. http://profs.logti.etsmtl.ca/claporte/English/VSE/index.html
18. Laporte, C.Y., April, A.: Assurance qualité logicielle, vol. 2. Processus de support, Paris, Hermes (2011) (in French)
19. Laporte, C.Y., April, A.: Software Quality Assurance. Wiley, New York (2017)

20. Radice, R.A., Roth, N.K., et al.: A programming process architecture. IBM Syst. J. **24**(2), 79–90 (1985)
21. Systems Engineering Handbook: A Guide for System Life Cycle Processes and Activities, 4th edn., p. 304 (2015). ISBN:978-1-118-99940-0
22. Project Management Institute, Project Management Body of Knowledge Guide (PMBOK Guide), 5th edition. Project Management Institute, Newtown Square (2013)

A Multi-case Study Analysis of Software Process Improvement in Very Small Companies Using ISO/IEC 29110

Claude Y. Laporte[1(✉)] and Rory V. O'Connor[2]

[1] École de technologie supérieure, Montréal, Canada
Claude.Y.Laporte@etsmtl.ca
[2] School of Computing, Dublin City University, Dublin, Ireland
Rory.OConnor@dcu.ie

Abstract. The ISO/IEC 29110 Lifecycle profiles for Very Small Entities is a relatively new standard aimed at addressing the particular development needs of very small companies. Due to its relative youth in the standards domain there is a lack of detailed case studies surrounding its actual deployment in industrial settings. The purpose of this paper is to disseminate the early success stories from pilot trials of this new and emerging standard. The lessons learnt from these case studies should assist the adoption of this new standard in an industrial setting.

Keywords: Very small entities · ISO standards · ISO/IEC 29110 · VSE

1 Introduction

In the domain of software development, Very Small Entities (VSEs) - "an entity (enterprise, organization, department or project) having up to 25 people" [1] - have the challenge of handling multiple small-scale, fast-moving projects allowing little room for unwieldy management processes, but still requiring an efficient and straightforward monitoring process [2]. Moreover due to the small number of people involved in the project and the organization, most of the management processes are performed through an informal way and less documented [3]. The perception of heavyweight processes, especially in terms of documentation, cost and nonalignment with current development process, are among the reasons why the companies did not plan to adopt a lifecycle standard in the short to medium term [4, 5].

VSEs have unique characteristics, which make their business styles different to larger organizations and therefore most of the management processes are performed through a more informal and less documented manner [6]. Furthermore there is an acknowledged lack of adoption of standards in small and very small companies, as the perception is that they have been developed for large software companies and not with the small organisation in mind [7, 8]. As smaller software companies have fewer resources in term of people and money there are many challenges [9].

There is evidence that the majority of small and very small software organizations are not adopting [10] existing standards/proven best practice models because they perceive the standards as being developed by large organizations and orientated towards large organizations, thus provoking the debate the in terms of number of employees, size does actually matter [11, 12]. Studies have shown that small firms' negative perceptions of process model standards are primarily driven by negative views of cost, documentation and bureaucracy [13]. In addition, it has been reported that SMEs find it difficult to relate standards to their business needs and to justify the application of the international standards in their operations [14, 15]. Most SMEs cannot afford the resources for, or see a net benefit in, establishing software processes as defined by current standards and maturity models [16].

Accordingly, a new standard ISO/IEC 29110 "Lifecycle profiles for Very Small Entities" is aimed at meeting the specific needs of VSEs [17]. The overall objective of this new standard is to assist and encourage very small software organizations in assessing and improving their software process and it is predicted that this new standard could encourage and assist small software companies in assessing their software development process [18]. The approach [19] used to develop ISO/IEC 29110 started with the pre-existing international standards, such as the software life cycle standard ISO/IEC/IEEE 12207 and the documentation standard ISO/IEC/IEEE 15289.

The ISO/IEC working group behind the creation of this ISO/IEC 29110 is encouraging the use of pilot projects [20] as a mean to accelerate the adoption of the standard by VSEs. To date a series of individual pilot projects (such as [21–24]) have been completed in several countries, however this paper brings together a series of in-depth longer term case studies of ISO/IEC 29110 implementations into a more compressive case study setting.

1.1 The ISO/IEC 29110 Software Basic Profile

The basic requirements of a software development process are that it should fit the needs of the project and aid project success [26, 27]. And this need should be informed by the situational context where in the project must operate [28] and therefore, the most suitable software development process is contingent on the context [29, 30]. The core situational characteristic of the entities targeted by ISO/IEC 29110 is size. The Generic Profile Group a collection of four profiles (Entry, Basic, Intermediate, Advanced) providing a roadmap to satisfying a vast majority of VSEs worldwide.

At the core the Basic Profile of this standard is a Management and Engineering Guide, officially know as ISO/IEC TR 29110-5-1-2, which focuses on Project Management and Software Implementation as illustrated in Fig. 1. The purpose of the Basic Profile is to define Software Implementation (SI) and Project Management (PM) processes from a subset of ISO/IEC/IEEE 12207 and ISO/IEC/IEEE 15289 appropriate for VSEs.

A set of Deployment Packages (DPs) have been developed to define guidelines and explain in more detail the processes defined in the ISO/IEC 29110 profiles [20] A deployment package is not a complete process reference model. Deployment packages are not intended to preclude or discourage the use of additional guidelines that VSEs find useful. DPs were designed such that a VSE can implement its content, without having to implement the complete ISO/IEC 29110 framework, i.e. all the management

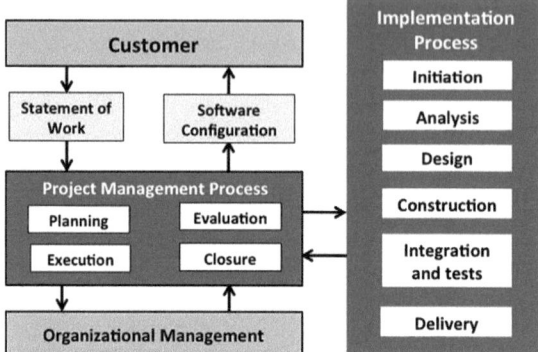

Fig. 1. Basic profile processes and activities [26]

and engineering activities, at the same time. A set of nine DPs have been developed and are freely available from [31]. They are available in Czech, English and Spanish.

2 ISO/IEC 29110 Industry Trial

In this section we will three detailed case studies of organizations that have implemented ISO/IEC 29110. The purpose of these trials is to illustrate the usage of this standard in an industrial context and to provide feedback to standards authors. Whilst not a detailed methodological approach to validation of this standard and whilst acknowledging the validation limitations, we believe that these high level results are useful to researchers and practitioners alike.

2.1 Case 1: Implementation in an IT Start-up

An implementation project has been conducted in an IT start-up VSE by a team of two developers [32]. Their web application allows users to collaborate, share and plan their trips simply and accessible to all. The use of the Basic profile of ISO/IEC 29110 has guided the start-up to develop an application of high quality while using proven practices of ISO 29110. The total effort of this project was nearly 1000 h. The two members of the team were assigned roles and activities of ISO 29110 (see Table 1). The management and engineering guide of the Basic profile lists the documents that have to be developed during a project as well as their typical content.

During the software development, a traceability matrix was developed between the software requirements, defined in the requirements specification document, and the software components. Since, in most projects requirements, defined in the requirements activity, are never finalized at the end of this activity, a traceability matrix is very useful. One advantage of such a matrix is the possibility of rapidly identifying the impacted software components when modifications, additions, deletions, of software requirements are done during a project.

Table 1. Allocation of ISO 29110 roles to the 2-member team [32]

Role	Identification
Analyst	A
Designer	B
Programmer	A/B
Project Manager	B
Technical Leader	A
Work Team	A/B

Verification tasks, such as peer reviews, were performed on documents such as the requirement specifications and the architecture. The team used the desk-check to review their documents which is inexpensive and easy to implement in any organization and can be used to detect anomalies, omissions, improve a document or present and discuss alternative solutions.

As defined in ISO/IEC 29110, the software integration and tests activity ensures that the integrated Software Components satisfy the software requirements. This activity provides [33]:

- Work team review of the project plan to determine task assignment.
- Understanding of test cases and procedures and the integration environment.
- Integrated software components, corrected defects and documented results.
- Traceability of requirements and design to the integrated software product.
- Documented and verified operational and software user documentations.
- Verified software baseline.

To manage the defects detected, a tracking tool was used. Such software allowed the team to do an inventory of problems found during the integration and testing activity, to track problems and to classify them, and to determine a priority for each defect found. In this project, the open source Bugzilla software tool had been used to manage the defects.

The test plan includes 112 cases which have been successfully completed with the exception test cases connected to one type of defect: the validation of the date format when manually entered by a user. Since this defect was classified as "minor", it was decided not to correct their instances during the first cycle of development. Figure 2 illustrates the percentage of defects detected during the execution of the tests for each category of defects.

The members of the start-up have recorded the effort, in person-hours, spent on tasks of the project to the nearest 30 min. For each major task, the effort to execute the task, the effort required to review a document, such as the software specification document, in order to detect errors and, the effort required to correct the errors (i.e. the rework). As an example, for the development of the software architecture document, it took 42.5 h to develop, an additional 1.5-hour to conduct a review and an additional 3.5 h to correct the errors.

As illustrated in Table 2 for this start-up project, about 8.9 % (i.e. 89 h/990.5 h) of the total project effort has been spent in prevention tasks such as the installation of

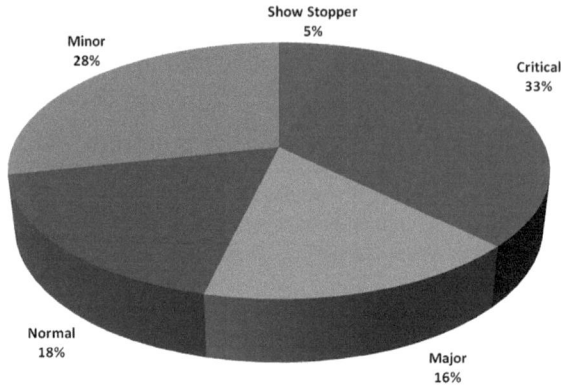

Fig. 2. Percentage of defects detected for each category of defects [32]

Table 2. Effort to execute, detect and correct errors by the 2-member team [32]

Title of task	Prevention (Hours)	Execution (Hours)	Review (Hours)	Rework (Hours)
Environment installation	89			
Project plan development		35	3	4
Project plan execution & project assessment/control		47		
Specification & prototype development		199.5	7	18
Architecture development		42.5	1.5	3.5
Test plan development		12.5	1	2
Code development and testing		361	47	96.5
Develop user guide & maintenance document		8	1	1
Web site deployment		8.5		
Project closure		2		
Total hours	**89**	**716**	**60.5**	**125**

the server, the workstations and the software tools; and only 12.6 % has been spent on rework (i.e. 125 h/990.5 h). This indicates that the use of appropriate standards, in this case for a start-up company, can guide all the phases of the development of a product such that the wasted effort (i.e. rework) is about the same as a more mature organization (i.e. about level 3 of CMM).

A large study was performed, in a large organization, to measure the cost of quality where 1100 software tasks were analysed on a software development project totalling 88,000 h [32]. As illustrated in Fig. 3, the distribution of development costs in the various categories of software quality and implementation cost. At the time the cost of quality study was performed, this organization was at level 3 of the CMM maturity model.

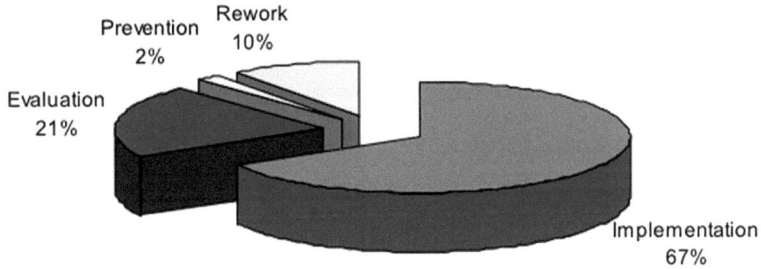

Fig. 3. Distribution of effort in the 88,000-hour project [32]

In most start-ups, the wasted effort, for a project similar to this one, would have added about 90 h (i.e. 30 % of 716 or 215 h – 125 h). This also implies, that for a net effort of about 6 h per member per day (if we subtract from an 8-hour day interruptions (e.g. phone call), answering emails, discussions in corridors, etc.), the product would have been ready for delivery to a customer about 15 days, of 6 h, later than with a project with only 12.6 % of waste.

These two projects have demonstrated that, by using ISO/IEC 29110, it was possible to properly plan the project and develop the software product using proven software practices documented in standards as well as not interfering with the creativity during the development of their web site. People who think that standards are a burden, an unnecessary overhead and a treat to creativity should look at this start-up project and revisit their results.

2.2 Case 2: A Large Canadian Financial Institution

The Cash Management IT department, of a large Canadian financial institution, is responsible for the development and maintenance of software tools used by traders. The software team is composed of 6 people. Each year, the division is faced with an increase in the numbers of requests to add, correct or modify features related to supported applications. Before the implementation of the ISO 29110-agile [25] process, customers had the following complaints:

- Very difficult to know the status of specific requests
- Very often, there is an incident when a change is put in production.
- There is a large number of faults detected by the quality assurance department
- The development process is painful and the documentation produced is not very useful.

In response to this problem, we evaluated our process by comparing the activities of the maintenance process to those of the Basic profile of the ISO/IEC 29110. Some shortcomings were found in the project management process and in the software implementation process. Figure 4 illustrates the coverage of the software implementation tasks to the Basic profile.

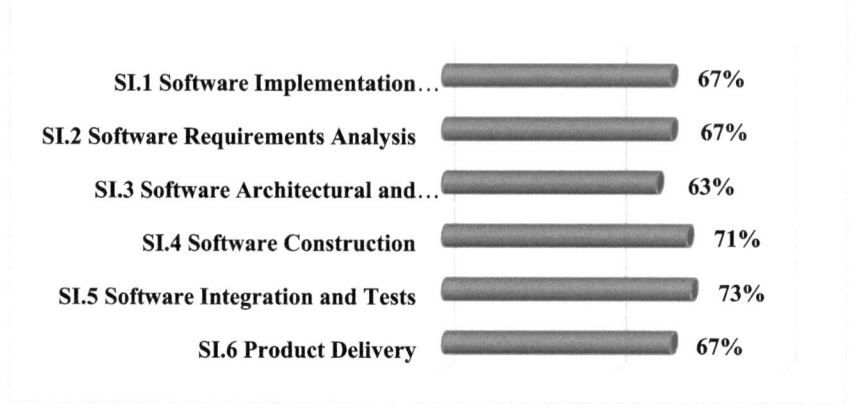

Fig. 4. Coverage of the initial software implementation tasks to the software Basic profile (Translated from [34])

The project management process has been adapted to the context of the division, by injecting a few tasks of the SCRUM methodology. The new agile process, using the Basic profile of the ISO 29110, has been tested on three pilot projects. In this organisation, an incident is classified as minor or major using a set of criteria such as the number of impacted systems, the severity, number of customers impacted and criticality of the impact. The criticality is evaluated on a 1 to 5 scale. Figure 5 illustrates the decrease in the numbers of systems impacted as well as in the total criticality level. In June, Fig. 6 illustrates that 5 systems were impacted and the criticality of those 5 incidents was of 17. About 9 months later, both the number of incidents and the criticality were very low (i.e. one incident and criticality level 1).

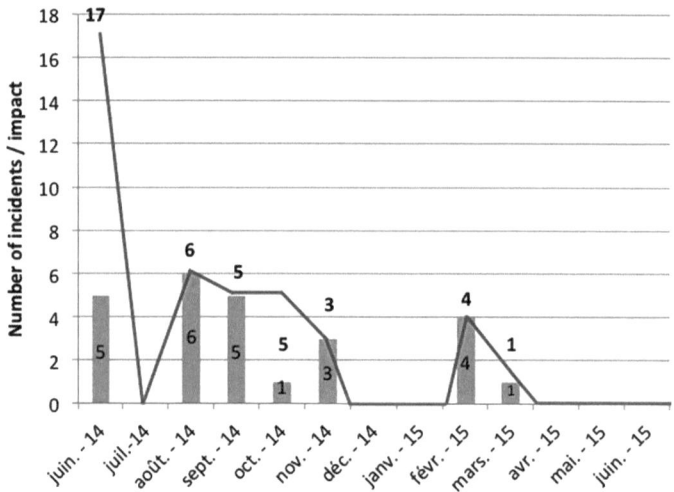

Fig. 5. Reduction of the number of monthly incidents (Translated from [34])

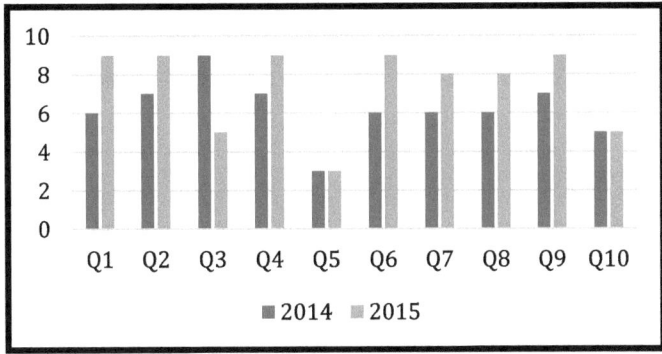

Fig. 6. Satisfaction level of traders (0 to 10 scale) before and after the implementation of the ISO 29110-agile process (Translated from [34])

The adoption of this agile approach, however, requires a higher availability from the users. Initially, this new approach presented a challenge. In some cases, a few users appointed a representative to play the role of head of product backlog. But, that person did not have adequate knowledge of the business domain. Also, the head of product backlog was not able to respond quickly to questions from developers about the requirements, and user stories were not sufficiently documented in advance to maintain the velocity of the team. Finally, representatives of the Project Office and the Audit Group required a few modifications to the new ISO 29110-agile process.

A survey has been conducted to measure the satisfaction level of traders after the deployment of the new ISO 29110-agile process. The following ten questions were asked to traders (on a 0 to 10 scale):

- How do you qualify the quality of our software upgrades (e.g. number of incidents recorded in production)?
- Are you well informed about the content of the next software upgrade?
- Is the frequency of delivery right for you?
- How do you trust the new process?
- How would you describe the ability of the new process to respond to your needs?
- How easy is it to consult the status of a change request?
- How much the new process prioritizes the added value for you as a trader?
- What is the quality level of upgrades?
- Are you satisfied with the productivity of the team in response to your needs?
- What is your overall level of satisfaction about the new process (e.g. quality, cost, return on investment)?

Figure 6 illustrates the increase in satisfaction level between the old process in 2014 and the new ISO 29110-agile process in 2015. The new ISO 29110-agile process has been tested on three pilot projects.

The new process helped to significantly reduce the number of major incidents caused by changes to the tools of the traders. The users are delighted with the new agile planning and control approach, which allows them to better manage their priorities and to always know the status of their requests. The maintenance team was also very pleased to see an improvement in the quality of the change requests, resulting in a noticeable decrease in the number of defects in the software tools handed to traders.

2.3 Case 3: The Implementation in a Division of an Engineering Enterprise

A Canadian division of a large American engineering company, the Transmission & Distribution of electricity division, has implemented a program to define and implement project management processes for their small-scale and medium-scale projects [35]. The firm already had a robust and proven process to manage their large-scale projects. The objectives of this process improvement project were to reduce cost overruns and project delays, standardize practices to facilitate the integration of new managers, increase the level of customer satisfaction and to reduce risk-related planning deviations. Their projects are classified into three categories as illustrated in Table 3. As illustrated in the table, over 95 % of the projects fall in the small- and medium-scale categories.

Table 3. Classification of projects by the engineering firm [35]

	Small project	Medium project	Large project
Duration	< 2 months	> 2 and < 8 months	> 8 months
Team size	<= 4 people	4–8 people	> 8 people
No. of engineering specialties	1	>1	Many
Engineering fees	$5,000–$70,000	$50,000–$350,000	> $350,000
Percentage of projects	70 %	25 %	5 %

Pilot projects have been conducted to test the project management processes and associated support tools (e.g. templates, checklists). The pilot projects consisted of running three different projects where project managers implemented the process and the associated tools. Managers then evaluated the proposed processes, identified problems and potential improvements.

The project management practices used by the company's managers were assessed against the ISO 29110 standard's Basic Profile. The division used the project management process of the Entry Profile of ISO 29110 to document their small-scale project management process and they used the project management process of the Basic profile to document their medium-scale project management process.

ISO has developed a methodology to assess and communicate the economic benefits of standards, which was used, by the engineering firm, to estimate the anticipated costs and benefits over a period of three years. The key objectives of the ISO methodology are to provide:

- A set of methods that measure the impact of standards on organizational value creation
- Decision makers with clear and manageable criteria to assess the value associated with using standards

- Guidance on developing studies to assess the benefits of standards within a particular industry sector

The approach used by the company comprises four steps:

1. Understanding the company's value chain
2. Analysing the value drivers
3. Identifying the impacts of standards
4. Assessing and consolidating results

The "value chain" is a concept can be used as a tool to understand the competitive advantage that a company can have in the actions it undertakes. The "value chain" is a representation of the different steps for an organization to create value in the form of goods or services to customers. Figure 7 illustrates the value chain of the company according to Porter's model. The performance of an activity can have an impact on cost and create a differentiation from competitors. Hence the advantage of using this tool to determine the impact of the project management improvement project to improve project management practices of the company.

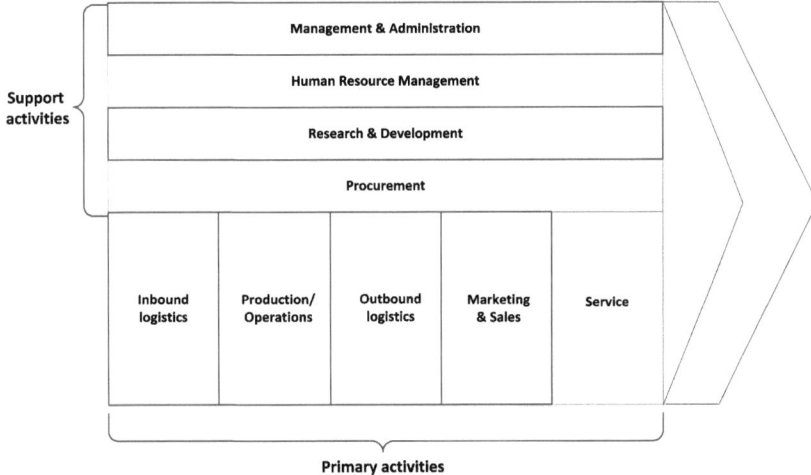

Fig. 7. Value chain of the engineering division (adapted from [36])

The sponsors of this process definition project made the estimates. The improvement program project sponsors made an estimate of anticipated costs and benefits over a period of three years. Table 4 shows the results for the first three years.

Pilot projects have been conducted to test the project management processes and associated support tools (e.g. templates, checklists). The pilot projects consisted of running three different projects where project managers implemented the process and the associated tools. Managers then evaluated the proposed processes, identified problems and potential improvements. The lessons learned sessions conducted at the end of the pilot projects have identified minor adjustments to the processes and tools.

Table 4. Costs and benefits estimations [35]

	Year 1	Year 2	Year 3	Total
Implement & maintain	59 600$	50 100$	50 100$	159 800$
Net Benefits	255 500$	265 000$	265 000$	785 500$

A section of the intranet, dedicated to project management, was created and served as a main access to project management documents such as project management process guides, checklists, forms and templates. Project managers were trained in the new processes and support tools.

The tools developed to support the project management processes proved very useful and helped the project managers rapidly integrate the knowledge required to execute the processes. The improvement program was so successful that managers of the company's other divisions have shown an interest in learning this approach in order to implement it within their respective divisions.

The engineering firm is planning to document and implement their systems engineering processes for the small-scale and medium scale projects using the ISO/IEC TR 29110-5-6-1:2015 Entry Profile [40] and ISO/IEC TR 29110-5-6-2:2014 Basic Profile [39] of the ISO 29110 systems engineering standard and guides.

Recently, the systems engineering Basic Profile of the ISO 29110 [39] has been implemented and successfully audited, by a team of 2 independent auditors, in a company involved in the design and production of subway system components [40ƒd].

3 Discussion and Future Work

The three case studies presented in this paper have demonstrated that by using ISO/IEC 29110, it was possible to properly plan and execute projects and develop products or conduct projects using proven system or software engineering practices without interfering with the creativity of developers. The relationship between the success of a software company and the software process it utilized has been investigated [33, 34] showing the need for all organizations, not just VSEs to pay attention to software process practices such as ISO standards.

As ISO/IEC 29110 is an emerging standard there is much work yet to be completed. The main remaining work item is to finalize the development of the remaining two software profiles of the Generic Profile Group: (a) Intermediate - targeted at VSEs involved in the management of more than one project in parallel with more than one work team and (b) Advanced - targeted at VSEs which want to sustain and grow as an independent competitive system and/or software development business.

Working Group 24 of ISO/IEC JTC1/SC7 was initially authorized to develop the ISO/IEC 29110 for software, was also assigned to develop a similar approach for VSEs involved in the domain of systems engineering [37, 38]. Recently the ISO published the systems engineering and management guides of the Basic profile [39] and Entry [41]. A German version of the Basic profile will be available in 2017 from the German standardisation organisation. The systems engineering and management guide of the Intermediate profile should be published by ISO in 2017.

Work currently underway on an assessment mechanism for ISO/IEC 29110 [42], a clear niche market need is emerging which may force the process assessment community to change their views on how process assessments are carried out for VSEs. It is clear that the process assessment community will have to rethink process assessment, new methods and ideas for assessing processes in VSEs.

In 2009, it was proposed to establish an informal interest group about education. Its main objective is to develop a set of courses for software undergraduate and graduate students such that students learn about the ISO standards for VSEs before they graduate. The role of education [43–46] is a significant issue in ensuring that the next generation of software project managers and software process engineers are both familiar with the benefits of standards, specifically in VSEs and the role of ISO/IEC 29110 in particular. In 2016, fifteen countries are teaching ISO/IEC 29110. As an example, ISO 29110 is taught in 10 universities of Thailand as well as in undergraduate and graduates courses in Canada [47]. Such education programmes may assist with addressing the perceived issues with standards adoption and the lack of managerial commitment [48, 49] in adopting VSE standards.

References

1. Laporte, Ç.Y., Alexandre, S., O'Connor, R.: A software engineering lifecycle standard for very small enterprises. In: O'Connor, R.V., Baddoo, N., Smolander, K., Messnarz, R. (eds.) EuroSPI 2010. CCIS, vol. 16, pp. 129–141. Springer, Heidelberg (2008)
2. Coleman, G., O'Connor, R.V.: An investigation into software development process formation in software start-ups. J. Enterp. Inf. Manag. **21**(6), 633–648 (2008)
3. Basri, S., O'Connor, R.V.: Evaluation on knowledge management process in very small software companies: a survey. In: 5th Knowledge Management International Conference, Terengganu, Malaysia, May 2010
4. Mora, M., O'Connor, R., Raisinghani, M., Macías-Luévano, J.: An IT service engineering and management framework (ITS-EMF). Int. J. Serv. Sci. Manag. Eng. Technol. **2**(2), 1–15 (2011)
5. Sanchez-Gordon, M.L., O'Connor, R.V.: Understanding the gap between software process practices and actual practice in very small companies. Softw. Qual. J. **24**, 549–570 (2015). doi:10.1007/s11219-015-9282-6
6. O'Connor, R., Laporte, C.Y.: Towards the provision of assistance for very small entities in deploying software lifecycle standards. In: Proceedings of the 11th International Conference on Product Focused Software (PROFES 2010). ACM (2010)
7. O'Connor, R., Coleman G.: Ignoring 'best practice': why Irish software SMEs are rejecting CMMI and ISO 9000. Australas. J. Inf. Syst. **16**(1) (2009)
8. O'Connor, R.V., Basri, S., Coleman, G.: Exploring managerial commitment towards SPI in small and very small enterprises. In: Riel, A., O'Connor, R., Tichkiewitch, S., Messnarz, R. (eds.) EuroSPI 2010. CCIS, vol. 99, pp. 268–279. Springer, Heidelberg (2010)
9. Basri, S., O'Connor, R.V.: A study of software development team dynamics in SPI. In: O'Connor, R.V., Pries-Heje, J., Messnarz, R. (eds.) EuroSPI 2011. CCIS, vol. 172, pp. 143–154. Springer, Heidelberg (2011)

10. Clarke, P., O'Connor, R.V.: An approach to evaluating software process adaptation. In: O'Connor, R.V., Rout, T., McCaffery, F., Dorling, A. (eds.) SPICE 2011. CCIS, vol. 155, pp. 28–41. Springer, Heidelberg (2011)
11. Coleman, G., O'Connor, R.: Software process in practice: a grounded theory of the Irish software industry. In: Richardson, I., Runeson, P., Messnarz, R. (eds.) EuroSPI 2006. LNCS, vol. 4257, pp. 28–39. Springer, Heidelberg (2006)
12. Basri, S., O'Connor, R.: A study of knowledge management process practices in very small software companies. Am. J. Econ. Bus. Adm. **3**(4), 636–644 (2012)
13. Petkov, D., Edgar-Nevill, D., Madachy, R., O'Connor, R.: Information systems, software engineering, and systems thinking: challenges and opportunities. Int. J. Inf. Technol. Syst. Approach (IJITSA) **1**(1), 62–78 (2008)
14. O'Connor, R., Basri, S.: The effect of team dynamics on software development process improvement. Int. J. Hum. Capital Inf. Technol. Prof. **3**(3), 13–26 (2012)
15. Larrucea, X., O'Connor, R.V., Colomo-Palacios, R., Laporte, C.Y.: Software process improvement in very small organizations. IEEE Softw. **33**(2), 85–89 (2016)
16. Laporte, C.Y., O'Connor, R.V., Paucar, L.H.G.: The Implementation of ISO/IEC 29110 software engineering standards and guides in very small entities. In: Maciaszek, L.A., Filipe, J. (eds.) ENASE 2015. CCIS, vol. 599, pp. 162–179. Springer, Heidelberg (2016). doi:10.1007/978-3-319-30243-0_9
17. O'Connor, R.V., Coleman, G.: An investigation of barriers to the adoption of software process best practice models. In: ACIS 2007 Proceedings, p. 35 (2007)
18. O'Connor, R.V., Laporte, C.Y.: Deploying lifecycle profiles for very small entities: an early stage industry view. In: O'Connor, R.V., Rout, T., McCaffery, F., Dorling, A. (eds.) SPICE 2011. CCIS, vol. 155, pp. 227–230. Springer, Heidelberg (2011)
19. ISO/IEC TR 29110-5-1-1:2011 – Software engineering – Lifecycle Profiles for Very Small Entities (VSEs) –Part 5-2-1: Management and engineering guide: Generic profile group: Entry profile, International Organization for Standardization/International Electrotechnical Commission: Geneva, Switzerland. http://standards.iso.org/ittf/PubliclyAvailableStandards/c051153_ISO_IEC_TR_29110-5-1_2011.zip
20. O'Connor, R.V., Laporte, C.Y.: An innovative approach to the development of an international software process lifecycle standard for very small entities. Int. J. Inf. Technol. Syst. Approach **7**(1), 1–22 (2014)
21. Laporte, C.Y., O'Connor, R., Fanmuy, G.: International systems and software engineering standards for very small entities. CrossTalk J. Defense Softw. Eng. **26**(3), 28–33 (2013)
22. Laporte, C.Y., Séguin, N., Villas Boas, G.: Seizing the benefits of software and systems engineering standards, ISO Focus +. International Organization for Standardization, pp. 32–36 (2013b)
23. O'Connor, R.V.: Evaluating management sentiment towards ISO/IEC 29110 in very small software development companies. In: Mas, A., Mesquida, A., Rout, T., O'Connor, R.V., Dorling, A. (eds.) SPICE 2012. CCIS, vol. 290, pp. 277–281. Springer, Heidelberg (2012)
24. Ribaud, V., Saliou, P., O'Connor, R.V., Laporte, C.Y.: Software engineering support activities for very small entities. In: Riel, A., O'Connor, R., Tichkiewitch, S., Messnarz, R. (eds.) EuroSPI 2010. CCIS, vol. 99, pp. 165–176. Springer, Heidelberg (2010)
25. Galvan, S., Mora, M., O'Connor, R.V., Acosta, F., Alvarez, F.: A compliance analysis of agile methodologies with the ISO/IEC 29110 project management process. Procedia Comput. Sci. **64**, 188–195 (2015)
26. Clarke, P., O'Connor, R.V.: The meaning of success for software SMEs: an holistic scorecard based approach. In: O'Connor, R.V., Pries-Heje, J., Messnarz, R. (eds.) EuroSPI 2011. CCIS, vol. 172, pp. 72–83. Springer, Heidelberg (2011)

27. O'Connor, R.V., Clarke, P.: Software process reflexivity and business performance: initial results from an empirical study. In: International Conference on Software and System Process (ICSSP 2015), 24–26 August 2015 (2015)
28. Clarke, P., O'Connor, R.V., Leavy, B., Yilmaz, M.: Exploring the relationship between software process adaptive capability and organisational performance. IEEE Trans. Softw. Eng. **41**(12), 1169–1183 (2015)
29. Jeners, S., Clarke, P., O'Connor, R.V., Buglione, L., Lepmets, M.: Harmonizing software development processes with software development settings – a systematic approach. In: McCaffery, F., O'Connor, R.V., Messnarz, R. (eds.) EuroSPI 2013. CCIS, vol. 364, pp. 167–178. Springer, Heidelberg (2013)
30. Clarke, P., O'Connor, R.: The situational factors that affect the software development process: towards a comprehensive reference framework. J. Inf. Softw. Technol. **54**(5), 433–447 (2012)
31. Deployment Packages repository. http://profs.logti.etsmtl.ca/claporte/English/VSE/index.html
32. Laporte, C.Y., Hébert, C., Mineau, C.: Development of a social network website using the new ISO/IEC 29110 standard developed specifically for very small entities. Softw. Qual. Prof. J. ASQ **16**(4), 4–25 (2014)
33. ISO/IEC TR 29110-1:2016: Systems and software Engineering - Lifecycle Profiles for Very Small Entities (VSEs) - Part 1: Overview. International Organization for Standardization (ISO), Geneva (2016). http://standards.iso.org/ittf/PubliclyAvailableStandards
34. Plante, F.: Développement et mise en oeuvre d'un processus de type agile au sein de la direction solution trésorerie du mouvement Desjardins. Rapport de projet de maitrise, École de technologie supérieure, April 2015 (in French)
35. Laporte, C.Y., Chevalier, F.: An innovative approach to the development of project management processes for small-scale projects in a large engineering company. In: 25th Annual International Symposium of INCOSE (International Council on Systems Engineering), 13–16 July 2015, Seattle, USA (2015)
36. Economic Benefits of Standards Methodology Handbook. International Organization for Standardization, Geneva, Switzerland (2010). http://www.iso.org/iso/home/standards/benefitsofstandards/benefits-detail.htm?emid=6
37. Laporte, C.Y., O'Connor, R.V.: Systems and software engineering standards for very small entities: implementation and initial results. In: 9th International Conference on the Quality of Information and Communications Technology (QUATIC), 23–26 September 2014, pp. 38–47 (2014)
38. O'Connor, R.V., Sanders, M.: Lessons from a pilot implementation of ISO/IEC 29110 in a group of very small Irish companies. In: Woronowicz, T., Rout, T., O'Connor, R.V., Dorling, A. (eds.) SPICE 2013. CCIS, vol. 349, pp. 243–246. Springer, Heidelberg (2013)
39. ISO/IEC TR 29110-5-6-2:2014 - Systems Engineering – Lifecycle Profiles for Very Small Entities (VSEs) – Part 5-6-2: Systems engineering - Management and engineering guide: Generic profile group: Basic profile. International Organization for Standardization/International Electrotechnical Commission, Geneva, Switzerland. http://standards.iso.org/ittf/PubliclyAvailableStandards/c063371_ISO_IEC_29110-5-6_2_2014.zip
40. Laporte, C.Y., Tremblay, N., Menaceur, J., Poliquin, D.: Implementing the new ISO/IEC 29110 systems engineering process standard in a small public transportation company. In: 23nd European Conference on Systems, Software and Services Process Improvement (EuroSPI 2016). Springer-Verlag, September 2016

41. ISO/IEC TR 29110-5-6-1:2015 - Systems and software engineering – Lifecycle Profiles for Very Small Entities (VSEs) –Part 5-6-1: System engineering Management and engineering guide: Generic profile group: Entry profile. International Organization for Standardization/ International Electrotechnical Commission, Geneva, Switzerland. http://standards.iso.org/ittf/PubliclyAvailableStandards/index.html
42. ISO/IEC 29110-4-1:2011: Software Engineering – Lifecycle Profiles for Very Small Entities (VSEs) - Part 4-1: Profile specifications: Generic profile group. International Organization for Standardization (ISO), Geneva (2011)
43. Laporte, C.Y., O'Connor, R.: Software process improvement in graduate software engineering programs, In: O'Connor, R.V., Mitasiunas, A., Ross, M. (eds.) Proceeding of the 1st International Workshop on Software Process Education, Training and Professionalism (SPETP 2015), vol. 1368, pp. 18–24. CEUR Electronic Workshop Proceedings (2015)
44. Laporte, C.Y., O'Connor, R.V.: Software process improvement in graduate software engineering programs. In: Proceedings of the 1st International Workshop on Software Process Education, Training and Professionalism (SPETP 2015), pp. 18–24. CEUR Workshop Proceedings (2015)
45. Ribaud, V., Matthieu, A.B., O'Connor, R.V.: Process assessment issues in a bachelor capstone project. In: Proceedings of the 1st International Workshop on Software Process Education, Training and Professionalism (SPETP 2015), pp. 25–33. CEUR Workshop Proceedings (2015)
46. Laporte, C., O'Connor, R., Garcia Paucar, L., Gerancon, B.: An innovative approach in developing standard professionals by involving software engineering students in implementing and improving international standards. Stand. Eng. J. SES (Soc. Stand. Prof.) **67**(2), 2–9 (2015)
47. Laporte, C.Y., O'Connor, R.V.: Software process improvement in industry in a graduate software engineering curriculum. Softw. Qual. Prof. J. ASQ **18**(3), 4–17 (2016)
48. Sanchez-Gordon, M.-L., O'Connor, R.V., Colomo-Palacios, R.: Evaluating VSEs viewpoint and sentiment towards the ISO/IEC 29110 standard: a two country grounded theory study. In: Rout, T., O'Connor, R.V., Dorling, A. (eds.) SPICE 2015. CCIS, vol. 526, pp. 114–127. Springer, Heidelberg (2015)
49. Basri, S., O'Connor, R.: Organizational commitment towards software process improvement an Irish software VSEs case study. In: 4th International Symposium on Information Technology 2010 (ITSim 2010), Kuala Lumpur, Malaysia, June 2010

Communication and Team Issues in SPI

Refactoring Software Development Process Terminology Through the Use of Ontology

Paul M. Clarke[1,2], Antoni Lluís Mesquida Calafat[4], Damjan Ekert[5], J.J. Ekstrom[6], Tatjana Gornostaja[7], Milos Jovanovic[4], Jørn Johansen[8], Antonia Mas[4], Richard Messnarz[5], Blanca Nájera Villar[9], Alexander O'Connor[1,3], Rory V. O'Connor[1,2(✉)], Michael Reiner[10], Gabriele Sauberer[9], Klaus-Dirk Schmitz[11], and Murat Yilmaz[12]

[1] Dublin City University, Dublin, Ireland
{paul.m.clarke,alexander.oconnor,rory.oconnor}@dcu.ie
[2] Lero, The Irish Software Research Centre, Limerick, Ireland
[3] ADAPT, the Global Centre of Excellence for Digital Content Technology, Dublin, Ireland
[4] Universitat de les Illes Balears, Palma, Mallorca, Spain
{antoni.mesquida,milos.jovanovic,antonia.mas}@uib.es
[5] ISCN, The International Software Consulting Network, Graz, Austria
{dekert,rmess}@iscn.com
[6] Brigham Young University, Provo, UT, USA
jekstrom@byu.edu
[7] Tilde Company, Riga, Latvia
tatjana.gornostaja@tilde.com
[8] Whitebox Aps, Hørsholm, Denmark
jj@whitebox.dk
[9] TermNet, The International Network for Terminology, Vienna, Austria
{bnajera,gsaubere}@termnet.org
[10] European Certification and Qualification Association (ECQA), Krems, Austria
michael.reiner@fh-krems.ac.at
[11] Technical University of Cologne, Cologne, Germany
klaus.schmitz@th-koeln.de
[12] Çankaya University, Ankara, Turkey
myilmaz@cankaya.edu.tr

Abstract. In work that is ongoing, the authors are examining the extent of software development process terminology drift. Initial findings suggest there is a degree of term confusion, with the mapping of concepts to terms lacking precision in some instances. Ontologies are concerned with identifying the concepts of relevance to a field of endeavour and mapping those concepts to terms such that term confusion is reduced. In this paper, we discuss how ontologies are developed. We also identify various sources of software process terminology. Our work to date indicates that the systematic development of a software development process ontology would be of benefit to the entire software development community. The development of such an ontology would in effect represent a systematic refactoring of the terminology and concepts produced over four decades of software process innovation.

Keywords: Software engineering · Software development process · Software development roles · Specialised communication · Terminology · Ontology

1 Introduction

Given that software development is a complex undertaking [1] which is human-centric in nature [2, 3], it follows that the consistent use of language and terminology should be an important consideration for software development. However, on the evidence of our initial research, it would appear that the software process domain suffers from an inconsistent use of terminology, to the extent that there may be large latent terminology problem concerning software development activities and roles [4]. That a terminology problem exists in our domain may to some extent be expected – since we have witnessed significant expansion over the past forty years. This expansion has been accompanied by innovation in the use of language and it is for this reason that we have *iterations* that are sometimes called *cycles*, *team leaders* that might be considered to be *project managers*, *features* that some might confuse with *user stories*, and *processes* that some refer to as *methods*. This expanse of terminology is not always accompanied by expansion of the underlying concepts and therefore, it could be claimed that new terminology is not always needed or helpful.

The consistent application of terminology is of concern to many fields of endeavour with the result that techniques have been developed to help address issues related to conceptual and terminological diversity. Ontological frameworks can be employed to reconcile diverse terminology through the systematic elaboration of the concepts of concern, while in parallel determining terminology-to-concept relationships. Once developed, an ontological framework can help to ground the language usage in a field, while it can also allow users of overlapping terminology to approximate where the conceptual scope of one term ends and another starts. Thus, a software process ontological framework could enable users of one software development process lifecycle to interact more smoothly with those using a different software development approach, while at the same time allowing all software developers to examine and clarify their own use of terminology and language. In previously published related work [4], the authors have elaborated on some examples of inconsistent terminology in the software process domain (refer to Fig. 1). In this paper, we provide some additional information on how ontologies are constructed and utilised, while also providing a brief overview of some of the present sources of software development process terminology, including books/bodies of knowledge, taxonomies and international standards.

This paper is structured as follows: Sect. 2 outlines the ontological approach and demonstrates how this technique can be of benefit to the software development community. Section 3 presents a brief overview of some of the sources of software process terminology, including an examination of the semantic distance that can be observed where multiple conflicting definitions are provided for the same term. Section 4 contains a discussion and conclusion.

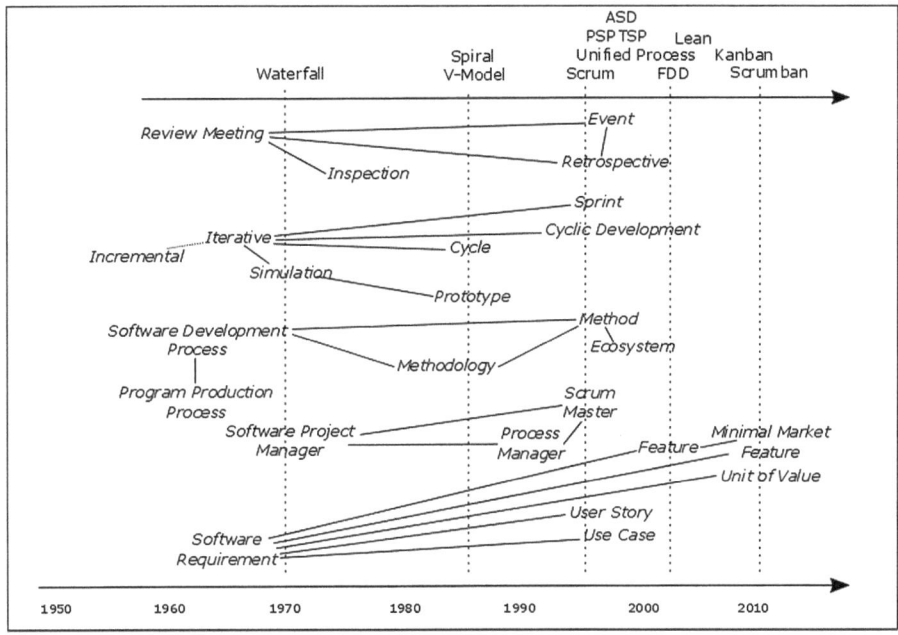

Fig. 1. Software terminology landscape – a process and role viewpoint

2 Terminology and Ontology

According to ISO 1087-1 [5], terminology work is the systematic collection, description, processing and presentation of concepts and their designations. This means that terminology is concerned with concepts and conceptual systems, making them explicit by means of definitions and designations as well as phrases within languages for special purposes. Terminology science provides the basic concepts and best practices for terminology work and terminography, i.e. for the systematic documentation and maintenance of terms. There are different ways to approach terminology work, as for example ad-hoc terminology management that focuses on solving instant problems and it is seen as a part of another process. On the other hand, systematic terminology management is based on the consistent application of working methods for a domain knowledge-oriented approach in order to harvest all the relevant concepts for a specific subject field.

In order to reduce the software development process terminological challenge, the concept orientation and the systematic terminology work approach are key: A systematic study of the field of knowledge that allows the collection of the concepts and terms and, thus, to develop a conceptual structure of the domain in the form of a concept system. The goal of our intended work, which we refer to as the SYNTHESIS Initiative, would be not only to enable clear communication between experts, but also to achieve the unique representation of concepts by avoiding redundancies, if possible, by setting a set preferred usage. This means, from the descriptive to the prescriptive work.

In order to develop this methodology for the successful harmonisation of the terminology for software development processes and roles, there is no need to start from scratch. Firstly, there are already existing standards from which to build the base for a solid terminological work (for example, ISO 704:2009 Terminology work — Principles and methods [6], and ISO 26162:2012 Systems to manage terminology, knowledge and content — Design, implementation and maintenance of terminology management systems [7]). And secondly, many terms, glossaries and resources for software development are already in use (and which in some cases are causing conflicts or unnecessary ambiguity).

Because of this, the first step would be to evaluate and assess available glossaries, documentation and resources and their reliability, information coming from authoritative bodies, any terminology work done by other institutions (for example, the ISO terminology about software process, to be found in the official ISO Online Browsing Platform [8] or the International Software Testing and Qualifications Board Glossary [9]). The reliability of such resources is a key factor while retrieving information. The assessment of the field of knowledge and identification and evaluation of the most relevant resources in the field of knowledge relating to software process terms build the basis for the ontological work. This can include domains such as security, reliability, methodology-specific terms and their interrelationship.

An ontology is the collection of concepts and terms in a certain language in a specific subject field, but also the formal, explicit (conceptual) models of object ranges in a computational representation [10]. According to the ISO, a model of product knowledge is achieved by a formal and consensual representation of the concepts of a product domain in terms of identified characterisation classes, class relations and identified properties [11]. An ontology also gives an indication about the degree of necessity of a prescriptive approach as it will show if there is a proliferation of terms for one concept, why this happens and which term candidate is the most adequate in each case. It should be highlighted that there is no single approach to ontology development that is universally applied, and that tooling can be utilised in order to support the development task [12].

According to ISO 704 [6], "it is necessary to bear in mind the subject field that gave rise to the concept and to consider the expectations and objectives of the target users, in organizing concepts into a concept system. The subject field shall act as the framework within which the concept field, the set of thematically related but unstructured concepts, is established … Characteristics shall be used in the analysis of concepts, the modelling of concept systems, in the formulation of definitions."

The terminology of a subject field always follows a concept system based on the relations existing between concepts. The unique position of each concept within a system is determined by the intension and the extension. In the case of concept systems based on generic relations, the concept system also reflects inheritance systems, because specific concepts inherit characteristics from their generic super-ordinates. The set of characteristics that come together as a unit to form the concept is called the *intension*. The objects viewed as a set and conceptualized into a concept are known as the *extension*. The two, the intension and the extension, are interdependent. For example, the characteristics making up the intension of 'mechanical mouse' determine the extension or the objects that qualify as mechanical mice. In some fields a distinction is made between necessary, sufficient and essential characteristics. However, explaining this in this paper would exceed the scope of the same [6].

The effectiveness of ontologies in addressing terminology concerns has been demonstrated in many fields [12] and given the type of findings outlined in Sect. 1, there are therefore good reasons to consider its use in the software development process space. Indeed, the use of ontology is already being considered as a technique for the harmonisation of terminology in ISO/IEC Joint Technical Committee 1, Subcommittee 7 (JTC1 SC7) [13]. This ontology approach to the software process conceptual structure would also help to delimit and clarify roles and tasks in the working environment being an innovative and comprehensive approach in order, not only, to harmonise the existing resources, but also standardise curricula and skills for professions related to knowledge-driven software development.

A canonical software development process and roles ontology would be linked or embedded in a terminological database that would also give information about the terms behind the concepts, their definitions and characteristics that would improve the specialised communication among not only software developers, engineers, project managers, business managers and trainers, but would also provide an updated, centrally managed, comprehensive, online available resource for everyone (even laypersons).

Last but not least, the role of the experts is essential in this process. The terminologist can only draft the methodology for a successful terminology project. But the software process engineers are the experts that have the knowledge to select the best term candidates, draft definitions and validate relevant information. However, it is often the case that experts lack the basic skills and knowledge to carry out systematic terminology work. Therefore, it will be important to develop and implement an integrated, cross-disciplinary, and market-oriented training programme to create a new skills and qualifications portfolio for these professionals. This would be subject of a new ECQA [14] job role: the ECQA Certified Terminology Professional for Software Process Engineering certification and training.

3 Sources of Software Development Process Terminology

We do not want to give the impression that there is anything surprising in the current state of software development process terminology. Teams form around specific problems and projects and evolve a terminology for their community of practice [15]. Since the team faces common problems inside of a common set of constraints they naturally evolve a dialect that facilitates efficient communication for them. They may even publish ontological artifacts that aid others in joining the community, since turnover on teams is common.

Neither do we want to give the impression that no work has been done to create a common conceptual framework for Software Engineering. Two efforts stand out as particularly important to the development of an accepted formal vocabulary for Software Engineering: The Software Engineering Body of Knowledge (SwEBoK) [16] and the Software and Systems Engineering Vocabulary (SEVocab) [17]. The SwEBoK is a long term effort by the IEEE-CS to create a standard taxonomy for what a Software Engineer ought to know 4 years into her/his career. SEVocab is an edited aggregation of ontological artifacts from over 100 ISO/IEC/IEEE standards. It has the appearance of a glossary since its basic organisation consists of terms followed by a list of definitions. However, since it includes *synonym* and *see-also* links to other terms it should probably be viewed as a topic map.

Professional societies can be classified as a formal communities of practice that form around a domains of expertise. Working Groups in those societies are chartered to create ontological artifacts for specific areas of interest or expertise. Since these ontological entities (Standards, Technical Reports, etc.) are designed to document a specific area of knowledge or expertise, they often contain a glossary of terms associated with the concepts used in the document. Examples include:

- ISO/IEC 24744:2007 Software Engineering–Metamodel for Development Methodologies [18]
- ISO/IEC 2382-20:1990 Information technology–Vocabulary–Part 20: System development [19]
- ISO/IEC TR 14471:2007 Information technology–Software engineering–Guidelines for the adoption of CASE tools [20]
- IEEE 1074-2006 IEEE Standard for Developing a Software Project Life Cycle Process [21]

In spite of these and many other efforts to document a standard terminology for areas in the discipline of Software Engineering, communities of practice continue to form, evolve, and create semantic drift. How many practitioners are aware that there is a standard metamodel for development methodologies? More instructive questions include: Does software development terminological semantic drift concern practitioners? Is semantic drift a latent as opposed to an open concern? Is semantic drift a worthy concern other than on large multi-supplier projects? These are questions that our ongoing efforts seek to explore.

As a measure of this drift in the system and software engineering space consider the SEVocab project. It is a database consisting of terms and definitions from 124 ISO/IEC/IEEE standards. Some terms have 7 or more associated concepts *after common definitions have been merged*. And this is from an aggregation of *formal standards*. If we are to reduce the entropy in software development process terminology, it will require significant human input even though there are some natural language processing and machine learning techniques that can reduce the manual effort. Some work has been accomplished but there is much more to be done. The Termediator project [22] currently has aggregated approximately 500 glossaries from domains closely related to Information Technology (Fig. 2 provides some background as to the types of sources of terminology incorporated into Termediator). The tool provides cluster analysis for concepts associated with a term which can aid in locating terms that are so over-used that they should be avoided as well as terms that are accepted as labels for a common concept across all of the domains represented. It also provides for rudimentary synonym analysis. This prototype demonstrates the utility of automated approaches to the initial analysis, but requires development to productise the implementation and add features to aid in analysis specific to the creation of an ontology for software development process terminology.

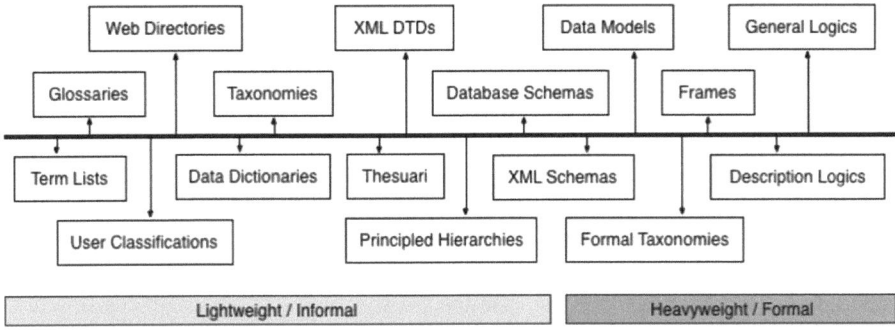

Fig. 2. Spectrum of software development process terminology sources

4 Discussion and Conclusion

According to the late-Enlightenment philosopher Georg Wilhelm Friedrich Hegel, *truth is found neither in the thesis nor the antithesis, but in an emergent synthesis which reconciles the two*. And this is precisely the type of truth that can be pursued in matters of language, as language is a representation of a concept, a concept has at its genesis an idea, and ideas do not lend themselves to perfectly complete definition or interpretation. Correspondingly, we can expect that a certain tension will necessarily arise between the correctness and common usage of terms such that absolute adherence to either is neither desirable nor advisable. So, our job with terminology is to bridge the gap from an idea to its representation, and to do so with a level of precision that is useful and effective for those who utilise the terms.

In earlier work, we demonstrated that there is a latent problem concerning the use of terminology for software development process and roles [4]. The purpose of this paper is to expand upon the ontology approach, explaining how it is suited to addressing the challenge of unifying the existing terms and concepts into a canonical software development process reference model. Such a model would also facilitate accurate interrelating of terms from different software development processes and methods, thus making it easier to understand how different software development models are similar, with positive benefits for those wishing to adapt processes or tailor processes [23]. Since such adaptive capability has been shown to be positively associated with business performance [24–26], any initiative which facilitates adaptation should be welcome. Furthermore, the reportedly high levels of SPI occurring in practice [27, 28], coupled with the rich variation in software development contexts [29] (which themselves are constantly changing [30]), suggests that greater consistency in terminology application would benefit the broader software development community.

A canonical model would also enable future software development process and method innovations to be readily interrelated to the large body of software process know-how that predated its arrival (something that is not easily achieved today). It would further have the benefit of revealing the genuine *newness* in newly proposed software development models and methods, as the conceptual mapping to the pre-existing concepts and terminology would be enabled through the ontology. This might not meet with the approval of software process entrepreneurs seeking to cash-in on *new* approaches but it would certainly benefit the millions of software development practitioners who seek to understand each other and to robustly evaluate newly proposed approaches for (1) differences from their existing processes, and (2) integration into their present processes. Indeed, in the fullness of time, newly proposed approaches might demonstrate their uniqueness/newness through formally elaborating on the relationship to the canonical model – this way, genuine process innovation can be supported and promoted, and poorly constructed or ill-informed process innovation can be identified.

Since ontology development requires specific expertise and may be costly, it is important that we first examine the case for a software development process ontology prior to embarking on its development. Perhaps the primary benefit of ontologies is the creation and provision of intelligent, knowledge-based systems by "translating data into actionable insights for decision making" [31]. Earlier published research has reported numerous direct benefits from ontology adoption, including increased productivity of both information workers and software engineering (cost and time reduction, quality improvements) [32]. It has also been demonstrated that in safety critical and security application development, the use of ontology is crucial to fulfilling the objectives of the development work [33]. Beyond software engineering, there is widespread adoption of ontologies in domains such as biomedicine [34], oil extraction [35], and the automotive industry [36], where ontology has been shown to be an effective way of identifying, naming and relating concepts within processes and domains.

While advocating the use of ontology, we also seek to highlight that this is not simply a problem with terminology, it is a greater problem whereby we have not as a community managed to render the core concepts of our field in a universally digestible form. Added to this mix is the possibility that there may even an issue concerning appropriate levels of completeness of individual understandings of the various software development process models that are routinely adopted (or referred to). Take for example the Waterfall model which would appear to have become associated with single-pass, sequential software development in some quarters [4, 37, 38], even though Royce's original model explicitly recognises the need to utilise multiple iterations in software development (those seeking clarification on this point should refer to [39]).

For the software process improvement community, there can be a challenge when formulating discussions with individuals and organisations in order to establish precisely the extent to which a process is enacted, or to understand the boundary to individual roles within companies. Therefore, the challenge of process improvement can potentially be reduced through the introduction of mechanisms to improve the consistency of use of related terminology. It should be noted that our proposed undertaking is neither small nor simplex. Correspondingly, we have assembled a cross-disciplinary team and it is also our intention to pursue a community-led approach to the work program, including engagement with large numbers of software development experts so as to systematically agree concepts, terms and definition. Naturally, within individual software development approaches where clarity exists in relation to software process terms, we would not seek to redefine individual terms – but rather clearly identify their relationship to other process models. Furthermore, work of the proposed nature requires many participants and many years, and therefore substantial funding, the pursuit of which is ongoing.

In software development, the importance of source code refactoring is well understood [40], without it source code can eventually become unmanageable (or at least economically challenging to maintain and extend). Terminology is no different, if allowed to drift unchecked, eventually the terminology and concepts become more and more confusing. The authors therefore propose that the time is anon to consider refactoring our software development process terminology, and that this is best achieved through the adoption of ontology.

References

1. Clarke, P., O'Connor, R.V., Leavy, B.: A complexity theory viewpoint on the software development process and situational context. In: Proceedings of the 2016 International Conference on Software and System Process (ICSSP 2016). IEEE, San Francisco (2016)
2. Yilmaz, M., O'Connor, R.V., Clarke, P.: A systematic approach to the comparison of roles in the software development processes. In: Mas, A., Mesquida, A., Rout, T., O'Connor, R.V., Dorling, A. (eds.) SPICE 2012. CCIS, vol. 290, pp. 198–209. Springer, Heidelberg (2012)
3. Yilmaz, M., O'Connor, R., Clarke, P.: Software development roles: a multi-project empirical investigation. ACM SIGSOFT Softw. Eng. Notes **40**(1), 1–5 (2015)
4. Clarke, P., et al.: An investigation of software development process terminology. In: Clarke, P.M., O'Connor, R.V., Rout, T., Dorling, A. (eds.) SPICE 2016. CCIS, vol. 609, pp. 351–361. Springer, Heidelberg (2016). doi:10.1007/978-3-319-38980-6_25
5. ISO: ISO 1087-1:2000 terminology work – vocabulary – part 1: Theory and application, 1st edn. ISO, Geneva, Switzerland (2000)
6. ISO: ISO 704:2009 terminology work — principles and methods, 1st edn. ISO, Geneva, Switzerland (2009)
7. ISO: ISO 26162:2012 systems to manage terminology, knowledge and content — design, implementation and maintenance of terminology management systems, 1st edn. ISO, Geneva, Switzerland (2012)
8. ISO: Online Browsing Platform. https://www.iso.org/obp/ui/#home
9. ISTQB, Standard Glossary of Software Testing Terms. http://www.istqb.org/downloads/glossary.html
10. Budin, G.: Methodology for dynamic ontology creation from terminologies to ontologies – tools of knowledge organization. In: Proceedings of International Terminology Summer School 2009, TermNet, Cologne, Germany (2009)
11. ISO: ISO 13584-32:2010 - industrial automation systems and integration - OntoML: Product ontology markup language, 1st edn. ISO, Geneva, Switzerland (2010)
12. Aardi, G., de Almeida Falbo, R., Pereira Filho, J.G.: Using objects and patterns to implement domain ontologies. J. Braz. Comput. Soc. **8**(1), 43–56 (2002)
13. Henderson-Sellers, B., McBride, T., Low, G., Gonzalez-Perez, C.: Ontologies for international standards for software engineering. In: Ng, W., Storey, V.C., Trujillo, J.C. (eds.) ER 2013. LNCS, vol. 8217, pp. 479–486. Springer, Heidelberg (2013)
14. ECQA: European Certification and Qualification Organisation. www.ecqa.org
15. Wenger, E.: Communities of Practice: Learning, Meaning, and Identity, 1st edn. Cambridge University Press, Cambridge (1998)

16. IEEE: Guide to the software engineering book of knowledge (SWEBOK). IEEE Computer Society, Los Alamitos (2004)
17. IEEE/ISO/IEC, SE Vocab - Software and Systems Engineering Vocabularly. https://pascal.computer.org/sev_display/index.action
18. ISO/IEC: ISO/IEC 24744:2007 software engineering–metamodel for development methodologies, 1st edn. ISO/IEC, Geneva, Switzerland (2007)
19. ISO/IEC: ISO/IEC 2382-20:1990 information technology–vocabulary–part 20: System development, 1st edn. ISO/IEC, Geneva, Switzerland (1990)
20. ISO/IEC: ISO/IEC TR 14471:2007 information technology–software engineering–guidelines for the adoption of CASE tools, 1st edn. ISO/IEC, Geneva, Switzerland (2007)
21. IEEE: IEEE 1074-2006 IEEE standard for developing a software project life cycle process, 1st edn. IEEE, Washington, DC (2006)
22. Riley, O., Richards, J., Ekstrom, J., Tew, K.: Termediator II: measuring term polysemy using semantic clustering. In: Proceedings of 3rd Conference on Research in Information Technology (RIIT 2014), pp. 81–86. ACM, New York (2014)
23. Coleman, G., O'Connor, R.: Investigating software process in practice: a grounded theory perspective. J. Syst. Softw. **81**(5), 772–784 (2008)
24. Clarke, P., O'Connor, R., Leavy, B., Yilmaz, M.: Exploring the relationship between software process adaptive capability and organisational performance. IEEE Trans. Softw. Eng. **41**(12), 1169–1183 (2015)
25. O'Connor, R.V., Clarke, P.: Software process reflexivity and business performance: initial results from an empirical study. In: Proceedings of the 2015 International Conference on Software and System Process, pp. 142–146. ACM, New York (2015)
26. Clarke, P., O'Connor, R.V.: The influence of SPI on business success in software SMEs: an empirical study. J. Syst. Softw. **85**(10), 2356–2367 (2012)
27. Clarke, P., O'Connor, R.V.: An empirical examination of the extent of software process improvement in software SMEs. J. Softw. Evol. Process **25**(9), 981–998 (2013)
28. Clarke, P., O'Connor, R.V., Yilmaz, M.: A hierarchy of SPI activities for software SMEs: results from ISO/IEC 12207-based SPI assessments. In: Mas, A., Mesquida, A., Rout, T., O'Connor, R.V., Dorling, A. (eds.) SPICE 2012. CCIS, vol. 290, pp. 62–74. Springer, Heidelberg (2012)
29. Clarke, P., O'Connor, R.V.: The situational factors that affect the software development process: towards a comprehensive reference framework. J. Inf. Softw. Technol. **54**(5), 433–447 (2012)
30. Clarke, P., O'Connor, R.V.: Changing Situational Contexts Present a Constant Challenge to Software Developers. In: O'Connor, R.V., Umay Akkaya, M., Kemaneci, K., Yilmaz, M., Poth, A., Messnarz, R. (eds.) EuroSPI 2015. CCIS, vol. 543, pp. 100–111. Springer, Heidelberg (2015). doi:10.1007/978-3-319-24647-5_9
31. Stanford Center for Biomedical Informatics Research (BMIR) at the Stanford University School of Medicine, Protégé. http://protege.stanford.edu/about.php
32. Oberle, D.: How ontologies benefit enterprise applications. Semant. Web **5**(6), 473–491 (2014)
33. Greciano, G., Budin, G.: Designing linguistic support for risk management communication. https://www.uibk.ac.at/translation/aktuelles/aktuelles/unterlagen/papergrecianobudineumedinhbsept2006.pdf
34. Hoehndorf, R., Schofield, P.N., Gkoutos, G.V.: The role of ontologies in biological and biomedical research: a functional perspective. Briefings Bioinform. **16**(6), 1069–1080 (2015)

35. Kharlamov, E., et al.: Ontology based access to exploration data at Statoil. In: Arenas, M. (ed.) ISWC 2015. LNCS, vol. 9367, pp. 93–112. Springer, Heidelberg (2015). doi:10.1007/978-3-319-25010-6_6
36. Rychtyckyj, N., Klampfl, E., Gusikhin, O., Rossi, G.: Application of intelligent methods to automotive assembly planning. In: 2007 IEEE International Conference on Systems, Man and Cybernetics, pp. 2479–2483. IEEE, New Jersey (2007)
37. Molokken-Ostvold, K., Jorgensen, M.: A comparison of software project overruns - flexible versus sequential development models. IEEE Trans. Softw. Eng. **31**(9), 754–766 (2005)
38. Larman, C., Basili, V.R.: Iterative and incremental development: a brief history. IEEE Comput. **36**(6), 47–56 (2003)
39. Royce, W.: Managing the development of large software systems: concepts and techniques. In: Western Electric Show and Convention Technical Papers. IEEE Computer Society, Los Alamitos (1970)
40. Mens, T., Tourwe, T.: A survey of software refactoring. IEEE Trans. Softw. Eng. **30**(2), 126–139 (2004)

Cardion.spec: An Approach to Improve the Requirements Specification Written in the Natural Language Through the Formal Method

Masao Ito[✉]

Nil Software Corp., Tokyo, Japan
nil@nil.co.jp

Abstract. As the reliability and safety of a system become more important, we need the requirement specification that is clear to read and has no error. So far several approaches have been proposed; the formal modelling technique is one of the effective approaches to get the correct specification. But, in the embedded system field, we cannot expect that the most of system engineers know about the formal specification technique. They are the experts of the system, not the specialist of system or software engineering. In our paper, we provide the new approach to mitigate this problem. The user uses only the natural language, and a tool provides the check the text on the fly and points out the sentence that has a problem. The formal model is constructed in the background. The user doesn't need to know the description of the formal model. In this paper, we introduce this approach and the tool, Cardion.spec that we implement our idea.

Keywords: Requirements specification · Natural language · Formal specification · SPARK · Six-variable model

1 Introduction

In the safety-critical system, such as the airplane, automobile, railroad and so on, the reliability and safety is the important factor. The error that affects them in the early development phase increases the cost of re-work, and sometimes it is hard to do it again because the development time is usually very long. And, of course, if we cannot notice the error, it affects the reliability and safety of the system.

To solve this problem, many methods are being proposed up to now. Formal approach is the powerful approach to create the correct requirement specification because it has a mathematical background (e.g. axiomatic set theory, algebra, logic and so on). The people of formal method people say that the formal approach provides the better way to improve the quality of specification and eliminate the error in it. But usually the requirements specification is written in the natural language [1].

In this chapter, we briefly check the several issues of the natural language text and formal method. And at the end of this section we introduce the SPARK language [2], which we choose for the formal approach for our approach. The point is that the formal approach works in the background in it.

1.1 Issues of the Requirement Specification Written in Natural Language

In the IEEE 830 guidelines [3], the eight guides on describing the requirements specification is provided:

- Correct
- Unambiguous
- Complete
- Consistent
- Ranked for importance and/or stability
- Verifiable
- Modifiable
- Traceable

First, we focus on the unambiguousness. This guideline says, "Requirements are often written in natural language (e.g., English). Natural language is inherently ambiguous (4.3.2.1)". And, if we can write the requirements formally we can eliminate the ambiguity, but "one disadvantage in the use of such languages is the length of time required to learn them. Also, many non-technical users find them unintelligible." That is, requirements written formally are good in the viewpoint of ambiguity, but practically we cannot expect that every people learn and use it immediately in practice. So, we have to manage to write good requirements in natural language without the ambiguity. The other example is shown in [4]. In this paper, authors define the quality model of documents and check them to select the documents that need further review. The quality has nine attributes.

- Atomicity
- Unambiguity
- Conciseness
- Testability
- Traceability
- Consistency
- Formal Correctness
- Correctness
- Completeness

They check the review results of the "automotive specifications of the Mercedes-Benz passenger car development (PCD)" and find that "the majority of defects are assigned to content quality-attributes like completeness, correctness and consistency" [5]. From this result, we focus on the consistency with unambiguity. Other attributes are also important, but they have the difficulty to check. For instance, completeness means the lack of information for a specification, but only the author knows whether it is true or not.

1.2 Formal Approaches

By using formal methods, we can eliminate the ambiguity and keep consistency in a model because of the mathematical-based formality. For example, Z language [6] is based on the axiomatic formal theory, and use the set as a type of data (i.e. abstract data type). The function is a given by the relationship between sets. If there is a violation of the type, tool can indicate it.

So far, there are several applications built with the formal method and the books [7, 8] show the successful result. For example, in the airplane field, the mission computer of C-130 was developed using the SPARK language. In the SAET-METEOR project, B method was used.

But there is a weak point on applying the formal approach. As IEEE 830 says, it needs the long learning period to start using a formal method. There are many people to write and read the requirements specification, for example, the hardware/software designer, supplier, testers, manufacturing engineer. At least, they can read the documents written in formal approach correctly at the same time.

And we have another difficulty. There is no universal formal approach. If the problem or solution domains differ, the suitable formal method might differ. For example, Z language, that is one of the famous state-based formal ones, is suitable for the domain that expresses the requirements with the idea of the set. The event based language, like statechart or SCR (Software Cost Reduction) [9] is applicable for the state transition based system. So, we also might need to learn the several formal languages.

1.3 Spark

We choose the SPARK language [2] as the formal language in our approach. SPARK (latest version is SPARK 2014) is the subset of ADA language [10], and we can use it for specifying and/or designing and implementing an application, especially high-integrity one. As we shown before, it is already used and has got good achievements.

To prevent the misuse of language, there are several restrictions in comparison with the ADA language[1].

- The use of access types and allocators is not permitted.
- All expressions (including function calls) are free of side effects.
- Aliasing of names is not permitted.
- The goto statement is not permitted.
- The use of controlled types is not permitted.
- Raising and handling of exceptions is not currently permitted.

The SPARK language has already several tools, such as GNATprove. It provides the many checking mechanism. Most notable checking is the flow analysis. The short example is showing below.

The keyword "Depends" shows the dependency between the variables. For example, "X => Y" means "X depends Y", that is, the value of X is determined by the value of Y. This description is useful to analyse of data flow (Fig. 1).

---

[1] http://www.univ-orleans.fr/sciences/info/ressources/webada/doc/spark/ug/language_subset.html#introduction-to-spark.

```
procedure Swap (X, Y : in out Integer)
    with Depends => (X => Y, Y => X)
is
    T : Integer;
begin
    T := Y;  ── should be T := X;
    X := Y;
    Y := T;
end Swap;
```

q.adb:4:20: warning: unused initial value of "X" [unused_initial_value]
q.adb:5:12: warning: missing dependency "null => X" [depends_null]
q.adb:5:32: warning: missing dependency "Y => Y" [depends_missing]
q.adb:5:32: warning: incorrect dependency "Y => X" [depends_wrong]
...

Fig. 1. Flow analysis

2 Method

In our approach, we analyze the requirements specification in natural language, and increase the quality of documentation incrementally. We use the SPARK language in this process, but user doesn't have to know this language. Only the tool uses it for background checking.

First of all, we show the basic flow of our approach. As we focus on the requirements specification of the embedded system, especially the system on the automobile. The model we use in our approach is mainly the finite state machine (FSM) model.

2.1 Outline of Our Process

There are three steps to improve the quality of the documents. First of all, we try to find the simple error in the sentence. Next, we extract the static and dynamic model. The dynamic model is important in the embedded system. The last phase, we generate the SPARK codes and make an effort to find the problematic points.

Tool doesn't automatically correct the error. It just points it out. And it might provide the candidate sentence, if possible. It is up to the user whether he/she revises it or not.

(Step1). The input is the requirements specification written in natural language (currently, we test only Japanese documents). We do the lexical analysis to get the chunks of a sentence with the word class, and do the syntactic parsing to get the modification structure. In Japanese the lexical analysis is very important, because the Japanese sentence has no space between words in a sentence. Next, we check the text and find the problematic points by using the basic information of text, such as;

(a) Long phrase/sentence
(b) Consecutive kanji/hiragana/katakana characters
(c) Lack of the object of the verb

(Step2). After the first step, we extract the static and dynamic elements to create the FSM model. As for static elements, we distinguish the other system and find the input data for the target system and output data to the other system(s). The dynamic elements is directly relating to the FSM. We extract the state and transition between states with the event/guard condition/action. The input and output of the static model is relating to the action of state transition.

Then we create a dictionary between natural language (Japanese) phrases to an English word. For example, "Clear the setting speed" is assigned into the SET_SPEED_CLEAR or "SET_SPEED = 0"

(Step3). Finally we convert the FSM into the SPARK codes, and compile them. If we encounter the compile error, our tool interprets it and indicates the user the problematic part.

2.2 Static Model

The aim of the static model is finding the system boundary of the target system and other system, and designating the data across the system boundary.

If there is no supporting information (e.g. system structure), it is hard to identify the outer parts of the target system. For example, when we read the sentence "output the target acceleration into the engine control", we may easily understand that the engine control is outer part of the cruise control system. Because the system engineer usually knows the structure of the system. But for the tool it is difficult to know it automatically if it doesn't have the knowledge of the system structure. So, this is the first point that the tool asks for the specification writer.

If the system boundary becomes clear, the flow of data across it is easy to capture.

2.3 Dynamic Model

For the embedded system, the dynamic behaviour is important because it is usually a reactive system. And the interaction between human and the machine is also essential in the recent complicated system.

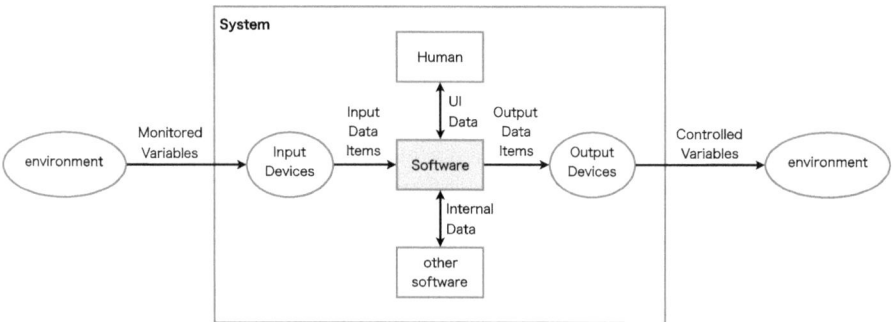

Fig. 2. Six-variable model

Before entering into the detail of the dynamic model, we'll explain the six-variable model of the system structure in this paper. In general, four-variable model is used; monitored and controlled variables and input and output data items [9]. But we use the six-variable model; we add the interaction of human-system (software) and the internal data to other part/system (Fig. 2). The four-variable model [11] is obviously the subset of six-variable model in a simple system that has no human interaction.

2.3.1 State
The Σ is the set of state. And we define the helper function for the state.

$id(\sigma)$	:id
$name(\sigma)$	:name
$parent(\sigma)$	:super-state
$children(\sigma)$	:sub-state
$type(\sigma)$	:"basic" or "super"
$default(\sigma)$	:is default state?

This is the simple definition of the state. We do not use the entry action/exit action/activity.

2.3.2 Transition
The T is the set of transition. And we define the helper function for the transition.

$src(\tau)$	:source state of transition
$trig(\tau)$	:trigger event
$cond(\tau)$	:condition
$act(\tau)$	:action
$dest(\tau)$	:destination state of transition
$prty(\tau)$	:priority

In the high-level requirements specification, the priority is seldom used.

2.3.3 Mapping
Basically the elements of the transition are expressed like <*src*, *trig*, *cond*, *act*, *dest*>. It means that "if we are in the *src* state and *trig* event comes when the condition *cond* satisfies, the system does *act* asynchronously and go to the *dest* state." We extract each element of transition from the analyzed text.

Previously, we see the six-variable models. The software is relating to the four direct variables of the six-variable model. They are;

(1) Observed variable
(2) Controlled variable
(3) User-input variable
(4) External-system variable

It is possible to think that the user-input variable is a kind of the input data, but we have to remember that the input data come from the environment. So, it is appropriate to think it is the different variable.

Next we show the patterns that define the way to set the transition according to the difference of the four variables.

(1) Pattern 1: Observed variable (comes from Environment). We consider the following example: "In the constant speed mode, if the system find the 5 km/h difference between the speed of the self-car and the setting speed, the system clear the setting speed and go to the standby state". In this example, the speed of the self-car is the observed variable. The setting speed is an internal variable.

We assume that the observed variable are monitored periodically, so, we introduce the special keyword PERIODICAL as the trigger of the transition.

$src(\tau) = s11$, $name(s11) = $ "Constant_Speed"
$trig(\tau) = $ PERIODICAL
$cond(\tau) = $ "5 km/h difference between the speed of the self-car and setting speed"
$act(\tau) = $ "Clear_Setting_Speed"
$dest(\tau) = s12$, $name(s12) = $ "StandBy"

(2) Pattern 2: Controlled variables. We think about the next sentence; "In the constant speed mode, the system calculates the target acceleration and output it to the engine control."

This sentence shows that system execution an action of calculation and output to engine control periodically.

$src(\tau) = s21$, $name(s21) = $ "Constant_Speed"
$trig(\tau) = $ PERIODICAL
$cond(\tau) = $ nil ("nil" means no object)
$act(\tau) = $ "calculates the target acceleration and output to engine control"
$dest(\tau) = s22$, $name(s22) = $ "Constant_Speed"

(3) Pattern 3: User-input variable. The user input causes the trigger of a transition; "In the standby mode, when user push down the AR(Accel/Resume) switch, the system moves to the constant mode."

$src(\tau) = s31$, $name(s31) = $ "StandBy"
$trig(\tau) = $ "AR_Switch"
$cond(\tau) = $ nil
$act(\tau) = $ nil
$dest(\tau) = s32$, $name(s32) = $ "Constant Speed"

(4) Pattern 4: External-system trigger. In this final pattern, the outside of the system gives a trigger; "In the cruise control operable mode, if there is an error notification from other system, the system cancel the constant speed mode, clear the setting speed and transit to error state."

src(τ) = s41, name(s41) = "cruise control operable mode"
trig(τ) = "Malfunction Notification"
cond(τ) = nil
act(τ) = "cancel the constant speed mode, clear the setting speed"
dest(τ) = s42, name(s42) = "Error"

2.4 Ask the Author

The state and the transition might not be decided certainly from an analysis of the natural language sentences automatically. So, the tool question the author of the requirements specification in order to fill the missing elements or select one from the multiple candidates of possibilities.

First, the integrity of the state transition is checked;

- Does all the states have the IN or/and OUT transition (except for the default state and the start/exit state)?
- Is there a unique default state?
- Is there an unconditional transition? When many transitions between the same states, there is a transition that hasn't the event and condition.

The more complicated example is relating to the nesting (hierarchical) state transition. For example, consider the next sentence: "go to main_switch_on state and transit to standby state". There are two possibilities. One is just transit to main_switch_on state and then standby state unconditionally. Another is transiting to main_switch_on, which is the super-state of standby state, and then transit to standby state from the default state of main_swtich_on state. In this case, the tool asks the author which is right.

2.5 Tool

We build the tool, Cardion.spec, to validate our idea. It consists of several parts. Checker does the basic verification of Japanese text from the viewpoint of readability (Sect. 2.1 Step1). The analyser creates the FSM internally from the results of the checker. The generator creates the various codes. One is the PlantUML[2] codes to visualize the FSM diagram, the second is the SPARK codes; both specification (ads) and body part (adb) (Fig. 3).

2.5.1 Dictionary

Dictionary is the user dictionary and has two roles. First, currently our tool analyses only Japanese requirements specification, so it converts Japanese text to English to generate the SPARK codes. Another purpose is creating the variable from the Japanese phrase to which FSM is relating. For example, the phrase "ON state of the engine switch"

---

[2] http://plantuml.com/.

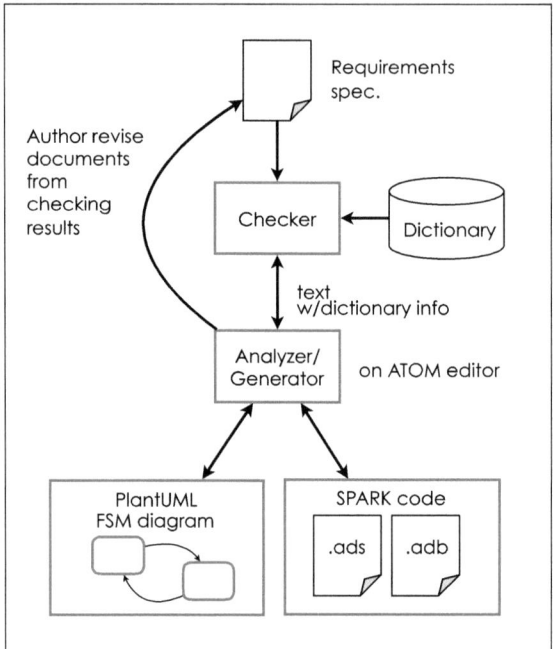

Fig. 3. Structure of Cardion.spec tool

becomes the variable name "S_IG_ON". In this process in which the user chooses the appropriate name, it is also good timing for the user to rethink the use of words to avoid the subtle fluctuation of words.

Here is the example of user dictionary (actually, the left part of list is the Japanese word).

@start cardion_jdic ("@start" is the keyword to indicate the start of the user dictionary)
Initial state, S_INIT
ON state of engine switch, S_IG_ON
OFF state of engine switch, S_IG_OFF
Standby state, S_NORMAL_RUN
Const speed state, S_CRUISE
Error state, S_CC_ERR
Engine switch ON, E_Ig_On

As this example shows that the state has a prefix "S_", and the event has a prefix "E_". It helps the analyzer to inspect the requirements specification.

2.5.2 Generation of SPARK Codes

To generate SPARK codes from FSM, we use some rules. In specification part, we define the type of the event, the state and the function as the action of transition (Fig. 4).

The transition is defined by the procedure that accepts the event and sets the new state (Fig. 5).

```
type Event_Type is (E_Ig_On, E_Ig_Off,
                    E_Cc_Sw_On, E_Cc_Sw_Off,
                    E_Ar_On, E_Cs_On,
                    E_Brake_On, E_Cancel_On,
                    E_Detect_Error);
```

Fig. 4. Example of generated definition of event type (specification part)

```
procedure State_Transition (E  : Event_Type) is
begin
    case IState is
        when S_INIT =>
            IState := S_IG_OFF;
        when S_IG_OFF =>
            case E is
                when E_Ig_ON =>
                    IState := S_IG_ON;
                when others =>
                    null;
            end case;
        when S_Ig_On =>
            IState := S_CC_NO_ERR;
        when S_CC_NO_ERR =>
            IState := S_CC_SW_OFF;
        when S_CC_SW_OFF =>
...
```

Fig. 5. Example of generated state transition (body part)

We expect that the generated codes are valid as the SPARK codes, and the tool, Cardion.spec, automatically compile them. And if there are some errors, we use this error information to refine the requirement specification. For example, if the event is defined in the specification part and all events don't appear in the body part, compile create error and the tool warn the user that the event is defined correctly.

There are two possibilities of problem that we have to consider as for warning to the author. One is that the document is not appropriate and the tool issued right warning. The second is the tool cannot analyze the document correctly. The latter is the false-positive indication. In our experience, it isn't possible to make this false-positive ratio into zero. But we noticed, through our experiment for one year, that it is acceptable to the author when the ratio is below the quarter of the correct indications.

3 Conclusion

In this paper, we explain an approach to improve the requirement specification written in natural language. In this approach, we have three steps to improve the document. First, we analyse the document by the lexical analysis and syntactic parsing to find out the simple problematic parts. As the second, we create the finite state machine and find the lack of elements (e.g. no out transition from the normal state). Finally, when compiling the generated SPARK codes from the FSM, compile errors are the candidate of error of documentation.

Simple, we can write the requirements specification in a formal specification language from the beginning. So, it becomes possible to process the requirements specification automatically by machine, and it is advantageous. But it is difficult for every people (i.e. writer/reader) to become familiar with the formal approach. If the reader doesn't understand the specification language correctly, he/she might misunderstand the correct document.

Our approach uses the formal approach in the background, so the user can concentrate on the natural language document and our tool assists this activity.

Appendix

A user writes the specification in the natural language (Fig. 6, left). Cardion.spec creates the SPARK codes (Fig. 6, upper right) and FSM model (Fig. 6, lower down) internally. The user does not need to see those representations, could focus on the natural language text.

But we could use the SPARK codes for the validation purpose.

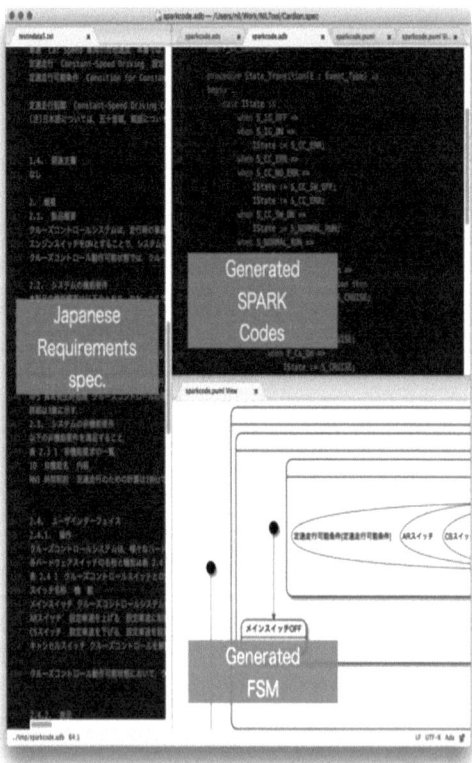

Fig. 6. Cardion.spec tool image

References

1. Sikora, E., Tenbergen, B., Pohl, K.: Industry needs and research directions in requirements engineering for embedded systems. Requirements Eng. **17**(1), 57–78 (2012)
2. McCormick, J.W., Chapin, P.C.: Building High Integrity Applications with SPARK. Cambridge University Press, Cambridge (2015)
3. IEEE: IEEE Recommended Practice for Software Requirements Specification (IEEE Std 830-1998). IEEE (1998)
4. Ott, D.: Automatic requirement categorization of large natural language specifications at Mercedes-Benz for review improvements. In: Doerr, J., Opdahl, A.L. (eds.) REFSQ 2013. LNCS, vol. 7830, pp. 50–64. Springer, Heidelberg (2013)
5. Ott, D., Raschke, A.: Review improvement by requirements classification at Mercedes-Benz: limits of empirical studies in educational environments. In: 2012 IEEE Second International Workshop on Empirical Requirements Engineering (EmpiRE). IEEE (2012)
6. ISO/IEC, ISO/IEC 13568:2002: Information technology – Z formal specification notation – Syntax, type system and semantics, ISO (2002)
7. Boulanger, J.-L.: Industrial Use of Formal Methods: Formal Verification. Wiley, New York (2013)
8. Iordache, O.: Methods. In: Iordache, O. (ed.) Polystochastic Models for Complexity. UCS, vol. 4, pp. 17–61. Springer, Heidelberg (2010)
9. Heitmeyer, C.L., Jeffords, R.D., Labaw, B.G.: Automated consistency checking of requirements specifications. ACM Trans. Softw. Eng. Methodol. (TOSEM) **5**(3), 231–261 (1996)
10. Barnes, J.: Programming in Ada 2012. Cambridge University Press, Cambridge (2014)
11. Parnas, D.L., Madey, J.: Functional documentation for computer systems engineering: version 2. McMaster University, Faculty of Engineering, Communications Research Laboratory (1991)

Establishing Effective Software Development Teams: An Exploratory Model

Mirna Muñoz[1(✉)], Jezreel Mejia[1], Adriana Peña[2], and Nora Rangel[3]

[1] Centro de Investigación en Matemáticas, Av. Universidad no 222, 98068 Zacatecas, Mexico
{mirna.munoz,jmejia}@cimat.mx
[2] CUCEI Universidad de Guadalajara, Blvrd. Marcelino García Barragán #1421, esq. Calzada Olímpica, 44430 Guadalajara, Jalisco, Mexico
adriana.pena@cucei.udg.mx
[3] Centro de Estudios e Investigaciones en Comportamiento de la Universidad de Guadalajara, Calle Francisco de Quevedo # 180, Col. Arcos Vallarta, 44130 Guadalajara, Jalisco, Mexico
norarangel@cucba.udg.mx

Abstract. Nowadays software represents an important piece to support a wide diversity of industrial needs in different domains. However, software development is not always a successful task, mainly for human related reasons. A problem that deeply affects small and medium enterprises (SMEs), particularly when they invest in software process improvement or to get high performance technology. The development of software is teamwork; unfortunately, not all teams manage themselves to achieve an effective performance. This paper aims to show a proposal of a model to integrate highly effective teams for software development. The proposed model focuses on three factors: skills, interactive styles and knowledge; with an innovative way to integrate teams by avoiding the use of traditional questionnaires. The paper includes both the background for this research and a global view of the model fundamentals. A discussion of the components of the model is also included.

Keywords: Human factor · Small and medium enterprises · SMEs · Software development · Effective teams · Teamwork

1 Introduction

There are a number of factors that affect the software development process. As Clarke and O'Connor in [1] stated out, development software is a complex, human centric activity, subject to many pitfalls if not properly organized; their reference framework distinguished 44 factors and 170 sub-factors in eight categories, including personnel factors related to software development. Within the personnel sub-factors are: team size, culture, experience, cohesion, skills, and disharmony, among others; which emphasize the current model of software development team-based.

Teamwork improves outcomes through its members' diverse skills and knowledge. However, even following a set of quality models and standards for improving the software development process such as CMMI [2], ISO 15504 [3], Moprosoft [4] or ISO 29110 [5], which aim to provide best practices that help organizations to achieve efficient and quality process; the success of a team is highly reliant on the human factor. In some cases, it appears that human aspects can become more relevant than technological ones in the team's performance [6, 7]. That is, not only the team members' capabilities influence the group performance, but their interactions, behaviors and dynamics [8–10]. As a result, a not proper performance of the team may be the product of a not proper members' composition.

Guinan et al. in [6] compared software development team's performance during requirements definition; in their study they examined 66 teams from 15 companies to contrast group process theory, the interaction and dynamics among the team members with technical factors as tools and methods, in high-performance software development teams. The results showed that, although technology factors have an important impact, processes had a major influence on the team's performance.

The rest of the paper is organized as follows: Sect. 2 covers the background of this research including an overview of the importance of work in teams, as well as the current identified problems related to integration of teams; Sect. 3 shows the proposal of a model to establish effective software development teams; Sect. 4 presents a discussion of this research area, and finally, Sect. 5 shows conclusions.

2 Research Background

Nowadays most of the software is developed by teams. Therefore, software engineers require knowledge on how to work in teams [11]. In this context, a lot of organizations have discovered that working in groups allows a higher people commitment, and that the implementation of changes is faster. Therefore, countries such as Mexico, Colombia, Japan, USA and India to name some, are investing in integrating competitive teams of engineers through their training in engineering practices [12]. To achieve that, the focus is on the implementation of methodologies such as Team Software Process^{SM} (TSP^{SM}) from the Software Engineering Institute [13] in an effort to provide a set of engineering best practices to develop software through teams.

According to Lopez in [12], of a total of 1,544 organizations that had been certified in TSP, Mexico has the first place with 979 organizations certified. Taking this information into account, this research arises due to the importance of achieving an effective configuration of teams. According to Cuevas et al. in [11], the required steps to integrate teams are not as obvious as we could expect, and frequently new teams spend a lot of time working in teamwork techniques. Besides, failures in software projects have been claimed to be the result of teamwork factors more than technical factors [11].

Regarding team problems, author such as Ribaud et al. [14] highlighted the importance of personality types and their relation with Information and Communication Technology (ICT) competences; and Yilmaz, Al-Taei and O'Connor [15] stated the importance of taking into account the team members' personality to integrate the team, in order to improve the effectiveness in software development teams.

Besides, two of the most known instruments related to personality and team's performance are the Tuckman's model [16] and the Belbin's team roles [17]. According to the Tuckman's model [16, 18] all groups have a set of developmental stages related to interpersonal and task-activity realms aspects; a team task is completed while the members relate to one another. This model is for small-group development, and it is aimed for the organizations to understand three main aspects: (1) set the current stage of the group; (2) identify the realm in which the group behavior falls, taking into account task and interpersonal realms; and (3) the next position of the group regarding the developmental sequence [16]. However, it does not cover the selection of the right members in order to succeed in getting a high performance team from a starting point.

Belbin [17] argued that at work people tend to behave, contribute, and interrelate with others in certain distinctive ways, they take a team role. A balanced combination on these roles is expected to result in a more successful team than those with an unbalanced composition. Designed questionnaires is the method used to identify the role a person will take in a team. This approach has been related to software development activities [19].

Self-reports, mainly questionnaires and scales, have been broadly employed in the study of personality or the identification of competences. Santacreu, Rubio and Hernández in [20] pointed out that this practice might obey to the consideration that every aspect related to personality is knowledge accessible only to the own individual, although they disagree on that. In any case, a self-report is a relatively easy and non-invasive method for the behavior and personality research that can provide a great amount of data in a short time.

However, this information can be influenced by the individual's social desires, memory and/or motivations [21]. Furthermore, it has been found a lack of correspondence between the objective measures of behavior and self-reports obtained as an evaluation instrument [22, 23].

Based on the above mentioned, this research aims to develop a proposal of a model for integrating high effective teams for software development, focusing on three factors: skills, interactive styles and knowledge. The model is described in Sect. 4.

3 Software Development Teams

Software development refers to a systematic production for developing quality software within a limit budget and time [15], and very important, it is developed by teams. According to Yilmaz et al. in [15], a significant number of researchers have suggested that most of the software development issues have a sociological nature. And therefore, it is crucial to analyze what concerns to work in teams.

A team for software development is a group of individuals working together and performing a work that involves a project. It is composed by individuals, with specific knowledge in specific subject and with specific skills to carry out that work [24].

Teams in organizations allow carrying out organizational and psychological functions regarding the development of software such as [11]:

- *Increment the time available to attend to customer needs*: teams make that employees commit with the essential practices involved in software development such as a fast answer to requirements, meet deadlines, and develop quality software products and services, as fundamental parts of their work.

- *Generate new ideas and solutions*: the potentiality of a team is determined by the variety of knowledge, experiences and the closeness to problems that makes the team as the most complete instrument to solve problems.
- *Improve software process*: a team is a potential source to provide information of how a key organizational process can be optimized.
- *Implement complex decisions*: a team is a potential source to be involved in order to generate the decision-making as well as the implementation of the actions involved.
- *Perform complex or dependent tasks*: work performed in organizations is complex and it requires the maximum of capacities; there, the work in an isolated way performed by an individual is less efficient than the teamwork.
- *Perform coordination functions*: a team contains more than technical knowledge, therefore it performs activities such as: establish communication channels, collect and manage information, disseminate results, and implement changes.

Unfortunately, even in good performance projects, problems arise; sometimes because each member has different roles and each role has its own goals. Therefore, when the goals enter in conflict, disagreements appear. It has been identified that the problems do not only come from a lack of experience or knowledge, but from the background or the interactive style of the team members [11], resulting in the failure of projects.

The identified most common problems in software development teams are [11]:

- *Inefficient leadership*: when a team has a lack of leadership, it is common to have problems with complaining plans as well as with the personal discipline.
- *Failure of cooperation*: if a team member is not motivated he/she might not be able to cooperate with the team.
- *Unbalanced participation*: each team member has different abilities and capacities, as well as different motivations, energy and commitment levels; therefore, if this is not taken into account while a task is assigned, it can represent a serious problem.
- *Lack of resolution and trust*: this occurs when the team has established goals or milestones with a lack of leadership, clear goals of a process, or defined plans.
- *Deficient quality*: when a team does not use personal reviews and team reviews.
- *Expanding Requirements*: when a team does not have a clear division between the changes for the requirement interpretation and changes for expanding the requirements.
- *Inefficient personnel valuation:* when team makes misunderstanding assessment among their members, because most of the time this kind of assessments is perceived as not equitable.

4 Model to Integrate High Effective Teams

According to Santacreu et al. in [20], for traditional approaches to the personality study, behavior is just one indicator of many personality traits of the individual. As an alternative to the taxonomies of individuals classified in a category according to their personality traits without regard to singularity, Ribes [25] proposed the analysis of how the individual faces different situations, showing a personality as a result of the particular conditions in the individual development for the particular conditions. Accordingly, on each person can be identified certain interactive tendency on specific conditions.

When people collaborate with others, the point of interest in this project, Ribes [25] pointed out that interactions do not relay only on situational factors or the extrinsic contingencies they are facing, but also on the participants' interactive styles. People interactions are modulated by the way in which the participants' interactive styles are or not complemented with each other, in such a way that a collaborative work can be facilitated or seriously affected by them.

Besides, according to the team software process the selection of team members for a new or existing team should take into account the members' skills, aptitudes, interests and team working abilities [26]. In such a way that people with different forms of facing situations interact in different ways among them, and linked to the social contingency. Based on this, we proposed to explore the compatibility of the individuals' interactive styles that will be part of a team for software development and how that compatibility will facilitate or prevent their goal achievement.

For the accomplishment of that, this research work is aimed to build on a model to establish effective software development teams. The model focuses on three factors: skills, interactive styles, and knowledge, because we think those are key aspects that allow selecting the right people according to the context and specific needs of a project. Figure 1 presents an overview of the model. Then, each part of the model is briefly described.

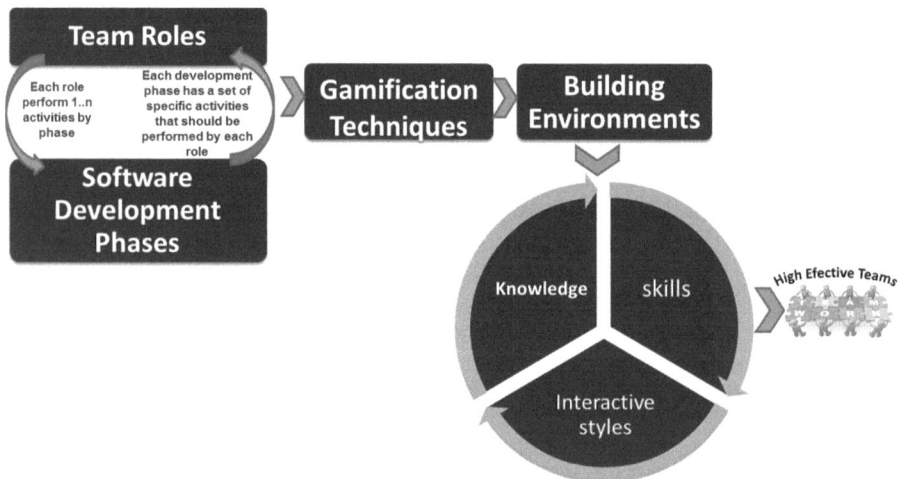

Fig. 1. Model to establish effective software development teams

As Fig. 1 shows, the model is composed of a set of phases for software development (each one with specific task to be performed by each role); and a set of roles required for the development of software by teams (each role should perform a set of specific practices depending on the software development phase). Based on these elements, the model builds different situations that each role of a team must face trough the software development stages. The situations are contextualized using gamification so that they provide an alternative and innovative way to analyze the knowledge, skills and interactive styles of each person in order to integrate high effective teams.

A high effective team, in here is considered as a team where its members have been selected according to their knowledge, skills and interactive styles, in such a way that they complement the required knowledge of the team; and, their types of interactive styles are in balance among all the members. Next sections present a brief description of each element of the model.

4.1 Software Development Phases

The first element of the model involves setting the phases of the software development as well as all activities a team should do through the software development cycle in order to create quality software. For this, the TSP methodology was taken as a base due to three factors: (1) the nature of the methodology is the development for software by teams; (2) the methodology provides a set of phases that cover the activities involved in the development of quality software; and (3) the methodology provides guidelines describing in detail the performed activities in each phase.

This research aims to help SMEs to ensure that the problems related to the human factor decreases. The goals by phases covered by our model are next briefly described [27]:

- *Launch*: this phase aims to launch the team. Its main activities are focused on documenting business goals, defining team member roles, and defining a schedule for monitoring the meetings.
- *Strategy*: this phase aims to provide a guide to establish a development strategy as well as early estimations of time and size. Its main activities are focused on defining a global development strategy, starting the risk management and the configuration management.
- *Planning*: this phase aims to provide a guide to produce the task plans, team and individual, as well as the quality plan. Its main activities are focused on adapting a defined process according to the project needs, establishing the planning of products related to the project, estimating the planning of products related to the project, defining the global quality plan, defining the global plan of the project, generating individual plans, and balancing the plans to distribute the workloads, and minimize schedules.
- *Requirement*: this phase aims to provide a guide during the requirements development and inspection. Its main activities are focused on analyzing the software needs, documenting the requirements, generating the system test plan, and updating the project baseline.
- *Design*: this phase aims to provide a guide during the inspection and development of the software design specifications. Its main activities are focused on specifying the design, and developing integration test plans and the project baseline.

- *Implementation*: this phase aims to provide a guide during the software implementation and inspection. Its main activities are focused on developing a detailed design, developing unit test plan, coding, performing unit test, reviewing quality criteria for components, and delivering components.
- *Test*: this phase aims to guide the team during the components integration and test. Its main activities are focused on integrating the product, performing the integration test, performing the system test, and developing user documentation.
- *Post-Mortem*: this phase aims to assess and analyze the project and team's performance at the end of each development cycle. Its main activities are focused on reviewing the process data to identify issues, identify improvements, and reviewing the roles performance.

4.2 Team Roles Activity by Phase

The second element of the model involves setting the roles of the software development to ensure the development of quality software. For this the TSP methodology was taken as base for three features: (1) the methodology nature is the development for software by teams; (2) the methodology provides a set of roles involved in the development of quality software; and (3) the methodology provides guidelines describing in detail the activities performed through the phases by each role.

Some of the responsibilities of the roles covered by our model are [27, 28]:

- *Team leader*: motivating team members, handling customer issues, protecting team resources, resolving team issues, reporting the status of the teamwork, and conducting meetings.
- *Planning manager*: leading the team to produce the task plan and schedule for each development cycle, leading the team to produce a balanced team development plan, and tracking the team' progress by analyzing planed and real values.
- *Quality manager*: leading the team to produce and track the quality plan, identifying issues in quality objectives, leading the team in the identification, documentation and maintenance of their processes as well as their development standards, and moderating and leading the teams' reviews and inspections.
- *Support manager*: leading the team to determine the support needs as well as to identify the tool and facilities needs, leading the development and management of change and or configuration management systems, and handling the team's issues and the risk tracking system.
- *Design manager*: leading the team in the design work, and ensuring that all appropriate design standards are being met and that the designs are properly recorded.
- *Implementation manager*: leading and monitoring the team through the overall quality of the team's implementation work, leading the implementation of a required standard, and monitoring the degree to which standards are followed.
- *Test manager*: leading the team to guarantee the quality of all testing and test related work for the project including testing standards, test plans, test procedures, and monitoring the degree in which testing work is done in accordance with the team and the organization's plan and standards.

4.3 Knowledge

The knowledge element of the model refers to the knowledge that an individual must have to perform specific tasks. It has its source in the best practices associated to the performance of the activities throughout a software development cycle.

Then, the knowledge required to execute the activities of each phase with the knowledge required by each role to perform each phase of the software development cycle is mapped.

4.4 Skills

The skills are related to the capacity of an individual to easily make something in a correct way. Then, this model element is based on the roles involved in organizational changes. When a change occurs in an organization, it is important to ensure a correct mixture of the involved profiles. A change in the plans involves getting the right people with the right attributes making correctly some function in the adequate moment at the right time [29].

The change of roles, necessary for change [29]: inventors, entrepreneurs, integrators, experts, managers, and sponsors are included in the model. Using this change, roles will enable us to get key behaviors or skills of each role; and therefore, to get information of the individuals so that their skills can be identified according to the needed roles.

4.5 Interactive Styles

The way in which an individual behaves in a specific situation is not good or bad; it is a metric of the natural preferences of each person.

The model uses personality interactive styles [25] to analyze the reaction of each individual facing specific situations but avoiding the use of questionnaires by using the gamification. This will allow us to build balanced teams where the individual's interactive styles can be complemented by the other team members, and as an objective measure of the individuals in the situation.

Through this model, it is possible to analyze the information of the personality profile and match it with the personality roles needed, so that, the roles would be assigned in a more adequate way; along with the compatibility among the interactive styles of the team members for software development; and how this can facilitate or obstruct the aimed achievement.

4.6 Building Environments

This element of the model is crucial for the proposed method because it should be able to apply gamification techniques in order to provide environments that reflect the main challenges a team must face throughout the phases of the software development cycle, but taking into account the individuals' knowledge, skills and capabilities; so that it can be possible to get the users' specific features while the individual is using such environments.

The knowledge required to perform each phase as well as the knowledge required to perform the activities of each role through the phases will provide the requirements to develop each phase environment with specific challenges.

4.7 Gamification

Some authors have highlighted the benefits of using gamification; particularly in the area of software engineering in process improvements [30, 31] implementation of models [32] and even in agile development [33], for example, gamification can help organizations to create environments with dynamic traditional actions regarding the software development cycle. In this proposed model, gamification aims to provide an alternative way to integrate teams for software development, avoiding the use of traditional questionnaires to integrate them.

Therefore, the alternative provided by the use of gamification techniques to build sceneries allows analyzing the individuals in an innovative environment so that their skills, capacities and knowledge can be collected and mapped, regarding the roles requirements in order to achieve the integration of high quality teams.

5 Discussion and Conclusions

In this paper is shown an overview of a proposed model for the integration of high effective teams for software development focusing on three factors: skills, personal interactive styles, and knowledge. The model is still under development; however, this paper presents its key elements in order to highlight its innovation.

This model arises from the hypothesis that if we help organizations in the identification of the right people according to the team's needs, the organization will be able to improve the team's performance. We believe that the implementation of the proposed method can help SMEs to improve the probability of success in their software teams, because the method is focused on human factors, which represents the main source of problems in teams most of the times.

Working within a team is becoming a critical factor for the development of high quality software, for this, it is important that teams can be integrated with a mix of members that can easily work along. A model like the one presented in this paper represents an important and innovative guide for team integration, avoiding the use of traditional questionnaires that might lead to misinterpretations by using a gamification method, and allowing diagnosis of human and task factors in similar situations that those presented in the real work environment.

Acknowledgements. CIMAT- Unidad Zacatecas, CUCEI and the Centro de Estudios e Investigaciones en Comportamiento de la Universidad de Guadalajara for the facilities to perform this research.

References

1. Clarke, P., O'Connor, R.V.: Changing situational contexts present a constant challenge to software developers. In: O'Connor, R.V., Umay Akkaya, M., Kemaneci, K., Yilmaz, M., Poth, A., Messnarz, R. (eds.) EuroSPI 2015. CCIS, vol. 543, pp. 100–111. Springer, Heidelberg (2015). doi:10.1007/978-3-319-24647-5_9
2. Chrissis, M.B., Konrad, M., Shrum, S.: CMMI for Development: Guidelines for Process Integration and Product Improvement. Pearson Education Inc., Massachusetts (2011)
3. International Organization for Standardization ISO/IEC 15504: 2004 Information technology – Process assessment (2004)
4. Oktaba, H., Vázquez, A.: MoProSoft: A Software Process Model for Small Enterprises. In: Software Process Improvement for Small and Medium Enterprises, Techniques and cases studies, (Information Science Reference eds), p. 170 (2008)
5. Laporte, C.Y., Alexandre, S., O'Connor, R.V.: A software engineering lifecycle standard for very small enterprises. In: O'Connor, R.V., Baddoo, N., Smolander, K., Messnarz, R. (eds.) EuroSPI 2008. CCIS, vol. 16, pp. 129–141. Springer, Heidelberg (2008)
6. Guinan, P.J., Cooprider, J.G., Faraj, S.: Enabling software development team performance during requirements definition: a behavioral versus technical approach. Inf. Syst. Res. **9**(2), 101–125 (1998)
7. Gorla, N., Lam, Y.W.: Who should work with whom?: building effective software project teams. Commun. ACM **47**(6), 79–82 (2004)
8. Hackman, J.R.: A Normative Model of Work Team Effectiveness. Technical report #2, School of Organization and Management, Research Program on Group Effectiveness, Yale University, New Haven, CT (1983)
9. Gladstein, D.L.: Groups in Context: A Model of Task Group Effectiveness. Admin. Sci. Q. **29**(1984), 499–517 (1984)
10. McGrath, J.E.: Groups: Interaction and Performance. Prentice-Hall, Englewood Cliffs (1984)
11. Cuevas, G., De Amescua, A., San Feliu, T., Arcilla, M., Cerrada, J.A., Calvo-Manzano, J.A., Garcia, M.: Teamwork and its techniques, Chap. 1. In: Centro de Estudios Ramón Areces, S.A. (ed) Software Process Management, pp. 1–29 (2002). ISBN 84-8004-546-9
12. Lopez, G.: How will Mexico achieve world-wide #1 in SW Quality? On TSP symposium, February 2016
13. Humprey, W.: The Team Software Process, Cargenie Mellon, Software Engineering Institute. Technical report CMU/SEI-2000-TR-023, ESC-TR-2000-023 (2000)
14. Ribaud, V., Saliou, P.: Relating ICT competencies with personality types. In: O'Connor, R.V., et al. (eds.) Systems, Software and Services Process Improvement. EuroSPI 2015. CCIS, vol. 543, pp. 295–302. Springer, Heidelberg (2015)
15. Yilmaz, M., Al-Taei, A., O'Connor, R.V.: A machine-based personality oriented team recommender for software development organizations. In: O'Connor, R.V., Umay Akkaya, M., Kemaneci, K., Yilmaz, M., Poth, A., Messnarz, R. (eds.) EuroSPI 2015. CCIS, vol. 543, pp. 75–86. Springer, Heidelberg (2015). doi:10.1007/978-3-319-24647-5_7
16. Tuckman, B.W.: Developmental Sequence in Small Groups. Psychological Bulletin **63**, 384–399 (1965). http://openvce.net/sites/default/files/Tuckman1965DevelopmentalSequence.pdf
17. Belbin, M.: Team Roles at Work. Elsevier Butterworth Heinemann, Oxford (1993)
18. Tuckman, W., Jensen, M.: Stages of small group development revisited. Group and Organization Studies **2**(4), 419–427 (1977). https://www.freewebs.com/group-management/BruceTuckman(1).pdf
19. Estrada, E., Peña, A.: Influencia de los Roles de Equipo en las Actividades del Desarrollador de Software. RECIBE **2**(1), II (2013)

20. Santacreu, J., Rubio, V., Hernández, J.M.: Evaluación objetiva de la personalidad: una alternativa a los cuestionarios. Análisis y Modificación de Conducta **30**, 803–825 (2004)
21. Arce, R., Velasco, J., Novo, M., Fariña, F.: Elaboración y validación de una escala para la evaluación del acoso escolar. Revista Iberoamericana de Psicología y Salud **5**(1), 71–104 (2014). http://www.redalyc.org/articulo.oa?id=245129173005
22. Hernández, J.M., Lozano, J.H., Shih, P.C., Santacreu, J.: Validez convergente de dos pruebas de evaluación de la minuciosidad. Psicothema **21**(1), 133–140 (2009)
23. Mischel, W.: Personalidad y Evaluación. Trillas, México (1980)
24. Project Management Institute (PMI): A Guide to the Project Management Body of Knowledge, 5th edn. Project Management Institute, Inc., Pennsylvania (2013)
25. Ribes, E.: Psicología General. Trillas, México (1990)
26. Humphrey, W., Chick, T., Nichols, W., Pomeroy-Huff, M.: Team Software Process Process^{SM} (TSP) Body of knowledge (BOK), Cargenie Mellon, Software Engineering Institute. Technical report CMU/SEI-2010-TR-020, ESC-TR-2010-020 (2010)
27. Humphrey, W.: Introduction to the Team Software Process. Addison-Wesley, Massachusetts (2006)
28. Humphrey, W.: TSP^{SM} Coaching Developments Teams. Addison-Wesley, Massachusetts (2006)
29. Kasse Initiatives: Process improvement means change. In: Change management tool kit. v2.0. (2008)
30. Yilmaz, M., Yilmaz, M., O'Connor, R.V., Clarke, P.: A gamification approach to improve the software development process by exploring the personality of software practitioners. In: Clarke, P.M., O'Connor, R.V., Rout, T., Dorling, A. (eds.) SPICE 2016. CCIS, vol. 609, pp. 71–83. Springer, Heidelberg (2016). doi:10.1007/978-3-319-38980-6_6
31. Gasca-Hurtado, G.P., Peña, A., Gómez-Álvarez, M.C., Plascencia-Osuna, Ó.A., Calvo-Manzano, J.A.: Virtual Reality as good practice for teamwork with engineering student. RISTI, No 16, 12/2015, pp. 76–91 (2015). doi:10.17013/risti.16.76-91
32. Oktaba, H., Kimenez, H.: Juego de cartas para identificar la salud de los proyectos de software. On TSP symposium (2016)
33. Jovanovic, M., Mesquida, A.-L., Mas, A.: Process improvement with retrospective gaming in agile software development. In: O'Connor, R.V., Umay Akkaya, M., Kemaneci, K., Yilmaz, M., Poth, A., Messnarz, R. (eds.) EuroSPI 2015. CCIS, vol. 543, pp. 287–294. Springer, Heidelberg (2015). doi:10.1007/978-3-319-24647-5_23

SPI and Assessment

Using a Process Assessment Model to Prepare for an ISO/IEC 20000-1 Certification: ISO/IEC 15504-8 or TIPA for ITIL?

Stéphane Cortina[✉], Béatrix Barafort[✉], Michel Picard[✉], and Alain Renault[✉]

Luxembourg Institute of Science and Technology, 5 Avenue des Hauts-Fourneaux,
4362 Esch-sur-Alzette, Luxembourg
{stephane.cortina,beatrix.barafort,michel.picard,
alain.renault}@list.lu

Abstract. Nowadays, whatever their domain of activity, the interest of the organizations for IT service management is growing. In that context, a certification of their service management system is seen as a good means to demonstrate their excellence in this discipline. Amongst all the existing process (assessment or maturity) models that could be used to support such a certification, two of them have been studied. This paper presents and compares the ISO/IEC 15504-8 and the TIPA for ITIL process assessment models, in order to determine their respective strengths and weaknesses when used for preparing an ISO/IEC 20000-1 certification.

Keywords: Process assessment model · IT service management · ISO/IEC 20000 · ISO/IEC 15504-8 · TIPA for ITIL · Certification · ITIL

1 Introduction

International standards specifying requirements for management systems are more and more popular: the number of companies seeking certifications for competitive advantage and gaining new markets is constantly increasing [1]. The flagship Management System Standard (MSS) is ISO 9001 for a quality management system with more than one million of certifications delivered in 2014.

In the Information Technology (IT) domain, two standards were published in 2005 (for their first version), the ISO/IEC 27001 for Information Security [2] and ISO/IEC 20000-1 [3] for IT Service Management (ITSM). This latter is the leading one in the series composed of nine parts describing requirements for defining a Service Management System (SMS), guidance, exemplar implementation plan, concepts and terminology, as well as a process reference model.

The expected benefits [4] for the companies seeking to certify their SMS against the ISO/IEC 20000-1 standard can be either internal (process and quality improvements) or external (marketing advantages) [5]. In order to get prepared for such a certification, an organization can assess the capability of its processes against a set of requirements. This has already been experimented for accreditation in [6, 7]. Moreover, a process assessment allows not only to get a clear view of the capability level reached by the assessed processes but also, through an in-depth examination of each of them, to analyze in detail how they have been implemented [8].

The ISO/IEC 33000 series of standards represents the state-of-the-art in the Process Assessment domain. It details the requirements for performing a process assessment (in ISO/IEC 33002 [9]) as well as those for designing a process assessment model (PAM): the main input needed to perform an assessment (in ISO/IEC 33004 [10]). Nowadays, there are many existing PAMs available, allowing to assess processes of various disciplines ranging from software [11] to ITSM [12]. To prepare for the certification of its SMS against ISO/IEC 20000-1, an organization can assess the capability of its ITSM processes, providing that it relies on a precise description of these ITSM processes, structured as a PAM. But how to select the model that will best support such a certification amongst the existing ones? The intent of this paper is to study two publicly available ITSM PAMs: the ISO/IEC 15504-8 [13] and the TIPA® for ITIL PAM [14], to identify their respective strengths and weaknesses. Since the mid-nineties, the authors of this paper (who are ISO JTC1/SC40 and JTC1/SC7 delegates, ITIL experts, and at the origin of the TIPA for ITIL framework) have been studying and using the ISO/IEC 15504 and 33000 standards for assessing IT Service Management processes. Based on that experience, they are now working to address the following problem statement: *amongst two existing process assessment models, which one brings the most value when preparing for an ISO/IEC 20000-1 certification?*

The paper is organized as follows: Sect. 2 describes the related work by surveying existing ITSM process assessment and maturity models. Section 3 presents in detail the ISO/IEC 15504-8 and the TIPA for ITIL PAMs studied in this paper as well as a comparison (that results from the analysis of the five characteristics considered as important for preparing an ISO/IEC 20000-1 certification). Then, Sect. 4 presents strengths, weaknesses and opportunities related to these models. Finally, Sect. 5 draws conclusions about the results and proposes some future work.

2 Related Work

Getting an ISO/IEC 20000-1 certification is a challenge that has been largely studied and various kinds of tools have been tested in order to support the preparation of such certifications.

On the one side, several guidance documents aiming at facilitating the implementation of a SMS have been published by the International Organization for Standardization (ISO) itself: ISO/IEC 20000-2 [15] provides assistance on the application of service management systems, ISO/IEC 20000-5 [16] gives an example of implementation plan, and ISO/IEC 27013 [17] offers help for an integrated implementation of both a service management system and an information security management system. Furthermore, the ISO/IEC 15504-8 standard provides an example of a PAM for IT service management that can also bring value when implementing an SMS.

On the other side, various types of maturity models have been designed to cover the ITSM aspects. Some of these models are based on the IT Infrastructure Library (ITIL®), the popular best practices set for managing IT services, and some others cover IT standards such as ISO/IEC 20000-1. Thus, in [18] the authors proposed a maturity model for ISO/IEC 20000-1 based on ITSM processes (derived from ITIL 2011 [19]) combined with management system activities (recommended by ISO in the Annex SL [20]). Additionally, there are also several maturity models for IT Service Management such as: IT Service Capability Maturity Model (ITSCMM) [21], Capability Maturity Model Integration for Services (CMMI-SVC) [22], Maturity Model for Implementing ITIL v3 [23]. However, even if all these maturity models are powerful tools for organizations that want to demonstrate their excellence through a staged approach, they cannot demonstrate an organization's readiness towards a requirements' standard such as ISO/IEC 20000-1.

Finally, as reported in [24], a process assessment performed with the help of a well-designed, ISO-compliant PAM can contribute to address both compliance and capability challenges to some extent. Having these findings in mind, we decided to analyze two existing process assessment models in order to determine the value that can be brought by each of them when preparing an ISO/IEC 20000-1 certification.

3 Preparing an ISO/IEC 20000-1 Certification Through an ITSM Process Assessment

Initially published in 2005, the first document of the ISO/IEC 20000 series, ISO/IEC 20000-1, has been revised in 2011. Its current version contains all the requirements for defining a SMS, and also includes service management related policies, procedures, plans, objectives, resources as well as processes. This part is normative, and consequently, is the one used for certification. The topics and processes described in ISO/IEC 20000-1 are depicted on Fig. 1 below.

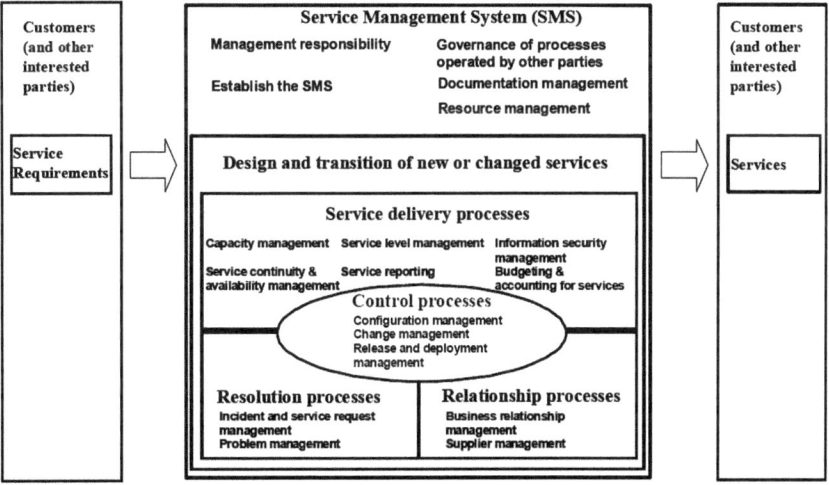

Fig. 1. A SMS according to ISO/IEC 20000-1:2011

Assessing the capability of the processes composing such an SMS is one of the effective ways for preparing certification. Indeed, it permits to get a clear view of the state of these processes and above all it identifies their inherent strengths and weaknesses. To perform that kind of assessment, the processes to be scrutinized need to be defined under the form of a PAM. In [25], the author describes how a bespoke PAM for ISO 20000 has been experimented during the course of consulting work. Being private, this model has not been included in the scope of this paper. On the contrary, the following sections describe two ITSM PAMs that are publicly available: ISO/IEC 15504-8 and TIPA for ITIL PAM. In order to determine which one should be used for preparing an ISO/IEC 20000-1 certification, five characteristics of these models have been systematically analyzed:

- the source documents,
- the process groups,
- the vocabulary used in each model for describing each process,
- the technique used to build the model,
- the coverage rate against the ISO/IEC 20000-1 requirements.

3.1 ISO/IEC 15504-8: An Exemplar Process Assessment Model for IT Service Management

ISO/IEC 15504-8 [13] is a Technical Specification document, enclosing an exemplar PAM for IT Service Management. Published in 2012, this document enables to assess the processes of ISO/IEC 20000-1:2011. It contains the description of 28 processes (see Fig. 2, below) considered to be necessary to meet ISO/IEC 20000-1 requirements (up to capability level 1). Each process is defined in terms of purpose and outcomes and includes two sets of process performance indicators: the process base practices, and their inputs and outputs. The description of these indicators is directly derived from the content of ISO/IEC 20000-2 and ISO/IEC 15289 [26]. These processes are grouped into six process groups whose names are identical to the components of an SMS presented in ISO/IEC 20000-1 and visible on Fig. 1. Moreover, as an ISO standard, ISO/IEC 15504-8 uses a standardized vocabulary. In other words, the terms used in this process model (such as '(service) management system', 'Plan-Do-Check-Act', 'Top management', or 'Internal audit') are typical ISO wording that can be found in the ISO/IEC 20000-1 requirements, and more generally in all MSSs.

ISO/IEC 15504-8 has been designed in such a way that it complies with the requirements from ISO/IEC 15504-2 [27]. This has two main consequences.

On the one side, the compliance of the model to ISO/IEC 15504-2 required that *"process descriptions shall be such that no aspects of the measurement framework beyond level 1 are contained or implied"*. In other words each source requirement (from ISO/IEC 20000-1) needed to be translated as a capability level 1 indicator (i.e. a base practice or input/output that demonstrates the achievement of the process purpose). It sometimes led to relocation of a business-related requirement (for example the maintenance of a work product) into the scope of the Information Item Management process (in order to avoid being considered as an indicator of capability level 2).

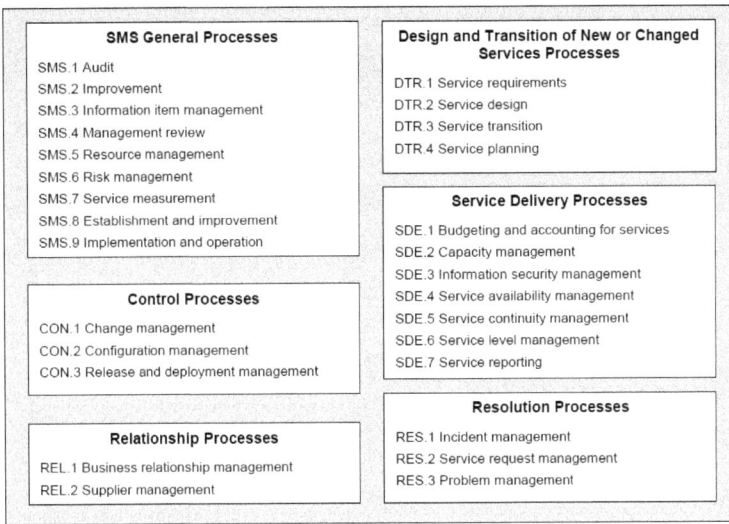

Fig. 2. ISO/IEC 15504-8 process map

On the other side, ISO/IEC 15504-8 *"shall provide an explicit mapping from the relevant element of the models [...] to the relevant process attributes of the measurement framework"*, as stated in ISO/IEC 15504-2. For that, ISO/IEC 15504-8 identifies (in its Annex C) a Process Capability Profile that is implied by the requirements associated with a Management System conformant to ISO/IEC 20000-1. As a result, an exhaustive list of all the links between each singular requirement contained in ISO/IEC 20000-1 and the base practices and their implied information item (input or output) in ISO/IEC 15504-8 is available in this annex. Furthermore, by design choice, each base practice describing a process within the model is linked to one and only one outcome of this process, which implies a simple heritage between this outcome and the set of related requirements. Thanks to this strict traceability between both standards, the ISO/IEC 15504-8 model offers the guarantee of covering 100 % of all the requirements enclosed in ISO/IEC 20000-1.

3.2 The TIPA for ITIL PAM: The Standard Description of the ITIL Processes in the TIPA Framework

The TIPA for ITIL PAM describes the ITSM processes based on ITIL 2011. This model is part of the TIPA framework, a standard-based method for the assessment of IT processes [28]. Published in 2005 after several rounds of experimentation, the first version of this PAM was initially targeting the ITIL v2 processes. Following the successive evolutions of ITIL, the TIPA for ITIL PAM (now licensed under a Creative Common Attribution) has continually evolved [29] and is now fully aligned with the 2011 version of ITIL. It describes 26 processes structured in 5 process groups similarly to the original ITIL publications. (see Fig. 3 below). In terms of vocabulary used, being

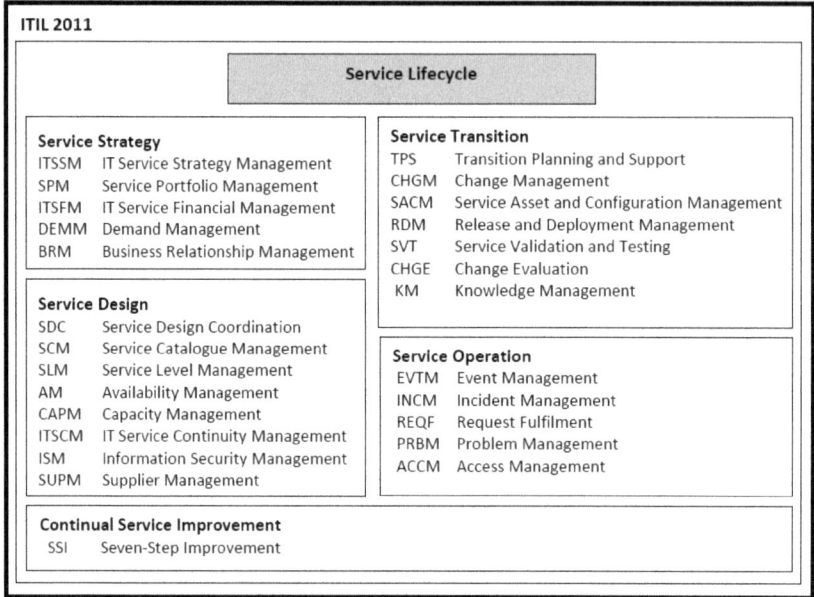

Fig. 3. TIPA for ITIL process map

"ITIL-oriented", the TIPA for ITIL PAM embeds much more technical and market-oriented jargon such as: "Return On Investment", "Strategic Assessment", or "Vision and mission").

The TIPA for ITIL PAM has been built using Goal Oriented Requirement Engineering techniques [30]. These techniques permit to trace in the model the multiple links that exist between one practice and several outcomes. In other words, each base practice can support more than one outcome which represents multiple heritages between this outcome and the set of related requirements. From an ITSM domain practitioner standpoint, this permits to depict the complex relations that today exist between the process activities and its expected results. Consequently, the assessment indicators contained in the model are seen as more representative of current working habits. The TIPA for ITIL PAM is thus more closely aligned with the business constraints and specificities of the ITSM domain.

To help us understand to which extent the TIPA for ITIL PAM covers the requirements from ISO/IEC 20000-1, we have analyzed the new ISO/IEC 20000-11 [31] titled "Guidance on the relationship between ISO/IEC 20000-1:2011 and service management frameworks: ITIL ®". Published in 2015 as part of the ISO/IEC 20000 series, this document provides guidance on how ITIL can be used to support efforts to demonstrate conformity to the requirements specified in ISO/IEC 20000–1. It also clearly correlates each of these requirements to one of the five ITIL core books. However, these correlations sometimes appear to be outside the perimeter of a process and consequently out of the scope of the TIPA for ITIL PAM (which only addresses the process-related chapter of each ITIL core book).

More precisely, we have analyzed all of the 419 elementary requirements contained in ISO/IEC 20000-1. This list of requirements has been built during the design of our maturity model for ISO/IEC 20000-1 (presented in [32]). For each requirement, we have examined how the related process is described within the TIPA for ITIL PAM. We have then determined if this particular requirement is addressed by one of the base practice of the TIPA PAM. This work was facilitated by the fact that the TIPA for ITIL PAM embeds a strict traceability between each base practice and the different ITIL core books. This analysis permitted us to determine that the TIPA for ITIL PAM covers 67 % of the requirements contained in ISO/IEC 20000-1 (mainly those included in clauses 5 to 9 addressing ITSM processes). Indeed, 282 requirements (out of a total of 419) are directly addressed by one of the 26 ITIL processes included in the TIPA for ITIL PAM. This results in a partial coverage of the content of ISO/IEC 20000-1 by the TIPA for ITIL PAM.

3.3 Comparison Between the Two Process Assessment Models

The Table 1 below summarizes the five characteristics of the two ITSM PAMs that have been analyzed.

Table 1. Key characteristics of the ISO/IEC 15504-8 and TIPA for ITIL PAMs

	ISO/IEC 15504-8	TIPA for ITIL PAM
Source documents	ISO/IEC 20000-1 ISO/IEC 20000-2 ISO/IEC 15289	ITIL 2011
Process Groups	SMS General processes	Service Strategy
	Design and Transition of New or Changed Services	Service Design
	Control processes	Service Transition
	Service Delivery processes	Service Operation
	Relationship processes	Continual Service Improvement
	Resolution processes	
Vocabulary used	ISO oriented	Market oriented
Building Technique used	Model built by mapping each requirement from ISO/IEC 20000-1 to an indicator that belongs to capability level 1	Model built using a specific TIPA transformation process (Goal-Oriented Requirement Engineering techniques)
ISO/IEC 20000-1 Requirements coverage	Fully (100 %)	Largely (67 %) (282/419)

When using a PAM for preparing a certification, the key characteristic that should be taken into account is the level of coverage of this model regarding the set of requirements against which the certification will be evaluated. However, the existence of a common vocabulary as well as of a common structure (clause names, process group titles...) between the set of requirements and the PAM should also be considered.

For all these reasons, the ISO/IEC 15504-8 model will provide more value compared to the TIPA for ITIL PAM, when preparing an ISO/IEC 20000-1 certification.

4 Discussions

The analysis of the two PAMs studied in this paper permits to highlight, for each of them, the strengths, weaknesses and opportunities described in the following sections.

4.1 ISO/IEC 15504-8: Strength, Weakness, and Opportunity

The key strength of the ISO/IEC 155504-8 PAM is its full coverage of all the requirements contained in ISO/IEC 20000-1 (as depicted in Table 1 of ISO/IEC 15504-8). Thus it is *de facto* the most appropriate tool that should be used by any organization willing to prepare for a certification of its SMS against the requirements of this standard.

However, due to the way the ISO/IEC 15504-8 processes have been designed (strictly following the requirements of ISO/IEC 15504-2) some of them can be difficult to assess. Indeed, each source requirement from ISO/IEC 20000-1 has been translated as an indicator of capability level 1 in ISO/IEC 15504-8. This implies that some business-process activities were included in the scope of non-business processes (to avoid them from being considered as indicators of a capability level > 1). As an example, in 15504-8 the *definition of a procedure to record, classify, assess and approve Requests for change* has been translated as a base practice of the "SMS.8 Establishment and Maintenance" process to avoid being considered as an indicator of capability level 3 of the "CON.1 Change Management" process. Another example is the *maintenance of a Capacity plan*, which falls under the scope of the "SMS.3 Information Item Management" process instead of being addressed by the capacity management process. Thus, when assessing the change management or the capacity management process, key business aspects such as the definition of the Request for change procedure or the maintenance of the capacity plan will not be scrutinized. From an ITSM practitioner point of view, this can be considered as a weakness of the ISO/IEC 15504-8 model.

The ISO/IEC 20000-1 standard is currently under revision. Indeed, since 2012, ISO has required that all the MSSs should be harmonized. For that, they should strictly follow the identical core text provided by the high level structure contained in the Annex SL [20]. Consequently, all the process assessment models targeting these harmonized MSSs will now include the same twelve management system processes. Such generic processes have already been described and included in the PAM for Information security management (ISO/IEC 33072 [33]). Thus, in the coming months, once the ISO/IEC 20000-1 will be reviewed and improved, it will be the opportunity for the ISO editors to update the associated PAM accordingly. This reviewed model (that will replace ISO/IEC 15504-8) will probably be included within the new ISO/IEC 33000 series of standards (whose long-term objective is to host a library of process models targeting various domains, including many management systems). Subsequently, this future ITSM PAM should benefit from both improvements: the revision of ISO/IEC 20000-1 on the one side, and the enhancements related to the new process assessment series of standards (ISO/IEC 33000) on the other side.

4.2 TIPA for ITIL PAM: Strength, Weakness, and Opportunity

The key strength of the TIPA for ITIL PAM is its market orientation. It is based on ITIL, the popular library of ITSM best practices. Being goal-oriented, the processes contained in the TIPA for ITIL PAM are both easy to understand by process practitioners, and easy to use by assessors. Aligned with the "adapt and adopt" philosophy advocated by ITIL, this model fits for many purposes. On the one side it can be used for supporting a pragmatic implementation of robust ITSM processes, based on a proven set of best practices. On the other side, the TIPA for ITIL PAM can also be used periodically, to both determine the initial starting point and evaluate the results of an improvement program.

Nevertheless, the analysis of its coverage rate regarding the SMS requirements showed the limits of the TIPA for ITIL PAM for preparing an ISO/IEC 20000-1 certification. Indeed, as exposed in Sect. 4.2, one third of the requirements contained in ISO/IEC 20000-1 (spread across Sects. 4, 6.3, 6.6, 7.1, 8.1, 8.2, 9.1, 9.2, and 9.3) is not covered by the TIPA for ITIL model. This is mainly due to the fact that the definition of the management system is not tackled by the ITIL publications and the TIPA for ITIL PAM is strictly aligned with ITIL processes. For example, the entire clause 4 of ISO/IEC 20000-1, which details the SMS general requirements, is obviously not addressed by any of the processes from the TIPA for ITIL PAM.

However this weakness can be mitigated by combining the TIPA model with management system processes such as those derived from the ISO annex SL. Expanding the TIPA for ITIL PAM with these common processes can considerably reduce the gap in term of coverage of the ISO/IEC 20000-1 requirements. Indeed, by doing so the number of elementary requirements covered would increase from 282 to 397 (which corresponds to a coverage rate of 95 %), and only 22 requirements (mainly related to the Change, Release, and Configuration management processes) would remain orphan. To address this problem, one solution could be to enrich the TIPA questionnaires (part of the TIPA for ITIL framework) for these three processes with new indicators targeting these orphan requirements. This would thus allow to use this expanded PAM (ITIL + management system processes) in a complete ISO/IEC 20000-1 certification context.

5 Conclusion

Assessing a process is a recognized means to get a clear view on the way it is implemented and on the way it is performed within an organization. A process assessment can thus be used for various purposes such as: certification preparation, capability determination, improvement follow-up, or supplier selection. Therefore, when applied to the ITSM domain, such assessments are helpful for preparing an ISO/IEC 20000-1 certification, providing they are based on the appropriate process assessment model. This paper studied and compared two publicly available ITSM models: ISO/IEC 15504-8 and TIPA for ITIL PAM. It permitted to highlight their strengths and weaknesses and to determine their respective preferred use cases. Thus, thanks to its close alignment with the targeted requirements, the ISO/IEC 15504-8 PAM is most likely candidate to best prepare an ISO/IEC 20000-1 certification. On the other side, the market-orientation of the TIPA for ITIL makes its usage very appropriate to support ITSM implementation and/or improvement initiatives. However, our current works precisely aim at including a new gap analysis tool within the TIPA framework. In the future, a combined use of this brand new tool for ISO/IEC 20000-1 with the existing TIPA for ITIL PAM will permit organizations to address both compliance and improvement challenges in one go.

References

1. ISO Survey (2014). http://www.iso.org/iso/home/standards/certification/iso-survey.htm
2. ISO/IEC 27001. Information technology – Security techniques – Information security management systems – Requirements. International Organization for Standardization, Geneva (2013)
3. ISO/IEC 20000-1. Information Technology — Service management — Service management system requirements. International Organization for Standardization, Geneva (2011)
4. Cots, S., Casadesús, M., Marimon, F.: Benefits of ISO 20000 IT service management certification, Information Systems and e-Business Management (2016). doi:10.1007/s10257-014-0271-2
5. Disterer, G.: Why firms seek ISO 20000 certification - a study of ISO 20000 adoption. In: ECIS 2012 Proceedings, Paper 31 (2012)
6. Renault, A., Picard, M., Ferrand, D.: Process assessment to support conformity assessment – experimentation of a PAM for accreditation conformity assessment. In: The International Conference SPICE 2008, Nuremberg, Germany (2008)
7. Jung, H.-W., Hunter, R.: The relationship between ISO/IEC 15504 process capability levels, ISO 9001 certification and organization size: an empirical study. J. Syst. Softw. **59**(1), 43–55 (2001)
8. Walker, A., Coletta, A., Sivaraman, R.: An evaluation of the process capability implications of the requirements of ISO/IEC 20000-1. J. Softw. Evol. Process **26**(12) (2014)
9. ISO/IEC 33002. Information Technology — Process assessment — Requirements for performing process assessment. International Organization for Standardization, Geneva (2015)
10. ISO/IEC 33004. Information Technology — Process assessment — Requirements for process reference, process assessment and maturity models. International Organization for Standardization, Geneva (2015)
11. Gresse von Wangenheim, C., Rossa Hauck, J.C., Salviano, C., von Wangenheim, A.: Systematic literature review of software process capability/maturity models. In: The International Conference SPICE 2010, Pisa, Italy (2010)
12. Mesquida, A.L., Mas, A., Amengual, E., Calvo-Manzano, J.A.: IT Service Management Process Improvement based on ISO/IEC 15504: A systematic review. Inf. Softw. Technol. **54**, 239–247 (2012)
13. ISO/IEC 15504-8. Information Technology — Process assessment — An exemplar process assessment model for IT service management. International Organization for Standardization, Geneva (2012)
14. http://bit.ly/23camL4

15. ISO/IEC 20000-2. Information Technology — Service management — Guidance on the application of service management systems. International Organization for Standardization, Geneva (2012)
16. ISO/IEC TR 20000-5. Information Technology — Service management — Exemplar implementation plan for ISO/IEC 20000-1:2011. International Organization for Standardization, Geneva (2013)
17. ISO/IEC 27013. Information Technology — Security techniques — Guidance on the integrated implementation of ISO/IEC 27001 and ISO/IEC 20000-1. International Organization for Standardization, Geneva (2015)
18. Picard, M., Renault, A., Barafort, B.: A Maturity Model for ISO/IEC 20000-1 Based on the TIPA for ITIL Process Capability Assessment Model. In: O'Connor, R.V., Umay Akkaya, M., Kemaneci, K., Yilmaz, M., Poth, A., Messnarz, R. (eds.) EuroSPI 2015. CCIS, vol. 543, pp. 168–179. Springer, Heidelberg (2015). doi:10.1007/978-3-319-24647-5_14
19. The Cabinet Office. ITIL Lifecycle Publication Suite. TSO Edition (2011)
20. ISO/IEC Directives, Part1, Annex SL. International Organization for Standardization, Geneva (2014)
21. Niessink, F., Clerc, V., Tijdink, T., van Vliet, H.: IT Service Capability Maturity Model, Vrije Universiteit (2005)
22. CMMI for Services, Version 1.3 (PDF). CMMI-SVC (Version 1.3, November 2010). Carnegie Mellon University Software Engineering Institute (2010)
23. Pereira, R., Mira da Silva, M.: A Maturity Model for Implementing ITIL v3. In: 6th World Congress on Services (SERVICES-1), USA (2010)
24. Clarke, P., Lepmets, M., Dorling, A., McCaffery, F.: Safety critical software process assessment: how MDevSPICE® addresses the challenge of integrating compliance and capability. In: Rout, T., O'Connor, R.V., Dorling, A. (eds.) SPICE 2015. CCIS, vol. 526, pp. 13–18. Springer, Heidelberg (2015)
25. Nehfort, A.: ISO 20000-PAM Process Assessment Model for ISO/IEC 20000-1, V051/006.11.2006, Nehfort IT-Consulting KEG (2006)
26. ISO/IEC/IEEE 15289. Information Technology — Systems and software engineering — Content of life-cycle information products (documentation). International Organization for Standardization, Geneva (2011)
27. ISO/IEC 15504-2. Information Technology — Process assessment — Performing an assessment. International Organization for Standardization, Geneva (2003)
28. Public Research Center Henri Tudor. ITSM Process Assessment Supporting ITIL. Van Haren Publishing (2009). ISBN: 9789087535643
29. Renault, A., Barafort, B.: TIPA for ITIL – from genesis to maturity of SPICE applied to ITIL 2011. In: The International Conference EuroSPI 2014, Luxembourg (2014)
30. Barafort, B., Renault, A., Picard, M., Cortina, S.: A transformation process for building PRMs and PAMs based on a collection of requirements – Example with ISO/IEC 20000. In: The International Conference SPICE 2008, Nuremberg, Germany (2008)
31. ISO/IEC TR 20000-11. Information Technology — Service management — Guidance on the relationship between ISO/IEC 20000-1:2011 and service management frameworks: ITIL ®. International Organization for Standardization, Geneva (2015)
32. Renault, A., Cortina, S., Barafort, B.: Towards a maturity model for ISO/IEC 20000-1 based on the TIPA for ITIL process capability assessment model. In: Rout, T., O'Connor, R.V., Dorling, A. (eds.) SPICE 2015. CCIS, vol. 526, pp. 188–200. Springer, Heidelberg (2015)
33. ISO/IEC TS 33072. Information Technology — Process assessment — Process capability assessment model for Information Security Management. International Organization for Standardization, Geneva (2016)

Towards Automated Traceability Assessment through Augmented Lifecycle Space

Miklós Biró[1,3(✉)], József Klespitz[2], Johannes Gmeiner[1], Christa Illibauer[1], and Levente Kovács[2]

[1] Software Competence Center Hagenberg, Hagenberg, Austria
{miklos.biro,johannes.gmeiner,christa.illibauer}@scch.at
[2] Óbuda University, Budapest, Hungary
klespitz.jozsef@phd.uni-obuda.hu,
kovacs.levente@nik.uni-obuda.hu
[3] Johannes Kepler Universität, Linz, Austria

Abstract. The assessment and improvement of the satisfaction of traceability requirements during the development of software in general and of safety-critical software in particular is demanding and costly. The special requirements are reflected in software process related general and industry specific standards and the popular agile approaches as well. It is imminent, for practical and logical reasons, that there is a need for the automation of the assessment of the completeness and consistency of traceability as far as possible. In addition to highlighting experienced weaknesses of current either homogeneous or heterogeneous tool environments intending to support development lifecycle traceability, this paper outlines new solutions and suggests the exploitation of emerging technologies for the automation of traceability assessment and improvement.

Keywords: Application lifecycle management · Process assessment · Process improvement · Open services for lifecycle collaboration · Tools integration · Heterogeneous tools environment · Existence · Non-existence

1 Introduction

Our research is motivated by the needs of embedded software development for active medical devices which are naturally safety-critical. Safety-critical systems have so high risk of causing harm that this risk must always be reduced to a level "as low as reasonably practicable" (ALARP) required by ethics, regulatory regimes, and standards (IEC 61508).

For the special case of medical software development, the standard IEC 62304 Medical device software - Software life cycle processes, was released in 2006, and is under review to be harmonized with ISO/IEC 12207:2008 (Systems and software engineering – Software life cycle processes).

MDevSPICE® [1, 2], released in 2014, facilitates the assessment and improvement of software development processes for medical devices based on ISO/IEC 15504-5, and enables the processes in the new release of IEC 62304 to be comparable with those of

ISO 12207:2008. The above points give just a glimpse of the changes heavily affecting software developers in the medical devices domain.

Instead of containing actual recommendations of techniques, tools and methods for software development, IEC 62304 encourages the use of the more general IEC 61508-3:2010 Functional Safety of Electrical/Electronic/Programmable Electronic Safety-related Systems – Part 3: Software requirements, as a source for good software methods, techniques and tools.

Bidirectional traceability is a key notion of all process assessment and improvement models. [3] reports about an extensive literature review which classifies the models involving software traceability requirements according to the scope of the model, that is:

- Generic software development and traceability including CMMI and ISO/IEC 15504 evolving into the ISO/IEC 330xx (Information technology – Process assessment) series of standards (SPICE).
- Safety-critical software development and traceability including DO-178C (Software Considerations in Airborne Systems and Equipment Certification) and Automotive SPICE.
- Domain specific software traceability requirements which, in the case of medical devices for example, include the already mentioned IEC 62304 (Medical Device Software – Software Life Cycle Processes), MDD 93/42/EEC (European Council. Council directive concerning medical devices), Amendment (2007/47/EC), US FDA Center for Devices and Radiological Health Guidances, ISO 14971:2007. (Medical Devices – Application of Risk Management to Medical Devices), IEC/TR 80002–1:2009 (Medical Device Software Part 1: Guidance on the Application of ISO 14971 to Medical Device Software), and ISO 13485:2003 (Medical Devices – Quality Management Systems – Requirements for Regulatory Purposes)

It is important to highlight that traceability is fully recognized as a key issue by the agile community as well [4, 5].

Unfortunately, complete and consistent traceability as well as the actual assessment of the satisfaction of the crucial traceability requirements is practically impossible to achieve with the heterogeneous variety of application lifecycle management (ALM) tools companies are using [6]. Following a manual approach, traceability assessors can only recur to sampling which has ultimate weaknesses detailed later in this paper.

It is evident that there are software development artifacts that can only be created by humans (customer, sales, marketing, etc.). Yet, there are other artifacts which can hardly be managed manually including for example the documentation of low level test results or results of automated testing (e.g. static and/or dynamic code analysis). Similarly, the number of relationships, including traceability links, between the different artifacts becomes prohibitive even in the simplest practical cases, so the handling and maintenance requires automated support.

Application Lifecycle Management systems (ALMs) are used to support the above mentioned processes. ALMs do not only cover the implementation, but the whole process starting from the initial idea, closing with the end of the product's life [7]. When a company chooses to set up an ALM, it can choose among numerous off-the-self or third party software systems and/or can decide to develop needed elements and optionally complement them with other management tools.

In this paper, after analyzing people and process challenges for achieving traceability in either homogeneous or heterogeneous tool environments, we point out fundamental logical and technical barriers for assessing and improving the completeness and consistency of traceability. Before introducing the suggested Augmented Lifecycle Space approach, we show relevant models which are good candidates to serve as its basis. Finally, RDF Triple Store (a purpose-built database optimized for the storage and retrieval of data entities composed of subject-predicate-object triples) is pointed out as the most suitable generic technology solution for representing artifacts and their relationships whose completeness and consistency must be verified by traceability assessors. RDF is at the core of the Linked Data paradigm the emerging cross-industry OSLC (Open Services for Lifecycle Collaboration) initiative is based on.

2 People and Process Challenges for Traceability in Either Homogeneous or Heterogeneous Environments

It is a fact that 50–60 % of software defects are related to requirements development [7]. Here, the rate of leakage (inherited defect which is detected only at a later stage) is 53 % in the requirements phase and 68 % in the design phase [3]. It is trivial that this fact raises the need for the improvement of current tools used to manage software development, especially requirements management.

Despite these facts, a significant proportion of people in charge of software development see traceability as a mandatory burden or as a useful but cumbersome duty [8–10]. The need for traceability being undeniable, full compliance is difficult to enforce in everyday practice [11]. An example of the need is a developer exploring the code for possible effects of code modification. But a new employee also needs the traceability feature to get familiar with the code and the system it models. Finally, assessors have to rely on the traceability system to ascertain about the capabilities of the processes [12].

The aforementioned problems coincide with our experiences. Although, senior management is most of the time aware of the importance of traceability, developers are naturally prone to neglecting it. Paradoxically, developers are the ones who first suffer from the deficiency of traceability (e.g. code fragments to redesign for satisfying requirement changes are difficult to find) and their productivity is definitely increased in case of a well-designed traceability environment.

In [13, 14], authors identify and analyze eight challenges for traceability from a goal-oriented perspective only briefly alluded to below:

1. Traceability should be fit-for-purpose and has to support stakeholder needs.
2. The ROI (return on investment) from using traceability has to be adequate.
3. Traceability has to be maintainable and able to accommodate changing stakeholder needs.

4. The stakeholders have to have full trust in traceability.
5. Varying types of artifacts have to be traceable at variable levels of granularity and quantity.
6. Traceability has to be portable.
7. Traceability has to be a strategic priority valued by all.
8. Finally, traceability has to be ubiquitous, but it is achievable only when it is established and sustained with near zero effort.

The above issues are present in the case of even homogeneous ALM environments which can and mostly do provide extensive support for implementing traceability. The issues are however amplified in the case of widely occurring heterogeneous tool environments.

The introduction of a variety of tools can be caused by many factors. The company may choose not to depend on a certain vendor and to consider its unique needs which can only be matched with the offers of different vendors. Similarly, heterogeneity might result if the tool system was established incrementally over time. Moreover, there is qualm about the loss of accumulated intellectual property. ALM systems store tremendous amount of precious information which might be damaged or lost in case of migration. Therefore, companies, most of the time, insist keeping well-tried solutions to avoid such scenarios. Finally, changing habits and getting used to new tools can be cumbersome for anybody even for developers.

In a diversified environment, traceability, consistency and usability issues are naturally amplified. In cross-tool relationships, where direct connections do not exist, (e.g. requirements and their tests may be present in different tools) aging will erode traceability, and can lead to inconsistencies. Thus, it is of upmost importance to create direct connections between artifacts in order to maintaining traceability and enabling consistency analysis. Furthermore, replication can be eliminated which further improves transparency and decreases the risk of introduced mistakes.

3   Logical and Technical Challenges for Assessing and Improving the Completeness and Consistency of Traceability

As already mentioned, ALM environments can and mostly do provide extensive support for creating traceability links and overviewing existing links.

There is however a fundamental difference between creating, overviewing links and proving that no links are missing which is the exact duty of the assessor and fully justifies the ultimate need for Automated Traceability Assessment.

The difference is a special case of the logical difference in mathematics between the proof of the existence of an object satisfying given properties and the proof of the non-existence of such an object. The existence ($\exists$) can be proven by showing an instance, while the proof of non-existence is equivalent to showing that the property is not satisfied by any object ($\forall$), which can obviously be much more difficult (Fig. 1).

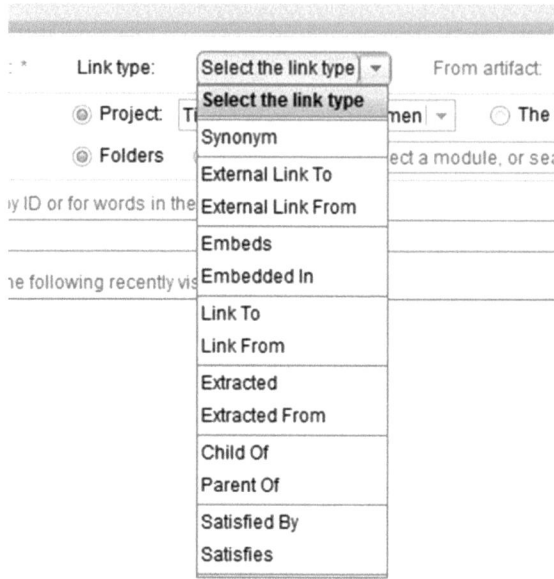

Fig. 1. Add a link to an artifact in IBM rational DOORS

The figures below show a glimpse to the technical support and windows that developers are faced with when creating and assessing traceability links between artifacts in a few popular tools:

Regarding the task of traceability assessors, the currently only possible manual approach they have to be content with is sampling which has ultimate weaknesses in addition to the logical difficulty of proving non-existence described before:

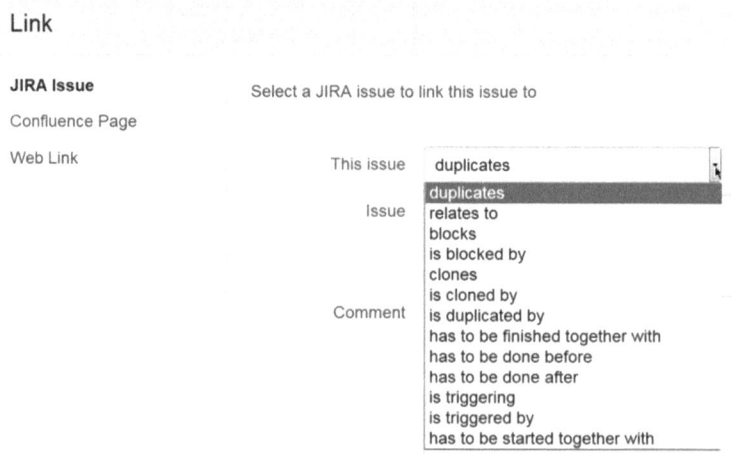

Fig. 2. Add a link to an issue in JIRA

- Traceability is basically restricted to the closed ALM system. Representational State Transfer (REST) APIs are mostly available for providing internal data. However, there is need for a standardized open form of exchange made possible by the emerging OSLC (Open Services for Lifecycle Collaboration) approach to be discussed (Fig. 2).
- Useful traceability reports including the traceability matrix can be generated. However, the manual processing of these reports, due to their size, is only possible with very small examples whose complexity is exceeded by the simplest industrial applications. The reports only contain already existing artifacts while missing artifacts can only be discovered by manual inspection. The reports are static while requirements and identified defects, for example, are very dynamically changing artifacts, and may even originate from outside the ALM system.
- Assessors and users may be easily confused by the complexity of the set of widgets, such as buttons, text fields, tabs, and links which are provided to access and edit all properties of resources at any time.
- Assessors and users need to reach destinations such as web pages and views by clicking many links and tabs whose understanding is not essential for the assessment (Fig. 3).

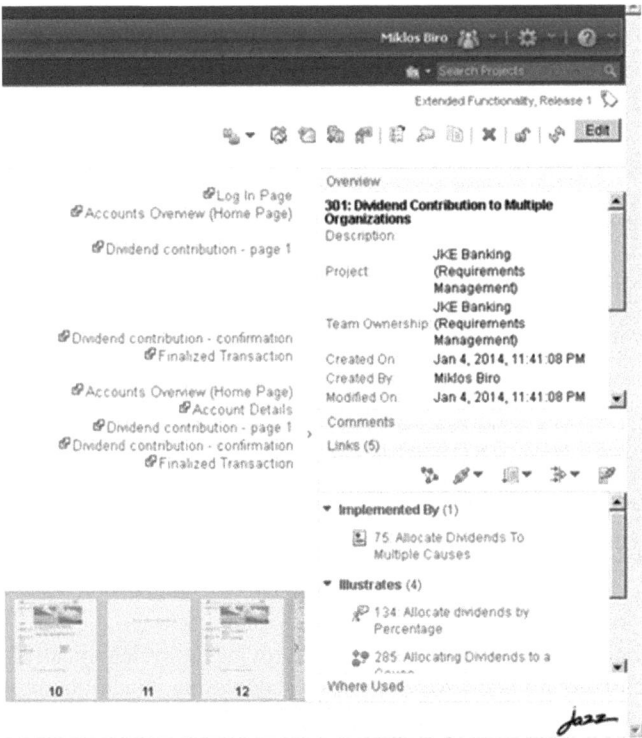

Fig. 3. Window fragment with traceability link in IBM rational CLM

In summary, the logical and technical challenges themselves, together with the people and process challenges, fully justify the need for the automation of the assessment and improvement of the completeness and consistency of traceability [15].

4 Considered Models Addressing Traceability

In this section, preparing the grounds for the following proposed solution, we refer to the general level V-model appearing in the most recent version of the already mentioned Automotive SPICE standard [16] also highlighted in the paper [17], as well as the engineering models developed by the SoQrates Working Group "Traces" also presented in the paper [17].

Figure 4 provides the overview of the bidirectional traceability and newly highlighted consistency requirements of version 3.0 of Automotive SPICE published in 2015.

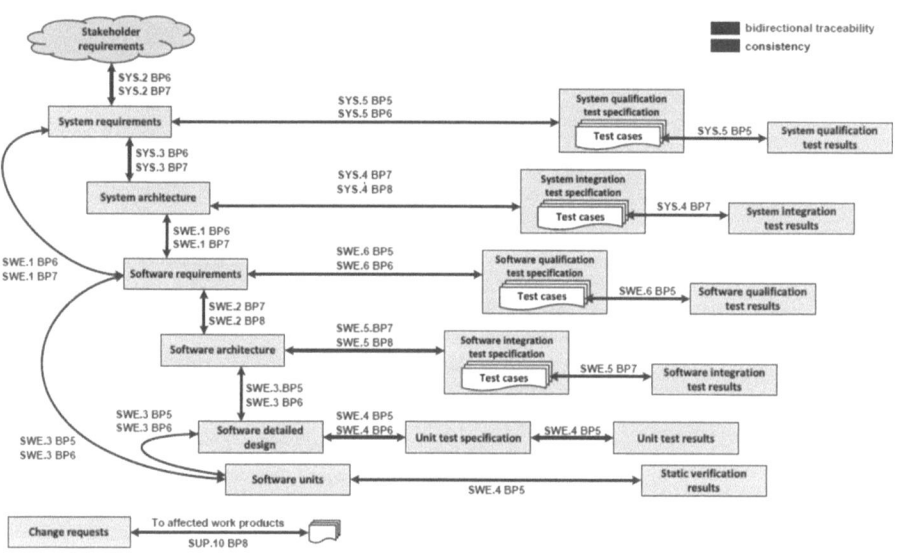

Fig. 4. Bidirectional traceability and consistency requirements of Automotive SPICE v3.0 [16]

The SoQrates Working Group "Traces" provides a systematically detailed engineering model including the traceability layer, addressing in addition reuse and variant management presented in the paper [17].

Both of the above models are good candidates to serve as base models for augmented lifecycle traceability described in the next section (Fig. 5).

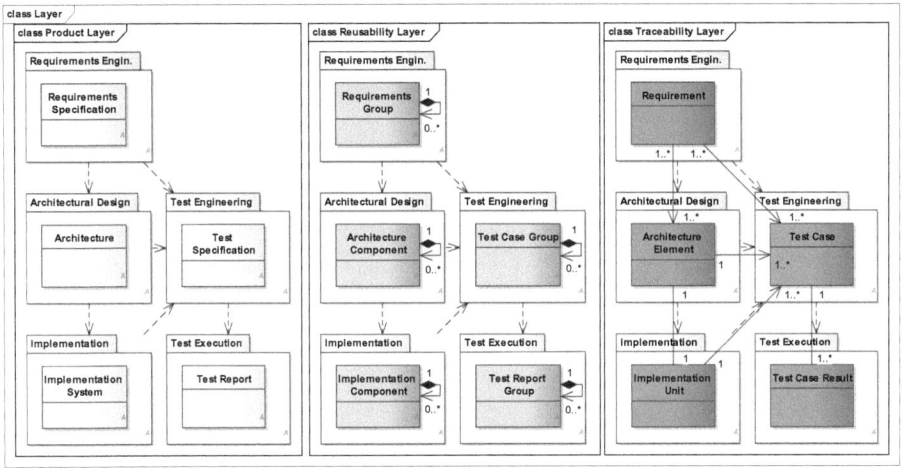

Fig. 5. Layers for product, reusability and traceability in the SoQrates Working Group "Traces" model [17]

5 Traceability Assessment through Augmented Lifecycle Space

As discussed earlier, the assessment of the completeness and consistency of traceability relationships materialized by links requires the proof that no links representing required traceability relationships are missing and that there are no inconsistencies among the links.

In case the proof process identifies missing or inconsistent links, a workflow can be automatically created to address the bridging of traceability gaps and/or remediation of inconsistencies.

The fundamental question is: **How to find missing links and artifacts which, by definition, do not exist**?

Let us define **Lifecycle Space** to be the set of lifecycle artifacts with their relationships which exist anywhere in the lifecycle environment.

The **Augmented Lifecycle Space** approach, sketched along the following steps, is the solution suggested in this paper:

1. Categorize all existing artifacts of the homogenous or heterogeneous tool environment according to the elements of the chosen model containing traceability requirements (e.g. requirement, architecture element, test case, etc.).
2. Analyze the existing relationships (links) and the artifacts in the system and identify those which are missing but should exist according to the traceability requirements of the model.
3. If one of the two artifacts necessary for a required relationship is missing, automatically augment the system with the corresponding artifact whose links will be initially missing of course.

4. Analyze the relationships (links) of the augmented system. If a relationship (link) required by the model is missing, then automatically generate the task of the workflow for bridging the relationship gap.
5. Execute the relationship gap bridging workflow generated in the previous step involving manual intervention if necessary.

The Augmented Lifecycle Space approach allows the assessment and improvement of the completeness and consistency of traceability in either homogeneous or heterogeneous tool environments.

The question the following section intends to answer: **how to technically access artifacts and their relationships in a homogeneous or a heterogeneous tool environment.**

6 Technical Approaches to Access Artifacts and their Relationships – the OSLC Initiative

A homogeneous tool environment usually contains an Application Programming Interface (API) which allows access to the artifacts and their relationships within the tool A itself. This tool-A-dependent API could then be used from any other tool B to build a specific interface between the tools A and B allowing access to the artifacts and relationships stored in tool A from tool B.

In the case of the very common heterogeneous tool environments, whose roots were discussed earlier, the artifacts and their relationships have of course to be accessed across the usually numerous tools applied at the company. It is apparent in this case that the just described point-to-point tools integration is professionally unreasonable.

The already mentioned Open Services for Lifecycle Collaboration (OSLC) cross-industry initiative was recently created to overcome the professionally unreasonable approach of point-to-point tools integrations.

OSLC's aim is to define standards for compatibility of software lifecycle tools to make it easy and practical to integrate software used for development, deployment, and monitoring applications. This aim seems to be too obvious and overly ambitious at the same time. However, despite its relatively short history starting in 2008, OSLC is the only potential approach to achieve these aims at a universal level, and is already widely supported by industry. The unprecedented potential of the OSLC approach is based on its foundation on the architecture of the World Wide Web unquestionably proven to be powerful and scalable and on the generally accepted software engineering principle to always focus first on the simplest possible things that will work.

The elementary concepts and rules are defined in the OSLC Core Specification [18] which sets out the common features that every OSLC Service is expected to support using the terminology and generally accepted approaches of the World Wide Web Consortium (W3C). One of the key approaches is Linked Data being the primary technology leading to the Semantic Web which is defined by W3C as providing a common framework that allows data to be shared and reused across application, enterprise, and community boundaries. And formulated at the most abstract level, this is the exact goal

OSLC intends to achieve in the interest of full traceability and interoperability in the software lifecycle.

Full traceability of a requirement throughout the development chain and even the entire supply chain was also a major focus point of the European CESAR project (Cost-Efficient Methods and Processes for Safety Relevant Embedded Systems) which adopted interoperability technologies proposed by the OSLC initiative [19].

Another important European project exploiting OSLC, was iFEST (industrial Framework for Embedded Systems Tools).

CRYSTAL (CRitical sYSTem engineering AcceLeration) is an ARTEMIS Innovation Pilot Project (AIPP) whose Interoperability Specification (IOS) is also based on OSLC [20].

In conclusion, the most suitable generic technology solution for representing artifacts and their relationships, that have to be accessed in any tool environment, is the RDF triple which is the object type the information in an OSLC resource is composed of and which is at the core of the Linked Data paradigm [21].

The technical manifestation in the OSLC paradigm of the Lifecycle Space, abstractly defined above, is the set of OSLC resources which all live in some OSLC ServiceProvider exposed by OSLC ServiceProviderCatalogs whose more detailed discussion is beyond the scope of this paper.

7 Conclusions and Further Works

The paper has shown that all approaches to achieving functional safety require the establishment of bilateral traceability between development artifacts and that the manual creation and maintenance of traceability links is possible, but the assessment of the completeness and consistency of traceability is not supported by current tools.

The Augmented Lifecycle Space approach, introduced in the paper, allows the automation of the assessment and facilitates the improvement of the completeness and consistency of traceability in either homogeneous or heterogeneous tool environments.

The technical solution suggested to handle artifacts and their relationships, in either homogeneous or heterogeneous tool environments, is OSLC (Open Services for Lifecycle Collaboration) which is based on the Linked Data paradigm.

Work is in progress targeting the implementation of the approach described in this paper in safety-critical software development environments.

Acknowledgement. The authors are grateful for the support of Research and Innovation Center of Óbuda University. The work is supported by the European Research Council Starting Grant ERC-StG 679681.

The research reported in this paper has been supported by the Austrian Ministry for Transport, Innovation and Technology, the Federal Ministry of Science, Research and Economy, and the Province of Upper Austria in the frame of the COMET center SCCH.

References

1. Lepmets, M., Clarke, P., McCaffery, F., Finnegan, A., Dorling, A.: Development of a process assessment model for medical device software development. In: Industrial Proceedings of the 21st European Conference on Systems, Software and Services Process Improvement (EuroSPI 2014), 25–27 June, Luxembourg (2014)
2. McCaffery, F., Clarke, P., Lepmets, M.: Bringing medical device software development standards into a single model - MDevSPICE. Ir. Med. Board Medi. Devices Newslett. **1**(40), 2–3 (2014)
3. McCaffery, F., Casey, V., Sivakumar, M.S., Coleman, G., Donnelly, P., Burton, J.: Medical device software traceability. In: Cleland-Huang, J., Gotel, O., Zismanm, A. (eds.) Software and Systems Traceability, pp. 321–339. Springer, London (2012)
4. Ambler, S.: Agile requirements best practices. In: Agile Modeling (2014). http://www.agilemodeling.com/essays/agileRequirementsBestPractices.htm. Accessed 08 Apr 2016
5. Ambler, S.: Tracing your design. In: Dr. Dobb's Journal: The World of Software Development (1999). http://www.drdobbs.com/tracing-your-design/184415675. Accessed 08 Apr 2016
6. Murphy, T.E., Duggan, J.: Magic quadrant for application life cycle management. In: Gartner (2012)
7. Chapman, D.: What is application lifecycle management? white paper (2010). http://www.davidchappell.com/writing/white_papers/What_is_ALM_v2.0–Chappell.pdf. Accessed 08 Apr 2016
8. Capers, J.: Software quality in 2011: a survey of the state of the ART. Capers Jones & Associates LLC (2011)
9. Nistala, P., Kumari, P.: Establishing content traceability for software applications: an approach based on structuring and tracking of configuration elements. In: 7th Workshop on Traceability in Emerging Forms of Software Engineering (TEFSE) (2013)
10. Bouillon, E., Mäder, P., Philippow, I.: A survey on usage scenarios for requirements traceability in practice. In: Doerr, J., Opdahl, A.L. (eds.) REFSQ 2013. LNCS, vol. 7830, pp. 158–173. Springer, Heidelberg (2013)
11. Biró, M.: Open services for software process compliance engineering. In: Geffert, V., Preneel, B., Rovan, B., Štuller, J., Tjoa, A.M. (eds.) SOFSEM 2014. LNCS, vol. 8327, pp. 1–6. Springer, Heidelberg (2014)
12. Panis, M.: Successful deployment of requirements traceability in a commercial engineering organization…really. In: 18th IEEE International Requirements Engineering Conference (RE), pp. 303–307. (2010)
13. Cleland-Huang, J, Gotel, O. C., Huffman Hayes, J., Mäder, P., Zisman, A.: Software traceability: trends and future directions. In: Proceedings of the on Future of Software Engineering, pp. 55–69. ACM (2014)
14. Gotel, O., Cleland-Huang, J., Huffman Hayes, J., Zisman, A., Egyed, A., Grünbacher, P., Dekhtyar, A., Antoniol, G., Maletic, J.: The grand challenge of traceability (v1.0). In: Cleland-Huang, J., Gotel, O., Zisman, A. (eds.) Software and Systems Traceability, pp. 343–409. Springer, Heidelberg (2012)
15. Regan, G., Biro, M., Mc Caffery, F., Mc Daid, K., Flood, D.: A traceability process assessment model for the medical device domain. In: Barafort, B., O'Connor, R.V., Poth, A., Messnarz, R. (eds.) EuroSPI 2014. CCIS, vol. 425, pp. 206–216. Springer, Heidelberg (2014)
16. Automotive, S. I. G., VDA QMC Working Group 13.: Automotive SPICE Process Assessment/ Reference Model, v3.0 (2015). http://www.automotivespice.com/fileadmin/software-download/Automotive_SPICE_PAM_30.pdf. Accessed 08 Apr 2016

17. Dreves, R., Hällmeyer, F., Haunert, L., Sechser, B.: Method to realize traceability in development processes. In: Proceedings of EuroSPI2 (2015)
18. OSLC Core Specification Workgroup.: OSLC core specification version 2.0. Open Services for Lifecycle Collaboration (2013). http://open-services.net/bin/view/Main/OslcCore Specification. Accessed 08 Apr 2016
19. Jolliffe, G.: Cost-efficient methods and processes for safety relevant embedded systems (CESAR)–an objective overview. In: Dale, C., Anderson, T. (eds.) Making Systems Safer, pp. 37–50. Springer, London (2010)
20. Pflügl, H., El-Salloum, C., Kundner, I.: Crystal, critical system engineering acceleration, a truly European dimension. ARTEMIS Mag. **14**, 12–15 (2013)
21. Biró, M.: functional safety, traceability, and open services. In: Madeyski, L., Ochodek, M. (eds.) Software Engineering from Research and Practice Perspective. Wyd. Nakom, Poznan, pp. 73–82. ISBN:978–83–63919–16–0 (2014)

Measuring Readiness for Compliance: A Gap Analysis Tool to Complete the TIPA Process Assessment Framework

Michel Picard[✉], Alain Renault[✉], Béatrix Barafort[✉], and Stéphane Cortina[✉]

Luxembourg Institute of Science and Technology, 5 Avenue des Hauts-Fourneaux,
4362 Esch-sur-Alzette, Luxembourg
{michel.picard,alain.renault,beatrix.barafort,
stephane.cortina}@list.lu

Abstract. The combination of conformity and process assessment is gaining interest among business organizations, and the IT Service Management (ITSM) field is no exception to this trend. We have designed a Gap Analysis tool enabling to translate the identified requirement gaps into a process perspective. The tool is based on the proces map from the Process Assessment Model (PAM) built on the same requirements set to provide the process view, and so it creates correlations and offers interesting complementarities with the related PAM. The Proof of Concept presented in this paper validates the design of such a tool. It opens the door to its application to the IT Service Management field and, in particular, its integration within the current Tudor's IT Process Assessment (TIPA) framework.

Keywords: TIPA · Conformity assessment · Requirements coverage · Gap analysis · Process approach · ISO/IEC 20000

1 Introduction

Process assessment has proved its value through a massive adoption in some sectors of the industry with the Capability Maturity Model Integrated (CMMI) Constellations [1–3], Automotive Spice [4], and more recently with the release of TIPA® for IT Infrastructure Library (ITIL) [5, 6]. Despite the valuable synergies existing between process assessment and management systems certification both approaches are seldom implemented complementarily.

In previous research works, the authors have made a first attempt to bridge the gap between process assessment and conformity assessment [7, 8]. They came to the conclusion that using a maturity model based on the TIPA for ITIL PAM [9] is not the best means to demonstrate an organization's readiness towards a requirements standard such as ISO/IEC 20000-1 [10]. This is due to the difference of granularity between the original requirements and the process assessment indicators, the difficulty to ensure straightforward traceability between both of them, and the inefficiency (low cost-benefit ratio) of the approach in comparison to an audit.

Other initiatives (Sect. 3) address the linkage existing between process and conformity assessment. However no generic framework supports the integration of process assessment and conformity assessment today. Hence, the research question is: *How to provide organizations with a tool translating the result of a conformity assessment in a process view?*

In this context, the paper presents a dedicated Gap Analysis tool and how such a tool can complement the TIPA framework to bring an answer to this question. In this paper, we first present in Sect. 2 terminology related to both conformity and process assessment domains and in Sect. 3 some related work. Section 4 is the description of the Gap Analysis deployed in the context of a Luxembourg regulation on e-Archiving. Section 5 presents discussions before conclusions given in Sect. 6.

2 Terminology

The concept of gap analysis and its positioning against a process assessment in a context of conformity assessment needs to be clarified to understand the contribution of our work and particularly its complementarity with the existing TIPA framework.

In the business world, a gap analysis *allows an organization to measure how it is performing versus its potential* (definition of the Cambridge Business English Dictionary © Cambridge University Press).

ITIL® 2011 in its Continual Service Improvement volume [11] defines a gap analysis as *"an activity that compares two sets of data and identifies the differences. A gap analysis is commonly used to compare a set of **requirements** with actual delivery."*

A gap analysis is commonly structured around a set of areas, topics or categories that make it efficient to use [12] (i.e. eliminate requirement redundancies, group requirements by organizational role...), and enable the overall result presentation. The term *"topic"* is used for designating the semantic grouping of requirements.

As defined in ISO 19011:2011 [13], an audit is a *"systematic, independent and documented process for obtaining audit evidence (records, statements of fact or other information which are relevant and verifiable) and evaluating it objectively to determine the extent to which the audit criteria (set of policies, procedures or requirements) are fulfilled."*

On the one hand, the ISO/IEC 17000:2004 [14] defines a conformity assessment as a *"demonstration that specified requirements relating to a product, process, system, person or body are fulfilled"*. The International Organization for Standardization (ISO) also specifies that the inspection is a specific form of conformity assessment, this latter being defined as *"examination of a product design, product, process or installation and determination of its conformity with specific requirements or, on the basis of professional judgement, with general requirements"*.

On the other hand, process assessment is defined in ISO/IEC 33001 [15] as a *"disciplined evaluation of an organizational unit's processes against a process assessment model"*, which is defined as a *"model suitable for the purpose of assessing a specified process quality characteristic, based on one or more process reference models"*.

Most organizations preparing the certification of a management system such as those described in ISO/IEC 20000-1 [10] or in ISO/IEC 27001 [16] first perform a gap analysis, in order to get a first and rapid summarized view on the requirements coverage. An internal audit is then performed when the gaps have been solved and the processes properly implemented, before the certification audits (third party audit) is done. So the gap analysis and (internal or third party) audit should be considered as different forms of conformity assessment (i.e. inspection) useful at different moments in the certification journey.

3 Related Work

Performing an audit is the commonly accepted way for determining compliance to requirements. But while ISO 19011 states that audit are systematic, formal and objective [13] we can also question their relevance regarding the way to support the sustainable improvement of an organization's processes.

A study performed in the early days of Software Capability Maturity Model (SW-CMM) has tried to explain how ISO 9001 could position compared to SW-CMM [17]. It has shown that ISO 9001 requirements were distributed between level 2 and 3 process areas. Deploying processes with level 3 was then supposed to support the compliance to the requirements of the management system standard. A similar study has established the relationship between ISO/IEC 15504 process capability levels and ISO 9001 [18]. The result was that the achieved capability level for each process was lying between 1 and 3 within ISO 9001 certified organizations.

The challenge to determine the capability level of an organization processes against a set of requirements or a requirement standard has also been tackled in various domains such as the accreditation [19], the information security management [12] and the IT service management domains [1, 20]. However, many of those attempts to combine the process assessment approach with compliance turned to be both heavy to develop and not very efficient in practice [8].

In 2014, ISO published a *"common and high level structure* for management systems" with *"identical core text and common terms and core definitions for use in Management Systems Standards"* [21], which all ISO management system standards have now to adopt. This intends to facilitate integration between various management systems. It may also facilitate the demonstration of compliance against one or several of these standards. This initiative raised a lot of interest in the ISO process assessment community and several process models are currently been developed (i.e. ISO/IEC 33072) or will be soon revised accordingly (i.e. ISO/IEC 20000-4 [22], ISO/IEC 15504-8 [23]).

Using process assessment for improvement purposes and preparing for regulation compliance has also been tackled in safety critical domains like Automotive [4] and Medical devices [24].

In the context of the recent MDevSPICE initiative [25] which integrates various medical device software standards within a single PAM, how to address the challenge of integrating compliance and capability has been described: reaching a capability level cannot ensure compliance against a standard.

Finally a part of the solution has already been explored and successfully tested while looking for a means to help small and medium-sized enterprises (SMEs) with limited resources getting prepared for a certification against the ISO/IEC 27001 standard [12]. A structured gap analysis tool was then designed. The gap analysis concept will be reused as a basis of our solution and will be adapted to better address our research question. It will particularly complement the TIPA process assessment framework.

4 The TIPA Gap Analysis

In order to answer our research question, we followed a structured method based on action research approaches [26] consisting of three major steps: 1. Requirements modeling, 2. Design of the tool, and 3. Experimentation [12].

The structure of the Gap Analysis tool such as presented in [12] has been complemented with a process view. This process view is a critical add-on for highlighting the correlation between elementary requirements from the original set of requirements and processes from the related PAM.

4.1 Requirements Modeling

The requirement's modelling is the most critical step of the method for making the Gap Analysis efficient. The *transformation process* applied to design the TIPA PAMs [7, 27, 28] includes dedicated steps for identifying, analyzing, and organizing the elementary (atomic) requirements originating from a collection of requirements. Figure 1 illustrates how the gap analysis development benefits from the transformation process.

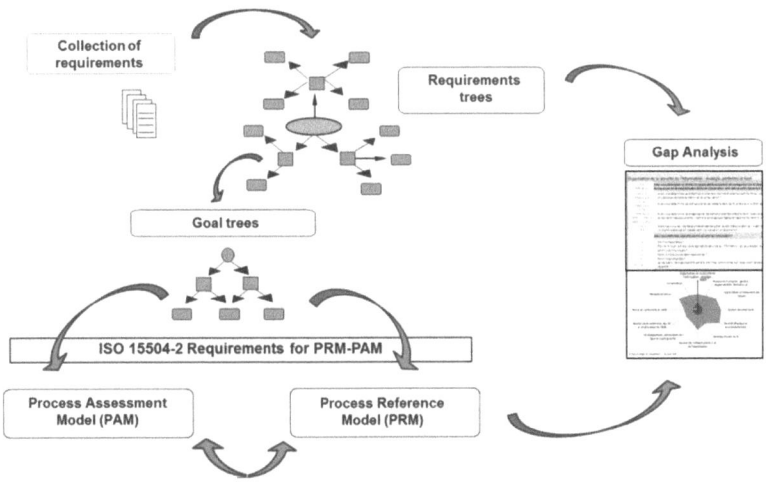

Fig. 1. How Gap Analysis benefits from the transformation process

The first step of the transformation process aims at identifying the elementary requirements contained in the source document (i.e. standard and/or regulation). Usually such a document contains a set of compound requirements identifying more than one obligation to be satisfied. Elementary requirements are created from compound requirements by separating out the distinct requirements [29]. For example, the sentence *"The service provider shall create, implement and maintain a service continuity plan(s) and an availability plan(s)"*, was decomposed into six elementary requirements: *The service provider shall create a service continuity plan(s)/The service provider shall implement a service continuity plan(s)/The service provider shall maintain a service continuity plan(s)/The service provider shall create an availability plan(s)/The service provider shall implement an availability plan(s)/The service provider shall maintain an availability plan(s).*

The TIPA *transformation process* provides us with an exhaustive inventory of the elementary requirements that need to be covered. The second step of the transformation process consists in organizing the elementary requirements around the objects they are targeting in order to build a set of requirement trees [27]. In the Gap Analysis context, this step was slightly adapted to gather the requirements around a set of topics (see terminology section) to sketch the structure of the Gap Analysis tool, rather than the set of objects targeted by the requirements. The Luxembourg regulation on e-Archiving being based on the ISO/IEC27000 series, the TIPA Gap Analysis reuses the 10 topics identified in [12] and adds two more topics, one for digitizing requirements and another for long-term storage requirements. The resulting requirement trees contribute directly to the three key steps for building an effective gap analysis tool [12]: 1. remove requirements redundancies, 2. structure the requirements by topic and 3. reduce the complexity of some requirements. In addition, the requirements trees provide a robust structure to what is required in [12] to actually build a Gap Analysis.

4.2 Design of the TIPA Gap Analysis Tool

The Gap Analysis Overview. The Gap Analysis is made effective thanks to a structured questionnaire organized by topic. The questionnaire is addressing the whole requirements set and is hierarchized to be efficient during the assessment. It is composed of general questions, providing an overview of the themes assessed in each topic that must be answered (and rated) during an assessment. These general questions are completed with more precise ones, assessing each elementary requirement individually, but used only if necessary (i.e. if the answer to the general question does not satisfy the assessor). Whatever the type of question, one or more elementary requirements are linked to each question to ensure the traceability. Concretely, an extract of such a questionnaire applied to the context of the Luxembourg regulation on e-archiving is shown in Fig. 2. It contains 359 questions for covering the 418 elementary requirements set forth in that particular regulation.

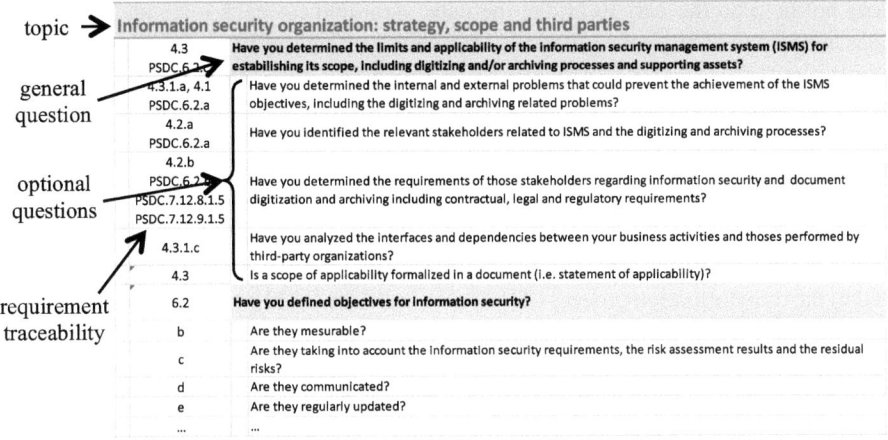

Fig. 2. TIPA Gap Analysis questions structured by topic

The questionnaire is supported by an automated MS Excel file in order to record the answers during the assessment process, rate the (general) questions and finally produce a radar chart as main result for the gap analysis. The radar chart summarizes the coverage rates of the organization practices against the elementary requirements related to each topic. The Fig. 3 shows an example of result in the context of the Luxembourg e-archiving regulation for which twelve topics were identified (see Sect. 4.1).

The Process View. The radar chart is structured around the topics identified during the design stage of the gap analysis. However, this topic-based presentation of the results

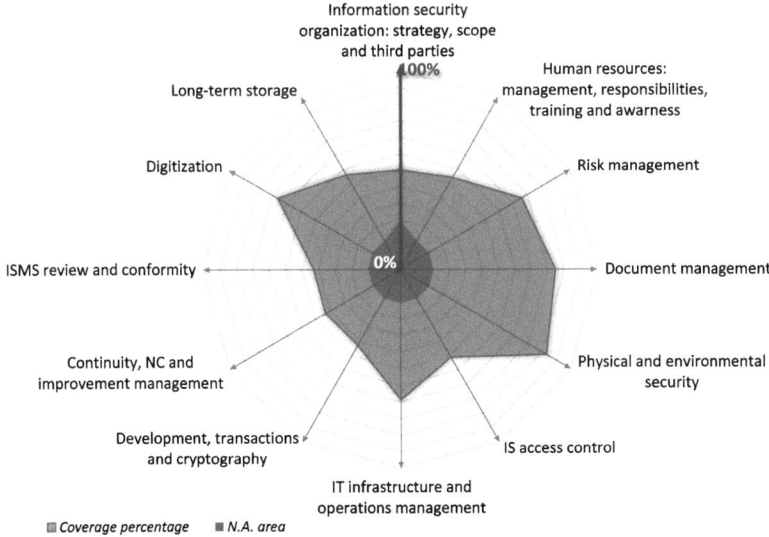

Fig. 3. Exemplar *radar chart* resulting from a TIPA Gap Analysis

does not help on the way to bridge the gaps identified for each topic and particularly does not help to identify the processes impacted by the unfulfilled requirement. In other words, the Gap Analysis tool as described above fails to actually support the process approach as a process view is missing. The *transformation process* is providing us with such a process view at a later stage, when the Process Reference Model (PRM) is designed (see Fig. 1). We can thus benefit again from its rigorous structure to complete the gap analysis with a *process view* as an additional perspective on the results. The development of this *process view* is made possible (and easy) thanks to the fact that a) the PAM is based on the same set of elementary requirements than the gap analysis tool, and b) the transformation process [27] used to build the PAM guarantees the traceability of these elementary requirements with the process base practices (assessment indicators) and *a fortiori* with the processes of the PAM.

It is thus possible to identify the set of elementary requirements that are related to each process of the PAM and then determine a requirements coverage rate for each process based on the answers given to the questions of the gap analysis tool.

Figure 4 gives an example of such a Gap Analysis *process view* that reuses the 25 processes from the PAM built on the Luxembourg e-archiving regulation. This example is based on the same data set as in Fig. 3. A different color (grey scale for this paper) is assigned to each process according to the coverage rate of the requirements it supports.

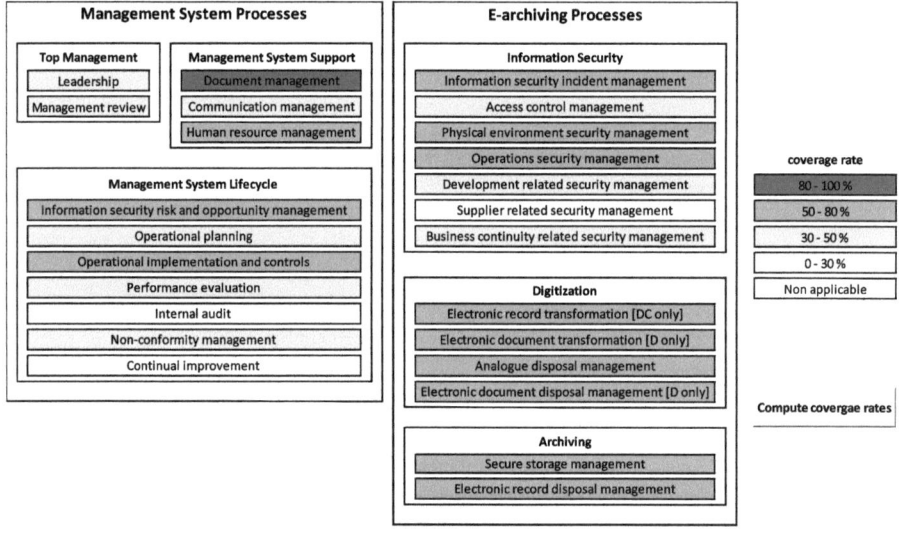

Fig. 4. Exemplar *process view* resulting from using the TIPA Gap Analysis

4.3 Experimentation

The third step of the research method consists in the experimentation of the tool in order to gather feedback and validate the solution. The tool has been designed in collaboration with a leading organization in Electronic Records Management (ERM) to better understand the impact of the Luxembourg e-archiving regulation on their functions and processes. The Gap Analysis tool is currently under experimentation within this organization. Their feedback based on first experiments confirms that the *process view* does indeed help to better understand the impact of the Luxembourg e-archiving regulation on their functions and processes, and thus help them to better assign their compliance actions to their existing process owners and management. By contrast in a common gap analysis tool, the result (presented by topic) should be investigated further to identify the person (i.e. role) in charge of compliance actions. Formal feedbacks are expected within the next months and will focus on the effectiveness of the Gap Analysis as a standalone tool.

Following this first experimentation stage, a second one is engaged to evaluate the way the tool effectively complements the existing TIPA framework (i.e. process assessment approach) and so contributes to validate its integration.

5 Discussions

Despite organizational benefits expected from combining conformity and process assessment approaches, the angle they each adopt to describe the organization status makes their combination a real challenge. The proposed Gap Analysis tool is only a first step in the integration of process and conformity assessment and some points have to be clarified to avoid disillusions.

Process assessment is expected to support sustainable process improvement within organizations [15] while the Gap Analysis is to quickly measure the compliance rate against a set of requirements [12]. The effective achievement of those objectives requires different types and amounts of resources for both developing and using each tool (i.e. process assessment and Gap Analysis). As an example, the ISO/IEC 27000 gap analysis described in [12] takes around 2h30 to get the whole questionnaire answered while in the TIPA context a sole interview covering one process of a PAM until capability level 3 takes almost as much time (and several interviews are usually advised to assess one process). The amount of resources required to perform a process assessment is an obstacle and restricts its use to some challenging business needs (e.g. improvement involving organizational changes, selection of critical service provider…) for which a gap analysis is less relevant and brings only a part of the solution. Moreover this is only true in cases where both PAM and gap analysis have been developed on the same (elementary requirements) basis. Indeed, the development of a gap analysis forces to identify a set of requirements but a library of best practices (i.e. ITIL) does not contain any, and it is intrinsically impossible to build a gap analysis on that basis alone since there is no formal set of requirements to satisfy (but ISO/IEC 20000-1 can help).

The cost of performing a process assessment based on individual interviews also constrains the possible scope of an assessment to a limited number of processes that are fully coherent with the target business needs. It is a different story for a gap analysis. Indeed its objective is to quickly establish the gap between a requirements set and the existing situation within an organization. This means that the gap analysis scope is somehow predefined by this requirements set and is usually broader than the one of a process assessment. Unlike a process assessment, a gap analysis is intended to be used as a whole and not for targeting a subset of the original requirements set.

One can argue that process assessment may be used to produce the same result than the one of gap analysis, but our past experience has shown that it is not cost-effective and finally not economically viable.

Moreover the Gap Analysis result shown through the *process view* should not be confused with a (TIPA) process assessment result. The level of details and the structure of the both results are highly different. Whereas process assessment is assessing the level of achievement of process and attribute outcomes to determine a capability (or another quality characteristic) level, the Gap Analysis *process view* provides only a view on the level of coverage of the requirements set related to the process. The information collected at the questionnaire level has to be further analyzed to find the rationale behind the requirement coverage rate of the process. By contrast, the process assessment result is fully structured around the processes and the collected evidences are subject to extensive analysis (i.e. Strengths-Weaknesses-Opportunities-Threats analysis and recommendations), providing organizations with enough inputs for improvement planning.

Nevertheless combining both the process assessment and the gap analysis results can bring valuable inputs to business organizations targeting both organizational improvement and certification. For this purpose, the *process view* added to the typical result of a gap analysis enables to embed the process lens in the result of a gap analysis and specifically create a bridge towards the PAM based on the same requirements set.

In addition, the fact that the Gap Analysis tool and the PAM are in this case based on the same set of elementary requirements enables to highlight correlations between both results. In the case of the Luxembourg e-archiving regulation, each elementary requirement has been linked to process performance indicators (i.e. base practices and work products) of the PAM that address the elementary requirements. Consequently, the coverage rate of requirements for each process in the *process view* gives some insight on the extent to which the process should achieve the capability level 1 during a process assessment. In that perspective, the Gap Analysis can be considered as bringing useful input to the definition of a (TIPA) process assessment scope. If we go even further, we can consider that a process assessment (partially) defined on the basis of the Gap Analysis' *process view* can aim at improving both the performance and the compliance of process at the same time.

6 Conclusion and Next Steps

The gap analysis is often conducted at the beginning of an organization's journey seeking compliance towards a set of requirements or standard. This paper has shown it is possible to expand the scope of such a tool and use it as a bridge towards a process-structured improvement approach. For that purpose, a TIPA Gap Analysis tool embedding a *process view* has been developed on the same foundation (i.e. elementary requirements set) that an ISO/IEC 33000 compliant PAM developed through the TIPA transformation process.

The Gap Analysis' *process view* reuses the process map of the related PAM in order to structure and present the gap analysis result through the process lens. These outputs can then be used to support the internal effort towards compliance. Despite this process perspective now provided, the Gap Analysis can however not compete with a traditional assessment of processes based on ISO/IEC 15504-33000 as it limits itself to making the inventory of the gaps identified against requirements. The *process view* enables just to structure these gaps differently.

The TIPA Gap Analysis should be considered as complementary to TIPA assessment framework, each providing a different view on the same actual situation. So the use of one or the other or both means for establishing a current organizational snapshot will directly depend on the business need of the target organization.

Even if the formal experimentation is still under progress, the TIPA Gap Analysis seems to be a promising add-on to the actual TIPA framework. The Proof of Concept (POC) presented in this paper will be shortly applied to the ISO/IEC 20000-1 standard while a formal correlation table (i.e. mapping) between the standard and the TIPA for ITIL PAM will be done. The combination of these two assets will provide the current TIPA and ITSM communities with a robust tool for jointly performing process and conformity assessment within their customer's organizations.

References

1. CMMI for Development, Version 1.3 (PDF). CMMI-DEV (Version 1.3, November 2010). Carnegie Mellon University Software Engineering Institute (2010). http://cmmiinstitute.com/resources/cmmi-development-version-13
2. CMMI for Acquisition, Version 1.3 (PDF). CMMI-ACQ (Version 1.3, November 2010). Carnegie Mellon University Software Engineering Institute (2010). http://cmmiinstitute.com/resources/cmmi-acquisition-version-13
3. CMMI for Services, Version 1.3 (PDF). CMMI-SVC (Version 1.3, November 2010). Carnegie Mellon University Software Engineering Institute (2010). http://cmmiinstitute.com/resources/cmmi-services-version-13
4. Automotive Spice. http://www.automotivespice.com/fileadmin/software-download/Automotive_SPICE_PAM_30.pdf
5. The Cabinet Office. ITIL Lifecycle Publication Suite. The Stationery Office Edition (2011)
6. Public Research Center Henri Tudor. ITSM Process Assessment Supporting ITIL. Van Haren Publishing (2009). ISBN:9789087535643
7. Renault, A., Cortina, S., Barafort, B.: Towards a maturity model for ISO/IEC 20000-1 based on the TIPA for ITIL process capability assessment model. In: Rout, T., O'Connor, R.V., Dorling, A. (eds.) SPICE 2015. CCIS, vol. 526, pp. 188–200. Springer, Heidelberg (2015)
8. Picard, M., Renault, A., Barafort, B.: A maturity model for ISO/IEC 20000-1 based on the TIPA for ITIL process capability assessment model. In: O'Connor, R.V. (ed.) EuroSPI 2015. CCIS, vol. 543, pp. 168–179. Springer, Heidelberg (2015). doi:10.1007/978-3-319-24647-5_14
9. TIPA for ITIL Process Assessment Model. http://bit.ly/23camL4
10. ISO/IEC TR 20000-1:2011. Information Technology — Service management — Service management system requirements. International Organization for Standardization, Geneva (2011)

11. The Cabinet Office. ITIL - Continual Service Improvement volume. The Stationery Office Edition (2011)
12. Valdevit, T., Mayer, N.: A gap analysis tool for SMEs targeting ISO/IEC 27001 compliance. In: The International Conference ICEIS 2010, Funchal, Portugal (2010)
13. ISO 19011. Guidelines for auditing management systems, Geneva (2011)
14. ISO/IEC 17000. Conformity assessment – Vocabulary and general principles. International Organization for Standardization, Geneva (2004)
15. ISO/IEC 33001. Information Technology — Process assessment — Concepts and terminology. International Organization for Standardization, Geneva (2014)
16. ISO/IEC 27001. Information technology – Security techniques – Information security management systems – Requirements. International Organization for Standardization, Geneva (2013)
17. Paulk, M.C.: Comparing ISO 9001 and the capability maturity model for software. Softw. Qual. J. **2**(4), 245–256 (1993)
18. Jung, H.-W., Hunter, R.: The relationship between ISO/IEC 15504 process capability levels, ISO 9001 certification and organization size: an empirical study. J. Syst. Softw. **59**(1), 43–55 (2001)
19. Renault, A., Picard, M., Ferrand, D.: Process assessment to support conformity assessment – Experimentation of a PAM for accreditation conformity assessment. In: The International Conference SPICE 2008, Nuremberg, Germany (2008)
20. Walker, A., Coletta, A., Sivaraman, R.: An evaluation of the process capability implications of the requirements of ISO/IEC 20000-1. J. Softw. Evol. Process **26**, 1316–1326 (2014)
21. ISO/IEC Directives, Part1, Annex SL. International Organization for Standardization, Geneva (2014)
22. ISO/IEC TR 20000-4:2010. Information Technology — Service management — Process reference model. International Organization for Standardization, Geneva (2010)
23. ISO/IEC 15504-8:2012. Information Technology — Process assessment — An exemplar process assessment model for IT service management. International Organization for Standardization, Geneva (2012)
24. Clarke, P., Lepmets, M., Dorling, A., McCaffery, F.: Safety critical software process assessment: how MDevSPICE® addresses the challenge of integrating compliance and capability. In: Rout, T., O'Connor, R.V., Dorling, A. (eds.) SPICE 2015. CCIS, vol. 526, pp. 13–18. Springer, Heidelberg (2015)
25. MDevSPICE. http://www.mdevspice.com/
26. Susman, G., Evered, R.: An assessment of the scientific merits of action research. Adm. Sci. Q. **23**(4), 582–603 (1978)
27. Barafort, B., Renault, A., Picard, M., Cortina, S.: A transformation process for building PRMs and PAMs based on a collection of requirements – Example with ISO/IEC 20000. In: The International Conference SPICE 2008, pp. 12–21, Nuremberg, Germany (2008)
28. Cortina, S., Picard, M., Valdés, O., Renault, A.: A challenging process models development: the ITIL v3 lifecycle processes. In: The International Conference SPICE 2010, pp. 59–66, Pisa, Italy (2010)
29. ISO/IEC/IEEE 29148. Software and systems engineering - Life cycle processes - Requirements engineering. International Organisation for Standardisation, Geneva (2011)

SPI in Secure and Safety Critical Environments

Development and Production Processes for Secure Embedded Control Devices

Tobias Rauter[(✉)], Andrea Höller, Johannes Iber, and Christian Kreiner

Institute for Technical Informatics, Graz University of Technology,
Infeldgasse 16, Graz, Austria
{tobias.rauter,andrea.hoeller,johannes.iber,christian.kreiner}@tugraz.at

Abstract. Security is a vital property of SCADA systems, especially in the context of critical infrastructure. In this work, we focus on distributed control devices for hydro-electric power plants. Much work has been done for specific lifecylce phases of distributed control devices such as development or operational phase. Our aim here is to consider the entire product lifecycle and the consequences of security feature implementations for a single lifecycle stage on other stages. In particular, we discuss the security concept used to secure our control devices in the operational stage and show how these concepts result in additional requirements for the development and production stages. We show how we meet these requirements and focus on a production process that enables the commissioning of secrets such as private keys during the manufacturing phase. We show that this can be done both, securely and with acceptable overhead even when the manufacturing process is handled by a contract manufacturer that is not under full control of the OEM.

1 Introduction

The growth of the renewable energy sector has a high impact on the technology of hydropower plant unit control systems [6]. Today these must react to power grid changes in time to achieve overall grid stability. As a consequence, control devices (depending on the provided functionality, they are also referred to as Remote Terminal Unit (RTU) or Programmable Logic Controller (PLC)) in single power plants, as well as control devices of different power plants have to cooperate in order to achieve the system-wide control goal. These requirements lead to networks of small, embedded control devices and heavyweight Supervisory Control and Data Acquisition (SCADA) servers and clients. At the same time, these power plants represent critical infrastructures that have to be protected against the recently emerging risk of security attacks [1,7].

Much work in the field of security for control systems has already been done for this reason. However, only very few investigations have so far focused on the implication of implemented security features for the development and manufacturing stages of these control systems.

In this work we examine these requirements and show how we tackled the challenges in a real product lifecycle:

- We describe the security architecture in an actual SCADA system used in the field of hydroelectric power plants.
- We then focus on the product lifecycle of the distributed control devices. These devices are part of critical infrastructure and are not produced in great quantities, but vary in their configuration for each customer.
- Based on the security features which are actually in place during operation, we identify requirements for earlier product lifecycle stages, specifically in the development and production phase.
- We show how we implemented an extended risk assessment process that enables lean privilege separation in the software architecture. This is essential for handling the complexity of the security architecture at a later stage.
- Moreover, we show how we enable the commissioning of secrets during the manufacturing process in such a way, that not even the manufacturers themselves are able to reveal critical information in a practicable manner. In contrast to recent studies [11], we show that for our system it is indeed reasonable and possible with low management overhead to implement such processes prior the deployment of control devices. This is also true if the production process is out-sourced to contractors that are not under control of the Original Equipment Manufacturer (OEM).

The rest of this paper is organized as follows: Sect. 2 describes the analyzed system, the introduced security concept and highlights the implications for development and production processes. Section 3 describes how we tackled these challenges in both lifecycle stages and Sect. 4 concludes the paper.

2 System Security Concept

This section the actual system that resulted in the requirements that initiated our security lifecycle processes. We provide a rough overview of the system and the implemented security enhancing technologies. A detailed description on how we identified the threats and requirements that led to these design decisions is beyond the scope of this paper. Here, we focus on the requirements for the earlier lifecycle stages arising from the introduction of such technologies.

2.1 System Overview

Figure 1 shows an exemplary SCADA system architecture. One central SCADA client is used to supervise RTUs of different plants at different sites. The RTUs are the actual control devices that execute the control strategy and interface with the environment (i.e., communicate with sensors and actuators). Since the control strategy could be distributed, the RTUs have to communicate directly with each other. In addition to the normal client that is used to supervise the system, there exists a maintenance terminal. These terminals are used to configure and deploy the control tasks to the RTUs.

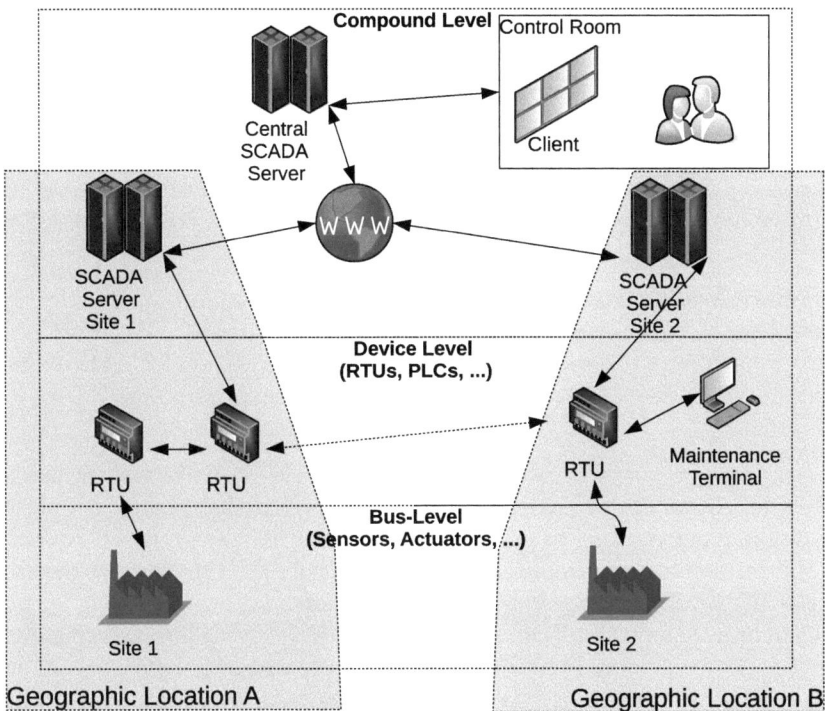

Fig. 1. Overview of an exemplary SCADA system which is used to control power plants at different locations

2.2 Security Concept

We were able to determine security and design requirements for the overall system with the help of a comprehensive risk and threat analysis based on STRIDE [14]. On an architectural and design level, the security enhancing technologies can be split into four groups: communication channels, interactions between devices, user interactions and system integrity verification.

Communication Channels. All our communication channels are based on Ethernet. While communication between different RTUs on the same site is often protected to a certain degree by the operator's network infrastructure, connections between different SCADA servers often use public infrastructures. We thus need to protect confidentiality and integrity of the sent information. In our system, we use Transport Layer Security (TLS) to ensure these properties.

Interaction Between Devices. Ensuring integrity and confidentiality on the communication channel alone is not enough. Devices have to be authenticated to ensure the proper source and destination of data flows. This can be achieved with TLS and the use of a Public Key Infrastructure (PKI) for point-to-point connections. Authentication is also a requirement to enable authorization in the system.

In some cases data may be sent via multiple hops. For example, a firmware update from the device OEM is sent to the plant operator. This operator uses the maintenance client to update the firmware. However, the OEM wants to ensure, that the operator is not able to run non-licensed or manipulated software on a RTU. Therefore, in addition to authentication and integrity checks on the channel, end-to-end verification is needed. This is achieved by the use of cryptographic signatures. Again, a PKI is needed as supportive technology.

User Interaction. Similar to device-to-device interaction, authentication is needed whenever a user wishes to interact with the system. We solve this by password-based and token-based authentication and a central login-server, which provides access-tokens that are used for authorization later on.

System Integrity Verification. The technologies described so far improve the authentication of devices and the integrity and confidentiality of their communication. However, due to software bugs or security design flaws, adversaries may still be able to compromise parts of the system. We thus need to ensure the integrity of the devices. Each device has to enforce its own integrity by means of adequate measures. Additionally, devices need to check the integrity of their communication partner. Figure 2 shows the basic integrity measures at device level. To achieve integrity verification, each device uses secure boot and sandboxing (if applicable). In order to attest integrity to communication partners, we use remote attestation. We use Integrity Measurement Architecture (IMA) [12] as a basis for this part. Basically, *Device 2* checks the integrity of *Device 1* by analyzing the software components running on *Device 1*. Traditionally, this is achieved by comparing the hash values of the running executables to reference values. However, such an approach is not feasible for networks with many devices since the reference values have to be updated every time the configuration of one device changes. Therefore, we use extensions such as OEM-signatures and the analysis of software privileges to reduce the size and dynamics of the reference values [8].

2.3 Security Requirements for Earlier Lifecycle Processes

The proposed approaches raise requirements for the development and production phase of the system. The key-based authentication techniques, the secure channels, the end-to-end verification of firmware updates as well as the integrity checks (secure boot and remote attestation) rely on the initial bootstrapping of security credentials (i.e., private keys and certificates).

Sandboxing is only useful when the separated software modules follow the principle of least privilege. This enables the efficient separation of software modules regarding their privileges. Therefore, the software components have to be designed with this principle in mind. Also our remote attestation concept profits from components with limited privileges.

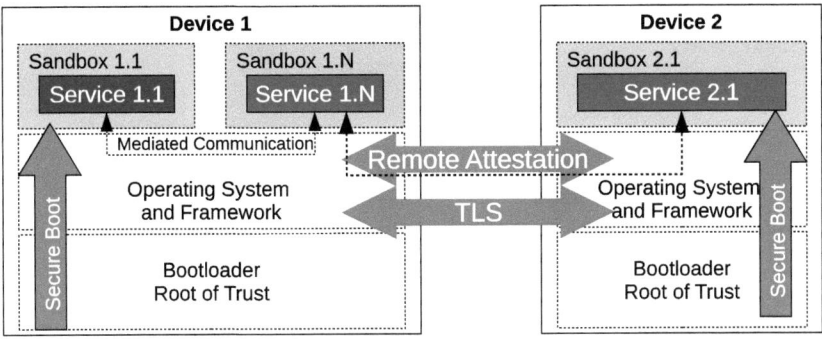

Fig. 2. Overview of the integrity verification at device level. While we can use state-of-the-art technologies such as Secure Boot and Sandboxing for INTEGRITY PROTECTION, we had to come up with a feasible ourselves solution for INTEGRITY ATTESTATION.

Moreover, subsystems with high privileges (especially the security relevant parts such as authorization modules) have to be considered for rigorous design and code reviews to minimize the risk of compromises.

3 Lifecycle Support

This section shows how the requirements described in the last section are addressed in our system lifecycle. We show how we addressed the need of privilege separation in the development process and how we integrated commissioning of private key material into the manufacturing process.

3.1 System Lifecycle

To describe our processes, we use the basic product lifecycle model illustrated in Fig. 3. The OEM develops a system and outsources the production to a contract manufacturer. In order to build a secure system, the development stage has to be augmented with security-enhancing processes such as threat analysis and mitigation. However, as shown in the last section, the integration of security measures in the operational phase requires the introduction of additional processes in earlier stages.

To reflect this in the development process, risk management processes (e.g., ISO/IEC 27005 [4]) propose an iterative approach. We will show how we integrated the risk management process into the development process to achieve both, privilege separation and a classification of subsystems regarding their security criticality. Based on this classification, we can identify the subsystems that need in-depth threat analysis and code reviews. Moreover, the process provides a list of privileges each component requires and thus eases the generation of sandboxing policies.

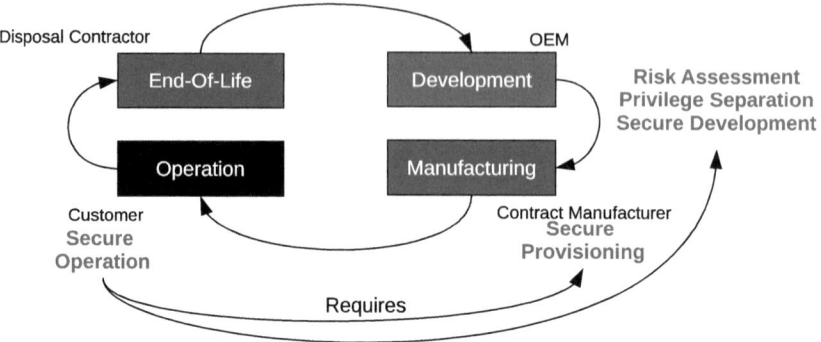

Fig. 3. The basic product lifecycle model and the stakeholders which are in place at each stage.

The lifecycle of the security credentials typically consists of four steps [2]: As a first step, keys have to be generated (1). In order to bind keys to a platform, they have to be certified (2). Moreover, they have to be distributed (3) and stored (4) on the platform. The first three steps are necessary to bootstrap trust of a device. We show how we integrate these processes into the manufacturing stage of the system lifecycle. We enable an OEM-controlled trust provisioning process of diverse systems even though the manufacturer is an external entity.

3.2 Asset-Based Component Rating and Privilege Separation

In order to enable the delineation of trust domains and the identification of critical software components, we proposed the integration of software risk assessment into organizational-level risk assessment processes [10]. Figure 4 illustrates, how our approach fits into the standard risk management process. After all assets and their risk ratings are identified, the assets are mapped to the software architectural model. Here, the privileges of the components are classified based on the assets they are able to access. Components that share their privileges are part of the same trust domain. In order to reduce the attack surface, the size of trust domains with high privileges should be minimized. Therefore, the software and/or security architect is able to introduce filter components, which are able to transform assets regarding their criticality. An authenticator, for example, may reduce the asset 'all private data' to 'data of a specific user'. We plan to automate the positioning of filter components into the architecture to optimize trust boundary sizes automatically in future work. Based on the final classification, additional assessment methodologies such as threat modeling can be prioritized. The output of this sub-process comprises additional threats to the assets that can be used for further evaluation.

Figure 5 shows how the process is applied to a simplified system architecture of a control device. We consider two assets: The values of the data points (information asset, 'Datapoints') and the function of changing the control program

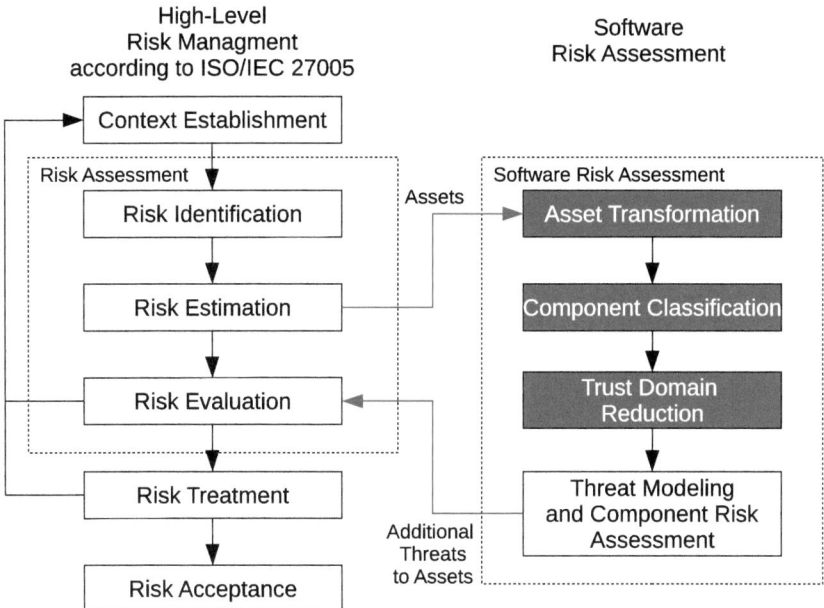

Fig. 4. A simplified risk management process according to ISO/IEC 27005 [4] (left), and how our approach is used to generate additional possible threats to assets that may originate from vulnerabilities in software components.

and data point values (function asset, 'Control Interface'). The system provides a proprietary interface, which supports authentication. Moreover, legacy communication partners that do not support such features have to be accepted. In the original system architecture (upper part of the figure), all services have access to both assets and thus all services are in the same (critical) trust domain. The introduced authentication filter component maps the original assets to new assets with lower criticality based on the logged on user (lower part of the figure). The legacy interface, for example, only has access to a subset of the data points and does not have write access to any critical component.

With the introduction of filter components, this process thus supports privilege separation of components, which is needed to set up useful sandboxing policies. Moreover it provides a classification of the privileges of components (i.e., which assets a component has to access) that eases the generation of sandboxing policies. Additionally, the resulting classification is fed back into the overall risk-management process. This supports the evaluation of which components are of high risk and should be considered for in-depth evaluation like comprehensive threat modeling or code review.

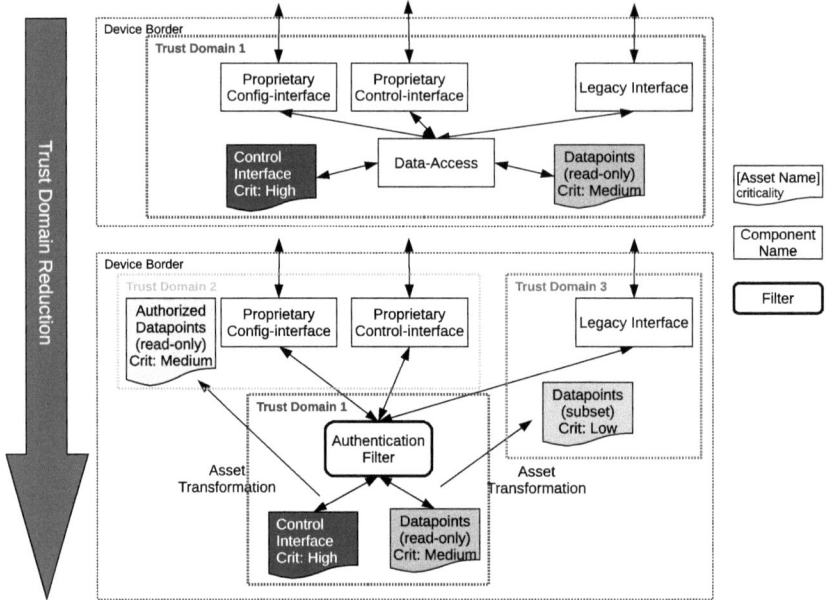

Fig. 5. Prior to the trust domain reduction (upper part), all services have access to all assets. The introduction of an authentication filter reduces the criticality of the accessible assets and separates the trust domains by their privileges.

3.3 Support for the Provisioning Process

Since all of the proposed methods rely on asymmetric cryptography for authentication and message integrity verification, we have to provide a process that securely distributes secrets such as private keys to a variety of devices. Here, two main challenges must be faced: First, even the manufacturer may be (partly) compromised. We thus have to ensure that the access to private key material is as difficult as possible during the production process. Moreover, a large number of different and customized devices has to be built and provided with key materials: In our scenario, a RTU consists of a variety of different components which are in charge for communication, the actual execution of the control task or access to I/O devices. They all have some similarities (e.g., a MCU that is executing a specific firmware) but vary in features, configuration and also security requirements. Moreover, the configuration of the RTUs (i.e., which sub-components are in place) varies depending on the customer's needs. At the same time, the manufacturing process for all these different devices should be as lean and possible. Moreover, functional integration tests should be performed at manufacturing time for all possible configurations.

In order to tackle all of these challenges, we created a Manufacturing and Test Environment (MaTE) [9] that is trusted by the OEM and delivered to all manufacturers as shown in Fig. 6. With these entities and a certification

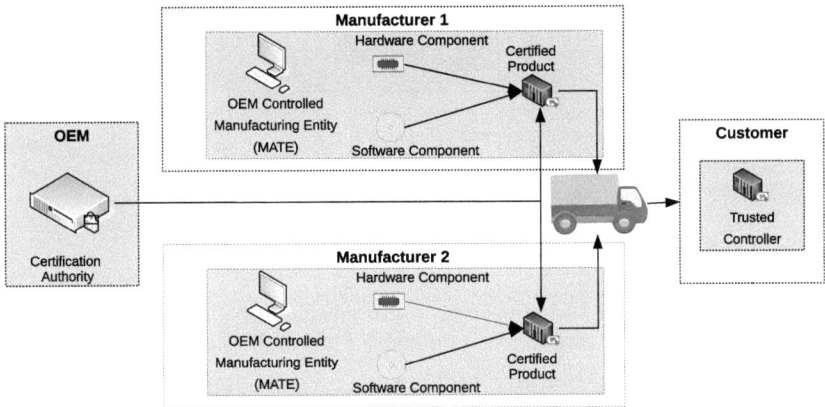

Fig. 6. The distributed production process based on OEM-provided manufacturing and test entities

authority located at the device OEM, we are able to generate a distributed production process that enables secure provisioning of secrets.

Production and Test Entity. As shown in Fig. 7, MaTE builds upon a generic production process [5]. Basically, an operation is performed on a set of (sub-)components. The output of one production step is a new component. In our process, the output is a 'new' component C' even if the input only consists of a single component C. The operation may have changed the component's configuration or, at least, retrieved some information (e.g., the component C has passed all functional tests). The resulting component C' may be completely manufactured device, as well as an input for a following production step. The actual operation may be a manufacturing step (automated or manual), a functional test step, a calibration step or a combination of these.

In MaTE, however, the operation is not defined directly. The operation is computed based on a generic model of the test procedure and a model of the actual system under test, i.e. the actual components which are used. An example for a test procedure may be 'deploy firmware and execute memory tests'. However, the memory, Central Processing Unit (CPU) and firmware varies based on the actual component. This is where the strength of the approach comes into play. The process template needs to be defined only once and MaTE generates the actual manufacturing procedures on the fly. The framework thus also enables secure provisioning of different types of devices in a unified way.

Secure Provisioning. As mentioned above, there are some requirements concerning the secure provisioning process: Since even the manufacturer may be compromised, the process should protect the key material in a manner that makes it impractical to reveal it for the manufacturer. Moreover, the device OEM must have control over which and how many devices he wants to trust.

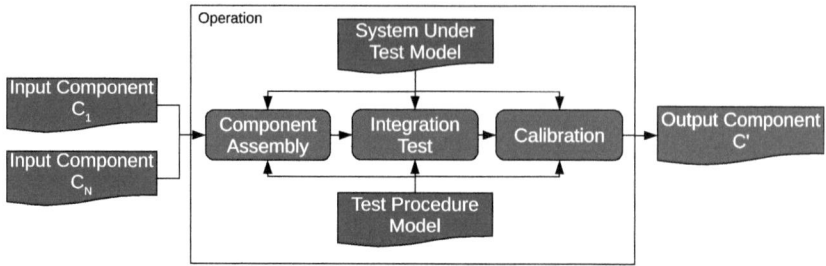

Fig. 7. In a basic manufacturing process, a procedure of operations (e.g., assembly or test) is performed on one to many components. The result is a (new) component that may be the input of the next production step.

Again, these requirements should be fulfilled for a variety of devices with different hardware features. Since our manufacturing tool is able to handle such variances, we can directly integrate our secure provisioning into the manufacturing process, as shown in Fig. 8.

MaTE itself is a small embedded computer that provides the user interface for the manufacturing process and all I/O connections required to instrument the manufactured devices (Device Under Test (DUT)). Since the OEM provides MaTE, it has full control over its function. To enable the secure provisioning process, MaTE requires some type of Hardware Security Module (HSM). This module needs to provide at least a tamper-proof storage for signature keys and a protected signature module that prevents software from reading the keys. This functionality is required since MaTE is exposed to a possible adverse environment. Typically, a Trusted Platform Module (TPM) could be used as HSM. However, using programmable solutions based on ARM TrustZone could be beneficial, because it would enable the integration of production contingents (e.g., the manufacturer is only allowed to produced 1000 items of product X per month).

As part of the usual manufacturing process, MaTE initiates the secure provisioning process (1). The DUT generates its own private key pair (2). Depending on the device type, this is done in software or on a dedicated hardware (typically a TPM). Using a TPM in the DUT enables tamper resistant storage and, in case endorsement key certificates are provided by the TPM-manufacturer, a root of trust for the platform identity. As a next step, the DUT sends its public key to MaTE (3). MaTE checks whether the current manufacturer is allowed to produce this type of device and signs the DUT's public key with its own private key (4). Both, the signature and the key is sent to the OEM's certification authority (5), which checks and certifies the request if everything is valid. Subsequently, the certificate is forwarded to the DUT (6 and 7). With the use of MaTE, we are able to use this unified process for different types of devices. Moreover, since the device OEM provides the manufacturing device, it has full control over the process. From a security perspective, this is enabled by the dedicated HSM that is used for critical checks such as the manufacturer's contingents. Moreover, the

OEM is able to check whether a certificate signing request is placed by one of its trusted manufacturing devices. Since the private key material used by the manufactured devices is generated directly on the device, there is no unnecessary exposure of critical information. Since this action is part of the production process, the required harnesses (i.e., components which are used to generate the key) can only be placed temporarily on the device and can be automatically deleted in the next production step. Whenever IP protection is important and the manufacturer should not be allowed to produce an unlimited amount of devices, TPMs with endorsement key certificates can be used. In this case, the OEM can check whether the device key of the signing request is generated by a TPM and can thus ensure that only one device is able to use the signed key[1]. Although the end-of-life phase is beyond the scope of this work, it should be mentioned that a tamper resistant storage also protects sensitive information at this stage. The proposed approach has the fundamental disadvantage that the manufacturer requires a permanent network connection to the OEM's servers. However, since MaTE uses a central database on the OEM site in any case, the secure provisioning process does not result in new requirements here.

In [3] different approaches for trust provisioning in the context of industrial automation are discussed. The conclusion is that a manufacturer-based approach for bootstrapping is most suitable for this domain. However, the assumption is made that the OEM and the manufacturer are one and the same company and thus do not need to take the additional management complexity into account. Other approaches suggest trust establishment based on physical contact of devices [13] or based on the interaction with an employee of the plant [11]. Both argue on the basis of the high complexity and costs in manufacturing-based approaches. Our approach, however, tackles this problem with the provision of the manufacturing entity by the OEM.

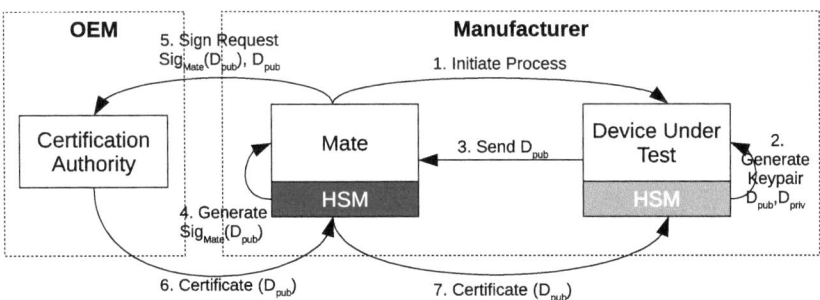

Fig. 8. Overview of the secure provisioning process.

---

[1] An adverse manufacturer might otherwise create a 'fake' device that generates a keypair and trick the OEM into signing it. Then, he could use this key for an unlimited number of pirated devices.

4 Conclusion

Security features that protect a device during the operational lifecycle raise the need for additional requirements in earlier product lifecycle phases such as development and production. Based on the security concept of distributed control devices in a SCADA architecture for hydropower plants, we demonstrated typical candidates for such requirements, such as privilege separation and the presence of pre-commissioned trust (in the form of secret key material). We showed how we meet these requirements in our development stage with a previously introduced extension of common risk management technologies. Moreover, we showed that it is indeed possible to integrate the initial commissioning of trust into the production process, even if a contract manufacturer is used that is not fully under control of the OEM.

In future, we plan to automate the process for the introduction of filter components based on the data flow graph and additional meta-information (e.g., what assets are needed by which components) of the software architecture to optimize the size and quality of trust domains. Moreover, we plan to investigate additional approaches for the commissioning process to evaluate their impact on the system's security properties and deployment costs. Based on these extensions, we intend to provide proposals for securing systems that take the complete product lifecylce into account, instead of the operational phase only.

References

1. Electricity Information Sharing and Analysis Center: Analysis of the Cyber Attack on the Ukrainian Power Grid (2016)
2. Fischer, K., Gesner, J.: Security architecture elements for IoT enabled automation networks. In: IEEE International Conference on Emerging Technologies and Factory Automation, ETFA (2012)
3. Fischer, K., Geßner, J., Fries, S.: Secure identifiers and initial credential bootstrapping for IoT@Work. In: Proceedings - 6th International Conference on Innovative Mobile and Internet Services in Ubiquitous Computing, IMIS 2012, pp. 781–786 (2012)
4. International Organization for Standardization (ISO): ISO/IEC 27005: 2008 - Information technology - Security techniques - Information Security Risk Management (2008)
5. Jørgensen, K., Petersen, T.: Product family modelling for manufacturing planning. In: International Conference on Production Research (2011)
6. Liserre, M., Sauter, T., Hung, J.: Future energy systems: integrating renewable energy sources into the smart power grid through industrial electronics. IEEE Ind. Electron. Mag. **4**(1), 18–37 (2010)
7. Miller, B., Rowe, D.: A survey SCADA of and critical infrastructure incidents. In: Annual Conference on Research in Information Technology, p. 51 (2012)
8. Rauter, T., Höller, A., Iber, J., Kreiner, C.: Thingtegrity: a scalable trusted computing architecture for resource constrained devices. In: EWSN (2016)
9. Rauter, T., Höller, A., Iber, J., Kreiner, C.: Using model-based testing for manufacturing and integration-testing of embedded control systems. In: 19th Euromicro Conference on Digital System Design (2016)

10. Rauter, T., Kajtazovic, N., Kreiner, C.: Asset-centric security risk assessment of software components. In: 2nd International Workshop on MILS: Architecture and Assurance for Secure Systems (2016)
11. Ray, A., Akerberg, J., Bjorkman, M., Gidlund, M.: Employee trust based industrial device deployment and initial key establishment. Int. J. Netw. Secur. Appl. **8**(1), 21–44 (2016)
12. Sailer, R., Zhang, X., Jaeger, T., van Doorn, L.: Design and implementation of a TCG-based integrity measurement architecture. In: USENIX Security (2004)
13. Stajano, F., Anderson, R.J.: The resurrecting duckling: security issues for ad-hoc wireless networks. In: International Workshop on Security Protocols (2000)
14. Swiderski, F., Snyder, W.: Threat Modeling. Microsoft Press, Redmond (2004)

Situational Factors in Safety Critical Software Development

Risto Nevalainen[1(✉)], Paul Clarke[2,3], Fergal McCaffery[3,4],
Rory V. O'Connor[2,3], and Timo Varkoi[5]

[1] FiSMA Association, Espoo, Finland
risto.nevalainen@fisma.fi
[2] Dublin City University, Dublin, Ireland
{paul.m.clarke,rory.oconnor}@dcu.ie
[3] Lero, the Irish Software Research Centre, Limerick, Ireland
[4] Regulated Software Research Centre,
Dundalk Institute of Technology, Dundalk, Ireland
fergal.mccaffery@dkit.ie
[5] Spinet Oy, Espoo, Finland
timo.varkoi@spinet.fi

Abstract. The generic software development situational factors model has been developed in order that environments within which software is developed can be profiled and better understood. Situational context is a complex concern for software developers, with a broad set of situational factors holding the potential to affect any one software development project. Safety critical software development is broadly similar to other kinds of software development/ engineering. But there are some additional or more dominant situational factors. In this article we conduct a conceptual experiment to define safety critical software development context using situational factors. Eleven such factors are identified, with some of the factors requiring elaboration beyond the detail presently available in the generic situational factors model. We firstly discuss the appropriateness of the selected factors in generic safety critical software development context. Thereafter we apply the selected factors to the medical device and nuclear power domains. Selected situational factors can be used as a high level profile and starting point for more detailed process and safety assessment. Discussion about potential use cases and further development needs is also presented.

Keywords: Situational factors reference model · Safety context · Safety critical software development

1 Introduction

Software development is a complex activity [1] and there are a rich variety of products, applications and domains for which software can provide effective solutions. In an initial effort to identify the factors of a context (such as the product or application or domain) that affect the manner in which software is developed, the situational factors model [2] was produced (by the authors of this paper) as a generic set of high level concerns that may influence the choice and form of software development processes.

For the avoidance of confusion, we wish to explicitly identify "environment", "setting" and "context" as synonyms of "situation" in this instance and therefore, we may also refer to these factors as "contextual factors" or "environmental factors" or "factors of the setting" but our preference is to use the term "situational factors" as this is the terminology used in the most complete reference for such factors [2].

The safety critical domain is concerned with "systems whose failure could result in loss of life, significant property damage, or damage to the environment" [3] and software may form part of such systems, for example in anti-lock braking systems (ABS) in cars and in flight control systems in airplanes and rockets. All safety critical software therefore has certain common situational factors that strongly influence the choice of software development processes. For example, it is common for safety critical software systems to be subject to regulation/legislation which demands that risk management is actively and robustly implemented throughout the software development lifecycle (as a mechanism to reduce the risk of events occurring that will adversely affect safety) (Fig. 1).

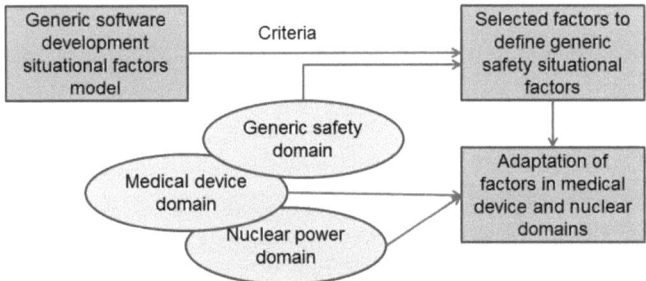

Fig. 1. Rationale in our conceptual experiment

2 Situational Factors in Software Engineering

Although numerous earlier attempts hinted at the existence of (or provided only partial descriptions of) certain contextual factors that affected software development, the situational factors reference model [2] represents the first substantial initiative to unify all factors into a single, comprehensive model. This unified situational factor reference model contains 44 individual factors (and a further 170 sub-factors), and serves to demonstrate that there are a large number of situational variables to be considered when defining and elaborating software development processes (refer to Fig. 2), perhaps too large to perfectly satisfy as it has also been shown that the interaction between a software process and its context is analogous to a complex system [1]. Complex systems are characterised by emergent behaviour, which essentially means that our ability to predict and control complex systems may be limited, as is evidenced in ecosystems where a single change holds the potential for unforeseeable, far-reaching and large-scale effects [4]. It is perhaps for this reason that process adaptive capability has been shown to be positively associated with business performance in the general software engineering field [5]. Clearly, however, emergence is not a behavioural property that we want to foster in safety critical systems and it is (at least partially) for this reason that there are a reduced number of dominant situational factors that affect safety critical software development processes. For this reason, we also find that processes are often formally defined and audited in safety critical domains. The reduced set of safety critical situational factors is perhaps so dominant that they almost eclipse other factors (or they least exercise significant priority over the other factors). We elaborate more on these factors in Sect. 3.

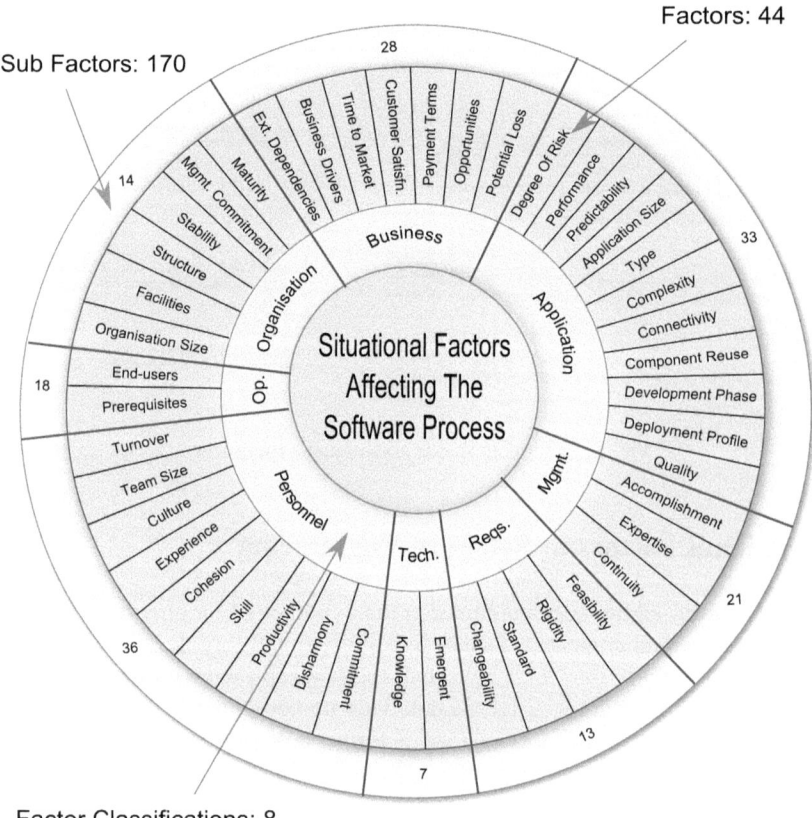

Fig. 2. The situational factors affecting software development

3 Dominant Situational Factors in Safety Critical Domains

3.1 Criteria for Identification of Specific Situational Factors in Safety Critical Software Development

The starting point in this article is that software development for safety critical systems is quite similar to any other context. So, what is said about software development at general level is valid also in safety domains. Most software safety standards specify additional requirements and do not repeat the basic principles. Otherwise the standards would be very long, heavy and difficult to use. Of course, there is still some overlap between generic and safety contexts.

Furthermore, different traditions exist in different safety related domains. For historical and regulatory reasons, some requirements that may be highly relevant in one safety related domain may not be considered to be highly relevant in another domain.

The generic situational factors model (refer to Fig. 2) is wide and quite detailed. Obviously, some selection criteria are needed to focus on such factors in safety contexts which are more specific from a scoping perspective. Our criteria are the following:

- High importance for safety, based on normative sources (standards, regulations)
- Scalability according to safety requirements (at various safety levels etc.)
- High safety impact and potentially in overall quality of software and also system
- Possibility to create, establish and manage safety culture

The expectation in our experiment is that the following differences between generic and safety context factors may occur:

- Selected safety critical situational factors will remain the same as in the generic sense, but the abstraction level may vary. Typically, a safety context factor may be more detailed and may also be more constrained. We mean that individual factors in the generic model [2] may require further detail for application to a safety critical domain, while at the same time, many of the factors in the generic model can be descoped in light of safety critical concerns. (Ref. Table 1).
- Selected generic safety critical situational factors are partially the same, but the language and definition should be different to be accurate and best aligned with each safety community. A good example of this is the fact that what the medical device domain refers to as "risk" management is referred to in certain other domains as "safety" management [6]. Furthermore, the application of safety levels depending upon the potential for harm can vary between domains.
- A safety critical situational factor may be so different from the generic situational factors model as to be considered additional. It may be also candidate to be added in the generic situational factors model in due course.

3.2 Selected Situational Factors for Further Elaboration

Given the argument that there are certain situational factors that dominate safety critical software development, our initial efforts focused on the identification of these factors.

Table 1. Mapping from generic situational factors to generic safety critical situational factors

Factor	Description	Sub-factor(s)	Argument(s): why dominant in a safety context
(Operational) Prerequisites	Concerns that must be satisfied prior to operationalisation	Applicable standards; Applicable laws	Safety manual/plan required; Separate safety lifecycle for software development; Degree of required rigour; Degree of independence in functional safety assessment; Degree of independence in V&V
(Application) Type	Nature of the application	Application domain; Application criticality	Degree of safety criticality
(Application) Quality	Application/Product quality characteristics	Required product quality	Degree of diversity (or diverse software); Defence in depth design and programming
(Requirements) Standard	Standard of application/product requirements	General quality of input and output requirements	Detailed requirements especially for outputs and safety properties in almost all software safety standards
(Application) Reuse	Extent to which existing proven software is reused	Required reuse; Extent of utilisation of externally sourced components	This is typically not a separate requirement in safety context, but strict requirements are defined in most safety standards to manage external components (may be called COTS, RUPS, PDS, SOUP etc.)
(Business) Magnitude of potential loss	Impact of negative events	Loss of human life	Magnitude of potential loss
(Business) External Dependencies	Dependencies outside of the business	Dependency on outside suppliers	Tool confidence level (or similar); Degree of COTS/RUSP qualification
(Personnel) Culture	The culture that exists among the personnel	Team culture	Safety culture

Following a number of concept elaboration sessions, each of the factors in the generic situational factors reference model was evaluated for its relevance to the safety critical domain.

From a total of 44 factor classifications in the generic situational factors model, 8 have been identified as being particularly important for safety critical software development situations, the corresponding analysis for which was performed by the authors given their experience in both safety-critical software development and situational factors affecting software development processes. The exercise to identify the situational factors involved an iterative process whereby the creators of the generic situational factors reference framework proposed factors that might affect generic safety critical software development, following which the authors most familiar with safety critical software development evaluated the proposed factors for relevance and importance in safety critical domains. A total of three iterations were required to render the results published in this paper. From the 8 generic situational factor classifications, a total of 11 situational sub-factors have been identified (refer to column 3 of Table 1).

4 Elaboration of Situational Factors in Safety Critical Software Engineering

What we are assuming is that "there are a reduced set of situational factors that dominate safety critical software development". Correspondingly, where the generic situational factors reference model highlights the need to consider the application degree of risk, it does not go so far as to elaborate on different degrees of risk depending on the risk classification of the safety critical software.

Since some safety critical software is more critical than other safety critical software, there is often a distinction drawn in various safety critical domains which has the impact of imposing more stringent safety oriented constraints for higher degrees of risk. For example, medical device software that is classified as safety classification A does not require that detailed designs are developed and verified for interfaces between software units whereas medical device software safety classification C does impose such constraints (according to IEC 62304 [7]). We can therefore see the benefit of identifying the dominant factors affecting safety critical software development and where appropriate extending some of those factors with the additional level of detail that is common in safety critical software. For example, the degree of risk associated with the application may be extended to take account of the various different levels of risk.

Process evaluation is also a common feature of safety critical software development and in certain domains there is a basic requirement to pass an independent external audit in order to legally supply software to the sector (as is the case in the medical device sector). However, process assessment can be adapted to satisfy the needs of process audit, since all of the regulatory requirements of an audit can be embedded in a process capability framework – such as is the case with MDevSPICE [8] and Nuclear SPICE [9]. With process assessments, various different types of process assessment can be undertaken, ranging from an internal, first party, informal process assessment to an assessment led by an independent, certified third party. Since it is envisaged that the safety critical situational factors reference model described in this work may be utilised for the purpose of identifying the key situational concerns in advance of a process assessment, the process assessment type is also included as a factor in the generic safety critical situational factors reference list (Table 2). Note that a total of 12 generic safety critical situational factors (Table 2) have been elaborated from the 11 generic situational factors identified in Table 1.

Our first step in adapting and applying the generic software development situational factors model to the safety critical domain is at a generic level, "generic safety critical software"[1]. We try to identify common factors in numerous domain-specific safety standards. Later in Sect. 5 we apply this generic set to two domains: medical devices and nuclear power. Our approach also allows a comparison between sector-specific profiles.

Many sector-specific safety standards and models have a long history and their own development community. In this paper, IEC 61508:2010 [10] is selected as the main source and reference for generic safety critical situational factors. More specifically, IEC 61508:2010 Part 3 is used, because it is a specific standard for safety related software development. In some sectors, this standard is reasonably well adopted and is the main starting point for sector specific additional requirements and adjustments. Good examples are the process industry (standard IEC 61511), automotive (standard ISO 26262) and railways (for example standards EN 50126, 50127, 50128). Medical device, space, avionics and nuclear sectors are somewhat distanced from IEC 61508, and use their own concepts. The nuclear sector goes further again and has separate standards for different safety classes (IEC 62138 and IEC 60880).

IEC 61508 is the main generic standard for functional safety. Software is only one element, the entire system (including hardware) must be considered. This is also the case in the nuclear sector, where IEC 61513 is the highest system-level standard (and it includes software). If system and software requirements are the same, then a system requirement is more valid. In the medical device sector however, software can be an independent of a physical (i.e. mechanical or electrical) medical device.

Our result from the first step is presented in Table 2. It is a shortlist of selected situational factors based on requirements in the generic safety standard IEC 61508:2010. This standard has a wide range of safety related requirements. For that reason and to make a comparison between sector profiles easier, we propose an ordinal scale for each of the selected factors. It is typically a 3-point or 4-point scale, see Table 2. We try to avoid a binary scale (for example No/Yes), because safety is rather a continuum than black or white. This is easily seen for example in safety integrity levels (SIL), which are in range 1–4.

In some cases, IEC 61508 does not have a direct requirement for some highly relevant factor. This may be true because no consensus is achieved as to how some requirement should be formulated. Diversity can be seen as one such factor. The other reason may be that a requirement or topic is not in the scope of IEC 61508 and is assumed to be valid only implicitly or indirectly. One such important topic is

---

[1] Such "generic safety critical software" may not exist, because most industry sectors use their own standards. Note also that terminology may vary in standards, for example "safety-related software" or "software important for safety".

Table 2. Safety critical software development, definition of generic profile

Generic safety situational factor (adapted from Table 1)	Source(s)	Range (ordinal scale if possible)
Separate safety lifecycle for software development	IEC 61508-3, Chapters 6, 7, 8	Not Required (NR), Recommended (R), Highly Recommended (HR)
Safety manual/plan	IEC 61508-1, Table A.3	Not Required (NR), Recommended (R), Highly Recommended (HR)
Degree of safety criticality	IEC 61508-1	SIL1...SIL4
Magnitude of potential loss, consequences	IEC 61508-1, 8.2.17	A, B, C, D
Degree of required rigour	IEC 61508-3, Annex C	R1, R2, R3
Tool confidence level (or similar)	IEC 61508-3, 7.4.4	T1, T2, T3
	IEC 61508-4, 3.2.11	See ISO26262 Part 8 for further details
Degree of independence in functional safety assessment	IEC 61508-1, Tables 4 and 5	1: independent person, 2: independent department, 3: independent organisation
Degree of independence in V&V (IV&V)	Is specified in many domain specific safety standards, not directly in IEC 61508	1: independent person, 2: independent department, 3: independent organisation
		Example: ISO 26262 Part 2: Table 1, Table D.1 and 6.4.6.4
Degree of COTS/RUSP qualification [a]	Is specified in many domain specific safety standards, not directly in IEC 61508	1: independent person, 2: independent department, 3: independent organisation
		Example: IEC 60880 Chapter 15
Degree of diversity (or diverse software)	Is specified in many domain specific safety standards, not directly in IEC 61508	Not Required (NR), Recommended (R), Highly Recommended (HR)
		Example: IEC 60880, Annex G.5. See also ISO26262 Part 6 method Table 5

(*Continued*)

Table 2. (*Continued*)

Generic safety situational factor (adapted from Table 1)	Source(s)	Range (ordinal scale if possible)
Defence in depth design and programming	Is specified in many domain specific safety standards, not directly in IEC 61508	Not Required (NR), Recommended (R), Highly Recommended (HR)
		Example: IEC 60880 Chapter 13 (prevention of common cause failures)
Safety culture	Is specified in many domain specific safety standards, not directly in IEC 61508	Not Required (NR), Recommended (R), Highly Recommended (HR)
		Example: ISO 26262 Part 2, Annex B

[a] COTS = Commercial off-the-self. RUSP = ready to use software product. In some standards, the abbreviation PDS (= pre-developed software) is used. Their meaning is equivalent in practice.

safety culture, which is a "soft" factor and may be implemented by organisational management rather than the development unit or project. Many such factors are in sector specific standards, and are therefore important to consider.

As we can see in Table 2, all factor candidates are not well (or directly) defined in the generic functional safety standard IEC 61508. Some are still kept in the list, because they are mentioned in several domain standards (see some examples and references in the range column). It is also possible that the generic IEC 61508 standard is incomplete because of the consensus-driven standardisation process.

5 Adaptation of Generic Safety Context Factors in Medical Device and Nuclear Domains

5.1 Safety Context Definition in Medical Device Domain

Table 3 is an adaptation of the generic safety situational factors (refer to Table 2) to the medical device domain. The medical device domain has long experience in safety standards (both in ISO, IEC and CENELEC) and regulatory body requirements (for example FDA in USA).

Whereas a number of other domains adopt IEC 61508 for the design of Safety critical software the Medical industry does not adopt this safety standard and has instead defined their own safety classification levels within the medical device software process lifecycle standard IEC 62304.

The three main elements within the IEC 61508 standard are addressed differently within a combination of three medical device standards: (1) IEC 62304 [7];

Table 3. Safety critical software development, adaptation of generic profile in medical device domain

Generic safety situational factor (see Table 2)	Additional source(s) in medical device domain	Range in medical device domain (ordinal scale if possible)
Separate safety lifecycle for software development	No lifecycle specified – but typically V-model seen as default IEC 62304 Annex C.4.2	Class A, B, C
Safety manual/plan	IEC 62304 Clause 5.1.1	IEC 62304 Clause 5.1.1 Note 1
Degree of safety criticality	IEC 62304 Clause 4.3	Class A, B, C
Magnitude of potential loss, consequences	IEC 62304 Clause 4.3	Class A, B, C
Degree of required rigour	IEC 62304 Clause 4.3	No scale. Class A, B, C can be used.
Tool confidence level (or similar)	Encourages use of IEC 61508 for tool advice	Proposed scale: Not Required (NR), Recommended (R), Highly Recommended (HR)[a]
Degree of independence in functional safety assessment	ISO 14971 Annex F.3	Proposed scale: NR, R, HR
Degree of independence in V&V (IV&V)	ISO 14971 Annex F.3	Proposed scale: NR, R, HR
Degree of COTS/RUSP qualification	IEC 62304 Clause 5.3.3 COTS is called SOUP in IEC 62304.	Proposed scale: NR, R, HR
Degree of diversity (or diverse software)	IEC 60601-1	Proposed scale: NR, R, HR
Defence in depth design and programming	IEC 60601-1	Proposed scale: NR, R, HR
Safety culture	ISO 14971 Clause 4.2	Proposed scale: NR, R, HR

[a] Medical device standards do not propose any scale for these factors. A scale from generic Table 2 is used here as an option.

(2) ISO 14971 [11] (the medical device risk management standard) and ISO 60601-1 [12] (the umbrella product level medical device standard).

The first of these areas that are covered within the IEC 61508 Risk Management lifecycle and lifecycle processes is covered in the medical device domain by IEC 62304 directly referencing the medical device standard for risk management (ISO 14971) as central to the IEC 62304 lifecycle process for medical device software. In fact, the risk management process in IEC 62304 references ISO 14971 and extends it only with additional software specific medical device elements that were not included in the more generic ISO 14971 standard.

The second of these 3 areas within IEC 61508 was the definition of Safety Integrity Levels (SILs). The medical device industry does not adopt SILs but instead uses the idea of software safety classes as defined in IEC 62304. Whereas, there are 4 SIL levels within IEC 61508 there are only 3 software safety classes of A, B and C within IEC 62304. Software safety class A means that no injury or damage to health is possible if the software system failed. Software safety class B means that non serious injury is possible if the software system failed. Software safety class C means that death or serious injury is possible if the software system failed. The main reason why the medical device domain uses these software safety classes as opposed to SILs is that SILs are based upon reliability which quantifies both the probability and the severity of harm caused by a software failure. This presents an issue within the medical device sector as the probability of failure of software is assumed to be 100 %. Therefore, within IEC 62304 a more simplified approach is adopted as prior to assignment of software safety classes only the severity of the harm that will be caused by a software failure is taken into consideration. Once a software system has been assigned one of the 3 software safety classes, different processes are required for each of the different software safety classes as IEC 62304 specifies what is required for each of the safety classes (for each process). Whenever, a software safety class has been assigned to a software system it is thereafter desirable to make efforts to further reduce the probability of failure of the software (if possible).

The third of these 3 areas within IEC 61508 relates to recommending methods, tools etc. for software development and also provides information in relation to the independence of personnel responsible for performing different lifecycle activities. This is not handled by an individual standard within the medical device domain but rather a combination of standards and in fact IEC 62304 recommends IEC 61508 as a good source for software methods, tools etc. In terms of the medical device sector, information relating to the independence of personnel responsible for performing different lifecycle activities is covered in ISO 14971 as opposed to IEC 62304. ISO 14971 contains requirements for the independence of those performing for example verification and safety assessments.

5.2 Safety Context Definition in Nuclear Domain

Table 4 is an adaptation of generic safety situational factors (refer to Table 2) to the nuclear domain. The nuclear industry also has long experience in safety standards (mainly IEC) and regulatory body requirements. Global cooperation is extensive, important and well established, for example the International Atomic Energy Agency (IAEA) based in Vienna. The national level is most important for regulatory issues, because each country wants to define their own policy in nuclear energy and safety. The Common Position [13] is an example of cooperation between authorities in selected European countries.

Table 4. Safety critical software development, adaptation of generic profile in nuclear domain

Generic safety situational factor (see Table 2)	Additional source(s) in nuclear domain	Range in nuclear domain (ordinal scale if possible)
Separate safety lifecycle for software development	IEC 60880 Clause 5.3; Annex A	Systems performing category A functions; safety class 1
	IEC 62138 Clause 4.3; 5; & 6	Systems performing category B or C functions; safety classes 2 and 3
Safety manual/plan	IEC 60880 Clause 5.5	Software quality assurance plan
	IEC 62138 Clause 5.1.1 & 6.1.1	Quality assurance plan (maybe part of System QA plan)
Degree of safety criticality	IEC 61226 [17]	Categories of functions A, B, and C for I&C functions important to safety
	IEC 61513	Safety classes of systems 1, 2 and 3; unclassified
Magnitude of potential loss, consequences	N/A	
Degree of required rigour	IEC 61513 Clause 6.4.1.2	Safety classes 1 & 2
Tool confidence level (or similar)	IEC 60880 Clause 14; Annex H	none
Degree of independence in functional safety assessment	N/A	
Degree of independence in V&V (IV&V)	IEC 60880 Clause 8; 10	By process requirements, verification team separate from the development management
Degree of COTS/RUSP qualification	IEC 60880 Clause 15	none
Degree of diversity (or diverse software)	IEC 60880 Clause 13.4; Annex G	none
Defence in Depth design and programming	IEC 61513 Annex A.3; Annex C	Safety classes and categories
	IEC 61226 Clause 5	Safety classes
	IEC 60880 Clause 13	Defence in Depth levels 1-5 in IAEA standard INSAG-10
Safety culture	Common Position Clause 1.6	none

A predominant feature in the nuclear domain is that the system life cycle and safety life cycle are considered separate. In practice, this means that functionality important to safety has independent systems from operational systems. Naturally, the same applies to software. Safety classes are numbered 1, 2 and 3, 1 denoting the highest safety class. Categories (A, B, C) – A being the highest – are assigned based on Instrumentation and Control (I&C) functions safety relevance.

IEC 60880 [14] covers the requirements for the software life cycle applicable in safety class 1. Additionally, it contains informal annexes on different special software qualification aspects such as defence against common cause failures, tools for software development and qualification, as well as requirements on pre-existing software. IEC 62138 contains graded requirements for software implementing category B and C functions [15]. IEC 60880 and IEC 62138 provide the principles and requirements for software safety classes. I&C functions of category A may be implemented in class 1 systems only, I&C functions of category B may be implemented in class 1 and 2 systems, I&C functions of category C may be implemented in class 1, 2, and 3 systems [16].

Standards in the nuclear domain focus on quality assurance and the prevention of failures rather than analysing the possible consequences of failures. The IEC 61513 standard states:

The highest practicable integrity is generally deemed necessary for any system which prevents or mitigates the consequences of radioactive releases. A lower level of integrity may be acceptable for systems which support protection against there being releases, but do not directly prevent or mitigate them. Consequently, there is not an equivalent scheme to the reliability/risk reduction SIL levels proposed in IEC 61508 in common use in the nuclear sector. This deterministic approach has been found generally sufficient in the nuclear industry and has resulted in practice in the setting of very high targets of all protective functions. However, the nuclear sector does recognise the numerical approach, and methods of probabilistic safety analysis (PSA) may provide clearer targets for the reliability of CB systems [16].

Defence in depth is required for all safety activities. IEC 60880 provides requirements for defences against software design and coding faults which can lead to common cause failures (CCF) of functions classified as category A [15].

6 Discussion and Conclusion

Our conceptual experiment demonstrates – and maybe validates to some extent - that the generic situational factors model can be used as the main source to define dominant safety factors. Adaptation and mapping is however, not straightforward. Most of the selected factors required further elaboration for generic safety critical situational factor identification. Some additional factors are also needed (Table 2). The authors also highlight that while we possess considerable expertise in both safety critical software development and software development situational factors, the exercise to elaborate the generic safety critical situational factors (from the generic software development situational factors) presently lacks an independent validation.

One idea in this experimental research was to propose an ordinal scale for selected safety factors. It would allow for a "safety profile" to be identified, a high-level common set of system/software specific normative requirements. When each factor value in an ordinal scale is aggregated further, it would be an overall indicator of safety in a given situation and for a given system/software.

Further adaptation of the selected factors from generic safety to domain-specific safety shows remarkable differences in results. Medical device software has much fewer requirements than nuclear domain. Major gaps also exist in the definition of the ordinal scale per each factor. At least, domain-specific standards may not even have such concepts. Maybe for historical reasons, different safety classifications are very popular. Unfortunately, they are quite different and not directly comparable. There may be benefits to adopting the generic IEC 61508 standard as a starting point and baseline in different domains, to improve comparability and cross-domain mapping of concepts and requirements.

Our research is still in early phase and remains highly conceptual. An in-depth validation is needed. Situational safety factors should be piloted and results should be compared between domains. Then it could be possible to improve comparability and better mapping between requirements in different standards.

A safety profile could be a first step in more detailed and well-established safety demonstration, such as safety case definition and assessment of system/software development processes. This is illustrated in Fig. 3. A safety profile can also be a separate result, some kind of quick analysis of system/software specific safety requirements and their achievement. Early identification of potential gaps could reduce risks in deliveries.

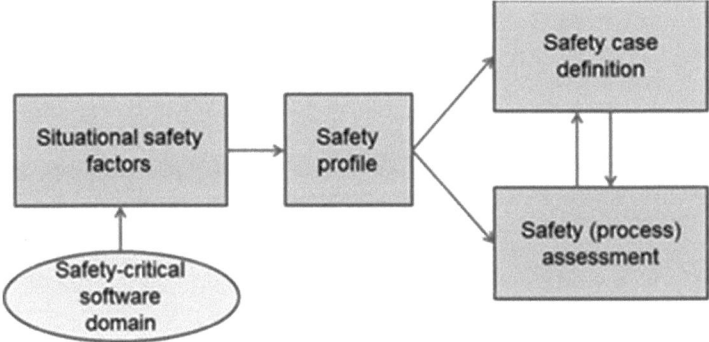

Fig. 3. Use of situational factors in defining a safety profile

The SPICE-based assessment approach is in use both in medical device and nuclear domains. Assessment methods are called with brand names such as MDevSPICE and Nuclear SPICE. The ISO/IEC 330xx family of standards is the main reference and starting point in both methods. Situational factors could extend the methods into earlier steps in supplier and system/software/platform selection.

The proposed safety situational factors contribute mainly in quality, for obvious reasons. They could be selected and elaborated further also by productivity and time criteria. It is a general trend in software and system markets that the overall success is much based on correct timing for markets. More agility is therefore also needed. In an ideal situation, quality and productivity factors would converge on a single point, and this is perhaps an outcome that can be achieved through the more aggressive adoption of technology-enabled software development processes [18] that we are starting to see emerging in the general software engineering field.

Acknowledgments. This research is supported in part by the Science Foundation Ireland Research Centres Programme, through Lero - the Irish Software Research Centre (http://www.lero.ie) grant 10/CE/I1855 & 13/RC/20194; and in part by the Finnish national nuclear safety program SAFIR2018 (http://safir2018.vtt.fi/).

References

1. Clarke, P., O'Connor, R.V., Leavy, B.: A Complexity theory viewpoint on the software development process and situational context. In: Proceedings of the 2016 International Conference on Software and System Process (ICSSP 2016). IEEE, San Francisco (2016)
2. Clarke, P., O'Connor, R.V.: The situational factors that affect the software development process: towards a comprehensive reference framework. J. Inf. Softw. Technol. **54**(5), 433–447 (2012)
3. Knight, J.C.: Safety critical systems: challenges and directions. In: Proceedings of the 24th International Conference on Software Engineering, pp. 547–550. IEEE (2002)
4. Manson, S.M.: Simplifying complexity: a review of complexity theory. Geoforum **32**(3), 405–414 (2001)
5. Clarke, P., O'Connor, R., Leavy, B., Yilmaz, M.: Exploring the relationship between software process adaptive capability and organisational performance. IEEE Trans. Softw. Eng. **41**(12), 1169–1183 (2015)
6. Clarke, P., Lepmets, M., McCaffery, F., Finnegan, A., Dorling, A., Eagles, S.: Characteristics of a medical device software development framework. In: Industrial Proceedings of EuroSPI 2014 conference, pp. 1–9 (2014)
7. IEC: IEC 62304 medical device software - software life-cycle processes. IEC, Geneva, Switzerland (2006)
8. Clarke, P., Lepmets, M., Dorling, A., McCaffery, F.: Safety critical software process assessment: how MDevSPICE® addresses the challenge of integrating compliance and capability. In: Rout, T., O'Connor, R.V., Dorling, A. (eds.) SPICE 2015. CCIS, vol. 526, pp. 13–18. Springer, Heidelberg (2015)
9. Varkoi, T., Nevalainen, R.: FiSMA report 2014-2. Advanced nuclear SPICE assessment process. Version 1.0, 2015-01-08. SAFIR2014. FiSMA, Espoo Finland (2015)
10. IEC: IEC 61508, functional safety of electrical/electronic/programmable electronic safety related systems. Parts 1 – 7. IEC, Geneva, Switzerland (2010)
11. ISO: ISO 14971 - medical devices - application of risk management to medical devices. ISO, Geneva, Switzerland (2009)
12. IEC: IEC 60601-1 - medical electrical equipment – part 1: general requirements for basic safety and essential performance. IEC, Geneva, Switzerland (2005)
13. BEL-V, BfS, CNSC: Common positio006E. Licensing of safety critical software for nuclear reactors. Common position of seven European nuclear regulators and authorised technical support organisations. Regulator Task Force on Safety Critical Software (TF SCS) (2013)
14. IEC: IEC 60880, nuclear power plants – instrumentation and control systems important to safety – software aspects for computer-based systems performing category A functions. IEC, Geneva, Switzerland (2006)
15. IEC: IEC 62138, nuclear power plants – I&C systems important to safety – software aspects for computer based systems performing category B and C functions. IEC, Geneva, Switzerland (2004)
16. IEC: IEC 61513, nuclear power plants – instrumentation and control for systems important to safety – general requirements for systems. IEC, Geneva, Switzerland (2001)

17. IEC: IEC 61226, nuclear power plants – instrumentation and control systems important for safety – classification of instrumentation and control functions. IEC, Geneva, Switzerland (2009)
18. Clarke, P., Elger, P., O'Connor, R.V.: Technology enabled continuous software development. In: Proceedings of the International Conference on Software Engineering (ICSE) Workshop on Continuous Software Evolution and Delivery (CSED). ACM / IEEE, New York (2016)

Supporting Cyber-Security Based on Hardware-Software Interface Definition

Georg Macher[1(✉)], Harald Sporer[2], Eugen Brenner[3], and Christian Kreiner[3]

[1] AVL List GmbH, Graz, Austria
georg.macher@avl.com
[2] pewag International GmbH, Graz, Austria
[3] Institute for Technical Informatics,
Graz University of Technology, Graz, Austria
{brenner,christian.kreiner}@tugraz.at

Abstract. The automotive industry has an annual increase rate of software implemented functions of about 30 %. In the automotive domain the increasing complexity of systems became challenging with consumer demands for advanced driving assistance systems and automated driving functionalities, and the thus broadening societal sensitivity for security and safety concerns, such as remote control of cars by hacking their IT infrastructure.

As vehicle providers gear up for the cyber-security challenges, they can leverage experiences from many other domains, but nevertheless have to face several unique challenges. The recently released SAE J3061 guidebook for cyber-physical vehicle systems provides high-level principles for automotive organizations to identify and assess cyber-security threats and design cyber-security aware systems in close relation to ISO 26262. Although functional safety and cyber-security engineering have a considerable overlap regarding many facets, such as analysis methods and system function thinking, the definition of system borders (item definition vs. trust boundaries) often differs largely. Therefore, appropriate systematic approaches to support the identification of trust boundaries and attack vectors for the safety- and cybersecurity-relates aspects of complex automotive systems are essential. In the course of this paper, we analyze a method to identify attack vectors on complex systems via signal interfaces. We focus on a central development artifact of the ISO 26262 functional safety development process, the hardware-software interface (HSI), and propose an extension for the HSI to support the cyber-security engineering process.

Keywords: ISO 26262 · SAE J3061 · Automotive systems · Hardware-software interfaces · Cyber-security · Functional safety

1 Introduction

The emergence of embedded automotive systems over the last decades has affected the development of vehicles, promising to improve the safety of drivers and support new applications. Exploiting the rising vehicle-to-vehicle and vehicle-to-infrastructure paradigms (growing to over 210 million Euros by 2016), future vehicles will have multiple inter-vehicle connections as well as capabilities for (wireless) networking with other vehicles and non-vehicle entities such as charging stations and traffic lights [1].

The resulting inter-connectivity increases attack surfaces and their damage potential, especially in light of the estimation that, worldwide, over a million people fall victim to cyber-crime every day, with a global cost of cyber-crime valued at 313 billion Euros in 2011 [2]. Embedded automotive system technologies offer great benefits, but they also bring new risks for users today, becoming critical for both quality and security performances.

Before the introduction of wireless connections and automated driving functionalities, vehicles were physically isolated machines with mechanical controls. Extra-functional properties of concern were mainly timing, reliability and functional safety. Today the automotive domain is focusing on adapting established functional safety processes and methods for security engineering (e.g. the recently available SAE J3061 [3]). Although functional safety and cyber-security engineering have a considerable overlap regarding many facets, the elements of concern are not identical in the two engineering disciplines. One example is the identification of trust boundaries for the safety- or cyber-security-related aspects of complex automotive systems and the definition of system borders in ISO 26262 context (item definition). Thus, appropriate systematic approaches to support the identification of trust boundaries are essential.

In the course of this paper, we analyze a way to identify trust boundaries and attack vectors on complex systems via signal interfaces based on the hardware-software interface (HSI), a central development artifact of the ISO 26262 functional safety development process. Furthermore, we propose an extension for the HSI to support the cyber-security engineering process.

The paper is organized as follows: Sect. 2 presents an overview of related works. In Sect. 3 a description of the proposed approach and detailed information about the individual items is provided. A brief evaluation of the approach is presented in Sect. 4. Finally, Sect. 5 concludes with an overview of the approach presented.

2 Related Work

An unambiguous definition of the hardware-software interface has become vital in the context of the road vehicles functional safety norm ISO 26262 [4]. But neither the functional safety standard nor automotive process reference model of Automotive SPICE [5] prescribe a specific methodology for the development of this artifact. Although an unambiguous specification of the various signals of embedded automotive systems to define the hardware/software interface is of high importance for the automotive domain, publications on HSI definitions are rare.

In the automotive domain hardware and software development cycle times differ significantly in length and software development is typically separated into several abstraction layers (such as application software (ASW), microcontroller abstraction layers (MCAL), basic functionality drivers (BSW)). This approach excludes hardware specific details and enables the establishment of focused software development teams (e.g., basic software developer, application software engineers, software integrators), but on the other hand it sometimes obfuscates the importance of HSI development.

In [6] a model-based development (MBD) approach for an ISO 26262 aligned HSI definition is presented. This work combines spreadsheet tools (such as Excel) and MBD tools in a bidirectional manner to enable a tool-independent method of engineering HSI definitions with spreadsheet tools and transformation of the generated information into a reusable and version-able model representation.

A domain-specific modeling approach for mechatronic systems with an integrated HSI definition feature is presented in [7]. The approach of this work has mainly been created for the development of embedded mechatronic based electric/electronic systems (E/E systems) in the automotive field and is based on a domain-specific language tailored for the specific needs of domain experts. The focus of this work was particularly set to simplify the work of domain experts who disfavor system modeling approaches (like UML or SysML). Other works postulate the problematic of defining HW/SW interfaces in the context of System on Chip (SoC) development [8], or are part of an emerging domain-independent paradigm for contract-based design. The contracts specify the input and output behavior of a component and provide a guaranteed behavior [9]. Such an approach can be used for software component safety contracts [10] as well as contract-based embedded system development [11,12]. Nevertheless, these approaches are not yet very common in the automotive domain.

2.1 HSI Relation to Automotive SPICE

The Automotive **S**oftware **P**rocess **I**mprovement and **C**apability Determination reference model [5] is based on the international standard ISO 15504 [13] and is primarily used in Europe, as well as in some parts of Eastern Asia. The reference model does not specify how processes have to be implemented. Instead, desired process outcomes are defined and described in more detail by best practice (BP) characterization (base or generic practices). The model does not address the demand for a hardware-software interface directly, but some guidance on HSI specification can be extracted from general interface topics of the system engineering processes (SYS) and software engineering processes (SWE).

- SYS.3.BP3, stipulates the definition (identify, develop, and document) of system element interfaces, which are equivalent to the hardware software interface.
- SYS.3.BP4 regards the description of the dynamic behavior of and between the system elements, which have to be taken into account in the HSI definition as well.
- SYS.4.BP3 postulates that the system integration test needs to provide evidence of consistency between the interfaces and the architectural design, which relates to the HSI definition.

- SWE.2.BP3 and SWE.2.BP4 can be interpreted in a similar way to their system level counterparts (SYS.3.BP3, SYS.3.BP4).
- SWE.2.BP5 regards the determination and documentation of the resource consumption objectives of all relevant software architectural design elements; to support this, the HSI definition shall include information on resource consumption.
- SWE.3.BP2, SWE.3.BP3 and SWE.3.BP4 can be interpreted in a similar way to their SW architecture counterparts (SWE.2.BP3, SWE.2.BP4 and SWE.2.BP5); nevertheless, signals communicated between the components on the most detailed software level do not directly belong to the HSI.
- SWE.5.BP3 requires a description of the interaction between relevant software units and their dynamic behavior, which can be interpreted in a similar way to its system level counterpart (SYS.4.BP3).

2.2 HSI Relation to ISO 26262

The HSI definition is one of the most important and essential work-products among the many required by ISO 26262. The HSI specifies the hardware and software interactions in consistency with the technical safety concept, which includes hardware components that are controlled by software and support the software execution.

The HSI document is the last development artifact of the system development phase and the starting point for parallel development of hardware and software. The HSI definition thus requires mutual domain knowledge of hardware and software and is usually the result of a collective workshop of hardware, software, and system experts. The HSI is the linkage between different levels of development and is used to align topics relevant to both hardware and software development. Furthermore, the HSI shall be continuously refined in the hardware and software product development phases, which are described in Parts 5 and 6 of the ISO 26262.

Although many best practice articles and books related to ISO 26262 have been published, the hardware-software interface has rarely been highlighted in any of these publications. This might be caused by the fact that HSI definition requires mutual domain knowledge and the responsibility for this artifact differs from company to company.

The majority of information concerning how to specify the interface in relation to functional safety can be found in Clause 7.4.6 of Part 4 of the standard. Additionally, the informative Annex B of Part 4 of ISO 26262 provides information concerning the possible content of the interface definition.

3 Hardware-Software Interface Definition with Security Extension

As mentioned previously, the HSI definition is probably the most crucial and essential work-product required by ISO 26262 related development approaches.

It requires mutual knowledge of hardware and software components and their interactions and needs refinement by these two development processes after initial establishment at the end of the system development phase. By now, the HSI specification no longer consists of only a single spreadsheet description of all signals from hardware to software and vice versa. Supplementary information, such as resource consumption objectives, HW specifics, and controller module configurations also need to be considered for an ISO 26262 or AutomotiveSPICE compliant HSI definition.

Table 1 itemizes a list of essential HSI attributes extracted from standards (ISO 26262 [4], AutomotiveSPICE [5], and SAE J3061 [3]), scientific papers [7,14], and the authors' experiences. Additionally, information has been added (marked with black boxes) to support security related identification of attack vectors on complex systems via their signal interfaces. The highlighted information can be used to identify attack surfaces and establish a defense in depth security pattern for specific signals.

To that aim, signals that are safety or cyber-security relevant inherit their ASIL from the hazard analysis and risk assessment (HARA; requested by ISO 26262) and/or their security level from threat analysis and risk assessment (TARA; requested by SAE J3061). Depending on the related security level / ASIL the signal shall be protected against cyber-security attacks according to a defense in depth pattern focusing on the (simplified) OSI model [16]. The OSI model is a conceptual model that partitions a communication system into abstraction layers (in the original version seven layers). Its goal is the interoperability of diverse communication systems with standard protocols. A layer serves the layer above it and is served by the layer below it.

In addition, the idea behind the defense in depth approach is to defend a system against any particular attack using several independent methods. If any of the layers fails to protect, then the next layer is in place to provide protection. Such a defense in depth approach is also proposed for automotive systems in general by [17,18] and for in-vehicle infotainment systems in particular by [19]. Another defense in depth approach for securing Ethernet communication for autonomous driving is presented in [20]. This work claims generally that enhanced connectivity and the dynamics of the security threats demand the establishment of several security barriers in order to avoid full exposure in case a security mechanism is bypassed.

Moreover, enhancing the HSI definition with supplementary cyber-security information and related signals helps to determine trust boundaries and attack vectors by focusing on signals and thus identifying controllers which can intervene with the involved signals. To that aim, all signals required for the system are analyzed and based on this analysis all control units, which have access to these signals are identified. These control units are within the same trust boundary. Systems within the same trust boundary are equally trusted. Access to the trust boundary is able only via dedicated devices (gateways) which have connections outside the trust boundaries. Thus, it is required that gateways prevent the misuse of trust and protect the control units within a trust boundary

Table 1. Essential HSI attributes, comments and origin

Layer	Attribute	Comment	Origin
conceptual	signal name	significant name	[14]
	signal description	short signal description	ISO 26262 Part 6
	signal direction	input or output	[14]
	signal source/sink	actuator or sensor related to signal	[7]
	ASIL	Automotive Safety Integrity Level	ISO 26262 Part 4
	Security Level (SecL)	security metric	SAE J3061, [15]
physical	supply voltage	-	[7]
	physical min value	-	ASPICE
	physical max value	-	ASPICE
	physical unit	-	ISO 26262 Part 6, ASPICE
	accuracy	% range of value	ISO 26262 Part 6
	HW interface type	digital, analog, bus ...	ISO 26262 Part 6, ASPICE
	HW pin	pin number or identifier	ISO 26262 Part 5
data	message ID	for bus communications	[7]
	message offset		[7]
	cycle time internal	xCU internal refresh rate	ISO 26262 Part 6, ASPICE
	cycle time external	cycle time of digital signal from external	[7]
	trigger	identifier of trigger	ISO 26262 Part 6
	operation mode	information if any special operation mode required	ISO 26262
	HW diagnostic feature	diagnostic feature description	ISO 26262
	memory type	-	ISO 26262
	data protection	special security information	ASPICE
	timing dependencies and sequence order	-	ASPICE
presentation	SW signal name	signal identifier for ASW	[14]
	initial value	-	[7]
	SW data type	-	ASPICE
	scaling LSB	fixed-point arithmetic scaling	[14]
	scaling offset		
	SW min value	-	ASPICE
	SW max value	-	ASPICE
	SW accuracy	% range of value	ISO 26262
	SW unit	physical unit representation	ASPICE
	default value	default value in case of invalid signal	[14]
	detection time	time to fault diagnosis	ISO 26262
	reaction time	reaction time after fault detection	ISO 26262

from attacks. This identification of trust boundaries and gateways which protect the boundaries is both crucial and cumbersome for complex system and network structures. Therefore, using the HSI definition provides a structured and methodical pattern for identification.

4 Application of the Proposed Approach

This section demonstrates the application of the presented approach for a representative safety and security relevant automotive embedded system. To that aim a basic concept of an electronic steering column lock (ESCL) has been chosen. This use-case is an illustrative example, reduced for training purposes and is not intended to be exhaustive or representing leading-edge technology or solutions.

Figure 1 shows a block diagram depiction of the use-case from a safety perspective (item definition). The depiction shows all involved components of an ESCL from sensors to actuators. As can be seen, the actuator is simply an electric motor which moves the bolt, controlled by a motor controller and an electric control unit (ECU). The required sensor signals are (a) a feedback channel of the bolt position (represented via endpos signal), (b) power supply and ignition key status information (CL30 and CL15), and (c) vehicle status information via CAN bus (ignition key status, vehicle speed signal, gear lever position).

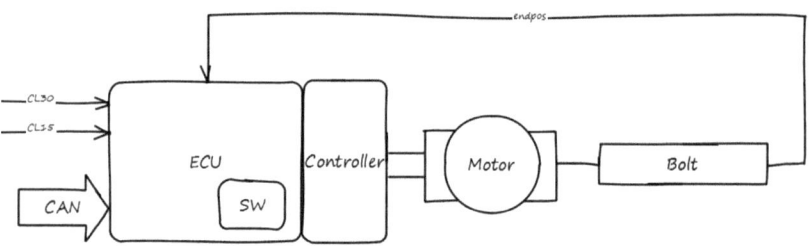

Fig. 1. Block diagram depiction of use-case (Item definition)

An excerpt of an ESCL HARA and TARA analysis [21] (using a combined approach by applying the SAHARA method [15]) reveals the security threat 'SH_1: spoofing of key-less-go off signal, vehicle speed 0kmph and gear lever in park position', resulting in $SecL = 2$ (security level) and security goal 'prevent spoofing of steering column lock signals', and is also related to safety goal 'SG1: prevent unwanted steering column locking' with $ASIL\ D$.

The use-case example represents a safety-critical and cyber-security related component and requires the application of an ISO 26262 aligned development process. Complying with ISO 26262 aligned development process requirements, the HSI artifacts for the ESCL system depicted in Fig. 2 are generated at the end of the system development phase.

#	HSI		ESCL					
1								
2	Signal name		CL30	CL15	endpos	ignition key status	vehicle speed signal	gear lever position
3	signal description	common	supply voltage signal from battery	ignition-starter switch signal	end position signal of ESCL bolt	ignition-starter switch signal	actual vehicle speed	actual gear lever position
4	Sensor/Actuator		CL30	CL15	endpos1	--	--	--
5	Direction		in	in	in	in	in	in
6	ASIL		ASIL B	ASIL B(D)	ASIL B	ASIL B(D)	ASIL B(D)	ASIL B(D)
7	SecL		0	0	0	2	2	2
8	Source(CAN/ANA/DIG)		ANA	ANA	DIG	CAN	CAN	CAN
9	physical unit		V	V	--	--	--	--
10	physical range lower limit		0	0	0	--	--	--
11	physical range upper limit	physical	12	12	12	--	--	--
12	supply voltage		12	12	12	--	--	--
13	signal tolerance %		5	5	--	--	1	--
14	interface		analog in	analog in	digital in	CAN A	CAN A	CAN A
15	pin		Port A11	Port A12	Port A15	Port B12	Port B12	Port B12
16	refresh rate ms		--	--	--	100	100	100
17	cycle time ms		10	10	10	10	10	10
18	message ID		--	--	--	0x100	0x100	0x100
19	message offset		--	--	--	0	0	0
20	trigger	data	--	--	--	--	--	--
21	operation mode		normal	normal	normal	normal	normal	normal
22	HW diagnostic		ref. Voltage	ref. Voltage	--	CRC	CRC	CRC
23	register-type		RAM	RAM	RAM	RAM	RAM	RAM
24	data protection		--	--	--	--	--	--
25	dependency		--	--	--	--	--	--

Fig. 2. Excerpt of the HSI definition of the ESCL use-case

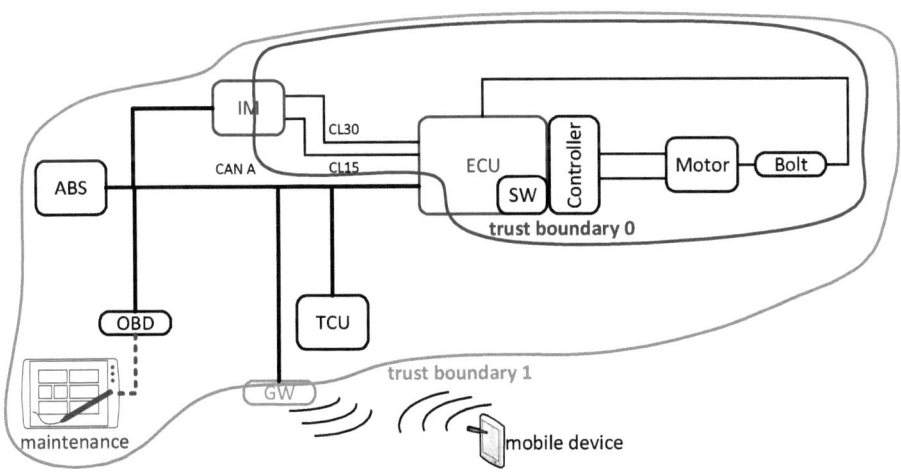

Fig. 3. Trust-boundary layers of use-case

As can be seen in Fig. 2, the *SecL* of the three directly connected signals (endpos, CL30, and CL15) are treated as 0 (not security relevant). This due to the fact that in order to mount a security attack, these signals would have to be manipulated in the vehicle directly at the ESCL system and that these signals are within the same trust boundary 0 (see Fig. 3). On the other hand, the three signals provided via CAN bus (thus provided from outside of trust boundary 0 of Fig. 3) are assigned a $SecL = 2$. This *SecL* indicates a possible cyber-security vulnerability and thus requires built-in security solutions exhibiting a defense-in-depth approach.

The realization of these protections in vehicle systems requires the coordinated design of multiple security technologies (such as isolation of safety critical systems, secure boot, tamper protection, message authentication, network encryption and many others). More details on these automotive security technology best practices, and how and which to choose for different security levels are out of the scope of this work, but can be found, among others, in [17,19]. Currently no standardization for the coordination of security designs has been established and it is up to the manufacturers to decide how to provide a secure context. Thus, we established the following design guideline for signal security for the different security levels (based on [22]):

Layer	Attribute
$SecL = 0$	no additional requirements
$SecL = 1$	verify origin of message
	verify integrity of message
$SecL = 2$	check volumes of messages
	detect abnormal behavior
	immutable device identification
	intrusion detection
$SecL = 3$	encrypted communication
	data encryption
$SecL = 4$	establishing of private communication channel
	correct cycle detection
	blocking of unapproved and inappropriate messages

For the example, the three CAN signals required by ESCL (assigned $SecL = 2$) have to be verified by the origin of message (this requires an immutable device identification) and message integrity (e.g. CANs CRC). Also, a detection of abnormal behavior of the CAN bus including a check of message repeat rate and intrusion detection is required.

Based on the HSI identification of the interfaces providing the signals (see Fig. 2 - line 15), devices connected to this interface can be easily identified and trust-boundaries for the specific system identified. This enables a complete identification of involved controllers for a further analysis of interfaces and the establishment of barriers for cyber-security attacks. To do this, we started with the ISO 26262 item of the ESCL system (Fig. 1) and filtered the content of the HSI for signals related to the ESCL system (Fig. 2). In the first step we identified controllers which have access to these signals. These controllers (depicted in Fig. 3) either generate the signals directly (such as the vehicle immobilizer (IM)) or are connected to the same communication bus (antilock braking system (ABS), on-board diagnosis connector (OBD), transmission control unit (TCU) and wireless gateway (GW)). For the second step we identified the inner trust boundary 0 which includes signals directly connected to the electric control unit (ECU). Simultaneously, gateways to the trust boundary 0 are identified (IM and ECU), which are required to ensure protection of the integrity of the trust boundary 0. In the next step the trust boundary of the remaining signals is established. Figure 3 shows a depiction of the first trust-boundary layers of the use-case. As can be seen in the depiction, trust boundary 1, which covers the first layer of all signals related to the ESCL system, also includes the wireless gateway (GW), which appears as a gateway to trust-boundary 1 and therefore enables remote cyber-security attacks on the ESCL. Additionally, if the on-board diagnostic connector (OBD) does not provide protection mechanisms for trust-boundary 1 (usually the case in common vehicle designs), maintenance systems are included in trust boundary 1 as well; a fact that could be easily overlooked and enabled security attacks recently described in [23,24].

5 Conclusion

Vehicle manufacturers are currently gearing up for the newly arising cyber-security challenges. Although they can leverage experiences from many other domains, nevertheless they have to face several unique challenges. Security standards do not need to be created from scratch for the automotive domain and are frequently strongly related to the safety processes.

Functional safety and cyber-security engineering have an overlap regarding many facets, but some development artifacts (such as the definition of system borders (item definition vs. trust boundaries)) often differ completely. To that aim, we have proposed a way to identify trust-boundaries and security design guidelines for the signal security of complex systems via signal interfaces defined in the hardware-software interface (HSI) definition. The application of the approach presented has been demonstrated based on a representative safety and security relevant use-case, an electronic steering column lock (ESCL). Although this use-case is intended for training purposes and represents neither an exhaustive nor a commercially sensitive project, the main benefits of the approach have been made evident.

Acknowledgments. This work is supported by the EMC^2 project. The research leading to these results has received funding from the ARTEMIS Joint Undertaking under grant agreement nr 621429 (project EMC^2) and from the Austrian Ministry for Transport, Innovation and Technology (BMVIT) in the Program IKT der Zukunft under FFG grant agreement nr 842537.

References

1. Bisson, P., Martinelli, F., Granadino, R.R.: Cybersecurity Strategic Research Agenda-SRA. In: European Network and Information Security (NIS) Platform NISP-Working Group, 3 (WG3), vol. v0.96, pp. 1–201, August 2015
2. Cercone, M., Ernst, T.: An EU cybercrime centre to fight online criminals and protect e-consumers. European Commission-Press release, March 2012
3. Vehicle Electrical System Security Committee, SAE J3061 Cybersecurity Guidebook for Cyber-Physical Automotive Systems
4. ISO-International Organization for Standardization, ISO 26262 Road vehicles Functional Safety Part 1–10 (2011)
5. The SPICE User Group, Automotive SPICE Process Assessment/Reference Model V3.0, July 2015
6. Macher, G., Sporer, H., Armengaud, E., Kreiner, C.: A versatile approach for ISO26262 compliant hardware-software interface definition with model-based development. SAE Technical Paper, SAE International (2015)
7. Sporer, H., Macher, G., Kreiner, C., Brenner, E.: Resilient interface design for safety-critical embedded automotive software. In: Zizka, J., et al., (eds.) Sixth International Conference on Computer Science and Information Technology, CCSIT 2016, Zurich, Switzerland, pp. 183–199. Academy and Industry Research Collaboration Center (AIRCC) (2016)
8. King, M., Dave, N., Arvind: Automatic generation of hardware/software interfaces. In: Proceedings of the Seventeenth International Conference on Architectural Support for Programming Languages and Operating Systems, ASPLOS XVII, New York, NY, USA, pp. 325–336. ACM (2012)
9. Cimatti, A., Tonetta, S.: A property-based proof system for contract-based design. In: 2012 38th EUROMICRO Conference on Software Engineering and Advanced Applications (SEAA), pp. 21–28, September 2012
10. Soderberg, A., Johansson, R.: Safety contract based design of software components. In: 2013 IEEE International Symposium on Software Reliability Engineering Workshops (ISSREW), pp. 365–370, November 2013
11. Damm, W., Hungar, H., Josko, B., Peikenkamp, T., Stierand, I.: Using contract-based component specifications for virtual integration testing and architecture design. In: Design Automation Test in Europe Conference Exhibition (DATE) 2011, pp. 1–6 (2011)
12. Iber, J., Höller, A., Rauter, T., Kreiner, C.: Towards a generic modeling language for contract-based design. In: 2015 Workshop Proceedings 2nd International Workshop on Model-Driven Engineering for Component-Based Software Systems (ModComp), p. 24 (2015)
13. ISO-International Organization for Standardization, ISO/IEC 33000 Series on Process Assessment (2014)
14. Macher, G., Sporer, H., Armengaud, E., Brenner, E., Kreiner, C.: Using model-based Development for ISO26262 aligned HSI Definition. In: EDCC Conference Proceedings (2015)
15. Macher, G., Sporer, H., Berlach, R., Armengaud, E., Kreiner, C.: SAHARA: a security-aware hazard and risk analysis method. In: Design Automation Test in Europe Conference Exhibition (DATE) 2015, pp. 621–624 (2015)
16. ISO-International Organization for Standardization, ISO IEC 7498–1 Information technology-Open Systems Interconnection-Basic Reference Model: The Basic Model (1994)

17. Brown, D., Cooper, G., Gilvarry, I., Rajan, A., Tatourian, A., Venugopalan, R., Wheeler, D., Zhao, M.: Automotive Security Best Practices, White Paper, pp. 1–17 (2015)
18. Hahn, T., Matthews, S., Wood, L., Cohn, J., Regev, S., Fletcher, J., Libow, E., Poulin, C., Ohnishi, K.: IBM Point of View: Internet of Things Security, White paper, April 2015
19. Windriver, Improving Android Security for Automotive with a Defense-In-Depth Strategy, White Paper (2013)
20. Pallierer, R., Ziehensack, M.: Secure Ethernet Communication for Autonomous Driving, February 2016
21. Macher, G., Riel, A., Kreiner, C.: Integrating HARA and TARA-How does this fit with Assumptions of the SAE J3061, Software Quality Professional (2016)
22. Otsuka, S., Ishigooka, T., Oishi, Y., Sasazawa, K.: CAN Security; Coste-Effective Intrusion Detection for Real-Time Control Systems, SAE Technical Paper 2014–01-0340 (2014)
23. Greenberg, A.: Hackers cut a Corvette's brakes via a common car gadget, November 2015
24. Mahaffey, K.: Hacking a Tesla Model S: What we found and what we learned, August 2015

SPI Initiatives

Collective Intelligence-Based Quality Assurance: Combining Inspection and Risk Assessment to Support Process Improvement in Multi-Disciplinary Engineering

Dietmar Winkler[1,2(✉)], Juergen Musil[2], Angelika Musil[2], and Stefan Biffl[2]

[1] SBA Research gGmbH, Favoritenstrasse 16, 1040 Vienna, Austria
dwinkler@sba-research.org
[2] Institute of Software Technology and Interactive Systems, CDL-Flex,
Vienna University of Technology, Favoritenstrasse 9/188, 1040 Vienna, Austria
{juergen.musil,angelika.musil,stefan.biffl}@tuwien.ac.at

Abstract. In *Multi-Disciplinary Engineering* (MDE) environments, engineers coming from different disciplines have to collaborate. Typically, individual engineers apply isolated tools with heterogeneous data models and strong limitations for collaboration and data exchange. Thus, projects become more error-prone and risky. Although *Quality Assurance* (QA) methods help to improve individual engineering artifacts, results and experiences from previous activities remain unused. This paper describes a *Collective Intelligence-Based Quality Assurance* (CI-Based QA) approach that combines two established QA approaches, i.e., (Software) Inspection and the *Failure Mode and Effect Analysis* (FMEA), supported by a *Collective Intelligence System* (CIS) to improve engineering artifacts and processes based on reusable experience. CIS can help to bridge the gap between inspection and FMEA by collecting and exchanging previously isolated knowledge and experience. The conceptual evaluation with industry partners showed promising results of reusing experience and improving quality assurance performance as foundation for engineering process improvement.

Keywords: Collective intelligence system · Defect detection · Engineering process · Improvement · FMEA · Inspection · Review · Risk

1 Introduction

In *Multi-Disciplinary Engineering* (MDE) environments, different stakeholders have to collaborate along the project course [1]. Examples for MDE environments include the engineering of automation systems, such as production automation systems, steel mills, or hydro power plants. For instance, plant planners are responsible for the basic configuration of a plant, mechanical engineers design the physical setting of the planned plant, electrical engineers provide electrical and wiring plans, and software engineers design the control software for operation [2].

In MDE projects, engineers typically follow a sequential process approach with parallel discipline-specific engineering tasks and isolated *Quality Assurance* (QA) activities [1]. Thus, engineering projects typically suffer from limited data exchange capabilities and become more error-prone and risky [3]. Figure 1 illustrates an example of a sequential engineering process observed at an industry partner, key deliverables, related stakeholders, and isolated QA activities. Examples of isolated QA activities are reviews/inspections [4, 5], Software and System Testing [6, 7], *Failure Mode and Effect Analysis* (FMEA) [8, 9], the *Fault Tree Analysis* (FTA) [10], or the *Defect Causal Analysis* (DCA) method [1, 11]. While reviews/inspections and testing focus on defect detection, FMEA, FTA, and DCA focus on assessing risks and on identifying root causes of defects. Typically, these QA approaches focus on individual engineering artifacts with limited data exchange and knowledge and experience reuse. However, knowledge and experience from method applications can provide a valuable input for improving QA methods. For example, defect lists (a key outcome of inspection) can drive the FMEA to assess related risks; candidate risks (a key outcome of the FMEA) represent knowledge that can be reused to improve inspection processes.

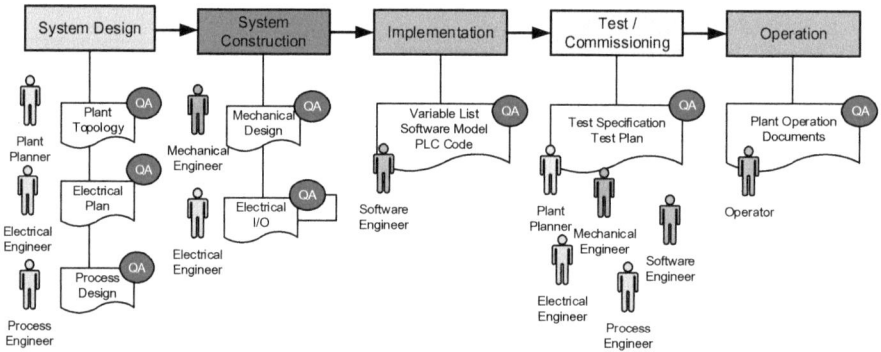

Fig. 1. Sequential engineering process in multi-disciplinary engineering projects [1].

However, individual QA methods are applicable for different types of engineering artifacts. For instance, reviews/inspections are well established in Software Engineering [4] and focus on early defect detection in various types of engineering artifacts, e.g., text documents, images, engineering plans, or software code. In Systems Engineering, e.g., in the Automotive Systems Domain, the FMEA is an established approach for risk assessment with focus on design, product, and process requirements [8]. Although reviews are used in Systems Engineering, more structured approaches, such as inspections, are rarely applied. Further, to the best of our knowledge, there are only limited attempts to combine different QA approaches, such as reviews/inspections and the FMEA, to gain additional benefits derived from applied methods. The combination of reviews/inspections and the FMEA can enable engineering process improvement in terms of using defect lists (derived from review/inspection approaches) as input for the FMEA; identified risks and countermeasures can be re-used in an inspection approach to improve review and inspection processes. However, main challenges include how to combine review/inspection processes and the FMEA in terms of improving QA mechanisms. More specifically, (a) how to reuse results from review/inspection in the FMEA (and vice versa) and (b) how to collect, aggregate, disseminate, and reuse engineering knowledge coming from method applications. The reuse of engineering knowledge can improve individual methods and increase method application performance. A type of software system that could address these capabilities are *Collective Intelligence Systems* (CIS), which are a particular kind of collaborative, social platform that focus on aggregation and dissemination feedback loops of user-generated content [13]. In software engineering, CIS have been sustainably integrated as tool support in best-practice software development processes, such as bug tracking (*Jira*[1]), code reviews (*Gerrit*[2]) or wide-scale software repository reuse (*GitHub*[3]). Therefore, CIS seems to be a promising starting point to bridge the gap between the aforementioned, so far isolated approaches. This paper addresses the challenges of combining inspections and FMEA on a conceptual level to provide a mechanism for reusing knowledge in engineering projects to (a) improve the engineering product and (b) to improve methods for defect detection (i.e., inspection) and risk management (i.e., the FMEA) processes by using a *collective intelligence system*.

The remainder of this paper is structured as follows: Sect. 2 presents related work on reviews and (software) inspection, the FMEA, and collective intelligence systems. Section 3 presents the research issues. Section 4 introduces to the concept of collective-intelligence driven defect detection and risk management based on required capabilities. Section 5 presents an initial concept evaluation. Finally, Sect. 6 discusses strength and limitations of the approach and concludes the paper.

2 Related Work

This section summarizes related work on (software) inspections for early defect detection (Sect. 2.1), the FMEA for systematic risk assessment (Sect. 2.2), and *Collective Intelligence Systems* (Sect. 2.3) to capture, manage, and reuse engineering knowledge for better supporting both inspection and FMEA processes.

2.1 Reviews and (Software) Inspections

Software reviews and inspections are well-established formal defect detection approaches in Software Engineering [4] to identify defects early and efficiently. Reviews and inspections follow a defined process executed by defined stakeholders. Figure 2 presents a common inspection process [14] including related roles.

The traditional inspection process includes six steps [14]: *Inspection Planning* (1) is based on project/quality plans or driven by a decision to conduct an inspection for a specific engineering artifact. A moderator is responsible for planning tasks, i.e., assessing inspection artifacts (e.g., based on inspection entry criteria), providing method support (e.g., reading techniques), and organizing team members and inspection

---

[1] Software tool *Jira*: https://www.atlassian.com/software/jira.
[2] *Gerrit*: https://www.gerritcodereview.com.
[3] *GitHub*: https://github.com.

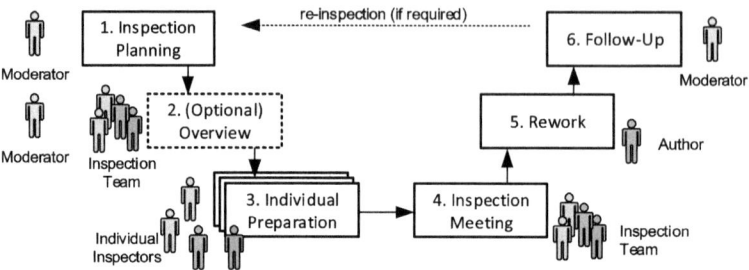

Fig. 2. (Software) Inspection process steps with related stakeholders [14].

activities. Depending on the experience of the team members and the complexity and novelty of the engineering artifacts, an *Optional Overview* (2) meeting helps inspection team members to get familiar with the provided inspection package. Note that inspections can also facilitate knowledge exchange and learning [15]. *Individual preparation* (3) takes as input the inspection package and delivers a set of individual defect lists provided by inspectors of the inspection team. The main goal of an *Inspection Meeting* (4) is to derive an agreed team defect list from the discussion of individual defect lists. In the *Rework* (5) phase responsible authors fix reported defects in their engineering artifacts and provide updated engineering artifacts. Finally, during the *Follow-Up* (6) phase the moderator checks these modifications and decides on (a) releasing the engineering artifact or (b) scheduling another inspection cycle (i.e., re-inspection), if quality criteria are not acceptable. Reasons for a re-inspection are based on too many reported defects or critical issues that might cause risks or have an impact on other engineering artifacts.

Reading techniques are supporting guidelines that guide a team of inspectors through the reading process and support them in detecting defects in various engineering artifacts, e.g., specification documents, models, diagrams, or software code. A reading technique is a structured approach on how to review/inspect a specific engineering artifact [16, 17] and thus, represent engineering knowledge for inspection application. Several studies investigated different reading techniques and reported on strength and weaknesses in different study contexts [4, 16, 18]. A *Checklist-Based Reading* (CBR) technique approach consists of a set of sequential and domain-specific tasks that enables inspectors stepping through the inspection artifacts and report candidate defects. *Usage-Based Reading* (UBR) focuses on prioritized use cases [14] and apply business-critical scenarios for defect detection. The application of *Perspective-Based Reading* (PBR) enables defect detection from various perspectives, e.g., developer, tester, or system architect [19]. Although reading techniques are popular in software engineering, they are not widely used in MDE. In the context of MDE, perspectives seem to be a promising approach, because engineers from different disciplines can take their individual viewpoints on engineering artifacts and report candidate defects. Winkler and Biffl [20] proposed the focused inspection approach with tool support that enables the application of perspective-based reading in MDE contexts.

Beyond improving products (artifacts) in Software Engineering, inspections, results of inspection process steps represent *explicit knowledge* on engineering artifacts (e.g., entities or relationships) or the application domain (e.g., architecture best practices). However, this explicit knowledge typically is lost after inspection and is only rarely used for improving processes or for supporting related engineering or QA activities.

2.2 Failure Mode and Effect Analysis

The main goal of the *Failure Mode and Effect Analysis* (FMEA) focuses on (a) the assessment of product reliability and (b) the early identification of risks, which can have a critical impact on the customer and use of the product [8]. FMEA team members identify and assess risks, candidate defects, and countermeasures based on system requirements, required features, and proposed solutions. During risk assessment, the FMEA team estimates probability (P), severity (S), and detectability (D) of candidate defects on a linear scale from 0 to 10^4 for every single requirement/feature and derives the *Risk Priority Number (RPN)*: RPN = P*S*D. In the context of an FMEA, probability refers to the likelihood of defect occurrence in the final product in the field; severity describes the consequences and the impact of a defect in the field; and detectability refers to complexity factors of identifying and locating the defect in the final product or artifact. The related RPN threshold values are defined in the project context to focus on the most critical issues. Based on this defined threshold value, RPNs above this value require countermeasures, RPN values below this threshold are accepted as risks and no actions are defined.

Figure 3 illustrates the basic FMEA process based on [9]: (1) *FMEA planning* is executed by the quality or project manager based on the application domain, requirements, or expected risks including scope definition, team composition and scheduling. In FMEA workshops, the team (often key stakeholders in MDE environments) identifies (2) *Key Components and Features* and determine (3) *Candidate Defects*. Candidate defects typically represent a list of risks and possible issues in context of the artifact or project. Experiences from previous projects often help to identify typical issues in the domain. However, this step often applies implicit experience and knowledge of experts in the FMEA team. (4) *Effect Assessment*. For every candidate defect the FMEA team determines defect probability, severity, and detectability and calculates the RPN based on expected defect effects. (5) The *Decision on Required Corrective Action* is based on the RPN, i.e., whether or not the RPN exceeds defined threshold values. (6) *Corrective Actions* (countermeasures) need to be identified and recommended by the FMEA team. (7) Implemented *Changes* require a re-assessment of the RPN. Note that this cycle could be repeated several times. Finally, the FMEA results in a (8) *FMEA Report*.

---

[4] Linear scale for probability, severity, and detectability: 0 stands for very low probability, severity, and detectability; 10 indicates critical probability, severity, and detectability. For example, the rating 10/10/10 means that candidate defects will definitely be in the final product (high probability) with a very critical impact (high severity) and it is very hard to identify the defect early (high detectability).

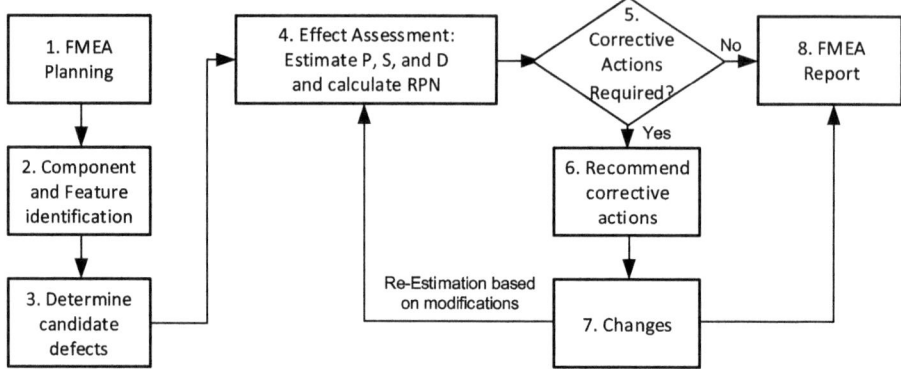

Fig. 3. Failure Mode and Effect Analysis (FMEA) process steps based on [9].

The FMEA has been successfully applied in systems engineering domains, such as automation systems, for early risk and defect assessment and prevention. However, existing experiences (from previous projects) or knowledge are typically embodied within FMEA team members but rarely made explicit for reuse in other projects or improvement of FMEA methods. CIS can help to make this implicit knowledge explicit.

2.3 Collective Intelligence Systems

Collective Intelligence Systems (CIS) are socio-technical platforms, which provide the efficient aggregation and dissemination of user-generated content and knowledge [13]. Representative examples of popular CIS are *Wikipedia, Twitter, YouTube* and the *Eclipse Marketplace*[5]. In addition, CIS possess effective self-organization capabilities, which are enabled by a characteristic feedback loop [12]. This loop coordinates the overall information flow between the platform users, thus enabling the division of labor and increased awareness of mission-relevant information.

Both inspection and the FMEA strongly rely on the interaction of human experts, who contribute to projects by applying best-practice methods. Often experiences and knowledge are implicitly embodied by experts but not explicitly expressed. Implicit knowledge hinder reuse of experiences and knowledge (a) in projects with similar method application and (b) across methods, here: inspection and the FMEA. Reusing experience and knowledge is an important foundation for engineering improvement. In context of information artifacts improvement efforts often focus on usability aspects (such as the cognitive dimensions framework [21]) to lower barriers for users to share and retrieve information. Another approach would be to address these issues on a systemic level. Thus, CIS capabilities could support human-centric activities, such as inspection and FMEA. In context of this paper, we consider a CIS as a "black box" and focus on the application of a CIS on a conceptual level for combining inspections and

---

[5] *Eclipse Marketplace*: https://marketplace.eclipse.org.

FMEA on process level to gain benefits from method application towards product and process improvement.

3 Research Issues

The isolated application of inspection for early defect detection in Software Engineering and the FMEA for early risk assessment in Systems Engineering helps to improve related artifacts in isolated phases. The combination of inspection and FMEA, powered by a CIS, aims at supporting project stakeholders in (a) improving methods based on the previous method application results, (b) making implicit process knowledge explicit for reuse purposes, and (c) gain additional benefits and synergies for method and process improvement. Therefore, we derive two research issues:

RI-1. How can a collective intelligence-based quality assurance (CI–based QA) approach support engineering process improvement in the MDE domain? The combination of inspection and the FMEA on process level can help to link results and experiences between both approaches. For instance, team defect lists (derived from the inspection process) can support guiding the FMEA process as foundation for determining candidate defects; results from FMEA application (candidate risks and defects) can support improving defect detection techniques to address these risks.

RI-2. What capabilities are required to enable CI-based QA for Inspection and the FMEA? Inspection, FMEA, and the combination of both approaches are typically human-centric application including high expert effort for inspection and FMEA processes. However, tool support aims at decreasing effort and cost, and increasing project, product, and method quality. Thus, the main question is which capabilities are needed for a tool solution, based on a CIS, to mediate the integrated quality assurance approach.

4 Collective Intelligence-Based Quality Assurance

The combination and integration of Inspection [18] and the FMEA [9] – as part of a *Collective Intelligence-based Quality Assurance* (CI-based QA) process – aims at including advantages of inspection and the FMEA, supported by a CIS. Advantages of software inspection include (a) early defect detection in various types of engineering artifacts by applying a structured process approach, (b) guidance of inspectors and teams of inspectors through the reading process by using reading techniques, and (c) making implicit knowledge explicit based on process steps, reading techniques (e.g., checklists or scenarios), and inspection outcomes (e.g., defect lists). Advantages of the FMEA include (a) early risk assessment of engineering artifacts, (b) list of components/features, related candidate risk/defect lists, RPN measures (see Sect. 2.2), corrective actions, and (c) process knowledge based on FMEA application process steps.

Figure 4 presents the combined inspection and FMEA process approach with a CIS including (A) inspection process steps (left hand side); (B) FMEA process steps (right hand side); and (C) *Collective Intelligence System* (middle part of Fig. 4). The *inspection process* (A in Fig. 4) takes as input the inspection object, e.g., an architecture design document and a set of requirements (A1). Note that typical inspections focus on the analysis of inspection objects in context of a stable reference document, i.e. requirements in this case. Reading techniques (A2) provide concrete guidelines for traversing the document under inspection, the perspective-based reading (PBR) approach in this example. Outcome of the inspection process is the agreed team defect list (A3) and engineering knowledge, represented by identified entities, relationships, typical defects, and explicit inspection knowledge (A4), such as dependencies between the architecture design and requirements or defects related to design elements. See Sect. 2.1 for details on the inspection process. The *FMEA process* (B in Fig. 4) takes as input requirements (common for inspection and the FMEA) and the team defect list (B1), which was the output of the inspection process, for FMEA execution. Furthermore, defined guidelines for risk assessment (B2), e.g., the *fault tree analysis* (FTA) approach, are used to identify additional candidate defects, root causes, and corrective actions. Outcome of the FMEA include RPN, risks, and corrective actions (B3). Furthermore, engineering knowledge represent explicit knowledge on how to derive risks, estimation values and experiences for RPN calculation, and how to identify corrective actions. See Sect. 2.2 for details on the FMEA process approach.

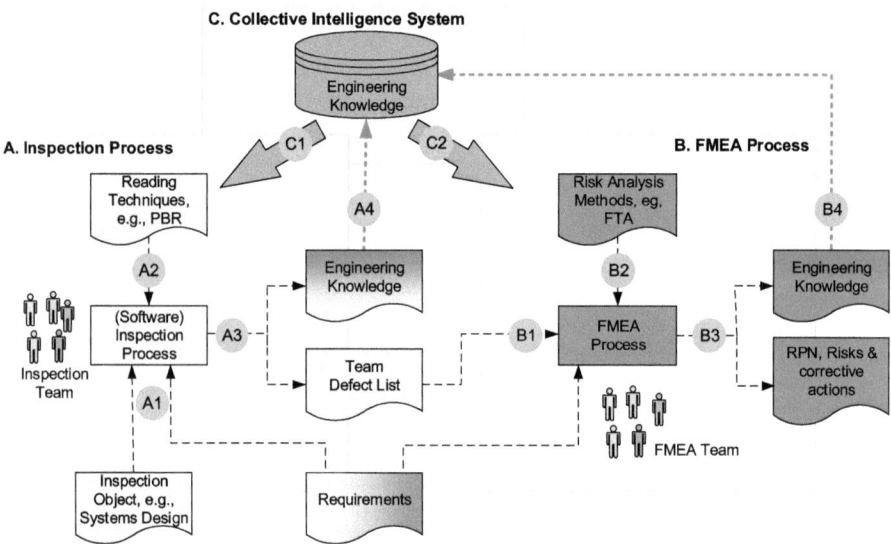

Fig. 4. Combined inspection and FMEA process bridged with a *Collective Intelligence System (CI-based QA)* with input/output artifacts.

Finally, the *Collective Intelligence System* (C in Fig. 4) aims at collecting experiences and knowledge from inspection processes (A4) and the FMEA process approach (B4). *Semantic Web Technologies*, e.g. based on [22, 23], can integrate and link explicit experience and engineering/process knowledge aspects from collected inspection results (e.g., requirements, defects, inspection process steps, and reading technique aspects) and FMEA results (e.g., risk, candidate defects, RPN estimations, and corrective actions). Combined/integrated engineering and process knowledge is used (a) to improve inspection processes and reading techniques (C1), e.g., to better address identified candidate defects (derived from FMEA processes), and (b) to improve FMEA processes by providing knowledge from inspection processes (e.g., scenarios that can support FTA). Knowledge and method engineers can use this experience/knowledge to improve the methods in their application domain.

However, method and process improvement (for future application) typically require time and effort to be implemented within an organization. The proposed approach gains immediate benefits that come from reusing results from previous tasks, here inspection results (i.e., team defect lists that represent real defects) in the FMEA approach to assess additional risks and identify corrective actions. Furthermore, inspection is well suited for training and learning purposes. Thus, immediate benefits can arise if new engineers have to be introduced to a project. Following the structured inspection approach, engineers will get familiar with engineering artifacts as "a by-product" of defect detection. Finally, in the MDE context, engineers are typically driven by mechanics and electrics and they are often familiar with the FMEA approach, while software inspection is not well established in this domain. Combining best practices from software engineering and automation systems development is a promising research direction to improve engineering projects and processes in MDE.

5 Tool Capabilities and Conceptual Evaluation

Inspection and the FMEA are important QA approaches in Software Engineering and the Automation Systems Domain. However, discussions with industry experts in the automaton system domain and research collaborators showed the need for process and tool support like a *CI-based QA* approach, e.g., combining inspection and the FMEA. For instance, customers of our industry partners claimed the need for FMEA for risk assessment. However, the application of a FMEA is time-consuming without capabilities for systematically reusing results or experiences from FMEA workshops. Thus, there is a clear need for providing method and tool support for FMEA execution. Software Inspection seems to be a promising approach to complement the FMEA to make implicit experience and knowledge explicit and to provide tool support for method application based on CIS, i.e., *CI-based QA*. Based on the conceptual process description (see Fig. 4), experiences with Software Inspection and the FMEA, and in discussions with our industry partners in the automation systems domain, we derived a set of capabilities needed for *CI-based QA* tool support:

Defect Detection Performance:
- Support for early defect detection and risk assessment to identify defects and risk early in the engineering process.
- Need for *effective and efficient* defect detection/risk assessment.

Risk Assessment:

- Need for *systematic* and *traceable* quality assurance processes, i.e., process steps and related outcomes have to be repeatable and traceable.
- Need for defined *responsibilities* and *roles* for method application, e.g., for planning, execution, and rework.
- Need for *guiding* less-experienced team members during method application.

Reuse of Experience and Tool Support for Engineering Process Improvement:

- Need for *reusing experiences and knowledge* from method application for engineering process improvement. This need includes the collection, aggregation, dissemination, and reuse of engineering knowledge to improve engineering methods.
- Need for *immediate improvements* of artifacts and engineering plans after method application, i.e., immediate effects of method application.
- Need for *tool support* to help inspection/FMEA teams in executing inspections/FMEA processes more effectively and efficiently.

Based on prototype evaluations and discussions with industry experts and research partners, we assessed the traditional inspection approach, the FMEA, and the *CI-based QA* process approach towards expected/needed key capabilities. Table 1 summarizes needs/capability considerations based on the initial evaluation of the process prototype and identified key capabilities towards a tool-support for CI-based QA.

Table 1. Needs/capabilities of Inspection, FMEA, and CI-based QA approach (++ strong support, o neutral or method-specific support, – weak support).

Needs/Capabilities	Inspection	FMEA	CI-Based QA
Effective & efficient **defect detection**	++	–	++
Effective & efficient **risk assessment**	o	++	++
Systematic quality assurance	o	o	++
Traceable results	o	o	++
Defined **roles and responsibilities**	o	o	o
Guidelines for method application (methodological support)	o	o	++
Reuse of Experiences and Knowledge	–	–	++
Immediate **artifact improvements**	o	o	++
Tool support	o	o	–[a]
Implementation/Application effort	o	o	o

[a] Tool support is currently under development.

Main results of the initial evaluation showed promising results for the *CI-based QA* approach because the approach combines/integrates best practices from both application methods, i.e., method support and processes from inspection and FMEA and process interfaces in between. However, typical applications focus on isolated improvements of artifacts rather than on a comprehensive view on linked methods. Therefore, in this paper we identified key needs and required capabilities for a comprehensive tool solution. A tool solution for the *CI-based QA* approach is currently under development.

6 Discussion, Limitations, and Future Work

In this paper, we introduced a *collective intelligence-based quality assurance* (CI-based QA) concept, an integrated approach for combining best-practice Inspection and the *Failure Mode and Effect Analysis* (FMEA). On a process level, both approaches can complement each other by reusing QA process artifacts, e.g., the team defect list (an important output of inspection) can help to drive the FMEA process based on identified defects in inspection objects. Both approaches, inspection and FMEA, come with comprehensive method support and guidelines, but there are limited exchange opportunities to benefit from each other. Based on guidelines and method best-practices, engineering knowledge is embodied in human experts and are not available explicitly. A CIS can help to make this knowledge explicit and available for (a) improving individual artifacts, (b) supporting individual methods for improvement, and (c) gain additional benefits from cross-method applications.

Research issue *RI-1* focuses on how a collective intelligence-based quality assurance *(CI-based QA)* approach can support engineering process improvement in the MDE domain. Figure 4 presents an integrated process approach for bundling benefits of inspection and the FMEA and support knowledge generation, aggregation, dissemination, and reuse based on a CIS. Discussions with industry experts and research collaborators found the approach promising for real-world application to improve defect detection and risk assessment based on experiences provided by CIS. However, tool support is needed to support CI-based QA. In addition, evaluations in industry contexts remain for future work.

Research issue *RI-2* focuses on required capabilities for a *CI-based QA* tool support. Table 1 summarizes the main capabilities derived from observations and discussions with industry partners and domain experts. This list of expected capabilities represents the foundation for implementing and evaluating a *CI-based QA* tool.

Limitations. Most important limitations of the approach focus (a) on limited tool support of the *CI-based QA* (currently under development) and (b) limited industrial evidence on benefits/limitations of the application of an integrated CI-based QA tool. First results in lab environments and during pilot tests at industry partners showed promising results. However, in-depth empirical studies are needed to investigate the impact of CI-based QA on defect detection and risk assessment.

Future work will include (a) definition of a *collective intelligence system* capable of supporting key capabilities, (b) implementation of the *CI-based QA* approach, (c) related pilot studies at industry partners, and (d) empirical evaluations in larger industrial contexts.

Acknowledgements. Parts of this work were supported by the Christian Doppler Forschungsgesellschaft, the Federal Ministry of Economy, Family and Youth, the Austrian National Foundation for Research, Technology and Development, and the TU Wien Doctoral College on Cyber-Physical Production Systems.

References

1. Kovalenko, O., Winkler, D., Kalinowski, M., Serral, E., Biffl, S.: Engineering process improvement in heterogeneous multi-disciplinary environments with defect causal analysis. In: Barafort, B., O'Connor, R.V., Poth, A., Messnarz, R. (eds.) EuroSPI 2014. CCIS, vol. 425, pp. 73–85. Springer, Heidelberg (2014)
2. Biffl, S., Lüder, A., Winkler, D.: Multi-disciplinary engineering for industrie 4.0: semantic challenges, needs, and capabilities. In: Biffl, S., Sabou, M. (eds.) Semantic Web for Intelligent Engineering Applications, Chap. 2. Springer (2016, to appear)
3. Biffl, S., Moser, T., Winkler, D.: Risk assessment in multi-disciplinary (Software +) engineering projects. IJSEKE **21**(2), 211–236 (2011). SI on SW Risk Assessment
4. Aurum, A., Petersson, H., Wohlin, C.: State-of-the-art: software inspection after 25 years. J. Softw. Test. Verification Reliab. **12**(3), 133–154 (2002)
5. Wiegers, K.: Peer Reviews in Software: A Practical Guide. Addison-Wesley, Boston (2001)
6. Broekman, B., Notenboom, E.: Testing Embedded Software. Addison Wesley, Boston (2002)
7. Myers, G.J., Sandler, C., Badgett, T.: The Art of Software Testing. Wiley, New York (2011)
8. Stamatis, D.H.: Failure Mode and Effect Analysis: FMEA from Theory to Execution. ASQ Quality Press, Milwaukee (2003)
9. Teng, S.-H., Shin-Yann, H.: Failure mode and effects analysis: an integrated approach for product design and process control. J Qual. Reliab. Mgmt. **13**(5), 8–26 (1996)
10. Ericson, C.A.: Fault Tree Analysis Primer. CreateSpace Independent Publishing, Seattle (2011)
11. Kalinowski, M., Card, D.N., Travassos, G.H.: Evidence-based guidelines to defect causal analysis. IEEE Softw. **29**(4), 16–18 (2012)
12. Musil, J., Musil, A., Weyns, D., Biffl, S.: An architecture framework for collective intelligence systems. In: 12th Working IEEE/IFIP Conference on Software Architecture (WICSA), pp. 21–30. IEEE (2015)
13. Musil, J., Musil, A., Biffl, S.: Introduction and challenges of environment architectures for collective intelligence systems. In: Weyns, D., et al. (eds.) E4MAS 2014 - 10 years later. LNCS, vol. 9068, pp. 76–94. Springer, Heidelberg (2015). doi:10.1007/978-3-319-23850-0_6
14. Laitenberger, O., DeBaud, J.-M.: An encompassing life cycle centric survey of software inspection. J. Syst. Softw. **50**(1), 5–31 (2000)
15. Carver, J., Shull, F., Basili, V.: Can observational techniques help novices overcome the software inspection learning curve? An empirical investigation. ESE J. **11**(4), 523–539 (2006)
16. Kollanus, S., Koskinen, J.: Survey of Software Inspection Research: 1991–2005, Working Papers WP-40, University of Jyväskylä (2007)
17. Travassos, G., Shull, F., Fredericks, M., Basili, V.R.: Detecting defects in object-oriented designs: using reading techniques to increase software quality. ACM SIGPLAN Not. **34**(10), 47–56 (1999). ACM
18. Biffl, S.: Inspection Techniques to support Project and Quality Management. Vienna University of Technology, Shaker, Maastricht (2001). Habilitation
19. Shull, F., Rus, I., Basili, V.R.: How perspective-based reading can improve requirements inspection. IEEE Comput. **33**(7), 73–79 (2002)
20. Winkler, D., Biffl, S.: Focused inspections to support defect detection in multi-disciplinary engineering environments. In: 16th International Conference on Product-Focused Software Process Improvement, Research Preview Paper (2015)
21. Blackwell, A., Green, T.: Notational Systems – The Cognitive Dimensions of Notations Framework, HCI Models, Theories, and Frameworks: Toward an Interdisciplinary Science. Morgan Kaufmann, San Francisco (2003)

22. Moser, T., Mordinyi, R., Winkler, D., Melik-Merkumians, M., Biffl, S.: Efficient automation systems engineering process support based on semantic integration of engineering knowledge. In: 16th International Conference on Emerging Technologies. and Factory Automation (ETFA) (2011)
23. Novak, P., Serral, E., Mordinyi, R., Sindelar, R.: Integrating heterogeneous engineering knowledge and tools for efficient industrial simulation model support. Adv. Eng. Inf. **29**(3), 575–590 (2015)

Automotive Quality Universities - AQUA Alliance Extension to Higher Education

Jakub Stolfa[1(✉)], Svatopluk Stolfa[1], Andreas Riel[2],
Serge Tichkiewitch[2], Christian Kreiner[3], Richard Messnarz[4],
Miran Rodic[5], and Monika Gaisch[6]

[1] Department of Computer Science, FEECS,
VSB-Technical University of Ostrava, 17. listopadu 15,
708 33 Ostrava-Poruba, Czech Republic
{jakub.stolfa,svatopluk.stolfa}@vsb.cz
[2] EMIRAcle AISBL c/o Grenoble Institute of Technology,
46 av Félix Viallet, 38031 Grenoble, France
[3] Institute of Technical Informatics, Graz University of Technology,
Rechbauaerstrasse 12, 8010 Graz, Austria
[4] ISCN Ltd., Florence House - Florence Villas 1, Bray, Ireland
[5] Faculty of Electrical Engineering and Computer Science,
University of Maribor, Smetanova ulica 17, 2000 Maribor, Slovenia
[6] University of Applied Sciences Joanneum, Graz, Austria

Abstract. This paper discusses the extension of AQUA (Automotive Knowledge Alliance AQUA – Integrating Automotive SPICE, Six Sigma, and Functional Safety) into the higher education studies. Follow-up project Automotive quality universities (AQU) aims to the adaptation of the AQUA integrated concept to the universities ECTS granted courses. The goal is to bridge the knowledge gap between the automotive industry needs and graduates capabilities in the area of Automotive SPICE, Functional Safety and Six Sigma. The integrated concept of AQU and AQUA complex approach to the education of graduates and engineers to enhance the knowledge in this area is described.

Keywords: Automotive · Automotive SPICE · Functional Safety · Six Sigma · Integrated approach · AQUA

1 Introduction

Assuring quality in Automotive has grown to a huge challenge and competition factor driven mainly by the permanent cost pressure in a mass market that is increasingly confronted with the safety criticality of various mechatronic systems and subsystems in a car. Nowadays electronics and software control more than 70 % of a modern car's functions, and several studies predict this share to grow to 90 % and more in the future [1]. This leads to a level of system and process complexity that has never been experienced before. There is a strong common agreement in the sector that interdisciplinary expertise is the absolutely indispensable fundamental basis for being able to tackle this complexity under the heavy pressure of shorter development and innovation cycles. International standards and norms about Development Quality (Automotive SPICE®, ISO/IEC 15504 [2]), Functional Safety (ISO 26262 [3], IEC 61508 [4]) and Six Sigma [5] (production and process quality) form the backbone of the European automotive and supplier industry. These standards make the smooth coupling of the different companies along the supply chain possible, and enable the successful integration of all parts and subsystems. In order to be eligible for OEMs, suppliers have to implement and master all these standards. The European automotive industry, however, is confronted with a lack of qualified specialists and even more so of interdisciplinary "all-rounders" that can act as the links between different expert groups.

Both, OEMs and suppliers, expect Automotive Quality Engineering skills from engineers, which is manifested by the increasing number of job vacancies for job roles with a high quality skills relevance (designers, developers, testers, functional safety experts and managers, quality managers, etc.). Faced with the complex challenges of holistic quality engineering taking into account mechanical and electrical/electronic hardware, software, as well as product design, development, and manufacturing, companies experience a substantial difference between the quality engineering skills and their actual needs and expectations. This difference leads to a significant decrease in their efficiency, effectiveness and therefore competitiveness.

One of the possible solutions to this situation is to prepare an integrated Automotive Quality Engineering education system for engineers and for graduates that envision their future career in the automotive industry. The education system should be able to address the needs of OEMs and suppliers in this field and be economically suitable.

Attempts to develop a new educational approach for automotive engineers already begun. The EU Erasmus + Sector-Skills-Alliance project AQUA (Automotive Knowledge Alliance AQUA – Integrating Automotive SPICE, Six Sigma, and Functional Safety, 2013–2014) first developed a curriculum (skill card), training material, and certificate for an "Automotive Quality Engineer Integrated" on Vocational education and training level (hereinafter VET) [6, 7]. This is based on a consistent and modular kit ("Baukasten") of training modules for Functional Safety, Automotive SPICE and Six Sigma, as well as on their integration that was developed (which is completely new on the training market) [6, 8, 9]. As a European Skills Alliance project, AQUA received high visibility by the European Commission, Automotive clusters, and industry, in particular suppliers and their European Association CLEPA.

The basis for the new educational approach in form of integrated teaching of standards and approaches was established [6] and now is the time to do the next step - AQUA alliance evolution - in terms of geographic coverage, by extending the initial focus on vocational training to cover also university and technical school education programmes, as well as extending the scope of topics, e.g. incorporating security design in practice to harden Automotive systems against malicious attacks. Follow-on project "Automotive Quality Universities" is currently rolling out and extending AQUA skills to Universities across Europe - to grow and strengthen the AQUA alliance.

In this paper, Automotive Quality Universities (hereinafter AQU) extension concept of AQUA to higher education level is presented and next development and visions about a possible orientation to the future is discussed. Section 1 describes the AQUA establishment idea and basic principles. Section 2 describes the AQUA basic idea and principles. Section 3 presents the AQU project goals and achievements and Sect. 4, Conclusion then summarizes the benefits and consequences of presented extension concept.

2 AQUA – Automotive Quality Integrated

In the past the role of an Automotive quality manager was based on standards like IEC 16949 and the implementation of a quality management system.

With the growth of complexity of car functionality and the increased use of electronics (more than 100 ECUs in cars are connected by a bus and each car function is mapped onto an ECU cluster) other rules came into existence. Automotive SPICE (ISO 15504) knowledge is meanwhile an important skill to assess Automotive systems which include both, electronics and software. Most of the manufacturers demand a SPICE level 3 from the suppliers.

Faults of electronic devices and software can lead to hazards (e.g. blocking wheels, unintended steering, no brake force, etc.) so that a new standard functional safety ISO 26262 has to be implemented. Systems that might cause a hazard get classified by an ASIL-A to D level. Therefore quality managers that have to release a product to the market must be familiar with the functional safety as well.

Quality management (specified in IEC 16949) has a responsibility for the entire product life-cycle, including the production part. Six Sigma is nowadays the most well-known method and statistical toolbox for quality control in production.

Automotive manufacturers (OEMs) demand from their suppliers increasingly high performance levels in all these three dimensions [10]. The most successful companies have an integrated view on this three-dimensional space. This essentially means that they achieve to take the related aspects into account in an integrated and systematic way from the very early design phases over the whole product creation cycle. In order to be able to do so, they have to qualify employees who are able to understand the essentials of the three aforementioned domains, and therefore act as links between the domain-experts. Furthermore, these employees also have an essential role in the project assessment processes that automotive suppliers have to undergo in order to be eligible for OEMs [11].

AQUA (Knowledge Alliance for Training, Quality and Excellence in Automotive) project, a pilot in the Erasmus + Sector Skill Alliances Program under the project number EAC-2012-0635, is the very first European qualification and certification program that addresses exactly this need and established an innovative modular teaching platform integrating following three dimensions on VET level:

- Automotive SPICE® (ISO/IEC 15504): Quality linked to the development process of software and electronics.
- Functional Safety (ISO 26262): Quality associated with the achievement of Functional Safety requirements.
- Design for Six Sigma: Focus on the reliability and robustness of products and production processes.

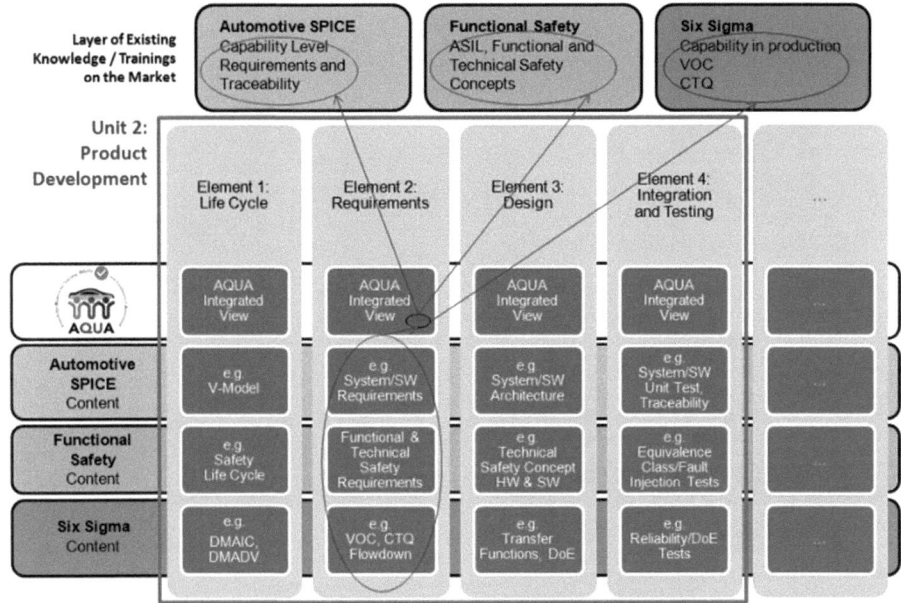

Fig. 1. Modular AQUA concept - unit 2 product development.

A Base layer of core modules was established and allows an integrated complementary view about these three approaches. Figure 1 illustrates the AQUA concept.

Specific content layers (Automotive SPICE, Functional Safety and Six Sigma) represent the particular approaches and the knowledge that is necessary for the specific element. The additional Integration AQUA layer then presents the integrated view, where common principles and paradigms of all approaches are linked, forming the holistic understanding of the presented contents.

This modular strategy allows companies to select each method separately or also to gain an advanced insight into how these methods in fact are joined together in advanced engineering companies. The AQUA unit content covers all the necessary knowledge: introduction of the approaches, product development, quality and safety management, and measurement.

In AQUA the concept of a new education for "Automotive Quality Manager with AQUA Skills" is formed and quality managers for the integrated understanding of the above three methods are trained [6, 12, 13].

3 AQU – Automotive Quality Universities

In the Automotive Quality Universities (Automotive Universe, hereinafter AQU) a ERASMUS+ project on Strategic Partnership for higher education, it is planned to launch the AQUA education at the universities, where ECTS (European Credit Transfer System) will be agreed to among a set of universities in Europe. The Automotive area is

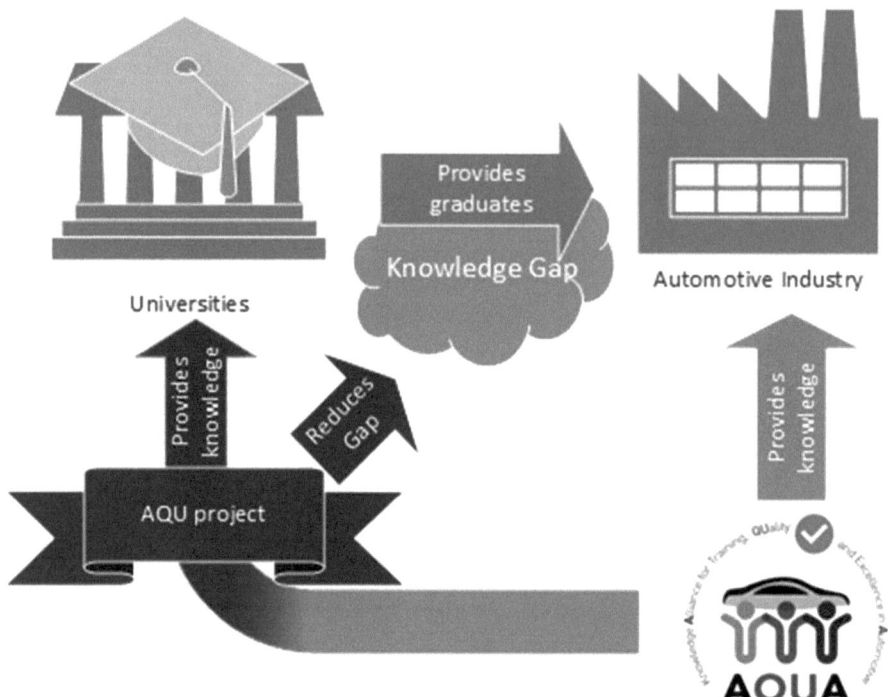

Fig. 2. Schematic view of AQUA, automotive industry, universities and AQU project relations

one of the European lead industries and employers, thus to provide the proper skills for staying competitive at the university level is a high demand across all member states.

Schematic view of relations between AQUA, automotive industry, universities and AQU project are depictured in the Fig. 2. On the top left of the figure universities as a provider of higher education are depictured. Universities provide graduates to the automotive industry, however like it was mentioned in the introduction, it is possible to identify some kind of knowledge gap in the area of automotive spice, functional safety and six sigma that are widely used and form the backbone of quality assurance in the automotive industry. Previously mentioned AQUA helps to increase knowledge level directly in the automotive industry by educating employees. AQU's goal is to reduce the knowledge gap between graduates of universities and required engineering and management skills in the industry. Anyway, the need for the application of selected approaches is relatively new even in the industry, so sometimes there are no engineers in the company, who would be skilled in this direction. With the combination of AQUA trainings at the industry and AQUA courses at the universities, prepared by AQU project, it is possible to bring a synergistic and homogenous solution to education of automotive spice, functional safety and six sigma in the automotive area.

The goal of AQU project is to establish the AQUA training at different universities as Automotive Quality Engineering oriented lectures. All universities agreed to provide

ECTS for the lectures and also agree to recognize ECQA as a supplementary industry certificate for the students. AQU project consortium includes:

- VŠB - Technical University of Ostrava, Czech Republic
- University of Technology Graz, Austria
- University of Applied Sciences Joanneum, Graz, Austria
- University of Maribor, Slovenia
- EMIRACLE (European Innovation in Manufacturing Association), Belgium, teaching students e.g. at Grenoble Institute of Technology, as well as professors and students in several French Engineering Schools (Ecole Centrale de Nantes, ENSAM ParisTech Aix en Provence, Université de Technologie de Troyes, Ecole Centrale de Lyon)
- ISCN/ECQA Online Campus for Industry.

It is also planned to establish an online Moodle based teaching platform where students from different universities can have joint subjects and exercises in the Automotive Quality area. The online campus will be integrated into the ECQA skills portals, learning portals and exam portals, allowing computer based learning and exams, and industry-recognized certificates in parallel to university ECTS.

The presented goals analysis showed that there are several challenges in adopting the originally VET oriented courses at the higher education level:

1. Process of integration to particular university (Integration of AQUA content to higher education).
2. Mapping AQUA ECVET to ECTS, curriculum adjustments.
3. Present knowledge on the level that is suitable for the students that are not experienced in the specific approaches.

To address this challenges, we have performed an analysis of needs, wishes, approaches and possible solutions for particular universities in particular countries. As a part of that analysis, educational programmes where the AQUA should be incorporated were compared as well. As the AQUA topic is broad wide and includes the possible application in electric, electronics and software development, requests and incorporation of proposals from participating universities also represent variety of possible inclusions into the different programmes.

3.1 Process of Integration to Particular Universities

Analysis and comparison of needs was performed at the project participating universities. The goal of the analysis was to get the information how the original modular AQUA course would be suitable for higher education studies in terms of modularity and content. Every university analyzed its needs and made a statement about the possible involvement of the AQUA to their programmes.

Basically, there are two possibilities of integration. First option is to take an AQUA course as a new subject and try to integrate it into the studies. Second approach is to use the big advantage of modularity and integrate an appropriate parts of the AQUA content to the current programme courses. Such an integration will be beneficial for understanding of the integration of AQUA related issues into the particular subjects on particular issues of development and quality in automotive industry.

AQUA as a Separate Course. AQUA project was first developed a curriculum (skill card), training material, and certificate for an "Automotive Quality Engineer Integrated" on VET level. To apply this course as a part of the higher education studies with ECTS granted, ECTS points have to be assigned to the course. The initial consideration of planned AQUA courses was already done. It is planned that if the course is taught as a pure AQUA course with the present content (Automotive SPICE, Functional Safety, Six Sigma), three AQUA subject will be suitable. Table 1 shows mapping of AQUA content to European Qualifications Framework levels (hereinafter EQF) [14]. It is divided to one bachelor course (3 ECTS), one master course (4 ECTS) and one doctoral course (5 ECTS). Bachelor courses content will be oriented more towards the theoretical aspects of integrated concept and even to the standards and approaches themselves, master courses will be oriented more to the practical aspects of integration and doctoral courses will allow research and development that deals with the integrated concept, standards and approaches.

Table 1. Mapping AQUA content to EQF levels

EQF level	AQUA content	ECTS
Level 6	Presentations/theory	3
Level 7	Presentations/theory	4
	Exercises to apply on an example (e.g. ESCL)	
Level 8	Presentations/theory	5
	Exercises to apply on an example (e.g. ESCL)	
	Implementation in a research at PhD level/with link to a real project	

Analysis was focused on the desired knowledge for each university programmes target groups and also based on desired AQUA elements teaching flows from particular universities. As an analysis output AQU project partners agreed on the selection of elements for the particular levels of studies. Bachelor level course will contain whole Unit 1 - introduction, Capability and Assessment and Audit elements from the Unit 3 – Quality and Safety Management and Concepts of some elements from the Unit 2 – Product and Development (Table 2). Master study subject then will contain especially all Unit 2 – Product and Development elements, that expect some level of practice and combination of gained knowledge from all other elements and other necessary Elements from the rest of element to be able to master the approach of integrated quality concept (Table 3).

AQUA Integration to the Currently Existing Courses. AQUA integration to the current courses will be the synergetic utilization of AQUA modular approach and as a matter of fact also a logical application of the original AQUA standards and approaches integration idea. In this case, the integrated standards and approaches concept will be included to the particular content where it should exactly be. This inclusion would

Table 2. Universities – AQUA content for Bachelor Level

Content Units of the training and skill card	Link Module / Integration View	ASPICE Module	Six Sigma Module	Safety Module
Unit 1 - Introduction				
U1.E1: Introduction	X	X	X	X
U1.E2: Organisational Readiness	X	X	X	X
Uni 2 - Product Development				
U2.E1: Life Cycle	X (concept)	X (concept)	X (concept)	X (concept)
U2.E2: Requirements	X (concept)			
U2.E3: Design	X (concept)			
U2.E4: Test and Integration	X (concept)			
Unit 3 - Quality and Safety Management				
U3.E1: Capability	X	X	X	X
U3.E2: Hazard and Risk Management				
U3.E3: Assessment and Audit	X	X	X	X
Unit 4 - Measure				
U4.E1: Measurement				
U4.E2: Reliability				

Table 3. Universities – AQUA content for Master Level

Content Units of the training and skill card	Link Module / Integration View	ASPICE Module	Six Sigma Module	Safety Module
Unit 1 - Introduction				
U1.E1: Introduction				
U1.E2: Organisational Readiness				
Uni 2 - Product Development				
U2.E1: Life Cycle	X	X	X	X
U2.E2: Requirements	X	X	X	X
U2.E3: Design	X	X	X	X
U2.E4: Test and Integration	X	X	X	X
Unit 3 - Quality and Safety Management				
U3.E1: Capability				
U3.E2: Hazard and Risk Management	X	X	X	X
U3.E3: Assessment and Audit				
Unit 4 – Measure				
U4.E1: Measurement	X	X	X	X
U4.E2: Reliability	X	X	X	X

bring us the benefit of complex understanding of the usage of standards, approaches and tools for the specific part of the development lifecycle at the right moment.

Acquisition of this approach needs besides other things reconsideration of each element from the higher education formal needs. Original AQUA VET course is very modular and consists of many elements grouped to several units. Every particular element and its content will be considered and at least appropriate amount working hours will be assigned to each module [15]. In that case we will be able to grant the amount of work that has to be done to master the element or its part and assign appropriate credits to the AQUA content as an included content. Then the particular selected subject can integrate the element or part of the element to its content and the amount of work that is needed will be clearly defined.

Analysis of the possible inclusion at particular universities that are partners in this project showed that there are really a lot of options, how and where to integrate the AQUA content.

3.2 Pilot Courses and Teaching

Some pilot AQUA courses were already held at the universities across the Europe – INP Grenoble, TU Graz, FH Joanneum and VSB-TUO. Trainers from AQUA taught these courses almost similarly as AQUA industry trainings and tested and observed the applicability of such a course in the higher education. Typical flow of teaching of VET course for not or little experienced target group concerning engineering practices that are showed on example is to start with U1. Introduction if necessary or skip it if not. Then continue with U2.E1: Life Cycle, then skip to U3.E2: Hazard and Risk Management, go back to the Unit 2 elements 2–4 and then do the U4 Measure. Such flow of teaching respect the development of practical example and simulates the usage of standards in time ordered usage of V-model in practice. AQUA trainers experienced that this flow of teaching is so far well accepted in VET courses and tried to apply this approach in the pilot courses. This typical flow is not the only one approach. As the AQUA courses are very modular, it always depends on the target group experience and trainer selection of appropriate modules and teaching flow.

Original course and its content is mostly oriented on the practical aspects for application in practice (Automotive SPICE, Functional Safety, Six Sigma so far). Such orientation that deals mostly with the essential question "how" is very useful for the application in the industry, where engineers and managers are mostly aware of answers to other essential questions "why" and "what for". Showing the practically applicable answer in form of approaches and methods to the "how" question for AQUA integrated concept is the key idea that leaded the development of this courses.

However, many reactions and other feedbacks from the universities showed, that students are not always aware of the needs that are requested by the automotive project's stakeholders. Thus students were able to learn the practical AQUA course content well, but are questioning and missing more information "why" and "what for" they should apply so many new concepts. Why to perform all of these integrated approaches if sometimes the task is easy and understandable and some methods seem to be redundant at first glance.

The conclusion for this finding is to prepare more "why" and "what for" oriented presentations for each element (e.g. add an elementary level layer to AQUA horizontal scheme), and thus to be prepared to show the answers to these essential questions and clarify the students understanding of common stakeholder needs. In the case of industry AQUA courses, such a presentation can serve as support materials in case that requirements are not properly understood by trainees, because stakeholder did not push them so far or they are novices in the automotive industry. Thus the AQUA courses will be suitable for trainees or students that are not award of necessary standards and are no or little experienced in automotive as well. Adding a content to the AQUA courses of course again increases the amount of time that is needed to go through the content and must be considered during the ECVET and ECTS considerations.

4 Conclusion

Currently the participating universities already offer programs dedicated to quality engineering in automotive. However, they are mostly based on older norms like TS 16949/ISO 9001 and do not consider the new challenges introduced mainly by the highly networked and complex electric/electronic/software subsystems in the vehicle. These challenges are certain to become even more important and difficult as the automotive industry committed to bringing the autonomous, networked vehicle on the market in 2021.

Mastering these challenges from an engineering point of view requires an integrated, systemic knowledge of the three fundamental fields: Automotive SPICE (capability of a company to develop software and electronics in a car, ISO 15504), Functional Safety (analysing and avoiding risks in the vehicle - e.g. self-steering leading to an accident or GM's ignition system problem which its impacts probably killed more than 100 people, ISO 26262), and Six Sigma (achieving a quantitative approach to production and product quality).

To support the European automotive industry (we are currently facing a paradigm change in industry, like it was the case in mobile phone technology when switching from mobile to smart phones) to stay competitive, it is extremely important to transfer this specific integrated knowledge to students thus empowering them to assume modern quality and safety related job roles in European automotive industry.

Very recently, the German Automotive Association (VDA) formed an Automotive Quality Alliance where all the major OEMs (car manufacturers) define assessment and selection criteria for suppliers mainly in terms of quality and safety [15]. This is another outstanding proof that all the automotive suppliers will need that knowledge, whatever subsystem they develop and produce. Consequently, a high demand for such skills is guaranteed in all regions of Europe where the automotive industry plays a key role as an employer.

This analysis corresponds to the motivation of the higher education institutions participating in the consortium of this project. Their particular interest is to considerably improve the automotive quality engineering education thanks to a new curriculum which represents current and future industry practice. They are convinced that the materials developed in AQUA provide the ideal basis for such a new programme. They will integrate the results of this project in their curricula leading to the education and certification of several hundreds of engineering students per year. As all these universities are highly networked in Europe and beyond, they will not only impact education on their national level, but also on European and international level. This will significantly contribute to bridging the knowledge and skills gap that actually exists between engineering education in automotive quality engineering and industry needs.

By aligning the programme with the ECTS scheme, it will be enabled for being adopted by several other universities in Europe, and also facilitated for being integrated in joint master programmes.

By associating to this programme a European ECQA certificate, which is officially recognized by leading industry, the new education programme will deliver outstanding added value to students and improve their competitive advantage on the job market.

Acknowledgement. This research was financially supported by the European Commission in the AQUA (Knowledge Alliance for Training, Quality and Excellence in Automotive) project as a pilot in the Erasmus + Sector Skill Alliances Program under the project number EAC-2012-0635. The special aspect of adapting the training program to higher education level, and its deployment in five European universities is financially supported by the European Commission in the Erasmus + Strategic Partnership project 2015-1-CZ01-KA203-013986 AutoUniverse (Automotive Quality Universities). This publication reflects the views only of the authors, and the Commission cannot be held responsible for any use which may be made of the information contained therein.

This research has been also supported by the internal grant agency of VSB-Technical University Ostrava, project No. SP2016/100.

References

1. Oliver Wyman Automotive: 2015 Car Innovation. A comprehensive study on innovation in the automotive industry. http://www.car-innovation.com. Accessed 11 Dec 2013
2. International Organization for Standardization: ISO/IEC 15504 International Standard "Information Technology – Software Process Assessment" (2008)
3. ISO, Road vehicles – Functional safety, ISO 26262, part 1–10, International standard under publication, Geneva (2011)
4. International Electrotechnical Commission, IEC/EN 61508: International standard 61508 functional safety: safety related systems. Second edn., Geneva (2010)
5. Theisens, D.: How Green is your Black Belt? In: Riel, A., O'Connor, R., Tichkiewitch, S., Messnarz, R. (eds.) EuroSPI 2010. CCIS, vol. 99, pp. 257–267. Springer, Heidelberg (2010)
6. Kreiner, C., Messnarz, R., Riel, A., Ekert, D., Langgner, M., Theisens, D., Reiner, M.: Automotive knowledge alliance AQUA – integrating automotive SPICE, six sigma, and functional safety. In: McCaffery, F., O'Connor, R.V., Messnarz, R. (eds.) EuroSPI 2013. CCIS, vol. 364, pp. 333–344. Springer, Heidelberg (2013)
7. The Vocational education and training level. http://ec.europa.eu/education/opportunities/vocational/index_en.htm. Accessed 08 April 2016
8. Messnarz, R., König, F., Bachmann, V.O.: Experiences with trial assessments combining automotive spice and functional safety standards. In: Winkler, D., O'Connor, R.V., Messnarz, R. (eds.) EuroSPI 2012. CCIS, vol. 301, pp. 266–275. Springer, Heidelberg (2012)
9. SOQRATES Safety Team, Messnarz, R., Ross, H.-L., Habel, S., König, F., Koundoussi, A., Unterrreitmayer, J., Ekert, D.: Integrated automotive SPICE and safety assessments. Wiley SPIP **14**(5), 279–288 (2009)
10. Rosnah, M.Y., Wan Nurul Karismah, W.A., Zulkifli, N.: Quality management maturity and its relationship with human resource development strategies in manufacturing industry. AIJSTPME **3**(3), 53–63 (2010)

11. Riel, A., Tichkiewitch, S., Messnarz, R.: Qualification and certification for the competitive edge in integrated design. CIRP J. Manufact. Sci. Technol. **2**(4), 279–289 (2010). Special Issue on Competitive Design
12. McDermid, J., Ripken, K.: Life Cycle Support in the ADA Environment. University Press, Cambridge (1984)
13. The European Qualifications Framework (EQF). http://ec.europa.eu/education/lifelong-learning-policy/eqf_en.htm. Accessed 08 April 2016
14. BE-TWIN Toolkit Bridging ECVET and ECTS – A Guide for Pedagogical Staff. http://www.ecvet-projects.eu/Documents/BeTWIN-Toolkit%20for%20trainers.pdf. Accessed 08 April 2016
15. Automotive Quality Alliance. http://www.automotive-quality-alliance.com/en/about-the-initiative/. Accessed 08 April 2016

How the Company Manages Critical Success Factors in Software Process Improvement Initiatives: Pilot Case-Study in Finnish Software Company

Jaana Pekki[✉]

Lappeenranta University of Technology, P.O. Box 20, 53851 Lappeenranta, Finland
Jaana.Pekki@lut.fi

Abstract. Software process improvement (SPI) has had its roots primarily in software engineering, nowadays this approach has grown and covers management of software companies - SPI is widely used in software companies to improve quality, stakeholders' satisfactions, reduce time-to-market, and introduce cost savings within the company. The current literature widely reports certain critical success factors (CSFs) of SPI initiatives; however, the number of publications concerning the topic of management of CSFs is limited. The objective of this paper is to identify and systemize critical success factors presented in the literature as well as to study how the case company manages CSFs in SPI. The case company evaluated the importance and current status of CSF of SPI activities and reported on management work toward performance improvement of CSFs. The main conclusion of this pilot study shows that proper management of CSFs increase usefulness of offering SPI to its key beneficiaries, thus stakeholders' values are taken into consideration.

Keywords: Software process improvement · Critical success factors

1 Introduction

For many years various software (SW) companies have put numerous efforts to mature SW development practices using different techniques and methods. The last decades were devoted mainly to the idea of software process improvement (SPI) [1]. SPI covers rather large number of approaches to improve software engineering practices. We discovered variety of SPI definitions but in this paper the following definition proposed by Hansen et al. [13] is used: "SPI is an applied academic field rooted in the software engineering and information systems disciplines. It deals with the professional management of software firms, and the improvements of their practice, displaying a managerial focus rather that dealing directly with the techniques that are used to write software".

Practitioners have an opinion that areas of the software development lifecycle that benefit from SPI include project management, requirements management, configuration management, software development, quality assurance, quality control, testing, risk management, acceptance and ongoing maintenance. Initially, SPI has had its roots primarily in software engineering, nowadays this approach has grown and covers, for example, management of software companies and plays a significant role in organizational change concept. SPI is considered as a complex action involving not only process improvement but also the organizational improvements. The improvement per se requires commitment from several departments including finances, human resources and senior management [16]. In this paper we admit this wide perception of SPI.

Numerous organizations reported the success of SPI, including examples from many industry case studies such as Alcatel [7], Ericsson [6], Hughes Aircraft [14], Motorola [8], and Onion [4]. A number of scholars [10–12, 17, 18] studied positive factors – critical success factors (CSF) influencing SPI. In this paper we adopt the perception of CSF in SPI proposed by Espinosa-Curiel et al. [15]: "SPI factor is any knowledge, competence, behavior, attitude, perception, feeling, situation, condition, or activity at personal, social, technical, or organizational level that influences the results of an SPI initiative." In other words, CSF is a factor that must present in SPI initiative or program. Scholars declare the organizational issues, change management and people involvement as the key elements of any SPI initiative. There are several distinct commonalities in the finding of aforementioned studies of CSFs which are discussed in section three of this paper.

The rationale of this article is to identify CSFs in SPI in the comprehensive literature, compare them and answer two research questions studied in the case company:

1. Does the case company manage critical success factors in software process improvement initiatives?
2. How does the case company manage critical success factors in software process improvement initiatives?

Why is it important to address those questions? The body of knowledge is CSF in SPI is well defined; however, the number of publications concerning the topic of management and stakeholder value recognition in CSFs in SPI is limited. We suppose that SPI initiatives are less effective if they are not useful to stakeholders. Stakeholders of SPI program or initiative are, for example, executives of all levels of organization, SW end-users or customers, programmers as well as other personnel of a company who are involved into SPI activities. Boehm [5] states that many failures in software projects and SPI initiatives are caused by value-oriented challenges when stakeholder values are not addressed or meat properly. In framework of this research stakeholder value is usefulness of offering SPI to its key beneficiaries, so they are fully involved into SPI activities which increases the success of those activities. Since many CSFs identified in the literature relate to people - SPI stakeholders, we plan to study in the case company are those factors important, what their current state is and how the case company manages them. This research is considered as a pilot case-study within one Finnish SW development company Developers Oy.

The paper is organized as follows: section two refers to the methodology used in the study, study limitations and case company description; section three identifies and analyzes the main studies on CSF in SPI; section four presents analysis of the case study; section five concludes the paper; section six suggests future research.

2 Methodology and Limitations

The body of knowledge on SPI CSFs is well shaped and developed. We studied the most relevant papers on the field to select and compare the identified CSFs for further investigation in the case company. The list of used scientific journals is limited to those: IEEE Software, Information and Management, Information and Software Technology, International Journal of Information Management, Journal of Empirical Software Engineering, Journal of Knowledge Management, Journal of Systems and Software, Scandinavian Journal of Information Systems, Software Process: Improvement and Practice, Software Quality Journal. Out of potentially interesting articles we included articles with direct focus on SPI critical success factors in general. As a consequence, we excluded articles focusing on more specific issues in SPI such as, for example, SPI success factors in small- and medium size companies, Web or agile software projects. We rationalize exclusion of the papers with narrow specialization because we assume the study done in this paper as a pilot one and general in its nature.

Table 1 shows the list of twenty two CSFs proposed by scholars and employed in this study. We analyzed the following factors, some factors are more general and some

Table 1. Critical success factors for SPI initiatives identified through selected publications

Factor/Publication	11	10	17	18	19	9
Senior management commitment	X	X			X	X
SPI goal distinction	X	X			X	X
Staff involvement	X	X	X	X	X	X
SPI personnel respect	X	X	X	X		
Compensated SPI responsibilities	X					
Dedication of resources/staff time	X	X		X		
Turnover	X	X				
Change agents/opinion leaders				X	X	
Encouraging communication					X	X
Managing the project					X	
Providing enhanced understanding/exploitation of existing knowledge					X	X
Stabilizing changed processes					X	
Tailoring improvement initiatives				X	X	
Unfreezing organization					X	
Awareness of SPI		X	X			X
Defined SPI implementation			X			
Reviews				X		
Standards/procedures, concern for measurement				X		X
Training and mentoring				X		
Focus		X				
Internal process ownership				X		
Exploration of new knowledge						X

of them are more detailed. We combined few detailed factors with general ones and proposed thirteen of CSFs for rating and analysis in the case company.

This case company is Finnish middle size SW development organization running SPI activities for several years. Five company's representatives: chief executive officer, SPI program manager, process engineer, SPI project manager, and senior product development manager participated in the evaluation. We asked them to estimate the importance of each factor for the company and current state each factor holds in the company at present. The scale from 1 to 5 is employed, where 1 is the lowest value and 5 is the highest. As the second part of the study we conducted an interview with senior product development manager who is in charge of SPI program to analyze the importance and current state of CSFs in the company and to report what managerial actions the case company makes to improve performance of those factors.

3 Critical Success Factors of SPI Presented in the Literature

Several studies have been undertaken on how SPI can result into success. However, as the goals of SPI vary according to context and company implementing it, the consensus on success factors may be problematic. Here, we review several key studies and report the success factors identified in each case. The accumulative Table 1 of factors found by researches stated below is presented in the end of this chapter.

Goldenson and Herbsleb [11] conducted survey of 138 respondents involved in 56 CMM programs in medium and large organizations. Based on that study they picked out more successful SPI initiatives. The factors proposed by them may be summarized as: senior management commitment; SPI goals distinction and understanding within the company; staff involvement (to what extend staff members participate in SPI initiatives); SPI personnel have to be of high respect within the company; dedication of resources and staff time; compensated SPI responsibilities.

El Emam et al. [10] conducted a study of factors influencing the success of SPI in 61 USA and Canada based medium and large software companies involved in SPI programs. They presented SPI success factors across organizational factors and process factors. Organizational factors are those that characterize the organization undergoing SPI and the characteristics of the organizational SPI effort itself. Process factors characterize activities of infrastructure that are believed to be necessary for successful SPI effort. Process improvement is more likely to be successful when there is a moderate amount of process focus. This research identifies several success factors that may influence successful SPI utilization: commitment (management interest and involvement into SPI initiatives); turnover (at the middle management and technical levels); politics (promoting of long-term benefits of SPI initiatives); respect (to what extend employees involved into SPI are respected in the company); focus (how deep the company is focused towards SPI activities.

Stezler and Mellis [19] reviewed case studies and reports of 56 medium and large organizations involved in SPI activities based on CMM or ISO 9000 improvement activities. They found the following factors that hold prospects for SPI success: change agents and opinion leaders (change agents supports the SPI activities at the company level, opinion leaders at the local levels); encouraging communication and collaboration (communication between the members of one team and members of different departments); management commitment and support (management interest and involvement into SPI initiatives); managing the improvement project (the level of effectiveness in SPI project management and control); providing enhanced understanding (existence of knowledge in current SW processes and business environment); setting relevant and realistic objectives (distinction and understanding of goals within the company); stabilizing changed processes (continuous support of SW processes, their maintenance and improvement at the local level); staff involvement (to what extend staff members participate in SPI initiatives); tailoring improvement initiatives (adaptation of SPI activities and needs of specific departments within the company); unfreezing the organization (readiness of the company to overcome "inner resistance" for change.

Hall et al. [12] conducted survey of 85 companies possessing different CMMI levels. They divided factors in across (1) human factors (for example, SPI leaders, management commitment, and staff involvement); (2) organizational factors (for example, communication and resources); and (3) implementation factors (for example, SPI infrastructure, setting objectives, tailoring SPI, evaluation). In their research they measured the use of implementation factors in the industry. Based on the study the success factors that may be considered are: resourcing (quantity of resources and time allocated for SPI in the company); quality of internal SPI staff; tailoring SPI (adaptation of SPI activities and needs of specific departments within the company); staff involvement.

Another study by Rainer and Hall [18] based on the survey of 85 companies complements the work of El Emam et al. [10], Stezler and Mellis [19] and Goldenson and Herbsleb [11]. Complementing factor was the specific attention to impact of success factors on levels of maturity in company. Factors found to be important in majorities of opinions are: reviews (regular review on current state of SPI program); standards and procedures (development of standards and procedures within SPI program); training and mentoring (training provided to the team of experts); experienced staff.

More matured companies considered the most valuable for successful SPI implementation the following: internal leadership; inspections (advanced reviews of the current status); internal process ownership (responsibility of particular process belongs to authorized person of team.

Dyba [9] performed quantitative research of 120 software and hardware companies of different sizes in Norway. The survey studied validity of several hypotheses presented by researcher and resulted in those key success factors for SPI initiatives: SPI success is positively associated with business orientation (the extent to which SPI goals are aligned with business goals and strategies); involved leadership (the extent to which leaders of all levels are committed and participate in SPI initiatives); employee participation (the extent to which employees use their knowledge and experience in SPI initiatives); concern for measurement – (the extent to which software company collects and utilizes quality data to guide and assess the effect of SPI initiatives); exploitation of existing knowledge; exploration of new knowledge. In general, study by Dyba [9] complements studies by Rainer and Hall [18], El Emam et al. [10], Stezler and Mellis [19] and Goldenson and Herbsleb [11]. However, it provides more detailed analysis of selected success factors.

Study by Niazi at el. [17] interviewed representatives of 29 medium and large companies involved into SPI programs. They identified success factors by empirical study and compare them to the factor the most frequently cited in the literature. However, authors state that in addition to success factors mentioned by El Emam et al. [10], Stezler and Mellis [19] and Goldenson and Herbsleb [11] there are two additional factors that may affect the success of SPI: awareness of SPI in the company (promoting of long-term benefits of SPI initiatives); defined SPI methodology (guidance on how to implement SPI activities).

One common observation from all studies presented in the section above is the necessity of senior management involvement into SPI initiatives. Additionally, the importance of clear vision and understanding of SPI goals should be considered. However, both technical and managerial human resources need to be involved in SPI program. All authors view staff involvement of all levels as extremely important success factor.

Dyba [9] suggests software organizations to "focus on both short-term and long-term alignment of SPI goals and business goals" and "share domain knowledge between software and business executives". Even though involved leadership assessed as success factor for SPI initiatives in his study, its importance stated less significant than in studies by Ryner and Hall [18], Stezler and Mellis [19] and followed findings by Abrahamsson [2] that "many SPI activities do not require management commitment beyond obtaining the resources needed". In Table 1 we unite factors of senior management commitment and involved leadership into one.

Technically it is possible to associate factor "focus" with such factor as "SPI goal distinction". The author supports the view of El Emam et al. [10]. The view reads: "an organization cannot be focused in its SPI effort if its improvement goals are not clearly stated and understood". So, first it is important to distinct SPI goals and then to focus the company into SPI effort. These are two different factors even though they are connected.

Niazi et al. [17] identify that awareness of SPI in the company is the novelty to the success factor list. However, Emam et al. [10] looked at the awareness issue, at least indirectly. For example, they report: "the general label for politically motivated activities and invectives that may promote or hinder SPI within an organization. This overlaps with the view of Niazi et al. [17] which reads: "by awareness we meant promoting through awareness events...among the higher management and the staff members of the organization". Niazi et al. [17] find that the awareness of SPI becomes important because it is a long-term activity and consumes finance. These potential benefits are not clearly seen at the beginning. By explaining and promoting advances of new initiatives credibility of SPI raises among staff members. Defined SPI implementation methodology is also reported to be new important SPI success factor to managers as in some cases managers lacked the knowledge of implementation of SPI activities. Thus, if implementation methodology is well stated it may help managers coordinate and steer the SPI activity.

Rainer and Hall [18] mention that their findings are not well comparable with factors identified by El Emam et al. [10], Stezler and Mellis [19] and Goldenson and Herbsleb [11]. However, our opinion is that factors such as "executive support and leadership", "change agents and opinion leaders", "experienced staff and personnel respect" correspond with the similar factors identified in earlier studies. They are integrated with those factors in the Table 1.

Dyba's [9] main contribution to the list of critical success factors in SPI is resulted in identification such factors as exploitation of existing knowledge and exploration of new knowledge. Exploitation of existing knowledge could be compared with key success factor "providing enhanced understanding" (existence of knowledge in current SW processes and business environment) by Stezler and Mellis [50] to some extent. However, the factor exploration of new knowledge is introduced by Dyba [9]. The main finding about those factors is that both forms of learning in organization are important for successful SPI initiatives and companies should find proper balance between them.

Table 1 accumulates critical success factors in SPI identified in the reviewed above studies and indicates authors that mentioned the factor.

4 Analysis and Discussion

Table 1 presents twenty two CSFs discovered by scholars. For evaluation in the case company Developers Oy we combine few detailed factors with general factors. Factor SPI personnel respect is united with factor change agents/opinion leaders; factor focus is united with factor defined SPI implementation; factors reviews and standards/procedures, concern for measurement are united with factor managing the improvement project; factors internal process ownership, turnover and compensated SPI responsibilities are united with staff involvement; factor exploration of new knowledge is united with factor providing enhanced understanding.

Five members of Developers Oy participated in the survey: chief executive officer, program manager, process engineer, SPI project manager, senior product development manager. They evaluated importance of each factor and current state each factor has in the company at present. The scale from 1 to 5 was used, 1 is the lowest value and 5 is the highest. Then we interviewed senior product development manager who is responsible for SPI activities to report what managerial actions the case company makes to improve performance of those factors.

Discussion below gives answers to our research questions.

"Management commitment" is management interest and involvement into SPI initiatives. It appears to be number one factor for success in SPI initiatives, it gets 4.4 average points. Practically all respondents perceive this factor as the most important. The current state in the company is evaluated as 2.8. Senior product development manager claims: "if you ask whether all managers ready to commit, the answer is no". Several top managers understand the benefits and accept the necessity of SPI initiatives. They lead their teams towards the right direction. However, most business executives who run global operations, global marketing and sales are interested primarily in product deliverables. The main challenge is that they are not directly involved into SPI activities; they have general perception on SPI which is not enough for valuable commitment. Nevertheless, Developers Oy found the way how to motivate those managers who commit in abridged way by: "showing the small improvements we can get, recording them; this is how they see what we did. It is about the measures, we try to build dashboards for different levels of organization, not to the SPI but the deliverables, the improved process. Let us say more visibility and more control for the R&D. I think that is the key issue, the only thing that they actually understand and can commit to".

The second most popular CSF is "unfreezing the organization" - readiness of the company to overcome inner resistance for change. Developers Oy evaluate this factor with importance equal to 4.4. However the situation in the company reaches the rate of 2.4. Almost all employees see the need for change, but as a cause of limited management commitment and rather low non-technical management involvement skeptical attitude toward SPI initiatives can be observed in some cases.

"Managing the improvement project" or the level of effectiveness in SPI project management and control is an important issue for the company, with average rating of 4 and 2.8 as for the current situation. Managers received training on SPI essentials: "we have given the training on the SPI model, how we are going to run it, how we are setting the target, how we are reporting the target, how we are doing those process improvements". Training is essential, so managers have the knowledge base for competent company running.

"Staff involvement" indicates to what extent staff members participate in SPI initiatives; it is granted with 4 points and 2.4 for the current situation. In Developers Oy the personnel is conditionally divided into several groups, each group receives information selected for it: "we built a dashboard, the dashboard is one of the ways of giving this information, and the higher you go in organization, on higher level those goals and measures actually are". In general, there is a process development team in the company, four people who are fully occupied with tasks related to SPI. Moreover, those employees have an option to develop SPI activities in some company's projects by involving extra human resources. That results in 30 % of all company personnel involved into some SPI initiatives and one team of professionals entirely working on those issues.

"Training and mentoring" refer to training provided to SPI team by experts. It gets 4 in average importance and 2.4 for the current situation. The factor is highly graded by the company representatives; however the situation with SPI policy is special and influences this factor. Developers Oy pilots SPI activities in two big projects: one is related to requirements engineering, the second to "formal workflow for actual software development, or so-called configuration management". Personnel working for these projects were specially selected for this purpose, meaning that: "they are not average people; they are well motivated and clearly understand advantages that the company receives by SPI initiatives". Those people do not need too much special mentoring. On the other hand, company provided some training to middle level management, but it was not quite successful: "unfortunately, we have some kind of failure there; we have done some internal training and motivation. It happened because this training was not enough and people were not willing to have it further".

"Change agents" normally support SPI activities at the company level, and "opinion leaders" at the local levels. This factor is evaluated as 3.8 by importance and 3 as on present. The overall attitude toward SPI specialists is ambiguous: "there are some people who are a little bit jealous to SPI team by not being involved; some who are afraid of changes and not willing to change any processes". Developers Oy does not have so-called change agents but few people on executive level who are "eager, well-committed and able to explain benefits SPI activities are targeted at. They are highly respected in the company".

"Awareness of SPI" shows how well SPI initiatives are promoted in the company as a short and long term beneficial activities. The factor is evaluated with importance of 3.6 and 3.2 for current situation. Developers Oy is rapidly growing SW company, getting more new employees and processes evolve, so people understand the necessity of change: "now when we have had some small evidence of success employees observe the benefits the whole company can get. There are concerns about technology and processes in use, but over all people see benefits of doing SPI". Globally, benefits for developers are perceived as following: "developers become professionals; they understand the essences of SW development, not the programming language, not as-it-is status, but on how to develop in more efficient way and improve the quality at the same time, so they do not need to debug few times".

"Resource allocation" defines how human and time resources are dedicated to SPI. The importance is graded with 3.6. Even though current state is the company receives only 3 points, senior product development manager declares: "in Developers Oy the situation is rather stable, we have enough resources".

"SPI goals" important to be distinguished and understood within the company. Developers Oy assesses it as 3.6 and 2.8 for the current state. Management of the company has clear and well explained position on the company's goals and future vision; business requirements normally derive from those goals, in turns processes appear from business requirements: "all SPI actions we perform are aligned with the strategy of the company". Senior product development manager claims that employees of engineering processes and support department (partly responsible for SPI activities) are well motivated and trained towards SPI goals and their correlation with the overall strategy of the company. At the same time personnel not involved into SPI activities on daily basis have challenges which are not a positive sign. Developers Oy needs certain measurements and evidence of successful SPI initiatives from other departments as well.

"Stabilizing change process" indicates continuous support of SW processes, their maintenance and improvement at the local level. This factor gets 3.6 points for importance and 2 for the current state. That factor assumes regular feedbacks from employees and management support. Developers Oy does not have feedbacks as widespread practice: "the only things that we have are wiki and common workplaces where we have discussions and comment projects; this is not obligatory, but we can have valuable feedback during meetings and reviews". Nevertheless, the company plans to introduce new questions on SPI to the mandatory internal satisfactory survey. As a motivation Developers Oy holds regular meeting on running SPI initiatives in the company where key players and opinion leaders present.

"Encouraging communication and collaboration" assumes communication between the members of one team and members of different departments. Developers Oy organizes regular meetings for the personnel and tries to increase interactivity and communication by introducing new and modern tools for expressing anonymous opinion and providing feedback. The company has kick off meetings for R&D department twice a year where they discuss achievements. Personnel exchange information primarily on project level, not much on business unit level.

"Providing enhanced understanding" correlates with a factor of "SPI goals" and means existence of knowledge in current SW processes and business environment. Some people in the company relate their contribution to SPI initiatives as to overall corporate mission and vision, some not.

"Tailoring improvement activities" is adaptation of SPI activities and needs of specific departments within the company. SPI activities effort to specific strengths and weaknesses of different teams and departments in Developers Oy: "it is a reality, all the teams are different and all of them have to be handled differently. It is done case by case, for example testing personnel has to be treated differently than program managers. Program managers are easy to explain why we do certain things, while testers mostly have distractive mindset and pessimistic to everything". In marketing department the situation is also challenging: "we have to motivate them heavily to get their stake of involvement".

"Defined SPI implementation methodology" is defined as guidance on how to implement SPI activities. Developers Oy organized seminar on SPI model used in the company disseminating how the company was going to run the model, how targets were settled, how the target would be reported, how process improvement was implemented and accepted to use. There two types of managers supporting SPI activities. First group is eager to share their practical knowledge by demonstrating how processes are performed; second group is well concerned about methods of work but delegate the guidance to responsible people.

5 Conclusions

In this research we conducted a pilot case-study on CSFs in SPI in Finnish software company Developers Oy to verify whether the company manages performance of CSF in SPI initiatives and how the company manages them.

By examining comprehensive literature we selected main papers on the topic. The CSFs in SPI found by scholars are different but mostly frequent mentioned are: senior management involvement in SPI initiatives, importance of clear vision and understanding of SPI goals, technical staff participation, and motivation for employees to be part of SPI initiative. Besides, both technical and managerial human resources need to be involved in SPI program. All scholars perceive the organizational issues, human involvement and change management as the key elements of any SPI initiative.

The factors selected from the literature generated the evaluation questionnaire on importance and as-it-is status of CSFs for the case company. Several case company representatives evaluated the list. CSFs were rated and commented by Developers Oy. We observe the main challenges with people and change management factors. The most important CSFs needed improvements are: management commitment, staff involvement, unfreezing the organization and stabilizing change process. Those factors are interrelated. Unfreezing the organization and overcome resistance for change within the whole company is problematic without proper management commitment. This commitment is needed at all levels of organization starting with higher management. In Developers Oy the situation on the higher level is rather promising, while middle management level is challenging one. The factor of staff involvement relates directly to management commitment. If managers do not motivate the personnel, do not provide support and personal example employees are not willing to take part into novelties and refuse changes. Therefore, it is basically impossible to have any positive feedback about SPI initiatives if regular workers do not get enough support. Based on the opinion of senior product development manager we conclude that one of the main challenges within SPI program is managing the change resistance. Currently, managers have no training how to handle various situations since all employees are different and should be treated differently. This kind of training is needed and for key SPI players as well. Managing the change resistance allows constructing initial improvement plan on that issue.

The main finding of this pilot study shows that proper management of CSFs increase usefulness of offering SPI to its key beneficiaries, thus stakeholders values are taken into consideration.

6 Future Research

The field of CSF in SPI is well developed and studied but there is limited number of research about CSF in SPI in small- and medium sized companies (SME). In addition we did not find many papers devoted to research in the field of CSF related stakeholders in SPI in SMEs. At the same time small – and medium size companies play significant role on the information technology world market. Based on the results of the current paper and domain observation we plan to conduct wide exploratory study with large sample of companies on CSF related to stakeholder in SPI activities in SMEs.

References

1. Aaen, I., Arent, J., Mathiassen, L., Ngwenyama, O.: A conceptual map of software process improvement. Scand. J. Inf. Syst. **13**, 123–146 (2001)
2. Abrahamson, P.: Is management commitment a necessity after all in software process improvement? In: 26th Euromicro Conference Proceedings, vol. 2, pp. 246–253 (2000)
3. Arent, J., Nordjerg, E.: Software process improvement as organizational knowledge creation: a multiple case study. In: Proceedings of the 33rd Hawaii International Conference on System Sciences, Maui, Hawaii, USA (2000)
4. Bazzana, G., Fagnoni, E.: Process improvement in the Internet Service Providing. In: Messnarz, R., Tully, C. (eds.) Better Software Practice for Business Benefit: Principles and Experiences. IEEE computer society, pp. 267–279 (1999)
5. Boehm, B.: Value-Based software engineering: reinventing "EarnedValue" monitoring and control. SIGSOFT Softw. Eng. Notes, **28** (2003)
6. Börjesson, A., Mathiassen, L.: Successful process implementation. IEEE Softw. **21**(4), 36–44 (2004)
7. Debou, C., Courtel, D., Lambert, H., Fuchs, N., Haux, M.: Alcatel's experience with process improvement. In: Messnarz, R., Tully, C. (eds.) Better Software Practice for Business Benefit: Principles and Experiences. IEEE computer society, pp. 281–301 (1999)

8. Diaz, M., Sligo, J.: How software process improvement helped Motorola. IEEE Softw. **14**(5), 75–81 (1997)
9. Dyba, T.: An impirical investigation of the key factors for success in software process improvement. IEEE Trans. Softw. Eng. **31**(5), 410–424 (2005)
10. El Emam, K., Goldenson, D., McCurley, J., Herbsleb, J.: Success or failure? modelling the likelihood of software process improvement. International Software Engineering Research Network Technical Report, ISERN-98-15 (1998)
11. Godelson, D., Herbsleb, J.: After the appraisal: a systematic survey of process improvement, its benefits, and factors that influence success, Technical report, CMU/SEI-95-TR-009, Software Engineering Institute, Pittsburg, 50 p (1995)
12. Hall, T., Rainer, A., Baddoo, N.: Implementing software process improvement: an empirical study. Softw. Process: Improv. Pract. **7**(1), 3–15 (2002)
13. Hansen, B., Rose, J., Tjørnehøj, G.: Prescription, description, reflection: the shape of the software process improvement field. Int. J. Inf. Manag. **24**(6), 457–472 (2004)
14. Humphrey, W., Snyder, T., Willis, R.: Software process improvement at Hughes aircraft. IEEE Softw. **8**(4), 11–23 (1991)
15. Espinosa-Curiel, I.E., Rodrıguez-Jacobo, J., Fernandez-Zepeda, J.A.: A framework for evaluation and control of the factors that influence the software process improvement in small organizations. J. Softw. Evol. Process **25**(4), 393–406 (2013)
16. McFeeley, B.: IDEAL: A User's Guide for Software Process Improvement. SEI, Pittsburgh (1996)
17. Niazi, M., Wilson, D., Zowghi, D.: Critical success factors for software process improvement implementation: an empirical study. Softw. Process: Improv. Pract. **11**(2), 193–211 (2006)
18. Rainer, A., Hall, T.: Key success factors for implementing software process improvement: a maturity-based analysis. J. Syst. Softw. **62**(2), 71–84 (2002)
19. Stelzer, D., Mellis, W.: Success factors of organizational change in software process improvement. Softw. Process: Improv. Pract. **4**(4), 227–250 (1998)

GamifySPI

Software Developer's Journey
A Story-Driven Approach to Support Software Practitioners

Murat Yilmaz[1,2], Berke Atasoy[3], Rory V. O'Connor[4,5](✉),
Jean-Bernard Martens[3], and Paul Clarke[4,5]

[1] Virtual Reality Laboratory, Çankaya University, Ankara, Turkey
[2] Department of Computer Engineering, Çankaya University, Ankara, Turkey
myilmaz@cankaya.edu.tr
[3] Technische Universiteit Eindhoven, Eindhoven, The Netherlands
berkeatasoy@gmail.com, j.b.o.s.martens@tue.nl
[4] Dublin City University, Dublin, Ireland
{Rory.OConnor,Paul.M.Clarke}@dcu.ie
[5] Lero, The Irish Software Engineering Research Center, Limerick, Ireland

Abstract. Agile development requires a highly iterative and collaborative design process, which relies on the successful interpretation of software development activities amongst team members throughout the overall process. However, contemporary methods and tools that support agile efforts provide little help in addressing context-specific tacit knowledge, which is difficult to externalize without a shared method of interpretation. Without a continuously updated interpretation of the project vision, it is difficult to claim a shared mental model, while this is actually vital for the success of an agile process. In this paper, we address this issue and seek guidance in an approach that is commonly used in film storycraft. Film production has ample experience with externalizing experiences with the help of visual planning tools and related techniques to orchestrate the creative efforts of vast interdisciplinary production teams. We therefore propose that methods and tools from visual storycrafting can be adapted to assist software developers, not only with externalizing and discussing context-specific tacit knowledge but also to keep them creatively engaged in the development process.

Keywords: Agile software development · Story-driven software development · Storycrafting · Software development process

1 Introduction

While agile methodologies have recently been proposed as a way to overcome challenges in the software development process, integrating agile approaches successfully into an existing company culture is actually a very challenging task.

Agile software development consists of a set of iterative software methodologies. Team-based production is advanced through collaborations of team members on the requirements that are collected from stakeholders [1]. It can be characterized by incremental development cycles, lightweight documentation, and face-to-face communication between team members. It requires teams that are capable of organizing themselves around cross-functional development activities by means of effective *tacit knowledge sharing sessions*. The basic assumption of agile methodologies is that effective software development relies on *context-specific tacit knowledge* that is at times hard to make explicit and share. The success of sharing such knowledge is affected by practitioners viewpoints, beliefs and value systems [2], as well as by their personalities [3]. Many development methodologies aim to support the conversion of tacit knowledge into formal and explicit system requirements that can in turn be converted into technical software specifications [4].

Many proponents of agile software development argue that it is more effective when a *shared mental model* [5] is developed by a team of practitioners who also have the technical skills to subsequently convert the shared objectives into technical specifications and implementations. Recent evidence suggests that this process of formulating and sharing (i.e. externalizing) tacit knowledge is actually much more difficult than the reverse transformation of explicit knowledge into tacit understanding (i.e. internalization). This latter method of knowledge transfer is known as hands on experience or learning by doing [6].

In storycraft there is a well-established tradition in representing and sharing tacit knowledge about human experiences by capturing such experiences in both textual and visual form (e.g., using storyboards). This tradition builds on the ability of most people to quickly sympathize, i.e., develop an emotional relationship, with the context and characters in a story, even in cases where this story has only been sketched in rudimentary form and has not been worked out in detail. Stories do not only convey functional information, such as the features of a new software program, but also propose contexts and users that can give meaning to such features. Stories can also assist in orchestrating team efforts, as team members develop an understanding of how they can contribute with their specific skills to the overall team objective, and possibly provide end-user value [7].

A quick, inexpensive and flexible parallel process to continuously translate tacit knowledge into explicit conversation can assist in capturing the essence of the motivation, and in understanding the impact of the actions taken by individual team members. The ability to think in terms of stories can help with externalizing context specific tacit knowledge and with coordinating the software developers' creative efforts.

From a software development point of view, storycrafting may assist the agile approach in several ways: (1) providing insight into the progress of the strategy behind the development process by visualizing not only actions and accomplishments but also the underlying reasoning and mindset, (2) providing engagement by visually capturing an explicit representation of the strategic moves between actions, (3) motivating and engaging team members into the overall process not just as *task responsibles* but also as *creative contributors*, (4) providing a common awareness of the impact of individual contributions throughout the whole process, (5) establishing a visual structure that engages practitioners not only practically but also emotionally in the task at hand.

The aim of the exploratory study that we report here was to assess the usefulness of storycrafting for improving the communication during an agile development processes. The more specific research question was whether or not we could improve an agile software development process by enhancing the visual communication process using story crafting techniques.

The remainder of the paper is organized in the following manner. Section 2 reviews relevant literature. Section 3 describes the details of our proposed approach. In the final section, we discuss the potentials and benefits of this approach.

2 Background

Agile development proposes the notion of *user stories* which describe planned features of the software artifact within a context, so that an understanding can be developed of the resulting customer experience (See Fig. 1). it has been empirically observed that this is an approach that is quite effective for capturing software requirements [8]. An important reason for this is that stories are an effective way of communicating a demand and hence an efficient way to exchange tacit knowledge [9].

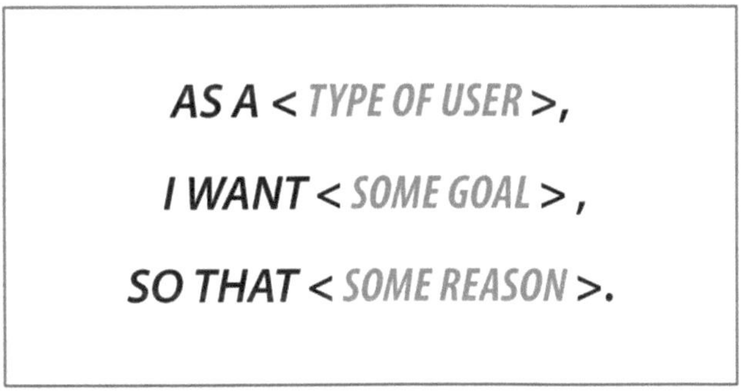

AS A < TYPE OF USER >,

I WANT < SOME GOAL >,

SO THAT < SOME REASON >.

Fig. 1. User story cards.

While the introducing *user stories* into an agile process has proven to be valuable, the full potentials of narrative imagining has not yet been accomplished. We are convinced that visual storycraft has much more to offer to an agile development process than is currently the case.

Storytelling is an explanatory activity that aims at providing a symbolic representation of a range of interactions and consequent emotions that an individual may experience with the software service under development. on one or more subjects. The contextual information within a story is important tacit knowledge that assist in developing a more explicit awareness of consumer value and the relevance of specific software requirements. Kalid and Saifullah [10] for instance proposed to use narratives as a way of capturing the tacit knowledge in a project, while Linde [11] argues that social knowledge can be transmitted effectively by using a narratives. Narratives provides a way to share tacit knowledge on socially relevant aspects such as lessons learned from previous projects, alternative ways of executing specific tasks, ways of resolving conflicts, etc.

Imagining in the form of stories is a rational thinking tool for looking into the future, predict, plan, and explain situations that do not yet exist [12]. All of the above are cognitive efforts and they require a common ground and a shared process to explicitly discuss, assess and decide. From a storycrafting perspective, agile efforts do not only promote interdisciplinary communication and process management of software development but also help to coordinate co-creative efforts towards innovative software design.

2.1 Storycrafting

Storycrafting takes various forms such as oral, written, theater and film [13]. Crafting a story does not entirely rely on the creative intuition of artistic minds. It relies on a well-established tradition in translating tacit knowledge into everyday thinking through structural frameworks and pre-defined guidelines and techniques. Aristotle maps the structure of actions in a story as a unified plot with a beginning, middle and end [14]. Propps Morphology of the Folktale establishes 31 commonly occurring themes that are called *story functions* which are classifiable actions that a protagonist can take in a story [15]. Campbell points out a common structure called Hero's Journey in every great story that has resonated through history [16]. Freytag describes a five-act structure to build a story that mostly applies to ancient Greek and Shakespearean drama [17]. Field's Paradigm establishes a three-act structure in which definitive moments called plot points control the change in direction of a story from the beginning till the end [16].

Certain forms of storycraft such as feature film-making have a proven record in managing and orchestrating highly complex production processes by interdisciplinary teams that passionately work and share an extremely complex process. Their process requires an interpretation of the tacit knowledge embedded in the scripts to be shared with a vast crowd of interdisciplinary workers. Visual planning such as story, e.g. through continuity boards, provides an efficient interface to explore options, reflect, discuss and detect problems and make changes quickly, easily and inexpensively [18].

2.2 Stories as Developer Experiences

Agile development is an exploratory process, which starts with a prioritization of aspects such as required collaboration and interaction in the software development process. Consequently, recent development and design challenges in software development require more human-centered approaches and the software industry is shifting its demands on software practitioners towards soft skills. In order to achieve sustainability in software decision making, practitioners should understand their dependence on their teammates, respect skills and approaches that they do not master themselves, and be able to cope with personality differences.

In this paper, we suggest that we should more rigorously organize software development experiences in terms of stories that can be used for communicating our development experience to other software practitioners. Furthermore, we suggest that agile software development demands a concrete but flexible way with a quick and inexpensive interface to externalize and capture the fleeting moments of discussion and decision-making in order to improve the quality of the design and development processes.

3 Software Developer's Journey

We propose a novel approach to assist teams in coordinating software development tasks by using a visual externalization process. The goal is to reveal important aspects of the software development progress in a visual environment with the intention to promote transfer of tacit knowledge. Software practitioners' experiences can be in the form of code snippets that solve a known issue, or propose an alternative approach towards resolving previously encountered problems.

Firstly, based on the notion of a shared metaphor that is one of the twelve practices in agile development [19], the second step in the process is to interpret the project tasks jointly with team members by exploring the potential statements in which such a metaphor is invoked. Here, we interpret software development as a theory building activity, which aims to bridge the gap between tacit knowledge and software project documentation by effectively capturing the design knowledge from an experience-focused perspective.

Secondly, a software team assesses the collected software development experiences into story elements such as *actors*, *domains* and *artifacts* in order to utilize them in the software design process. The tacit knowledge consists of a set of rules and procedures that can assist in reaching decisions on specific development tasks [20], and hence guides the overal software development process.

Thirdly, a software team identifies the key stakeholder(s), i.e., relevant personas and contexts as well as the intended experience. The demographics of the persona and his relationship to the software development tasks are essential for understanding what defines successful use of the software. Identifying stakeholder conflicts at an early stage can provide a software team with an understanding of the emotional consequences that completing or failing software tasks may have. There is evidence to suggest that such an understanding can have influence the success of a software project [21].

Fourthly, the projected experience can be contextualized through a visual representation of all actions that can shared, e.g., by means of an agile

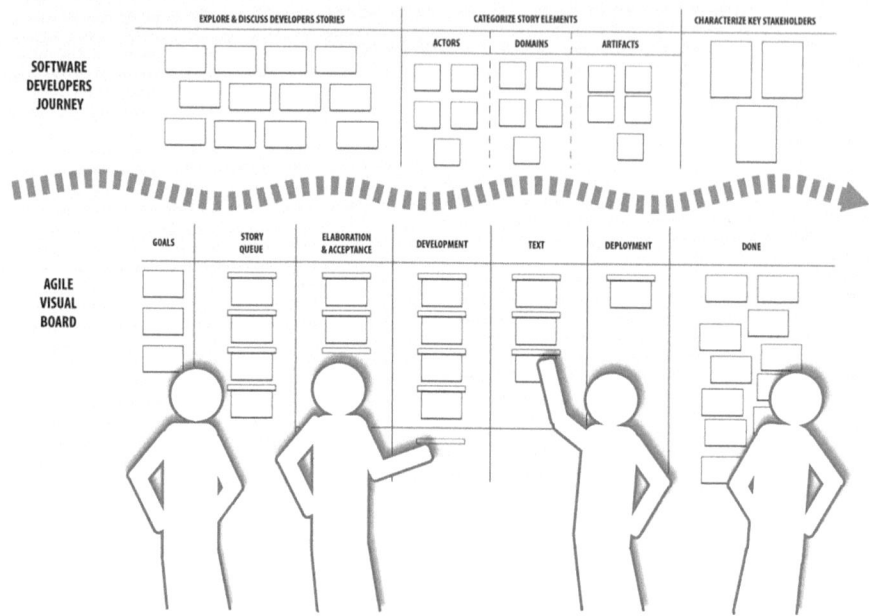

Fig. 2. The enhanced agile task-board.

task board[1], which may in turn help to coordinate the software development process (see Fig. 2).

To explore the feasibility of our approach, we initially subscribed to the guidance of a method called Storyply. This method explores the application of storycraft in user experience design in order to improve the focus of interdisciplinary design teams on the targeted end-user experience [22]. We appropriated certain stages of Storyply Method in order to test some of our claims on a senior graduation project conducted by a team of three novice researchers at Cankaya University Computer Engineering Department (see Fig. 3). The project group was developing a VR-based application for creating a virtual storytelling experience about GobekliTepe, which is a pre-historic site about 12000 years old at SanliUrfa, Turkey. The project lasted for a year and it was supervised by two of the authors.

The team used Scrumban, which is a combination of Kanban and Scrum, in their development process. We added two phases from the Backstage of Storyply, i.e., Insploration and Categorizing Story Elements, as well as a condensed version of the On-Stage phase. We were interested in observing the effects of the Storyply activities on the Scrumban methodology and on the team process and outcomes. Our preliminary results indicate the effectiveness of the proposed approach in several respects. Firstly, it helped the development team to build a shared metaphor. Secondly, the visual progress in the development phase was

---

[1] The task board is a visual display of the software development progress.

Fig. 3. Testing how storycraft resonates with software developers while conducting a scrumban process with support from storyply.

visible to all team members so that it could be used as a reference in the discussions. Thirdly, this approach helped the team to reveal already at an early stage the potential problems that needed to be resolved in the software development process.

4 Discussions

A story is a structural artifact which can effectively be used in software development. Software practitioners should focus on software development tasks where stories can act as a narrative asset that may improve visual planning of software development and to keep team motivation alive. Stories can guide software teams to give priority to the experiences of targeted customers already in the early stages of the design process.

Stories guide us to create a personal interpretation of a system metaphor, which is valuable for self-reflection of the software practitioners. A shared metaphor can help a software team explore the diversity of different perspectives and formalize a shared vision in very early stages of the development. This is inline with Beck [23] who already suggested that a team should simplify a software artifact to fit a a single metaphor. Software practitioners might agree that the design of a particular software service is similar to an assembly or product line or it may look like a coffee shop with service personnel and chiefs and customers. As it follows a storified life-cycle, the proposed approach also promotes that software teams may more easily claim ownership of the software artifacts.

An important goal of this preliminary study is to demonstrate the benefits of a story-driven software development. In fact it is important to capture and store the excessively valuable tacit knowledge using a rich story-based approach. Consequently, we claim the need for an emerging skill called *creatively engaged software practitioners* who also master the process of capturing software development experiences. Software practitioners will hopefully recognize the importance of such an approach and the potential benefits that it can bring.

Although this research envisions a preliminary framework that utilizes stories in an agile development, more qualitative and quantitative data should be collected on the proposed approach. In particular, this approach needs further testing with software teams conducting agile processes and experts should iterate on the apprach based on such observations. Most importantly, a future cross-national study involving various software development teams from different countries is essential. There is, therefore, a definite need for a complementary study that could also assess the long-term effects of using stories in agile software development.

References

1. Penkar, S.: From Projects to Programs: A Project Manager's Journey. CRC Press, Boca Raton (2013)
2. O'Connor, R.V., Yilmaz, M.: Exploring the belief systems of software development professionals. Cybern. Syst. **46**, 528–542 (2015)
3. Yilmaz, M., O'Connor, R.V., Clarke, P.: An exploration of individual personality types in software development. In: Barafort, B., O'Connor, R.V., Poth, A., Messnarz, R. (eds.) EuroSPI 2014. CCIS, vol. 425, pp. 111–122. Springer, Heidelberg (2014)
4. Nonaka, I., Takeuchi, H.: The Knowledge-Creating Company: How Japanese Companies Create the Dynamics of Innovation. Oxford University Press, New York (1995)
5. Larman, C., Vodde, B.: Practices for Scaling Lean & Agile Development: Large, Multisite, and Offshore Product Development with Large-Scale Scrum. Pearson Education, Upper Saddle River (2010)
6. Ryan, S., O'Connor, R.V.: Acquiring and sharing tacit knowledge in software development teams: an empirical study. Inf. Softw. Technol. **55**, 1614–1624 (2013)
7. Patton, J., Economy, P.: User Story Mapping: Discover the Whole Story Build the Right Product. O'Reilly Media Inc., Sebastopol (2014)
8. Cohn, M.: User Stories Applied: For Agile Software Development. Addison-Wesley Professional, New York (2004)
9. Groff, T., Jones, T.: Introduction to Knowledge Management. Routledge, London (2012)
10. Kalid, K.S., Saifullah, M.S.: Project story capturing system: the use of storytelling to capture tacit. In: Building a Competitive Public Sector with Knowledge Management Strategy, p. 315 (2013)
11. Linde, C.: Narrative and social tacit knowledge. J. Knowl. Manage. **5**, 160–171 (2001)
12. Turner, M.: The Literary Mind: The Origins of Thought and Language. Oxford University Press, New York (1998)
13. McClean, S.T.: Digital Storytelling: The Narrative Power of Visual Effects in Film. MIT Press, Cambridge (2007)
14. Hiltunen, A.: Aristotle in Hollywood: The Anatomy of Successful Storytelling. Intellect Books, Bristol (2002)
15. Hammond, S.P.: Children story authoring with propps morphology (2011)

16. Duarte, N.: Resonate: Present Visual Stories that Transform Audiences. Wiley, New York (2013)
17. Freytag, G.: Freytag's Technique of the Drama: An Exposition of Dramatic Composition and Art. Scholarly Press, New York (1896)
18. Glebas, F.: Directing the Story: Professional Storytelling and Storyboarding Techniques for Live Action and Animation. Taylor & Francis, New York (2009)
19. Cockburn, A.: Agile Software Development. Addison-Wesley Professional, Boston (2001)
20. Reber, A.S., Lewis, S.: Implicit learning: an analysis of the form and structure of a body of tacit knowledge. Cognition **5**, 333–361 (1977)
21. Boehm, B.: Value-based software engineering: reinventing. ACM SIGSOFT Softw. Eng. Notes **28**, 3 (2003)
22. Markopoulos, P., Martens, J.B., Malins, J., Coninx, K., Liapis, A. (eds.): Collaboration in Creative Design. Methods and Tools. Springer, Cambridge (2016)
23. Beck, K.: Extreme Programming Explained. Addison-Wesley, Reading (2000)

Gamification Proposal for Defect Tracking in Software Development Process

Gloria Piedad Gasca-Hurtado[1(✉)], María Clara Gómez-Alvarez[1], Mirna Muñoz[2], and Jezreel Mejía[2]

[1] Maestría en Ingeniería de Software, Facultad de Ingeniería,
Universidad de Medellín, Carrera 87 no. 30-65, Medellín, Colombia
{gpgasca,mcgomez}@udem.edu.co
[2] Centro de Investigación en Matemáticas, Av. Universidad no 222,
98068 Zacatecas, Mexico
{mirna.munoz,jmejia}@cimat.mx

Abstract. Software process improvement is an approach used by software industries to increase the productivity and quality of their processes and products. One important issue is the social interaction among the team members looking for productivity enhancement, motivation and training, among others. However, these social skills are difficult to train in a traditional way both in academic and industrial environments. This difficulty could be address-using gamification like a strategy to improve the social factors related to the software development process. In this paper, we present a gamification proposal focused on training in defect tracking. This training looks for evaluation, implementation and use of a pedagogical instrument (game) for train in defect tracking practices following the principles of gamification. Additionally this instrument promotes other skills like teamwork, negotiation and effective communication.

Keywords: Evaluation · Gamification · Software process improvement · Defect tracking

1 Introduction

Process improvement is an issue of software engineering that has gained great importance in recent decades, due to software development companies are in a continuous search of high quality software production. For this reason, companies make large investments to improve their processes, but they don´t always achieve the expected results [1].

This lack of success is reflected in reports like The Standish Group International, Inc 2015. This report shows that 6 % of projects in large companies were successful, 9 % for medium companies and 62 % for small businesses. In addition, other studies of The Standish Group states that 52 % of the projects faces changes of scope, time or budget, generating failure in pre-agreed functionality. On the other hand, 21 % of projects fail. This results in only 29 % of projects met the terms of quality, cost and time [2].

These indicators show problems related to technical difficulties of software engineering in areas such as requirements engineering, planning and project management, process improvement and software quality. These technical problems are associated with engineering social factors such as skills development in professionals needed to improve the performance of work teams and organizations [3]. For this reason, nowadays training strategies are applied in work teams to ensure the assimilation of technical concepts and skills development such as leadership, teamwork, effective communication and negotiation in professionals [4].

The gamification has become a strategy of facilitation of knowledge transfer incorporating dynamics associated with games.

This strategy allows achieving high levels of motivation to work with team members, integrate participants to increase technical knowledge and increase progress indicators of software process improvement needed for the success of the implementation of good practices in organizations [5].

The gamification is a trend in the area of software engineering and software development that offers interesting alternatives to face difficulties related to skills development.

In this paper, a gamification proposal is described to track software defects in the context of PSP/TSP framework. This proposal is designed trying to incorporate ten gamification principles, and a preliminary validation is proposed based on an empirical method for software engineering. Part of the validation is based on a questionnaire applied to professionals who have participated in the game application as a pilot study case.

In Sect. 2 the theoretical framework on which the proposal is based is presented. In Sect. 3 the gamification proposal is described to track software development defects, designed using a set of steps to establish the components of the game. In Sect. 4 a preliminary validation of the proposal from the selection of an empirical method for software engineering is described. Finally, in Sect. 5 the conclusions and future work are presented.

2 Theoretical Framework

Gamification has been described as the use of game elements to improve user engagement and experience with non-game initiatives [6]. For the application of gamification in several sectors like recruitment, planning, training and development of personal skills, among others, Oprescu *et al.* proposes ten principles [7]:

1. *Orientation:* the participant is the center of the experience for achieving engagement, sense of control and self-efficacy. In the same way, games encourage participants to progress through various levels with increasing difficulty.
2. *Persuasive elements:* through game elements, we can obtain certain information of participants or change their initial behavior.
3. *Learning orientation:* games can help developing skills, motivational outcomes and knowledge acquisition.
4. *Achievement based on rewards:* games could be oriented to a positive feedback related with goals achievement as a way to increase self-efficacy.

5. *Y Generation adaptable:* games allow Y generation individuals express their opinion in a fun, engaging and rewarding environment.
6. *Amusement factors:* games include humor, play and fun elements to increase participants' motivation and satisfaction.
7. *Transformative:* gamification combines competition and collaboration and could integrate moral decisions to enhance the desired skills in participants.
8. *Well-being oriented:* games could focus on personal and organizational well-being.
9. *Research generating:* games could allow participants to collaborate in order to identify future improvements in the application area.
10. *Knowledge-based:* gamification could be based on knowledge, either as an outcome or as feedback. In fact, educational games have learning goals related to concepts of a subject.

In the context of Software Process Improvement (SPI) Herranz et al. [8] show a high-level gamification framework for the adoption of process improvement culture. This proposal has six phases: (a) viability, (b) business goals, (c) user's objectives and motivations, (d) activities to enhance, (e) gamification proposal, (f) implementation and (g) assessment. Such gamification framework is oriented to organization needs and software teams involved in a SPI initiative. Taran proposes a board game to present the main concepts of risk management in software projects [9]. In the area of requirements engineering, Zapata et al. proposes requirements game for promoting teamwork, user needs analysis and cooperation [10]. Such approaches attempts to adapt gamification principles in the areas of software engineering and software process improvement.

3 Gamification Proposal to Track Software Defects

The gamification proposal is defined using the method for teaching instruments design [11]. This method is based on: (a) the experience as immediate and primary resource of human being and (b) the gamification in an educational environment as a strategy to stimulate and increase the motivation of participants. The method proposes to carry out a series of sequential steps to obtain a teaching instrument as shown in Fig. 1.

The following describes each one of the instrument components in a way that can be systematically applied in the training process of institutionalization of culture of defect tracking in software development teams.

3.1 Components of the Gamification Proposal

According to the method for teaching instruments design [11], the proposal presented below is equivalent to a teaching instrument, from now on called game for tracking defects in software development. The components of this game are shown in Fig. 2.

The following section describes in detail each one of the components that structure the gamification proposal.

Game Learning Goals. The first game component are the learning goals defined based on the recommendations of instrument design method [11]. For the selection of

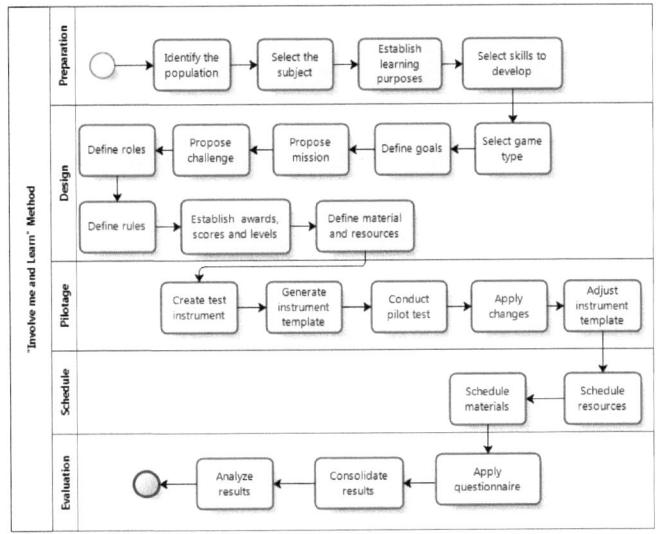

Fig. 1. Gamified method for teaching instruments design

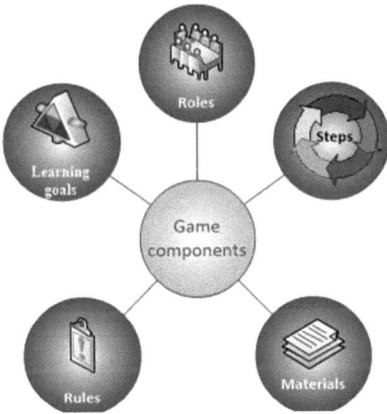

Fig. 2. Game components for tracking software defects

the learning goals, it is necessary to analyze the main concepts of the training subject and skills and abilities desired in the professionals. In the case of the game proposed in this paper the goals are:

Goal 1. Recognizing the roles of a software development team according to the PSP/TSP framework.

Goal 2. Identifying the responsibilities and goals to be achieved for each phase of a software development project.

Goal 3. Promoting social skills in teamwork that facilitate the interaction of its members such as negotiation, effective communication, teamwork and creativity.

Goal 4. Identifying business requirements in each phase and verifying such requirements from the results obtained.

Goal 5. Understanding the basic formulas for measuring defects and their importance in controlling the product quality.

Game Roles. The second component corresponds to the roles table (Table 1). It is important to define the following roles of the game taking into account the responsibilities of each team member.

Table 1. Roles and responsibilities of the development team

Role	Responsability	Function
Leader	Coordinate the development team. Understand and present the instructions and material for paper boats construction. Ensure that the acceptance criteria expected are met.	Team and work coordination. Leader cannot built paper boats during constructions periods.
Developer	Build origami paper boats based on the guidelines [12, 13].	Building paper boats following the guidance and acceptance criteria.
Tester	Verify the quality of the finished product and take measures.	Performing verifications of products from verifications guides (See Fig. 3). Registration of defect information and taking quality metrics.

Game Steps. The third component of the proposal are the game steps, which serve to facilitate the introduction of the basics concepts of defects tracking in software development. The game is based on an analogy that simulates a software development environment with paper boats construction. The steps to follow are:

Step 1. Establish work teams distributing participants to represent roles such as leader, developer and tester.

Step 2. Build paper boats during four iterative and incremental phases. During the phases it is included the defects feedback identified in built products. Feedback phases are established under the principles of software verification and taking measurements of product quality.

Step 3. Check the quality of the developed product and take metrics. Participants who have the role of tester take quality measures. These measurements are recorded in the registration defects templates (See Fig. 3d). For verification of the quality of the developed products, verification guides are used where the acceptance criteria are described. This process of verification, testing and taking measurements allows knowing the performance and productivity of work teams.

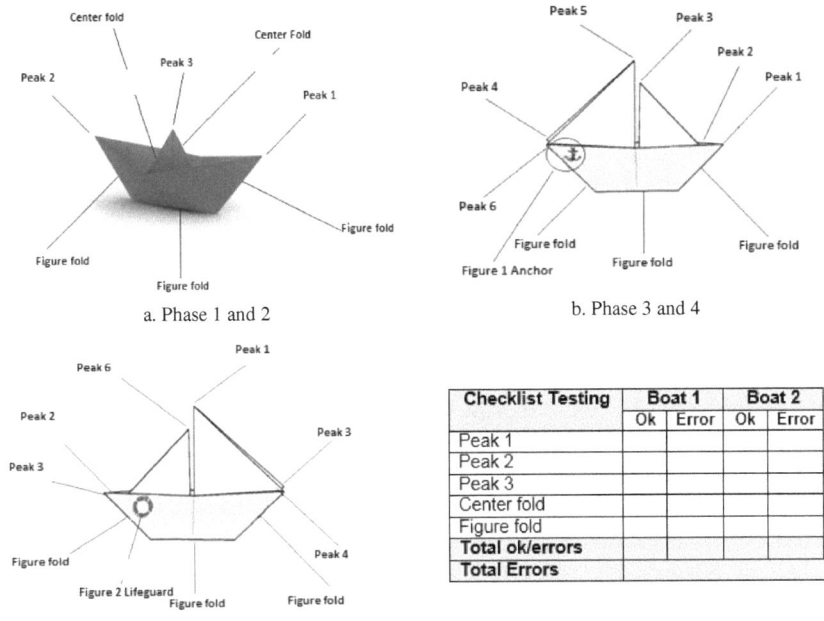

Fig. 3. Guidelines to verify and record information of paper boats built.

Game Materials. The fourth component of the game are the necessary materials, i.e. since the game consists in boat building from origami instructions as simulation of development of a software product, the required materials are: sheets of paper, pencils and sheet of origami instructions [12, 13].

Games Rules. The fifth component is the set of rules necessary to achieve the objective of the game, i.e. achieve the highest team performance and demonstrate improvements in the process of building paper boats.

Rule 1. Conform teams of at least three members with the following roles: (a) leader, (b) developer and (c) tester.

Rule 2. The facilitator defines and explains to the leaders acceptance criteria of paper boats. Such criteria refer to software quality requirements. In the game acceptance criteria relate to the folds, uniformity, wrinkles, false folds, brands and paper breaks.

Rule 3. The facilitator gives the leader the material and origami instruction sheet for building paper boats. Five units of white paper of 32 cm by 25.5 cm are provided in each phase.

Rule 4. Participants should build paper boats in a process consisting of four phases. Each phase has an origami instruction sheet for each product to build [12]. In phases 1 and 2 (See Fig. 3a) a paper boat of low complexity is built and in phases 3 and 4 (See Fig. 3b and c) participants build a paper boat of medium complexity.

Rule 5. The participant with the role of developer must build five paper boats per phase, taking into account: (a) acceptance criteria defined and explained by the facilitator, and (b) the duration of each phase. For phase 1 and phase 2 duration is 5 min, while for phase 3 duration is 15 min and for phase 4 duration is 20 min.

Rule 6. Upon completion of construction time, developers deliver finished products to the tester for verification, without the intervention of other team members. To perform this task, the tester has the verification guidelines for each phase as shown in Fig. 3.

Rule 7. The tester and the leader record the verification and validation metrics for each phase. In the template shown in Fig. 3d defects found are quantified according to acceptance criteria and the result of verification is recorded.

Rule 8. Once the information in the verification templates are registered, the tester and project leader measure defects according to formulas (1), (2) and (3).

$$PID = CT * (\frac{TPE}{PT}) \qquad (1)$$

Where, PID = Phase injected defects CT = Construction time, TPE = Total phase errors and PT = Phase Time

$$PRD = CT * [\frac{(PPTE - CPTE)}{PT}] \qquad (2)$$

Where, PRD = Phase removed defects, PPTE = Previous phase total errors and CPTE = Current phase total errors

$$PP = \frac{Removed\ defects}{Total\ injected\ errors} \qquad (3)$$

Note: Time variable in phase corresponds to the time of constructions plus time of verification for paper boats (5 min).

Formula (1) refers to defects injected in phases 1 and 3, where teams build a paper boat for the first time. This formula allows to determine the average of defects of each paper boat. This task pretends to simulate the way how injected defects into a software project are quantified.

In phases 2 and 4, partcipants build for the second time the same paper boat and removed defects are measured. This task is included in the game as a mechanism for evaluation of productivity and level of expertise achieved by the team with respect to the previous phase.

Through this metric, participants reflect on issues such as the importance of quality over quantity of developed features and the importance of building software products met the customer's quality requirements.

With such formulas is possible to obtain the value of process performance (PP) from the metric indicated in the formula (3).

Rule 9.   At the end of each phase, the tester shall submit to the team a report of the verification done and measures of injected and removed defects per phase. This game activity intends that participants recognize the performance achieved as a team and productivity improvements during different phases. In addition, this exercise helps to developing communication skills and teamwork between testers and developers.

Rule 10. At the end of the four phases, the facilitator should promote a space for reflection about issues such as learning achieved, the different performed roles, the strategy to follow in the game to achieve the highest productivity and lessons learned from teamwork.

The following section presents the preliminary validation of the gamification proposal. This validation consists in the establishment of the existing correlation between the gamification proposal and the gamification principles previously presented.

4 Preliminary Validation of Gamification Proposal

Because of the importance of human activities in software development, many of the research methods that are appropriate to software engineering are drawn from disciplines that study human factors. A study of selecting empirical methods for software engineering describes a set of empirical methods according to the type of research [14]. This paper is associated to a research project in an early stage of development, for this reason we are interested in establishing relationships between the gamification principles and the gamification proposal presented in this paper like a preliminary validation form.

4.1 Establishment of Relationships like Preliminary Validation

Before establishing relationships between the principles and the gamification proposal, we apply a questionnaire as a way to measure the student satisfaction regarding the gamification proposal. This exercise was a key input for the preliminary validation of the gamification proposal, because is considered an additional step in the the game development process. The questionnaire method was applied using non-probabilistic sample by means of snowball technique by identifying which individuals can participate in this pilot [15].

For the validation, we use the principles of gamification proposed by Oprescu *et al.* [7] to correlate them with the components of the gamification proposal through the question: *Is the gamification principle correlated to the gamification proposal components?*. We identify the correlation with the gamification proposal components through the analysis and comparison of each gamification principle. The purpose is validating the adoption of the gamification principles in the proposal to reach a gamified

Table 2. Preliminary validation of gamification proposal

Principle	Relationship	Score value				
		1	2	3	4	5
1	Rule 4	☐	☐	☐	X	☐
2	Rule 9	☐	☐	☐	X	☐
3	Learning goals	☐	☐	☐	☐	X
4	Rule 9	☐	☐	☐	X	☐
5	Rule 10	☐	☐	☐	X	☐
6	Materials, Rule 4 & Fun level	☐	☐	☐	☐	X
7	Rule 1 and 8	☐	☐	☐	☐	X
8	Rule 2 and 3	☐	☐	☐	☐	X
9	Rule 5, 6 and 8	☐	☐	☐	☐	X
10	Rule 8, 9 and 10	☐	☐	☐	☐	X

environment for defect tracking in software development. The results of this analysis are presented in Table 2.

In order to complement the validation using correlation elements as proposed by empirical research [14], an evaluation of the correlation level identified was realized. The last column of Table 2 shows the assessment established in a consensus with an experts focus group. For achieving this score, a qualitative assessment scale was defined according to a Likert scale (Table 3).

Table 3. Likert scale for score correlation value

Likert scale	Description
5	Exists a direct correlation between the gamification principle and the proposal evidenced on more than one of his components.
4	Exists a direct correlation between the gamification principle and the proposal evidenced only in one of his components.
3	Exists a direct correlation between the gamification principle and the proposal, but there is no evidence in his components. The evidence is present in the case study results.
2	Exists a subjective correlation without evidence in the proposal components.
1	Don't exist correlation between the gamification principle and the proposal.

4.2 Discussion

Researchers experts in software process improvement, software defects management and tracking, and gamification in software engineering participate in two work sessions. These experts evaluate five gamification principles by session. The input for this evaluation was the qualitative scale defined in Table 3 with the premise of group concensus. As a result of such sessions the score value for each gamification principle was assigned, marking with an x the agreed value.

The first principle has assigned a score value of 4 because exists a direct correlation between this principle and the proposal evidenced in Rule 4. Such rule refers to different levels of difficulty when participants construct paper boats in each phase.

The second principle has assigned a score value of 4 because exists a direct correlation between this principle and the proposal evidenced in Rule 9. This rule describes the tester feedback to the team about defects injected and removed in the product (paper boat). Such feedback helps to identify the importance of defect tracking process in product quality assurance.

The third principle has assigned a score value of 5, according to Likert scale (Table 3) because exists a direct correlation between this principle and the proposal evidenced by the five learning goals of the game. Learning goals show his educational purpose related to the identification of roles and responsibilities in software development teams according to the PSP/TSP framework.

The fourth principle has assigned a score value of 4 because exists a direct correlation between this principle and the proposal evidenced in Rule 9. This rule describes tester feedback to the team for improving the product. Such activity helps to develop strong relationships between different roles in a project team and improves team performance.

The fifth principle has assigned a value of 4, because it exists a direct correlation between this principle and the proposal evidenced in Rule 10. This rule determines that the facilitator should generate a reflection space more attractive looking for participants' responses about the learning achieved and lesson learned.

The other principles have assigned a score value of due to exists a direct correlation between the principle and the proposal evidenced on more than one of his components (Table 4).

Table 4. Correlation between Principles and Components

Principle	Component	Justification
6	Materials, Rule 4 and Fun level	The materials include origami instructions like a fun factor for participants.
		Rule 4 presents the construction of paper boats using these instructions.
		Fun level perceived for participants in the questionnaire results, where the 83 % of participants considers very good and excellent this variable for the pilot. This assessment is associated with the analogy between the paper boats construction and software development [15].
7	Rule 1 and 8	Rule 1 of the game establishes team structure and roles to cooperate in the teamwork.
		Rule 8 shows the metrics that must be applied for tester and leader in a cooperative way to improve product quality and team performance

(*Continued*)

Table 4. (*Continued*)

Principle	Component	Justification
8	Rule 2 and 3	Rule 2 describes that facilitator explain to team leader the acceptance criteria of paper boats.
		Rule 8 associated with the calculus of metrics for defect tracking.
		Such rules promote a secure simulated environment to make decisions by leaders, developers and testers.
9	Rule 5, 6 and 8	Rule 5 describes the process of paper boats construction by the developer.
		Rule 6 explains the interaction between the tester and the team for feedback about product quality.
		Rule 8 presents the metrics for defect tracking that must be calculated by the tester and the team leader.
		These rules define the responsibilities of developer, test and leader respectively and the collaboration dynamics. Such collaboration allows defining improvements in the paper boats construction.
10	Rule 8, 9 and 10	Rule 8 includes the basic metrics for defect tracking.
		Rule 9 promotes the feedback about product quality inside the team.
		Rule 10 promotes a reflection space to discuss learning achieved by the participants.
		Such rules shows the dynamics of defect tracking through metrics applied by tester and leader, the feedback of the tester about defects for the team and the reflection space to socialize the learning achieved by the participants. All these elements allow knowledge assimilation and socialization.

The values associated with the principles are 4 and 5 in all the cases, makes evident that the gamification proposal achieve simultaneously motivation, engagement, knowledge assimilation and social skills like teamwork and effective communication in participants.

5 Conclusions and Future Work

Software development companies have among their priorities the implementation of successful projects in terms of quality, cost and time. To achieve this purpose they are interested in topics such software process improvement. However, indicators related to failure of software development projects that show problems. Some of these problems are associated with human and social factors of process improvement such skills development in professionals. For this reason, it is important the ongoing search of strategies for software engineering where motivation, assimilation of concepts and development of skills such as leadership, negotiation and teamwork are achieved. These skills are essential for social interaction within development teams. The gamification proposal presented aims to achieve the development of social skills that emerge in teamwork, which are key to consolidating software development teams of high performance. From the analysis of the gamification principles in the game components proposed it is evident that the incorporation of elements such as amusement factors, well-being and knowledge oriented promotes training related to defect management and performance improvement of software development teams.

From the work done, future lines of work arises such as:

- Apply the game in business training processes seeking to present the basics concepts of defect tracking and development of social skills, which are a critical success factor for software project teams.
- Define a mechanism of formal validation of the gamification proposal which is supported on expert judgment and data collected from controlled experiments design in software development teams of professionals in training.

References

1. Rico, D.F.: ROI of Software Process Improvement: Metrics for Project Managers and Software Engineers. Ross Publishing, Richmond (2004)
2. Standish Group, 2015 Chaos Report, Standish Group International Inc. (2015)
3. Jensen, B.K.: Responding to the enrollment crisis: alternative strategies to increasing student interest in Computer Science. J. Comput. Sci. Coll. **21**, 8 (2006)
4. President's Council of Advisors on Science and Technology, Report to the president engage to excel: producing one million additional college graduates with degrees in science, technology, engineering, and mathematics. Executive office of the president, Washington, D.C. (2012)
5. Dorling, A., McCaffery, F.: The gamification of SPICE. In: Mas, A., Mesquida, A., Rout, T., O'Connor, R.V., Dorling, A. (eds.) SPICE 2012. CCIS, vol. 290, pp. 295–301. Springer, Heidelberg (2012)
6. Rednic, E., et al.: Organize distributed work environments in a game-like fashion. In: Chen, Z., Lopez-Neri, E. (eds.) Recent Advances in Knowledge Engineering and Systems Science, pp. 213–218. WSEAS Press, Cambridge (2013)
7. Oprescu, F., et al.: I play at work—ten principles for transforming work processes through gamification. Front. Psychol. **5**(14), 1–4 (2014)
8. Herranz, E., et al.: Gamification as a disruptive factor in software process improvement initiatives. J. UCS **20**, 885–906 (2014)
9. Taran, G.: Using games in software engineering education to teach risk management. In: Proceedings of the 20th Conference on Software Engineering Education & Training, Dubin, Ireland (2007)
10. Zapata, C.M., Awad, G.: Requirements game: teaching software projects management. CLEI Electron. J. **10**(1), (2007)
11. Gasca-Hurtado, G.P., et al.: Method of pedagogic instruments design for software engineering. In: 2016 11th Proceedings Presented at the Information Systems and Technologies (CISTI), Iberian Spain (2016)

12. Build origami boats basing on the guide-lines (2015). http://www.origami-fun.com/support-files/origami-boat-print.pdf. Accessed 31st Mar 2016
13. British Origami Society (2015). http://www.britishorigami.info/practical/diagrams/simple/sailboat.php. Accessed 31st Mar 2016
14. Easterbrook, S., et al.: Selecting empirical methods for software engineering research. In: Shull, F., Singer, J., Sjøberg, D.I.K. (eds.) Guide to Advanced Empirical Software Engineering, pp. 285–311. Springer, London (2008)
15. Losada, B.M., et al.: Assessment proposal of teaching and learning strategies in software process improvement. Rev. Fac. Ing. **77**, 105–114 (2015)

Process Improving by Playing: Implementing Best Practices through Business Games

Antoni-Lluís Mesquida[1(✉)], Milos Jovanovic[1,2], and Antònia Mas[1]

[1] Department of Mathematics and Computer Science, University of the Balearic Islands,
Cra. de Valldemossa, km 7.5, 07122 Palma de Mallorca, Spain
{antoni.mesquida,milos.jovanovic,antonia.mas}@uib.es
[2] Faculty of Technical Sciences, University of Novi Sad, Trg Dositeja Obradovica 6,
21000 Novi Sad, Serbia

Abstract. This paper demonstrates the use of business games in process improvement. Research method for selecting games and their tailoring to support the activities proposed by process reference models is described. In this research two major process categories for software development companies are considered: project management and software implementation. This article focuses on project management process category (the ISO 21500 international standard for project management is taken as a reference) while software implementation is left for future research. Concrete application of one business game to the activities suggested by ISO 21500 is presented in the paper, thus showing the project management process improvement possibilities with business games.

Keywords: Process improvement · Business games · Project management · ISO 21500

1 Introduction

It is widely accepted that engagement and commitment of the people involved in the process is one of the most important factors for a successful deployment and process improvement. In order to implement a process model, organizations should know the activities that may be used in practice in order to obtain the expected outcomes. Moreover, besides just knowing the expected outcomes they should poses the proper tools, techniques and perform adequate activities that can be useful in specific process implementation. In the case of software development company two main groups of processes should be taken into account: software implementation processes and project management process.

Agile practices are increasingly used by software development companies, and according to agile principles[1], all the team members should be involved in the implementation of the new processes at organizational or project team level. Keeping all the project stakeholders engaged and maintaining a ground where they can discuss and have fun at the same time is fundamental to continuously improve the processes established [2]. To achieve the stakeholder involvement, and increase their motivation, different business games may be applied to break the usual routine. These games can be considered as a good example of tools to be used for facilitating the implementation of the techniques recommended by process reference models.

In this paper we suggest that use of business games can be helpful in certain aspects of process deployment in software development organizations. Moreover, a research gap is identified and as a future work we propose to consider games as a proper tool to be used for process implementation and also for obtaining the recommended process outcomes. In line with that, we have planned to gather, analyse and tailor games for project management and software development best practices.

Using the experience and lessons learned from previous research initiatives [3], authors suggest that scope of this research should be divided in two parts: first part should investigate business games tailoring to facilitate project management processes implementation, and second part should investigate business games tailoring to facilitate technical processes implementation. In the first part we will demonstrate everything related to the project management process tailoring. We have decided to take as a basis the process reference model of the ISO 21500 international standard [4], aligned with the process map from the PMBOK Guide [5], which is accepted on the international level by both industry and scientific population. As stated in ISO 21500, "*the project management processes described by this standard need not be applied uniformly on all projects. Therefore, the project manager should tailor the management processes for each project by determining what processes are appropriate and the degree of rigor to be applied for each process*". We truly believe that the application of business games can be seen as an attractive way to tailor the best practices recommended by the ISO 21500 processes.

Our intention is to integrate games in the project management processes of the ISO 21500 standard, and in this paper we have made a first step towards that goal. Therefore, we show how games can be used as a new technique to facilitate the implementation of the processes proposed by ISO 21500.

The paper is structured as follows. Section 2 presents previous research and a selection of games that can be used to improve software processes. Section 3 introduces the ISO 21500 international standard for project management. Section 4 presents the research method to be followed in order to satisfy the goals proposed by this investigation and Sect. 5 shows an example of the research method application. Finally, Sect. 6 concludes the paper and opens discussion about the future research to be undertaken.

2 Games for Process Improvement

Project leader and project team as a whole, should be able to select the suitable set of the games depending on their experience, background and current phase or situation of the project. Size of the project team, physical location of team members (distributed – virtual teams or centralized – working together), time boxed meetings such as retrospective, are important factors in selecting the appropriate game. Moreover, games recommended in the research may be used depending on different situational factors [6].

Different game thinking approaches may be found in the literature, specifically in software development field. Theory of drama is used by Ogland to define a game for software development organizations consequently improving the software development process [7]. Software development may be observed as a game with project resources as a limitation [8]. Iterative and collaborative strategies of software development are brought in relation with invention and communication games.

Conceptual framework for responsible gamified enterprise systems development with four phases was proposed by Raftopoulos: discover, reframe, envision and create [9]. A software project may be observed as a balancing game based on skill decision making in software [10]. Scrumban integrated gamification approach was developed by Yilmaz to guide software process improvement [11]. Additional game elements are developed as an extension to the Scrumban framework with aim of addressing the software practitioners' social concerns.

Game elements used in Agile software development have recently entered in research focus, but it is evident that involving games in software development increases motivation of project team and helps people involved to focus on shortening the development tasks and define better objectives [11]. Agile approach is more than pure process following, it is rather effective communication and teamwork between the project team and the client [12]. There are lots of games such as: timeline driven by feelings or data, known issues problems and actions and 360 degree appreciation game, to be deployed during agile meetings to foster different features of a highly effective agile team [2]. Games used in agile meetings such as retrospective or review consist of simplified game elements, however they increase the overall team motivation and have an important impact on social behaviour and team building.

3 ISO 21500 Guidance on Project Management

The standard ISO 21500:2012 [4] provides generic guidance and a high-level description of the project management concepts and processes that have impact on the achievement of projects. It describes 39 processes for project management, which are similarly structured to the PMBOK Guide [5], to be used throughout the project lifecycle.

The project management processes may be viewed from two different perspectives: either as the management of the project in a timelier manner, described as *process groups* (Initiating, Planning, Implementing, Controlling and Closing), or presenting the processes as *subject groups*. There are ten different subject groups: Integration, Stakeholder, Scope, Resource, Time, Cost, Risk, Quality, Procurement and Communication. Each process is shown in the process group and subject group in which most of the activity takes place. Table 1 collects the 39 processes of ISO 21500 classified based on the process groups and subject groups.

The project management processes in ISO 21500 are defined and described in terms of the purpose, description, primary inputs and primary outputs. In the interest of brevity, the standard does not indicate the source of all primary inputs or where primary outputs go. Table 2 collects the information provided by ISO 21500 for an exemplar process, the *Define project organization* process (P16 in Table 1).

Table 1. ISO 21500 Project management processes cross-referenced to process and subject groups.

Subject groups	Process groups				
	Initiating	Planning	Implementing	Controlling	Closing
Integration	P1. Develop project charter	P2. Develop project plans	P3. Direct project work	P4. Control project work	P6. Close project phase or project
				P5. Control changes	P7. Collect lessons learned
Stakeholder	P8. Identify stakeholders		P9. Manage stakeholders		
Scope		P10. Define scope		P13. Control scope	
		P11. Create work breakdown structure			
		P12. Define activities			
Resource	P14. Establish project team	P15. Estimate resources	P17. Develop project team	P18. Control resources	
		P16. Define project organization		P19. Manage project team	
Time		P20. Sequence activities		P23. Control schedule	
		P21. Estimate activity durations			
		P22. Develop schedule			
Cost		P24. Estimate costs		P26. Control costs	
		P25. Develop budget			
Risk		P27. Identify risks	P29. Treat risks	P30. Control risks	
		P28. Assess risks			
Quality		P31. Plan quality	P32. Perform quality assurance	P33. Perform quality control	
Procurement		P34. Plan procurements	P35. Select suppliers	P36. Administer procurements	
Communication		P37. Plan communications	P38. Distribute information	P39. Manage communications	

Table 2. Information provided by ISO 21500 for each process.

Process:	Define project organization		
Purpose:	The purpose of Define project organization is to secure all needed commitments from all the parties involved in a project.		
Description:	Roles, responsibilities and authorities that are relevant to the project should be defined in accordance with the project's nature and complexity and should consider the performing organization's existing policies. The definition of the project organizational structure includes the identification of all team members and other persons directly involved in the project work. This process includes the assignment of project responsibilities and authorities. These responsibilities and authorities may be defined at the appropriate levels of the work breakdown structure. Those definitions usually include responsibilities to perform the approved work, manage progress and allocation of resources.		
Primary inputs:	Project plans	Primary outputs:	Role descriptions
	Work breakdown structure		Project organization chart
	Resource requirements		
	Stakeholder register		
	Approved changes		

4 Research Method

In this section exact steps of used research methodology are explained. Current and future research will be divided into four sequential stages (Fig. 1), described in continuation:

1. Gathering a complete set of games and filtering the adequate games to be used for Project Management Process Improvement.
2. Mapping selected games with some of the 39 ISO 21500 processes.
3. Tailoring of the games to fulfil the activities and to obtain the outcomes of the related ISO 21500 processes.
4. Creation of a new ISO 21500 process map including the games that can be used to fulfil their activities and to obtain their outcomes.

During the first stage we will perform a complete review of literature containing games that can be used for process improvement. Some of the preselected sources to be used at this stage are [13–18].

During the second stage, we will identify all the existing relations among the game objective and the elements of the process: purpose, description, input or output. Finding the game that could be used for obtaining a particular output required by the process would be the most valuable scenario for improving the standard of interest. However, it would be also useful to identify games that can be applied to execute some of the activities proposed by the related process.

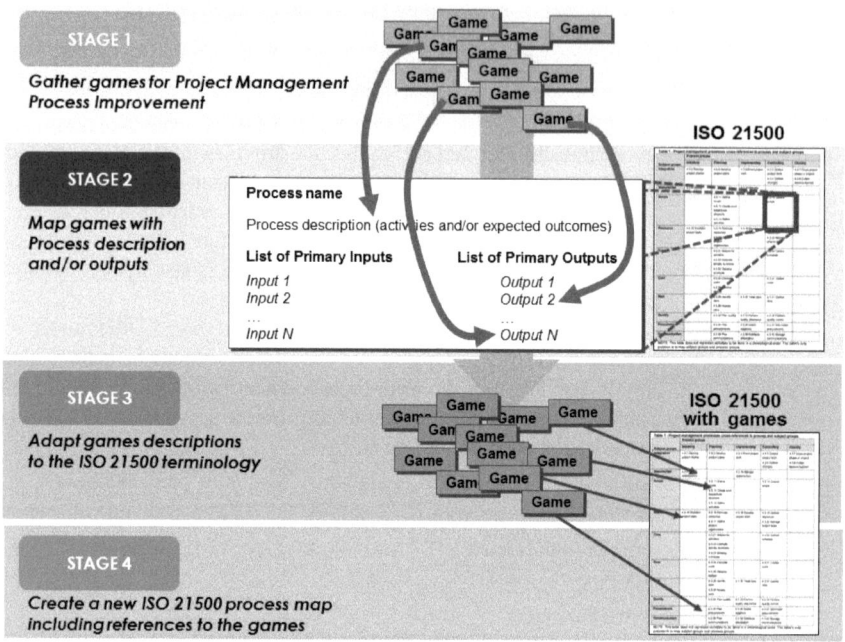

Fig. 1. Research method to be followed.

During the third stage, we will tailor the games to the related process purpose or output. Great number of existing games are quite general and applicable to many different objectives. The work at this stage will consist of customization of the game description, using the same vocabulary from the ISO 21500 standard.

Finally, during the last stage of the research, we will create a new ISO 21500 process map including games that can be used to fulfil the process reference model activities and to obtain the recommended outcomes.

5 Demonstration of the Research Method Application for One Specific Game

With the aim demonstrating the methodology of the research we plan to undertake in the future, this section shows the application of the research stages described in the previous section with one specific game. The game selected (from the ones that will be gathered during the first stage) is called *Role Expectations Matrix* [16] which is inspired by *Give-and-take Matrix* from [18]. This is a team-forming game that aims to map out the expectations among team members. It helps them to better define their roles and avoid future conflicts due to hidden or unknown expectations.

The steps to be followed in order to run this game are as follows:

1. Create a list of all the team members' roles.
2. Using the list, create a matrix with the list of roles along both horizontal and vertical axes. Label the vertical axis as "from" and the horizontal axis as "to".
3. Ask team members to write down (on separate post-its) their expectations to each one of the roles. These notes should go on the cells on a horizontal line for the team member role.
4. Discuss among the group the whole matrix. It is recommended to select one "from" role (a matrix vertical line) and then each person reads his/her expectation notes for that role. Repeat for all roles.

The objective of completing the matrix is to find the most complete picture of team members' expectations on each other.

When applying the second stage of the research method (mapping the games with process descriptions and outputs), the relations among the game and the ISO 21500 project management processes should be identified. In this case, the goal of the game can be easily linked to the process *P16. Define project organization* (see Table 2), whose purpose is "*to secure all needed commitments from all the parties involved in a project*".

In the process description it is stated that "*Roles, responsibilities and authorities that are relevant to the project should be defined in accordance with the project's nature and complexity and should consider the performing organization's existing policies*". All the roles relevant to the project should be identified by performing the steps 1 and 2 of the game.

The process description also states: "*[...] This process includes the assignment of project responsibilities and authorities. [...] Those definitions usually include responsibilities to perform the approved work, manage progress and allocation of resources*". By performing steps 3 and 4 of the game, the responsibilities and expectations for that role are identified and agreed.

Regarding the outputs of this process, by playing the game the two primary outputs (*Role descriptions* and *Project organization chart*) can be easily obtained. The Project organization chart is composed of the roles along the horizontal axis of the obtained Matrix. The Role descriptions can be completed by taking all the expectations and responsibilities written down in the post-its assigned to each role.

Moreover, the Role Expectations Matrix game can be used to widen the scope of the roles defined and include also the expectations of other external stakeholders, such as customers or providers. With this extension of the game, it could be used for the implementation of the process *P8. Identify stakeholders*, whose purpose is "*to determine the individuals, groups or organizations affected by, or affecting, the project and to document relevant information regarding their interest and involvement*". In that case, the obtained result from the game - Role Expectations Matrix could be considered as a *Stakeholder register*, the primary output to be obtained by applying this process.

During the third stage of the research (adapt games descriptions to the ISO 21500 terminology), the game should be tailored to better adapt to the two related processes *P16. Define project organization* and *P8. Identify stakeholders*. The main adaptation will consist of including the text "and other external stakeholders" in the game description after each appearance of "team members".

Finally, during the fourth research method stage (Create a new ISO 21500 process map including references to games), we will include in the new ISO 21500 process map a reference to the usage of the game Role Expectations Matrix to obtain the outputs of processes *P16. Define project organization* and *P8. Identify stakeholders*.

6 Conclusion and Future Work

In this paper it is presented how business games can be used as an additional technique for implementing the activities and best practices suggested by process models. We propose to undertake a research to show the steps to be followed by other academics and practitioners when using games for process improvement. In this research we will refer to two major process categories: project management and software implementation. Following this division, we have presented the tailoring of one concrete game (*Role Expectations Matrix*) to facilitate the implementation of two project management processes of the ISO 21500 international standard (*Define project organization* and *Identify stakeholders*).

Future work would consist in continuation of the proposed research method with aim of further adding of business games to ISO 21500 project management standard. Furthermore, the same research method will be used for the software implementation process category. After gathering the business games, as a result of the first stage of the presented research method, this game database can be used through stage two, three and four for mapping with both process standards: project management and software implementation.

Acknowledgments. This work has been partially supported by the Spanish Ministry of Science and Technology with ERDF funds under grants TIN2016-76956-C3-3-R and TIN2013-46928-C3-2-R.

References

1. Fowler, M., Highsmith, J.: The agile manifesto. Softw. Dev. **9**, 28–35 (2001)
2. Jovanovic, M., Mesquida, A.-L., Mas, A.: Process improvement with retrospectives gaming in agile software development. Commun. Comput. Inf. Sci. **543**, 287–294 (2015)
3. Mesquida, A., Mas, A.: A project management improvement program according to ISO/IEC 29110 and PMBOK. J. Softw. Evol. Process. **26**, 846–854 (2014)
4. ISO - International Organization for Standardization: ISO 21500:2012 Guidance on project management (2012)
5. Project Management Institute: A Guide to the Project Management Body of Knowledge (2013)
6. Clarke, P., O'Connor, R.V.: The situational factors that affect the software development process: towards a comprehensive reference framework. Inf. Softw. Technol. **54**, 433–447 (2012)

7. Ogland, P.: The game of software process improvement: some reflections on players, strategies and payoff. In: Norsk konferanse for organisasjoners bruk av informasjonsteknologi (NOKOBIT 2016), pp. 23–25, Trodenheim, Norway (2009)
8. Cockburn, A.: The end of software engineering and the start of economic-cooperative gaming. In: ComSIS, vol. 1, pp. 1–32 (2004)
9. Raftopoulos, M.: Towards gamification transparency: a conceptual framework for the development of responsible gamified enterprise systems. J. Gaming Virtual World. **6**, 159–178 (2014)
10. Pries-Heje, J., Baskerville, R., Levine, L., Ramesh, B.: The high speed balancing game. Scand. J. Inf. Syst. **16**, 11–54 (2004)
11. Yilmaz, M., O'Connor, R.V.: A scrumban integrated gamification approach to guide software process improvement: a Turkish case study. Teh. Vjesn. **23**, 237–245 (2016)
12. Špundak, M.: Mixed agile/traditional project management methodology – reality or illusion? Procedia Soc. Behav. Sci. **119**, 939–948 (2014)
13. Kua, P.: The Retrospective Handbook. Leanpub, Layton (2013)
14. Krivitsky, A.: Agile Retrospective Kickstarter. Leanpub, Layton (2015)
15. Gonçalves, L., Linders, B.: Getting Value Out of Agile Retrospectives. A Toolbox of Retrospective Exercises. Leanpub, Layton (2013)
16. Caroli, P., Caetano, T.: Fun Retrospectives - Activities and Ideas for Making Agile Retrospectives more Engaging. Leanpub, Layton (2015)
17. Esther, D., Larsen, D.: Agile Retrospectives - Making Good Teams Great. The pragmatic bookshelf, Dallas (2006)
18. Gray, D., Brown, S., Macanufo, J.: Game Storming - A Playbook for Innovators, Rulebreakers, and Changemakers. O'Reilly Media, Sebastopol (2010)

Gamification and Human Factors in Quality Management Systems: Mapping from Octalysis Framework to ISO 10018

Mary-Luz Sanchez-Gordón[1(✉)], Ricardo Colomo-Palacios[2], and Eduardo Herranz[1]

[1] Computer Science Department, Universidad Carlos III de Madrid,
Av. Universidad 30, Leganés, 28911 Madrid, Spain
mary_sanchezg@hotmail.com, eduardo.herranz@uc3m.es
[2] Faculty of Computer Sciences, Østfold University College, Postboks 700, 1757 HaldenNorway
ricardo.colomo-palacios@hiof.no

Abstract. Human factors are important in order to achieve outcomes which are consistent and aligned with organizational strategies and values. However, understanding how to successfully deal with human factors involved in a Quality Management System is a challenging issue. Therefore, there is a need to move beyond traditional mechanisms to manage human aspects. While much attention has focused on the motivation of people though gamification in recent years our mapping found that others human factors described in ISO 10018 such as communication, education, engagement and teamwork could be achieved. Nevertheless, getting the best out of people is not always easy and it is a challenge that cannot be ignored.

Keywords: Gamification · Octalysis · ISO 10018 · Human factors

1 Introduction

The overall performance of a quality management system and its processes ultimately depends on the involvement of competent people and whether they are properly introduced and integrated into the organization [1]. The involvement of people is important in order to an organization's quality management system (QMS) to achieve outcomes which are consistent and aligned with their strategies and values [1].

Gamification has gained noteworthy interest in industry and academic settings [2] being implemented in a panoply of settings. In the context of software industry, Gamification deserves special attention, given the human-intensive nature of software processes [3, 4]. Serious games are complete games whereas gamification is a way of designing products and services with the intention of a system that includes elements from games, not a full "game proper" [5]. Gamification is the use of game design elements in non-game contexts [5]. In recent years, there is a growing interest in gamification [3, 6] as well as its applications and implications in several fields such as education and software process improvement. However, to the best of authors' knowledge, given the relatively newness of the topic and the lack of formal guidelines for quality assessments in gamification settings in general, and applied to software industry in particular, there is a need to link mature efforts in the field of people and quality management and gamification environments. This paper is a first step towards this goal. In this paper, authors present a mapping on maybe the most mature framework on gamification and ISO 10018:2012 the standard on Quality management, providing guidelines on people involvement and competence.

The remainder of this paper is structured as follows: Sect. 2 presents the background of this study. Sections 2.1 and 2.2 outlines the ISO 10018 and Octalysis Gamification framework. In Sect. 3 we report on the results of the mapping. Section 4 summarizes a conclusion as well as outlines future work plans.

2 Background

2.1 ISO 10018

ISO 10018:2012, Quality management – Guidelines on people involvement and competence, is a new ISO standard for organizations of all sizes, types and activities [7]. It is designed to work in conjunction with ISO 9001 standard and help organizations involve their people in the QMS [8]. Two of the key definitions in ISO 10018 are:

- *Competence* is defined as the *"ability to apply knowledge and skills to achieve intended results"*
- *Involvement* is defined as *"engaging in and contributing to shared objectives"*

The contents of ISO 10018 follow the structure of ISO 9001 with the exception of Clause 4 Management of people involvement and competence. Others clauses are: 5 Management responsibility, 6 Resource management, 7 Product realization, 8 Measurement, analysis and Improvement. Most of the activities listed in clauses 5 to 8 can be used as a checklist to assess the current status of an organization regarding people involvement and competence [1]. In addition, ISO 10018 contains two annexes: *(a) Human factors that impact the QMS*, and *(b) Self-assessment*. Consequently, other important definition in this standard is:

- *Human factors* is defined as *"physical or cognitive characteristics, or social behavior, of a person"*

The following human factors are addressed in the ISO 10018 standard [1] (a full definition of the terms can be found in the standard): *Attitude and motivation*, *Education and learning*, *Empowerment*, *Leadership*, *Networking*, *Communication*, *Recruitment*, *Awareness*, *Engagement*, *Teamwork and collaboration*, *Responsibility and authority*, *Creativity and innovation*, and finally, *Recognition and rewards*.

2.2 Octalysis Gamification Framework

Octalysis is a complete gamification framework proposed by Yu-kai Chou [9]. We choose this framework because it is well known and has implemented at companies in the real world. In 2015, Chou won "Gamification Guru of the Year" award at the World

Gamification Congress which is the biggest event about this topic in Europe. According to its author, it can be used as a tool in applying gamification and analyzing a gamified product or service. Chou claims *"the gamification is design that places the most emphasis on human motivation in the process"*. In other words, he suggests that almost every game is "fun" because it appeals to certain core drives within human that motivate players towards certain activities [9]. In essence, Octalysis puts on a Human-Focused Design (as opposed to function focused design to get the job done quickly) [6]. There are five levels in total. Level 1 organizes systematically a list of gamified elements or cognitive drives. Previous studies have advocated that gamification can be used in software process development to make a set of task engaging and motivating [4, 10, 11]. The approach is based on an octagon shape hence its name with eight core drives represented by each side.

1. *Core drive 1: epic meaning and calling* is the need to contribute to something greater than oneself;
2. *Core drive 2: development and accomplishment* is about motivating people because they are feeling that they are improving, they are leaving up an achieving mastery;
3. *Core drive 3: empowerment of creativity and feedback* is the core drive that motivates people to incorporate their creativity, try different combinations and strategies, seek feedback and adjust;
4. *Core drive 4: ownership and possession* is the primary core drive that motivates people to accumulate possessions, improve it, protect it and get more;
5. *Core drive 5: social influence and relatedness* refers to the activities motivated by the influence of other people (e.g., based on social pressure and what other people think, do or say);
6. *Core drive 6: scarcity and impatience* is what motivates people to want something they cannot have (e.g., because it is not immediately or easily obtainable);
7. *Core drive 7: unpredictability and curiosity* is willingness to discover the unknown outcome and involve chance;
8. *Core drive 8: loss and avoidance* refers to the motivating factors that help people avoid a loss or situations they do not want happening (e.g., to die in a game).

The main benefit of this framework is the connections between the core drives and its facilitation in balancing them. The core drives on the right are considered Right Brain core drive and are related to creativity, self/expression, and social aspects. It implies motivation techniques that are more intrinsic which means that the motivation is the activity itself is rewarding on its own [12] (you do not need a goal or a reward). In contrast, the Left Brain core drives are associated to logic, calculations and ownership. They have a tendency of being more based on extrinsic motivation which means that the motivation is to obtain something, whether it is a goal, a good, or anything you cannot obtain [9]. However, Chou points out the Left/Right Brain Core Drives are merely symbolical as it makes the framework easier and effective when designing.

Moreover, Octalysis can be divided into two groups regarding their motivational urgency: white hat and black hat. White hat gamification contains the top core drives in the octagon. It is considered very positive motivations and provides people the feeling of being empowered and inspired. Also, it facilitates long term motivation and engagement. Conversely, black hat gamification contains the bottom core drives. It is considered more negative motivations and involves motives that drive active engagement based on uncertainty and the fear of losing something. It could create a high motivation for immediate tasks and drive short term results. However, the two core drives in the middle of Octalysis do not belong exclusively to white hat or black hat gamification. Those two core drives can go in both ways, depending on the applied game design elements and circumstances around the gamified process. To achieve a good Gamification process all eight core drives should be considered on a positive and productive activity so that everyone ends up happier and healthier [9].

Once Level 1 is mastered, one can then apply it to Level 2 Octalysis which tries to optimize experience throughout all four phases of a player's journey: Discovery, Onboarding, Scaffolding, and Endgame. Once you mastered Level 2 Octalysis, you can then push it one level higher to Level 3 and factor in different player types which is based on Bartle's Taxonomy of Player Types [13]: Achievers, Explorers, Socializers and Killers. Accordingly to Chou [14], Higher Level Octalysis processes are really there for organizations that are truly committed to making sure that they push their metrics in the right direction, while improving longevity of a gamified system.

Finally, our study is focused in Level 1 because it is usually sufficient for the majority of companies trying to create a better designed gamified product and experience. This framework contains an extensive list of game mechanics as well grouping them as to why they result in user engagement in a game. In the context of business and enterprise, a job would be considered gamified to the extent that mechanics are used to elicit engagement in the task.

3 Mapping

Although people are fundamental in the software process and in its assessment and improvement [15], enough attention to human factors is still not given [16–18]. Besides much research work has studied the application of gamification in software engineering (SE) for increasing the engagement and results of developers [3] but the existing research on gamification applied to SE is very preliminary or even immature, since most studies have been published in workshops or conferences, and few of them offer sound empirical evidence of the impact of their proposals on user engagement and performance. Therefore mappings allow the detection of differences and similarities between these approaches. Authors will follow the guidelines provided at [19] including these steps: (1) Analyze the models; (2) Design the mapping; (3) Carry out the mapping; (4) Present the outcomes and (5) Analyze the results. In what follows, the mapping performed is described using the method provided.

3.1 Models Analysis

The first activity is to analyze each reference model involved in a mapping process. Octalysis framework and ISO 10018 are studied in detail. An overview of these reference models are described in related literature section of this paper.

3.2 Mapping Design

Authors, following [19] carried out the following activities:

1. Identification of elements to be compared: Octalysis framework involves 8 core drives, and authors identified for each of them which human factors should be compared.
2. Direction of the comparison: the direction is from Octalysis framework to ISO 10018.
3. Comparison scale definition: authors use a "traffic light" scale for the one to one mapping. This scale is also used in the works of [6]:
   (a) E: explicit, the item has appeared in the framework's definition.
   (b) I: implicit, the item has not appeared explicitly in the framework definition. Inferred by the authors or referred inside a previous work of the authors.
   (c) U: unavailable, the item has not appeared anyway.
4. Comparison template definition: All these values are analyzed and checked from a holistic point of view and authors determine to what extent ISO 10018 human factors are fulfilled.

3.3 Mapping

This mapping is an iterative process in which authors analyze the Octalysis framework with ISO 10018. For Octalysis framework all core drives are studied. Authors identified specific techniques. The objective is not to set a naïve approach between Octalysis core drives' names and ISO 10018 human factors' names. In this mapping, authors analyze also whether specific techniques and human factors of the ISO 10018 are also meet. In order to carry out the mapping, a first relationship between reference models is defined. Then, a drilling down process analyzing in detail these relationships helps us to identify fine grained relationships. All these mapping are managed by using several spreadsheets where Octalysis core drives are displayed as rows, and ISO 10018 statements are displayed as columns. As a consequence of this process and given the relationship between Octalysis and ISO 10018, 77 techniques related to Octalysis framework are analyzed and compared to ISO 10018.

3.4 Outcomes

Following the guidelines provided in [19], the document Result of Comparison compiles the mapping and is shared and agreed among authors. Table 1 shows the resulting mapping for core drives. Each column has a fulfillment result based on the intersection of human factors. The comparison reveals that core drives do not include all human factors proposed in the ISO 10018. *Recruitment* is overlooked and *Awareness*, *Leadership*, *Networking* and *Responsibility* have appeared implicitly. Furthermore, it is not surprising that *Attitude and motivation* and *Recognition and rewards* are bringing in all core drives. Therefore the current mapping does not cover 100 % the ISO 10018. However, accordingly to Werbach and Hunter [20] game thinking can yield winning solutions to real-world so gamification can be applied to recruitment if managers and future co-workers can undertake some part of the recruitment process. That means that properly applied techniques, in a creative way, can enhance any human aspects but it will require a great deal of thought about the entire design of the system, including understanding the nature of users, thinking about what one would like them to do and how best to make them do it – among many other considerations [20].

Table 1. Mapping between Gamification elements to human factors of ISO 10018

OCTALYSIS FRAMEWORK	ISO 10018												
	Attitude and Motivation	Awareness	Communication	Creativity and innovation	Education and learning	Empowerment	Engagement	Leadership	Networking	Recognition and rewards	Recruitment	Responsibility and authority	Teamwork and collaboration
Epic Meaning & Calling	E	U	E	U	U	U	E	U	U	E	U	U	U
Developments & Accomplishment	E	U	I	I	E	U	U	U	U	E	U	U	I
Empowerment of Creativity & Feedback	E	U	E	E	E	E	E	U	U	E	U	U	U
Ownership & Possession	E	U	U	U	U	U	I	U	U	E	U	I	U
Social Influence & Relatedness	E	I	I	U	E	U	E	I	I	E	U	U	E
Scarcity & Impatience	E	U	U	U	U	U	U	U	U	E	U	U	U
Unpredictability & Curiosity	E	U	U	U	U	U	E	U	U	E	U	U	U
Loss & Avoidance	E	U	U	U	U	U	U	U	U	E	U	U	U

On the other hand, four core drives receive more coverage: *Epic Meaning and Calling*, *Developments and Accomplishment*, *Empowerment of Creativity and Feedback*, and *Social Influence and Relatedness*. When *Epic Meaning and Calling* is activated, participants choose to be members of your system and will take action not because it necessarily benefits them directly, but because it turns them into the heroes of the organization's story. *Developments and Accomplishment* stimulates positive emotions, building up a learning curve of the player who receives the feeling of moving forward and achieves a clear goal "satisfying work". In relation to *Empowerment of Creativity and Feedback*, the best way to implement it is by giving people a lot of choices or options to solve one problem. In a good designed gamification this process continuously reoccurs and provides a high engagement over a long time. *Social Influence and Relatedness* is related with the influence of other people, human desire to connect and compare with one another. This can be in order to impress other people, belong to a group and be conform to its social norms, or in order to avoid being excluded or mocked. However, it is mainly addressed in a way of teamwork, where they need or get help from others, and gaining recognition and respect. The power of this element is both in the motivation and satisfaction to belong and contribute to a group. Moreover, the engagement of actually inviting others to the game comes from the understanding the reason of doing so. They know how this benefits themselves.

4 Conclusions

In a work place environment, gamification can increase motivation. Nevertheless, the impact of gamification in the intrinsic motivation can also be negative. But it is not easy design an engaging gamified solution that also fulfills business metrics [9]. Although our current mapping does not cover 100 % of the ISO 10018 the insights of this study indicate that gamification can be designed for addressing all human factors. The mapping is defined and applied following Baldassarre et al. approach [19].

The main conclusion from this study is that gamification can be used as method for improving QMS in particular initiatives focus on software process. In fact, we are currently in the process to define and validate a framework that enables the integration of specific gamification mechanisms in the organizational change management of software process improvement (SPI) [10, 11]. However, there are still multiple questions unanswered in the context of applying and implementing gamified solutions in organizations. For instance, whether there is an economic value in applying gamification and how it can be measured. Whereas costs are probably easy to gather, the expected future profits are very difficult to value and the benefits are hard to express in monetary terms.

The results of the study can be used as a basis for further research in the area of gamification and its impact on human factors related to QMS. It is necessary to conduct further research that particularly addresses the effect of gamification in the long run with a focus on the impact on these human factors. Long term studies should be performed, in order to see the impact of repetition and possible boredom after some time. Further research is needed on the risk of alienating people, when the gamified tasks are customized to targeted test subjects.

References

1. ISO: ISO 10018 Quality Management - Guidelines on People Involvement and Competence, Geneva (2012)
2. Huotari, K., Hamari, J.: A definition for gamification: anchoring gamification in the service marketing literature. Electron. Mark. (2016, in press)
3. Pedreira, O., García, F., Brisaboa, N., Piattini, M.: Gamification in software engineering – a systematic mapping. Inf. Softw. Technol. **57**, 157–168 (2015)
4. Dorling, A., McCaffery, F.: The gamification of SPICE. In: Mas, A., Mesquida, A., Rout, T., O'Connor, R.V., Dorling, A. (eds.) SPICE 2012. CCIS, vol. 290, pp. 295–301. Springer, Heidelberg (2012)
5. Deterding, S., Dixon, D., Khaled, R., Nacke, L.: From game design elements to gamefulness: defining "gamification." In: Proceedings of the 15th International Academic MindTrek Conference: Envisioning Future Media Environments, pp. 9–15. ACM, New York (2011)
6. Mora, A., Riera, D., Gonzalez, C., Arnedo-Moreno, J.: A literature review of gamification design frameworks. In: 2015 7th International Conference on Games and Virtual Worlds for Serious Applications (VS-Games), pp. 1–8 (2015)

7. Merrill, P.: ISO 10018 The best of people. ISO Focus, pp. 28–31 (2012)
8. Merrill, P.: The people principle. Qual. Prog. **46**, 42–44 (2013)
9. Chou, Y.: Actionable Gamification: Beyond Points, Badges, and Leaderboards. Octalysis Media, USA (2015)
10. Herranz, E., Colomo-Palacios, R., de Amescua Seco, A.: Gamiware: a gamification platform for software process improvement. In: O'Connor, R.V., Umay Akkaya, M., Kemaneci, K., Yilmaz, M., Poth, A., Messnarz, R. (eds.) EuroSPI 2015. CCIS, vol. 543, pp. 127–139. Springer, Heidelberg (2015). doi:10.1007/978-3-319-24647-5_11
11. Herranz Sánchez, E., de Colomo-Palacios, R., de Amescua Seco, A., Yilmaz, M.: Gamification as a disruptive factor in software process improvement initiatives. J. Univ. Comput. Sci. **20**, 885–906 (2014)
12. Csikszentmihalyi, M.: Flow: the psychology of optimal experience. Harper Perennial Modern Classics, New York (2008)
13. Bartle, R.: Hearts, clubs, diamonds, spades: players who suit MUDs. J. Online Environ. **1**, 1–25 (1996)
14. Chou, Y.: Octalysis: Complete gamification framework (2013). http://www.yukaichou.com/gamification-examples/octalysis-completegamification-framework/
15. Sampaio, A., Sampaio, I.B., Gray, E.: The need of a person oriented approach to software process assessment. In: 2013 6th International Workshop on Cooperative and Human Aspects of Software Engineering (CHASE), pp. 145–148 (2013)
16. Baddoo, N., Hall, T.: De-motivators for software process improvement: an analysis of practitioners' views. J. Syst. Softw. **66**, 23–33 (2003)
17. Baddoo, N., Hall, T.: Motivators of software process improvement: an analysis of practitioners' views. J. Syst. Softw. **62**, 85–96 (2002)
18. Niazi, M.: Software process improvement: a road to success. In: Münch, J., Vierimaa, M. (eds.) PROFES 2006. LNCS, vol. 4034, pp. 395–401. Springer, Heidelberg (2006)
19. Baldassarre, M.T., Caivano, D., Pino, F.J., Piattini, M., Visaggio, G.: Harmonization of ISO/IEC 9001:2000 and CMMI-DEV: from a theoretical comparison to a real case application. Softw. Qual. J. **20**, 309–335 (2011)
20. Werbach, K., Hunter, D.: For The Win: How Game Thinking Can Revolutionize Your Business. Wharton Digital Press, Philadelphia (2012)

Gamifying the Onboarding Process for Novice Software Practitioners

Mehmet Kosa[1(✉)] and Murat Yilmaz[2]

[1] Department of Digital Game Design, İpek University, Ankara, Turkey
mkosa@ipek.edu.tr
[2] Department of Computer Engineering, Çankaya University, Ankara, Turkey
myilmaz@cankaya.edu.tr

Abstract. As the software development process becomes more complex, the adaptation challenges for novice software practitioners become magnified. In particular, an invisible adaptation barrier could have emerged between a software project and newly hired software engineers. This barrier needs to be overcome as soon as possible for the new comers to be productive and effective. To address this issue, we propose a tailored gamification process especially for novice software engineers so as to improve their onboarding process. The approach aims to provide the novice practitioners more motivation and less struggling, which promotes the utilization of "6D Gamification Framework" that is discussed as an example.

1 Introduction

Onboarding a novice software engineer is not a trivial task. Getting used to a new company culture as well as to a complex software project is generally not achieved in a day. This adaptation stage, until completed properly, keeps away the new comer from productivity for a significant amount of time. Both the companies' onboarding methods and the new comer's motivation play important role to get over this period. Methods and processes are proposed to ease this period however, to our knowledge, there has been no widely accepted framework for onboarding software engineers. Gamification frameworks, although developed for general purposes, may be of help for both the novice software engineers and enterprises.

The rest of the paper is organized as follows: Related work on onboarding is presented. Then, design principles and design considerations for onboarding games are discussed. Lastly, the conclusion and future studies are stated.

2 Related Work

Onboarding in this context is the process of helping the employee to get on track – that is to make her acquire the required skills, behaviors and knowledge – until she is fully equipped. The importance of onboarding is mentioned several times by the literature [6] and lots of attention has been invested on open source software projects rather than private company settings. Dai et al. [13] give a general review of onboarding by discussing key areas in onboarding, the reasons for onboarding, impact of successful onboarding, common mistakes and best onboarding practices. Depura et al. [14] in their study advocate using gamification, social media and mobile technology improves employee engagement and learning effectiveness based on quantitative results and qualitative surveys. When we boil down onboarding to software engineering domain, there are several studies regarding the onboarding process. Yates, as her PhD dissertation, although not touching the gamification concept, thoroughly discusses the onboarding process in software engineering which stands out as a valuable starting point [17]. Steinmacher et al. [7] categorized onboarding barriers as social interactions, newcomers previous knowledge, finding a way to start, documentation problems, and code issues where all of them have sub-issues. In another study, Steinmacher et al. [10] defines two more onboarding barriers that are building/setting up workplace issues and newcomer behavior. Another study reports that, to overcome these issues, a portal is developed that reported to increase the self-efficacy of the new comers [8]. Self-efficacy might have a prominent role in onboarding for the new comers since they need to feel that they are in control and capable to be effective. It has been found that the new comers have a better job satisfaction if they are more self-efficient [19] Games in this sense are excellent tools to provide players self-efficacy [18, 20] with its minimal, step-by-step goals and small victories leading to higher achievements. Flow, the optimal experience, [15] might also be mentioned here which is another construct that games are reported to provide [16]. Getting the junior software engineers into flow will mean that they are experiencing enjoyment which will lead to increased motivation and engagement levels. Begel et al. [9] reports some common misconceptions of newly graduated engineers which can also be taken into consideration and addressed by the onboarding games. To overcome the onboarding issues on of the main method reported is the mentoring [5, 11]. Other than that, presence of past social connections is reported to have positive effects on onboarding [12].

Not necessarily being directly related to onboarding, Herranz et al. [21] explained their gamification platform (for software process improvement) that harnesses the power of motivation of gamification for software process improvement. Yilmaz et al. [22] also stated in an empirical study that the gamification techniques helped a small-scaled company improved its processes.

Among the gamification application attempts [4], 6D framework from Werbach [1] is a well-known one which we have chosen to discuss for the purpose of this study.

3 Design Principles

Following Kevin Werbach's 6D framework, it has been adapted for onboarding software engineers [1].

Game designers who design for onboarding should first define business objectives (D1). The main objective can be selected that the company should be having sustainable policies, activities and culture on onboarding engineers.

Secondly, they need to delineate target behaviors (D2). Those behaviors that the designers want to leverage for our case might be the positive attitude and motivation of the new comers in a playful manner.

Next, they need to describe the players (D3). The "players" for an example case might be junior software engineers that are 22–30 years old with possible gaming history. The designers can also consider Bartle's types [2] not to left out any player type. Another useful source might be the Marczewski's player type framework for gamification design [3].

Then, the designers of such onboarding games should devise activity loops (D4). These loops are generally inspected under two categories: Engagement loops and progression loops. For the former, designers should think of motivating actions that they want the player to take, which causes the player to do the action, which causes a feedback that the designer will provide and in return will motivate the player to continue. "Immediate feedback" is the crucial part here therefore the new comer should not be left all alone to learn the codebase or company policies. For the latter loop, designers should be able to let the new comers win small battles (understanding part of a code and demonstrating by doing) which will eventually result in achieving final overarching goals which might be the main responsibility of that software engineer in the company.

As for the fifth principle, the designers should ensure that this altered process of onboarding is fun and good designers do not forget the fun (D5) factor of the system. Junior software engineers are going through onboarding process every day across the globe in traditional methods. This approach is to make these processes more motivating and engaging. Therefore the core motivating factor, fun, should be taken very seriously when designing such interactivities.

Lastly, designers of such games should deploy appropriate tools (D6). According to the framework, this comprises of three levels: Components, Mechanics and Dynamics. As for the components, they are the underlying level of the mechanics and dynamics and they should be decided depending on the other levels (virtual currency, levels are some examples for components). For the mechanics, achievements, discovery, ownership, progression, quests and rewards seem prominent and among those, discovery and quests may be selected as the driving mechanic. Lastly, for the dynamics, altruism, cooperation and related constructs should be put forward especially when a couple of software engineers are being on boarded.

Following on those 6 principles, engaging, game-like activities can be produced to increase the effectiveness of the onboarding process, which ensures the novice software engineers' effectiveness at once and provides a smooth transitioning in into the company culture (Fig. 1).

An example consideration of a gamification framework for the present problem is discussed above. However, this is not to mean that engineers and designers should strictly stick to this. Other gamification frameworks may also be considered to be applied for onboarding. Even, one can take a perspective from a serious game designer point of view and add gameplay on top of game thinking and game elements. Taking this, one step further, game design principles themselves can be applied rather than gamification frameworks which may result in better outcomes.

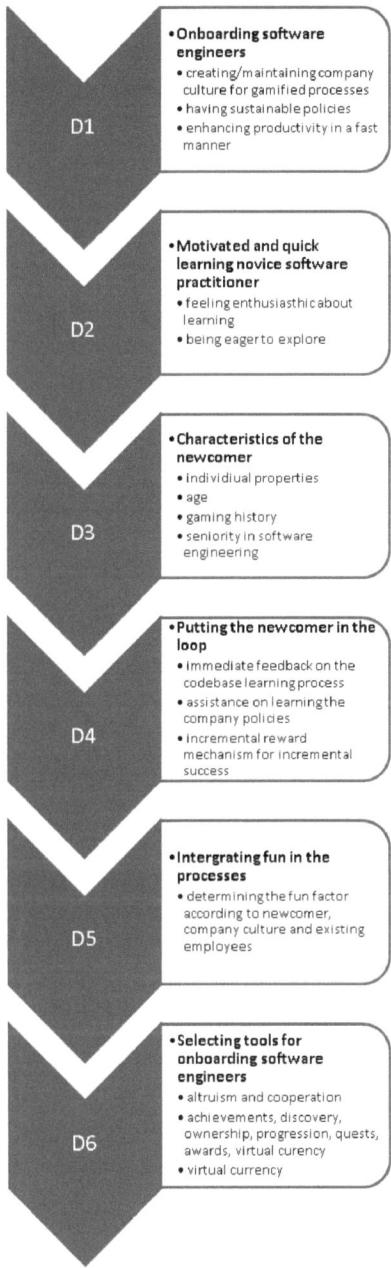

Fig. 1. Adapted gamification design framework (6D) [1]

Company culture can really be a thruster or a limiting factor for this kind of approach. If the new comers as well as the former employees can be directed in a playful mindset, the process will be beneficial for all, not just the new comer.

Pairing – matching the new comer with a responsible senior staff and mentoring in the onboarding process stands out as a prevailing method for newly hired software engineers to be on boarded. Therefore necessitating cooperative actions in onboarding games are highly advised.

4 Design Considerations

Some design considerations should be discussed while designing onboarding games. Some of them are summarized as follows:

- Will the novice software engineers be interacting/playing with the paired senior staff or with each other through the onboarding process?
- Will the novice software engineers be having virtual currency that creates endogenous value? How will they be able to spend it?
- How long the onboarding games should last? Mini-games that are played for short periods of time from time to time? Or long-running games that lasts for a week/month until the end of the onboarding process?
- Should there be a narrative integrated to the activities?
- How will the quick wins for the novice software engineers be provided so that she/he will be developing self-efficacy about the project?
- Which gamification frameworks are well-suited for onboarding?
- How can we test the validity of a gamification framework in this context?
- How can non-digital games be incorporated?

5 Conclusion and Future Studies

Applying gamification/game design principles to the onboarding process of software engineers to a company can be a great use for that company to increase productivity of newly hired employees at once which results in general productivity. The ideas in this paper are neither tested nor validated in this particular domain. Demonstration of empirical evidence of using games in these kinds of situations in software engineering domain is required. For that, detailed design of full-fledged series of games or game-like activities to orient and onboard novice software engineers should be presented in future studies. While contemplating about this, actual game tutorials can be a leading guide for new designers. How to design games to onboard junior software engineers for complex software projects, measuring the success of the methods and the performance of the newcomer remain problems to be solved.

References

1. Werbach, K., Hunter, D.: For the Win: How Game Thinking Can Revolutionize Your Business. Wharton Digital Press, Philadelphia (2012)
2. Bartle, R.: Hearts, clubs, diamonds, spades: players who suit MUDs. J. MUD Res. **1**(1), 19 (1996)

3. Marczewski, A.: User types. In: Even Ninja Monkeys Like to Play: Gamification, Game Thinking and Motivational Design, 1st ed., pp. 65–80. CreateSpace Independent Publishing Platform (2015)
4. Mora, A., Riera, D., González, C., Arnedo-Moreno, J.: A literature review of gamification design frameworks. In: 2015 7th International Conference on Games and Virtual Worlds for Serious Applications (VS-Games), pp. 1–8. IEEE, September 2015
5. Fagerholm, F., Johnson, P., Sanchez Guinea, A., Borenstein, J., Munch, J.: Onboarding in open source software projects: A preliminary analysis. In: 2013 IEEE 8th International Conference on Global Software Engineering Workshops (ICGSEW), pp. 5–10. IEEE, August 2013
6. Graybill, J.O., Hudson, M.T.C., Offord Jr., J., Piorun, M., Shaffer, G.: Employee onboarding: identification of best practices in ACRL libraries. Libr. Manag. **34**(3), 200–218 (2013)
7. Steinmacher, I., Gerosa, M.A.: How to support newcomers onboarding to open source software projects. In: Corral, L., Sillitti, A., Succi, G., Vlasenko, J., Wasserman, A.I. (eds.) OSS 2014. IFIP AICT, vol. 427, pp. 199–201. Springer, Heidelberg (2014)
8. Steinmacher, I., Wiese, I., Uchoa Conte, T., Aurelio Gerosa, M.: Increasing the self-efficacy of newcomers to open source software projects. In: 2015 29th Brazilian Symposium on Software Engineering (SBES), pp. 160–169. IEEE, September 2015
9. Begel, A., Simon, B.: Struggles of new college graduates in their first software development job. ACM SIGCSE Bull. **40**(1), 226–230 (2008)
10. Steinmacher, I., Wiese, I.S., Conte, T., Gerosa, M. A., Redmiles, D.: The hard life of open source software project newcomers. In: Proceedings of the 7th International Workshop on Cooperative and Human Aspects of Software Engineering, pp. 72–78. ACM, June 2014
11. Fagerholm, F., Guinea, A.S., Münch, J., Borenstein, J.: The role of mentoring and project characteristics for onboarding in open source software projects. In: Proceedings of the 8th ACM/IEEE International Symposium on Empirical Software Engineering and Measurement, p. 55. ACM, September 2014
12. Casalnuovo, C., Vasilescu, B., Devanbu, P., Filkov, V.: Developer onboarding in GitHub: the role of prior social links and language experience. In: Proceedings of the 2015 10th Joint Meeting on Foundations of Software Engineering, pp. 817–828. ACM, August 2015
13. Dai, G., De Meuse, K.P.: A Review of Onboarding Literature. Lominger Limited, Inc., A subsidiary of Korn/Ferry International (2007)
14. Depura, K., Garg, M.: Application of online gamification to new hire onboarding. In: 2012 Third International Conference on Services in Emerging Markets (ICSEM), pp. 153–156. IEEE, December 2012
15. Csikszentmihalyi, M., Csikzentmihaly, M.: Flow: The Psychology of Optimal Experience, vol. 41. Harper Perennial, New York (1991)
16. Chen, J.: Flow in games (and everything else). Commun. ACM **50**(4), 31–34 (2007)
17. Yates, R.Y.: Onboarding in software engineering (2014)
18. Meluso, A., Zheng, M., Spires, H.A., Lester, J.: Enhancing 5th graders' science content knowledge and self-efficacy through game-based learning. Comput. Educ. **59**(2), 497–504 (2012)
19. Song, Z., Chathoth, P.K.: An interactional approach to organizations' success in socializing their intern newcomers: the role of general self-efficacy and organizational socialization inventory. J. Hosp. Tourism Res. **34**, 364–387 (2010)
20. Allan, J.D.: An introduction to video game self-efficacy. Doctoral dissertation, California State University, Chico (2010)

21. Herranz, E., Colomo-Palacios, R., de Amescua Seco, A.: Gamiware: a gamification platform for software process improvement. In: O'Connor, R.V., Umay Akkaya, M., Kemaneci, K., Yilmaz, M., Poth, A., Messnarz, R. (eds.) EuroSPI 2015. CCIS, vol. 543, pp. 127–139. Springer, Heidelberg (2015). doi:10.1007/978-3-319-24647-5_11
22. Yilmaz, M., O'Connor, R.: A scrumban integrated gamification approach to guide software process improvement: a Turkish case study. Tehnicki Vjesnik (Technical Gazette) **23**(1), 237–245 (2016)

Functional Safety

Functional Safety Considerations for an In-wheel Electric Motor for Education

Miran Rodic[1], Andreas Riel[2(✉)], Richard Messnarz[3,4], Jakub Stolfa[5], and Svatopluk Stolfa[5]

[1] Faculty of Electrical Engineering and Computer Science, University of Maribor, Maribor, Slovenia
miran.rodic@um.si
[2] EMIRAcle & ISCN Group, Grenoble, France
andreas.riel@grenoble-inp.fr
[3] ISCN LTD, Bray, Ireland
rmess@iscn.com
[4] GesmbH, Graz, Austria
[5] Department of Computer Science, Technical University of Ostrava, VSB, Ostrava, Czech Republic
{jakub.stolfa,svatopluk.stolfa}@scoveco.cz

Abstract. The European Automotive Quality Sector Skill Alliance AQUA has been establishing practice-oriented education and training program on modern automotive engineering challenges since 2012. In the context of their most recent activity, they transfer their certified industry training program on integrated automotive quality engineering and management to higher education. This article introduces a practical example that is used in this new curriculum to explain the functional safety dimension of integrated automotive quality. Since the students are highly interested in electric and hybrid vehicles technologies, the example of an e-motor control for the drivetrain was chosen as a case study.

Keywords: Functional safety · Higher education · Quality in automotive

1 Introduction

As published in [1, 2], the European Automotive Quality Sector Skill Alliance AQUA aims at innovating and improving education and professional training of automotive engineering, with a particular focus on mechatronics systems engineering. One of their currently most outstanding initiatives is the transfer their certified industry training program on integrated automotive quality engineering and management to higher education [3]. The consistent use of practical examples from industry in order to explain the complex concepts of integrated automotive quality engineering to master students is a key element of the lecture program.

This article describes the quality challenges linked to functional safety using the example of an in-wheel electric motor, connected to the three-phase power electronics inverter. This example is very relevant for e-mobility. Elaborated as a consistent case study, this example turned out to be very effective practical complement to the lecturing material explaining the theory. The example can be useful for the students in their future careers, since the electric drives will become a common feature of various kinds of vehicles. As such it also brings in the added value by extending the knowledge about electrical motors and power electronics, as well as vehicle dynamics.

Section 2 of this article describes the system under investigation, for which a schematic circuit diagram, as well as an ISO 26262 compliant item definition is given in the Sects. 3 and 4, respectively. Section 5 discusses how to tackle the principal functional safety challenge linked to this example. Section 6 concludes and gives an outlook.

2 System Description

In-wheel motors are widely used in the scooters and small cars (where the speed is low, typically under 45 km/h), but in the normal cars they have been applied only in some experimental vehicles. However, their many advantages over the hub motors make them very interesting for the future.

Due to their high efficiency, high torque to mass and torque to volume ratio, permanent magnet synchronous motors are gaining popularity in electric vehicles drivetrains. They are powered by power electronics inverters, in which MOS-FETs or IGBTs are used as switches. The control is typically performed using a microcontroller or digital signal controller and is using field oriented control method [4, 5]. This method controls the torque of the motor through the control of phase currents.

The motor can rotate in both directions and can operate as a motor or a brake (generator). The three motor windings are wye-connected and only two of the currents would need to be measured. However, for the purpose of safe operation all three currents are measured, and their sum, which should be close to zero, is used for the purpose of plausibility check.

The use of in-wheel motors has several benefits over the hub motor. The most important one is that the space is saved. The wheel itself is also a motor and required power electronics devices are easier to place in a smaller space, leaving more room in the car for passengers and cargo. Additionally this gives additional freedom to the designers, which are not limited by the setup of the single drivetrain. However, this structure also brings several hazards into the operation of the vehicle. For example it can happen that due to the faults of sensors, power electronics switches, and/or control unit, the system becomes unstable and the wheel can even block in the worst-case scenario.

The electric vehicle under consideration is depicted in Fig. 1. It is a four-wheel drive vehicle, having in-wheel motors in all four wheels, which gives it a number of advantages regarding driving and controllability performance. In this vehicle, the e-motors are presented as M1 (front left wheel), M2 (front right wheel), M3 (rear left wheel), and M4 (rear right wheel). ECU1, ECU2, ECU3, and ECU4 represent the Electronic Control Units (ECU) controlling the motors M1, M2, M3 and M4, respectfully, whereas ECUC is a central control unit, responsible for the central control functions, power management etc. It is important to note that ECUs are not necessary physically separate units, as a typical microcontroller used for such a purpose can easily control two or even more motors. Microcontrollers existing on the market, like for example the ones by NXP ([6, 7]) and Texas Instruments ([8, 9]) are compliant with the requirements presented by ISO 26262 (certified for ASIL D) and have many additional safety-dedicated features, like ECC (Error-Correcting Code) on Flash and RAM Interfaces, Built-In Self-Test (BIST) for CPU and On-chip RAM, dual CPUs running in lockstep, etc.

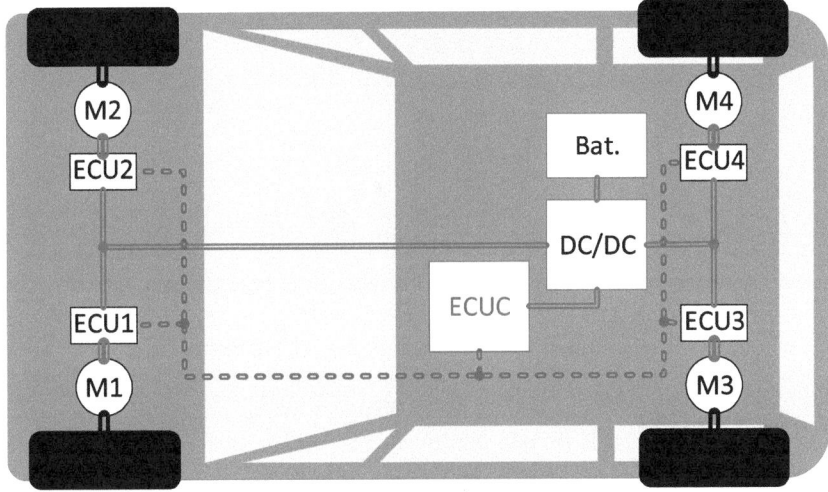

Fig. 1. Vehicle setup

The battery is presented as a block *Bat*, whereas the block *DC/DC* represents the DC/DC converter attached to it. Inverters are not represented on the figure for the clarity of the representation. The power transfer lines are represented with solid lines, whereas data transfer lines are represented with dotted lines.

Because of the steering the front wheels are more safety-critical than the rear ones, thus the hazard and risk analysis will be performed for the front left wheel, with the in-wheel motor presented as M1. In the case of the front right wheel the results would be the same, whereas for the rear wheels the required ASIL would be different, due to the lower influence of the rear wheels to the steering.

3 Electric Motor Circuit and Operation

The schematic circuit diagram of an electric motor based drivetrain, used for the driving of M1, is presented in the Fig. 2. It contains a power supply (which in this case is presented as a simple battery), power electronics inverter, sensors, and of course electric motor. The presented setup is a very basic explanation and some of the devices also applied in such inverter (like for example electrical brake) are not shown.

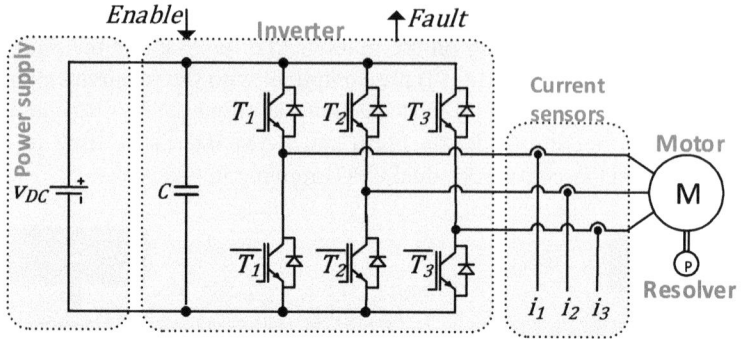

Fig. 2. Schematic circuit diagram of an electric motor based drivetrain

The inverter is constructed out of three legs, consisting of two switches each. The electric motor is connected between high and low switch, and thus the phase can be connected to either positive or negative electrode of the battery. The switches need to be controlled in such a way, that they are never turned on at the same time, since this would result in a short-circuit, permanently damaging the inverter. Additionally, a short time interval has to be inserted between the on-states of the switches due to their finite turn-on and turn-off times. Otherwise, the basic operation, as presented on the figure, is such that the high switch is on and the low switch off, or vice versa. Also an output, enabling the operation of the inverter is applied (*Enable*). The capacitor on the battery side of the inverter is used due to the poor dynamics of the battery.

The sensoric part of the drivetrain consists out of three current sensors, measuring the phase currents of the electric motor (i_1, i_2 and i_3), voltage sensor, measuring the voltage of the power supply (V_{DC}) and absolute encoder (typically resolver) measuring rotor position. Additionally a *Fault* input is connected to inverter circuit, providing the information regarding possible faulty operation.

Electronic control unit (ECU) is not presented in Fig. 2, but it is understood that it is used for performing measurements, control algorithms and driving actuators.

In the Item definition, presented in Fig. 3, sensors and actuators are presented as follows:

- S_C1.1 – current sensor, phase current 1 (i_1), motor M1,
- S_C1.2 – current sensor, phase current 2 (i_2), motor M1,
- S_C1.3 – current sensor, phase current 3 (i_3), motor M1,
- S_V1.1 – voltage sensor, voltage V_{DC}, motor M1,
- S_P1.1 – position sensor – position of rotor (P), motor M1,
- S_F1.1 – *Fault* input – from inverter, motor M1,
- A_L1.1 – output for inverter leg no. 1, T_1, motor M1,
- A_L1.2 – output for inverter leg no. 2, T_2, motor M1,
- A_L1.3 – output for inverter leg no. 3, T_3, motor M1,
- A_E1.1 – output for enabling the inverter operation, *Enable*, motor M1.

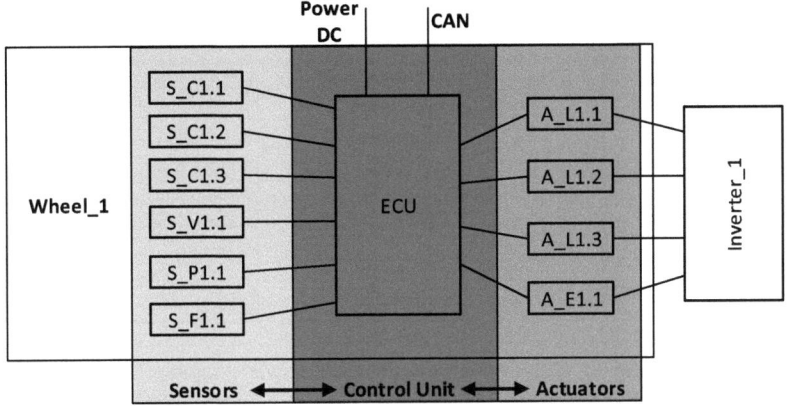

Fig. 3. Item definition of an electric motor based powertrain

This item definition will be the basis for the subsequent quality considerations in terms of functional safety.

4 Hazard Analysis and Risk Assessment

There are several risks connected to the use of permanent magnet synchronous motor in the drivetrain. In this paper due to the space limitations we will only focus on one of them, namely the case when one of the current sensors fails.

If it is assumed that such in-wheel motors are used for driving the front wheels in of the normal passenger car, capable of driving on the highway (with normal speed, 130 km/h), the following hazard case is identified: "Failure of one of the current sensors when driving a fully occupied vehicle at high speed." In this case the failure of the sensor can result in wrong torque of the motor, in worst case this could also result in blocking of the motor, consequently causing the loss of direction for a significant period of time.

First the severity of such a scenario is identified. Obviously the motor behaves in an uncontrolled way, the vehicle losses direction and an accident is imminent and fatal injuries can be expected. This gives the Severity classification S3. At this point it is important to note that during risk and hazard assessment the design is unknown and safety mechanisms are not taken into consideration.

The exposure classification is assessed based on the fact, that the driving wheel is driving the vehicle always when it is being driven, it is a case of normal operation. This gives the Exposure classification value E4.

The controllability classification can be simply assessed. If one of the front wheels is suddenly and unexpectedly blocked, only the very best (expert) drivers can keep the vehicle under control. This results in Controllability classification C3. With the use of ASIL table presented in ISO 26262 the determined ASIL value is ASIL D.

The assessment table is presented in Fig. 4.

Possible malfunction	Situation	S	Argument	E	Argument	C	Argument	ASIL	Safety Goal
blocking motor	fully occupied vehicle, high speed	3	possibility of blocking exists – fatal injuries can be expected.	4	drivetrain is normally operated during driving	3	uncontrollable situation – only expert drivers will manage the control of a car suddenly braking during acceleration	D	avoid blocking motor

Fig. 4. Hazard analysis and risk assessment (extract)

5 Functional Safety Strategy

The strategy to avoid this kind of risks and hazards is based on the basic Kirchoff laws. Namely, sum of all electric currents entering a junction or node is exactly equal to the sum of electric currents leaving the node. Since the motor is wye connected, the sum of all three currents should be zero. Of course due to the several effects like measurement gain and offset variation as well as measurement noise the value of zero is a too strict criteria. In practice the current sum has to be within the prescribed limits (I_{lim}):

$$-I_{lim} < i_1 + i_2 + i_3 < I_{lim} \tag{1}$$

Furthermore, in order to avoid the randomly occurring current spikes (a result of noise introduced into the circuit) starting the safety mechanism, the current sum has to be outside of the prescribed limits for a prescribed time. Because the currents flow through the windings, having the physical behavior of coils, they cannot rise immediately, but will do so with some transient, giving the safety system some time to evaluate behavior and respond with an appropriate action. In that time with some evaluation method the faulty sensor is determined and the operation is continued by simply calculating the current from the faulty sensor from the values of remaining two sensors. For example if current sensor measuring current i_3 fails, this current can be calculated as follows:

$$i_3 = -i_1 - i_2 \tag{2}$$

In this configuration motor can operate safely and it is only advisable that there is a warning light warning the driver that a visit to the repair shop should be made.

Some research regarding the above-presented issues has been presented in [10, 11].

At this point it is possible to define a safe state. If it is possible to determine the faulty sensor, the safe state could be determined as operation with the reduced speed.

If the faulty sensor detection and isolation are not performed, the safe state can be reached by simply turning off the motor and the remaining three drives can continue driving the vehicle, however, it is advisable to reduce the speed as well. The only real danger is that due to the false reading of current the motor is blocked or its torque reversed, which will not happen if the motor is not powered. The required response time in which this safe state is reached can be set to some ms (depending on the vehicle structure), since this is the range of time constants of the motor windings, determining the time in which the current and consequently torque can build-up to the possibly dangerous levels.

6 Conclusion

This paper presents one of the industrial case studies that are used in the AQUA education program for higher education in order to teach modern automotive quality engineering challenges to students. The experiences made in pilot lectures have been very positive with particular respect to the level of comprehension that the students developed for the complex engineering challenges that are associated to integrated automotive quality engineering. In the context of a European initiative, the education program is currently being deployed in five European universities of technology. The evaluation of the experiences gathered in this crucial phase will be reported in the next edition of the EuroSPI conference.

The given example can be simply altered by changing the configuration of the vehicle (e.g. to a two-wheeler – front and rear wheels powered) or performing the evaluation on the example of rear wheels. This gives many options to both, students and educators, to use the basically same example in many different variations.

The issue of reliability has not been addressed in this paper, even if it is surely important. For that purpose a good presentation is given in [12, 13]. A nice example of good data available to the customers is given on the webpage [14], which can be a good resource for the students and currently represents a state-of-art in the semiconductor industry.

Design of electric vehicles and their components is a promising future technology, which requires a multidisciplinary knowledge. In such an endeavor a multidisciplinary team consisting of electrical, mechanical and mechatronics engineers, as well as recently IT specialists, is required. However, even some basic knowledge on the matter can improve the cooperation thus leading to more successful cooperation.

Acknowledgements. This European initiative was financially supported by the European Commission in the AQUA (Knowledge Alliance for Training, Quality and Excellence in Automotive) project as a pilot in the Erasmus+ Sector Skill Alliances Program under the project number EAC-2012-0635. The special aspect of adapting the training program to higher education level, and its deployment in five European universities is financially supported by the European Commission in the Erasmus+ Strategic Partnership project 2015-1-CZ01-KA203-013986 AutoUniverse (Automotive Quality Universities). This publication reflects the views only of the authors, and the Commission cannot be held responsible for any use which may be made of the information contained therein.

References

1. Kreiner, C., Messnarz, R., Riel, A., Ekert, D., Langgner, M., Theisens, D., Reiner, M.: Automotive knowledge alliance AQUA – integrating automotive SPICE, six sigma, and functional safety. In: McCaffery, F., O'Connor, R.V., Messnarz, R. (eds.) EuroSPI 2013. CCIS, vol. 364, pp. 333–344. Springer, Heidelberg (2013)
2. Kreiner, C., Messnarz, R., Riel, A., Theisens, D.: The AQUA automotive sector skills alliance: best practice in an integrated engineering approach. ASQ Softw. Qual. Prof. (ASQ SQP) **17**(3), 35–45 (2015)
3. Riel, A., Tichkiewitch, S., Stolfa J., Stolfa S., Kreiner, C., Messnarz, Rodic, M.: Industry-academia cooperation to empower automotive engineering designers. In: Procedia CIRP (2016, in press)
4. Leonhard, W.: Control of Electrical Drives, 3rd edn. Springer, Berlin (2001)
5. Vas, P.: Sensorless Vector and Direct Torque Control. Oxford University Press, Oxford (1998)
6. Safety Manual for Qorivva MPC5643L, Freescale Semiconductor, MPC5643LSM, Rev. 2, April 2013
7. Qorivva MPC5643L Microcontroller Data Sheet, Freescale Semiconductor, MPC5643L, Rev. 9, June 2013
8. SafeTI™ Design Packages for Functional Safety Applications, Texas Instruments. http://www.ti.com/ww/en/functional_safety/safeti/SafeTI-26262.html
9. TMS570LS1227 16- and 32-Bit RISC Flash Microcontroller, TMS570LS1227, SPNS192B, October 2012. http://www.ti.com/lit/ds/symlink/tms570ls1227.pdf. Accessed Feb 2015
10. Gàlvez-Carrillo, M., Kinnaert, M.: Sensor fault detection and isolation in three-phase systems using a signal-based approach. IET Cont. Theory Appl. **4**(9), 1838–1848 (2010)
11. Meinguet, F., Gyselinck, J.: Sensor and open-phase fault detection and isolation for three-phase AC drives. In: Proceedings of the Power Electronics, Machines and Drives Conference (PEMD), April 2010
12. Chung, H.S., Wang, H., Blaabjerg, F., Pecht, M. (eds.): Reliability of Power Electronic Converter Systems. The Institution of Engineering and Technology, London, UK (2016). ISBN:978-1-84919-901-8
13. Lutz, J., Schlangenotto, H., Scheuermann, U., De Doncker, R.: Semiconductor Power Devices Physics Characteristics Reliability. Springer, Berlin (2011). doi:10.1007/978-3-642-11125-9. ISBN:978-3-642-11124-2
14. DPPM/FIT/MTBF estimator, Texas Instruments. http://www.ti.com/quality/docs/estimator.tsp

A Compact Introduction to Automotive Engineering Knowledge

Andreas Riel[1(✉)], Monique Kollenhof[2], Sebastiaan Boersma[3],
Ron Gommans[4], Damjan Ekert[5,6], and Richard Messnarz[5,6]

[1] InnoPlusPlus and Grenoble Institute of Technology, Grenoble, France
andreas.riel@grenoble-inp.fr
[2] Symbol BV, Enschede, The Netherlands
monique.kollenhof@symbolbv.nl
[3] ROC Summa College, Eindhoven, The Netherlands
sc.boersma@summacollege.nl
[4] ROC Ter AA, Helmond, The Netherlands
r.gommans@roc-teraa.nl
[5] ISCN LTD., Bray, Ireland
{dekert,rmess}@iscn.com
[6] GesmbH, Ebenfurth, Austria

Abstract. Professionals in the automotive industry, teachers at Vocational Education and Training institutions (VETs), and training and consulting organizations from all over Europe developed a curriculum of basic skills needed to assume modern Automotive Engineering job roles. Based on this curriculum, defined in the form of two skill sets, training materials, as well as a text book and exercise book have been authored. For VETs and industry pilot trainings were organized.

The training not only prepares automotive students for their future jobs in the automotive industry but also enables professionals in the automotive industry to teach their newly graduated engineering employees in specific and fundamental knowledge and skills that form the basis of the growing variety of engineering job roles in the automotive industry. This article describes the experiences so far and looks ahead to the near future. The proposed Automotive Engineering curriculum provides a value-added springboard for engineers to assume engineering job roles in the modern automotive industry.

Keywords: Automotive Engineering · Automotive professional · Vocational Education and Training

1 Introduction

As published in [1], a European consortium of training and consulting organizations in very close cooperation with major automotive OEMs and tier-1 suppliers, started developing a VET training that empowers recent graduates for assuming engineering job roles in the automotive industry [2]. This initiative is a strategic part of the European Automotive Quality Sector Skill Alliance AQUA [3] aiming at establishing a

Europe-wide agreed and industry-driven qualification program for modern automotive engineering skills at all education levels.

Based on the results of a vast needs analysis [1] we developed skill sets for foundation and practitioner levels of knowledge. These skill sets provide the fundamental basis for the creation of a curriculum and related training materials comprising a comprehensive text book "First Steps into the Automotive Industry", an exercise book, a trainers' guide, as well as training slides. The skill sets are also the basis for the development of a pool of test questions used for the certification of competences by the ECQA [4].

This paper elaborates on the established training program (Sect. 2), as well as on the experiences collected in the first pilot trainings in the Netherlands (Sect. 3), were the project coordinator and the participating VETs are located. It will also give an outlook on the further developments and Europe-wide pilot training activities.

2 Training Program

The basis of the training program specification are EQF-compliant skill sets [4] for foundation and practitioner levels, both consisting of a number of "Units", "Elements", and "Performance Criteria":

- Unit: On the topmost level, the skill set is presented by skill set areas, each called a 'Unit'. The chapters in the book "First Steps into the Automotive Industry" reflect the 'Units' described in this skill set.
- Element: Each 'Unit' consists of a number of "Elements". The paragraphs in each chapter of the book "First Steps into the Automotive Industry" reflect the "Elements" in this skill set.
- Performance Criterium: Each "Element" consists of a number of "Performance Criteria" and each "Performance Criteria" has an explanation. These describe the tools, techniques and competences that are required by automotive engineers.
- Level of Cognition: A "Cognitive Level" according to the Bloom's taxonomy of knowledge has been assigned to each "Performance Criterium". This defines at which level the Automotive Engineer is expected to apply the respective tool, technique or skill. This is the minimum level the Automotive Engineer must be able to demonstrate in order to be assessed as competent.

Besides the project consortium, professionals from the automotive industry were consulted multiple times in developing the skill set. Not only surveys were conducted but also interviews were held, both more than once. Overall Europe, 30 companies in automotive – OEM and Tiers – responded to the project consortium's questions suggesting topics and content that should be covered in the skill set and training material. Also the level of cognition was discussed. It took more than one year of collaboration and pilot testing before the skill sets were definitive. As the skill sets form the basis of the training material, their development was one of the most crucial tasks of this project.

The released skill sets are the result of mutual agreements of education organizations, the automotive industry, as well as training and consulting organizations.

They are the basis for the definition of a curriculum that is aimed at being integrated fully or partly in major European VETs. The following sub-sections will elaborate further on this curriculum.

2.1 Introduction to the Automotive Industry Sector

The program starts with a training unit giving an introduction to the automotive sector in terms of its history, evolution and future, as well as key terms and key challenges. Characteristics of the sector are discussed, in particular the supplier structure, product and releases, and the importance of customer focus. Typical automotive engineering job roles are introduced to help learners orient themselves towards specific fields of interest.

A learning element giving an overview of a small selection of the most important legal documents, regulations and standards relevant for the sector.

The importance and essence of processes and process thinking in the automotive sector is also elaborated in this introductory module. The increasing dominance of mechatronic subsystems in modern vehicles implies an outstanding of the role of multi-disciplinary challenges in engineering organizations and processes. This is also discussed in this introductory module, as is the important concept of simultaneous engineering. Table 1 summarizes these topics and the associated performance criteria.

Table 1. Elements of the training unit "Introduction"

Automotive Industry	
History and evolution	Recall the history and developments within the automotive industry
Definitions, terms, and abbreviations	Recall automotive definitions, terms, and abbreviations
Supply chain	Describe the supplier structure of the automotive industry
Key challenges	Understand the key challenges of the automotive industry
Automotive industry versus other branches	Understand the differences with others branches (e.g. aerospace, medical, defense, consumer electronics, etc.)
Evolution and future	Understand what the future of the automotive industry could be like (e.g. electric, hydrogen, self-driving car)
Characteristics in the Automotive	
Product and process release	Understand the product and process release and change notifications within the automotive industry
Customer focus	Recall the role of customers' expectations and specifications
Job roles	Understand the engineering job roles in the automotive industry and their differences
Specification documents	N/A

(*Continued*)

Table 1. (*Continued*)

Legislation, Regulations, and Standards	
Legislation and regulations	Recall the applied legislation and regulations in the automotive industry
Standards	Recall the key objectives and concepts underlying the several norms and standards, its complexity, and the relations between them
Process Thinking	
Primary process	Understand the primary process of a company
Automotive process landscape	Understand the automotive process landscape
Changes on product and process	Recall that changes on product and process have consequence(s)
Multidisciplinary approach & simultaneous engineering	Understand the multidisciplinary and simultaneous engineering approaches

2.2 Product and Process Development

The second unit focusses on selected engineering aspects of product and process development in the automotive sector. Departing from the explanation of the notion of the product life cycle and sustainability, a closer look is taken at the development phase of the product life cycle by discussing the development process, as well as the typical activities carried out in the context of this process. The notion of systems engineering is explained, as it is of particular importance in modern vehicles where system-level functions are implemented by numerous cooperating subsystems. The explanation of the V-cycle establishes the link between system-level and component-level development activities.

Functional safety, i.e., the safe behavior of subsystems in case of failure, is discussed in the context of a module on risk management. This module also contains an introduction to FMEA, i.e., Failure Mode and Effect Analysis, which is one of the most important methods of risk management on both product and process levels in automotive. Table 2 summarizes these topics and the associated performance criteria.

Table 2. Elements of the training unit "Product and Process Development"

Product Lifecycle Management	
Different levels	Understand the product life cycle and product life cycle management
Designing for end-of life	Understand the link between life cycle engineering and sustainability
Advanced Product Quality Planning (APQP)	
Objectives	Understand the objectives of APQP, why and when it is used
Phases	Identify the different phases of APQP

(*Continued*)

Table 2. (*Continued*)

Systems Engineering	
Breakdown structure of a vehicle	Understand the complexity of a vehicle and its systems
System level development	Understand product development process, and V-Model
Component level	Understand the development life cycle
Risk Management	
Risk management Process	Understand the risk management of A-SPICE. Project, process, organization
Failure mode and effect analysis	Understand failure mode effects and analyses. Understand the process FMEA and is able to interpret the process risks
Functional safety	Understand failure mode effects and diagnostic analysis. Interpret the hazard and risk analyses based on ISO 26262 and IEC 61508

2.3 Production

The third training unit deals with the automotive production process, with a particular focus on the quality assurance measures based on Six Sigma principles. The key topics here include the Process Capability (a measure for the variation in the process) and Process Control, mainly based on statistical tools applied to data measured in the process.

Since the suppliers have a key role in the automotive development and production process, the assurance of the quality they deliver is essential to the total quality management of the product creation process. This training element therefore discusses supplier control and assessment schemes, in particular Automotive SPICE ®, which is used by automotive OEMs to assess their suppliers' mechatronics development process quality worldwide.

Change management is an important activity throughout the entire product creation process, because changes can happen at every moment. Table 3 summarizes these topics and the associated performance criteria.

Table 3. Elements of the training unit "Production"

Process Capability	
Machine variation	Describe machine variation
Short term variation	Participate in collecting, measuring and interpreting data (interpret short term variation: C_{pk} and C_p)
Long term variation	Participate in collecting, measuring and interpreting data (interpret long term variation: P_{pk} and P_p)
Process Control	
Measurement system analysis	Explain what measurement system analysis is and is used for. Basics of measurement system analysis: participate and interpret measurements and analyses (e.g. Gage R&R, attribute agreement analysis report)

(*Continued*)

Table 3. (*Continued*)

Controlling processes	Describe how and why processes are controlled during production
Statistical process control	Describe what statistical process control is and is used for
Out of control action plan	Describe what a control plan and OCAP are, and what they are used for
Interactions between tools	Describe the relations between process FMEA, control plan, and OCAP's
Supplier Quality Assurance	
Controlling suppliers	Understand how suppliers are controlled in the automotive industry
PPAP and EMPB	Understand PPAP and EMPB and their differences
Auditing suppliers	Understand supplier audit (VDA 6.3)
Automotive spice assessment	Understand Automotive SPICE® and why Automotive SPICE® assessments are performed
Management of Change	
Risk of changes	Describe the risk of changes
Change notifications	Describe change notification, PPAP, and EMPB
Changes during design and development	Understand the interface with change management in design and development

2.4 Continuous Improvement

The fourth and last unit deals with continuous improvement as an intrinsic element of successful automotive development and production processes. The key elements are tools and methods for problem finding, analyzing, and solving, lean manufacturing (i.e., the minimization of non-value-adding activities in the manufacturing process), quality awareness, as well as approaches to sustaining improvements. Table 4 summarizes these topics and the associated performance criteria.

Table 4. Elements of the training unit "Continuous Improvement"

Problem Solving	
8D	Describe the 8D process
Containment actions	Identify containment actions (e.g. recall, corrective actions during service, etc.)
Root cause analysis	Knows tools that are used for root cause analyses (e.g. Ishikawa, 5Why, etc.)
Prevent re-occurrence	Describe the relations between problems, FMEA, and control plan
Lean Manufacturing	
Lean manufacturing in the automotive industry	Describe lean manufacturing and interpret lean manufacturing in the automotive chain
Appling lean manufacturing	Describe why lean manufacturing is applied in the automotive industry

(*Continued*)

Table 4. (*Continued*)

Quality Awareness	
Leadership and commitment	Describe the type of leadership needed in the automotive industry. Describe what commitment is and its importance
Team formation and team work	Participate in gaining commitment.
Cultural diversity and its Influence	Understand cultural diversity (not only nationalities but also between job roles)
Sustain Improvements	
Sustaining improvements and changes	Describe how to sustain improvements or changes. Understand the importance of lessons learned
Quality management	Describe the role of quality management

3 Experiences from Pilot Trainings in the Netherlands

The project consortium consists of seven partners including two VET organizations, ROC Summa College and ROC Ter AA. In February 2016, these two VETs started teaching their students the Automotive Engineering curriculum. Compared to the slides for higher education the slides for the VET students were especially developed for them. The slides were provided with lots of pictures. All training material was in English (book, slides, and exercises) but the spoken language was Dutch.

3.1 Pilot Training at Summa

Summa has taught 42 1st year students, and 33 2nd year students whose ages range from 16 to 19 years. They enter Summa when they are around 16/17 years of age and are expected to graduate 4 years later. Like the 2nd year students the 1st year students were very enthusiastic and eager to learn. One major difference was that the 1st year students had just finished their ISO/TS 16949 courses while the 2nd year students had not. For both groups this was the first year for ISO/TS 16949 to be taught.

The 1st year students did not have any problems following the Automotive Engineer training course, however the 2nd year students did. They were also struggling because as of the second year students are expected to work more and more independently, are less guided, and have less breaks during school. Also their homework is not guided anymore. During classes it was quite quiet, although 2nd year students asked more questions mainly because they are better in expressing themselves. The 1st year students asked most questions during assignments. 1st year students as well as 2nd year students had trouble with pictures/figures that had more than one concept in them, like the figures explaining the V-cycle. For this reason the teacher spent more time on these slides than expected.

Most students could handle the slides in English language even if they preferred the Dutch language. That is why different kind of techniques were practiced: after a 1 h lecture, during the same week all students had a 1 h exercise lesson. To practice the theory, an exercise book with a lot of exercises was developed by the project consortium.

These activities were very much welcomed by the students as it gave them the opportunity to experiment with their newly developed knowledge in a non-theoretical way.

Besides the exercise book also a teachers' guide was developed to guide teachers. Depending on the students the teacher choose to let them do their exercises individually or let them work in groups. All exercises were discussed during class, also students were discussing other students' answers to the exercises.

The skill set, including Bloom levels, not only was needed for developing the Automotive Engineering training course and lesson plans, but was also of great value for teachers and students. Using the skill set in organizing classes, developing lesson plans, and as a waypoint for the exams motivates students for leaning, but also gives them a tool to check if they are on the right path preparing for their exams. Like theory and practice, teaching and learning are two different things. The teacher teaches but the student "decides" if he/she is willing to listen, take the time to read and learn by heart.

In summary, the experiences of Summa with this Automotive Engineering course are very positive. As of next year for the 1st, 2nd, and 3rd year students all training material developed by the project consortium will become a part of their curriculum. The possibility of closing the training with a Europe-wide recognized certificate makes this course of great value for the students, Summa, and (international) internships. It also enlarges the students' chances of getting a job. The students of Summa will take their ECQA exam in June 2016.

3.2 Pilot Training at Ter AA

Ter AA has taught 24 students 2nd year students, and 7 3rd year students. Their ages range from 17 to 20 years. They enter Ter AA when they are around 16/17 years of age and are expected to graduate 4 years later. Like Summa Ter AA also decided to have one theory lesson and one exercise lesson every week. Unlike Summa all units and elements were new for the Ter Aa students. Some students were interested in all elements, while other would have preferred more technical subjects like engines and tuning methods.

During classes the interaction with the students was good, however the teacher was not able to stick to the lesson plan and had to slow down as preparing the students for the exam (skill set and Bloom levels) took more time than planned. "Characteristics in the Automotive" the students did not find interesting at all, the same for "Legislation, Regulations, and Standards". That is why the teacher choose for a different method after the first lesson of "Legislation, Regulations, and Standards". Instead of the teacher being the only one preparing the next lesson, the students were assigned certain slides of the next lesson. Their assignment was to gather additional information and also to compose a multiple choice question for slide's content. During the next lesson they had explain their slides to the class. The questions were all saved as a "Kahoot"-quiz, and will be used for classes in the future.

During the classes of the other units the skill set's performance criteria were used: students were assigned one of them and had to prepare and present their own slides. The students are very motivated to ultimately obtain an ECQA certificate. Not only passing the exam but also attending every class and doing all their homework according to plan is one of the criteria. The students of Ter AA will take their exam in June 2016.

Unlike other classes at Ter AA, all students did their homework without complaining. The book was only used for back up and doing homework. The slides were used in the lessons. In order to obtain a better understanding and attention of the students the teacher added some extra pictures to some elements' slides. It was a very useful feedback for the project consortium.

Training material in the English language turned out to be an obstacle for one student only. Most of the students even preferred doing their homework in English. The skill set turned out to be a very useful and needed tool for teachers and students. The fact that the project consortium spent a lot of time fine-tuning the skill sets was of great added value for teacher and students. Like Summa, also Ter AA decided that as of next year the Automotive Engineering training course will be part of the standard curriculum for 2nd and 3rd year students. They are also strongly recommending other VETs to do so.

3.3 Pilot Training at Symbol

At Symbol a 4-day Train-the-Trainer Automotive Engineering for 16 professionals working in automotive was scheduled for May and June 2016. The goal was not only to train employees (e.g. team leaders and teachers in automotive industry) in automotive engineering but also to empower them for being were able to teach their employees themselves, in particular new recruits Therefore, the Train-the-Trainer curriculum is at the level of higher education (Practitioner skill set). Symbol is used to working with skill sets, and trainees very much appreciated working with the Automotive Engineering skill set. Because of the success of this training a second Train-the-Trainer is scheduled at Symbol for September 2016, and a third one is envisaged for the end of 2016.

4 Conclusions and Outlook

In the context of the European AQUA automotive sector skill alliance [2], a European consortium of trainings providers, consultants and associated automotive tier-1 suppliers have created an agreed curriculum providing fundamental knowledge required in modern automotive engineering job roles. Based on the related foundation and practitioner level skill sets, a comprehensive text book, exercise book, as well as training slides, a teachers' guide, and a pool of exam questions have been created. All these materials will be made available for training, education and consulting organizations after their first officially published release in the last quarter of 2016.

Based on the experiences collected in pilot trainings so far, we may conclude that the Automotive Engineering curriculum had a warm welcome in VET and industry. Also higher education in the Netherlands, Austria, France, and Slovenia have shown their interest. In April 2016, ISCN organized an introduction course of the Automotive Engineering curriculum at the University of Maribor (Slovenia). In September 2016, the Automotive Engineering course will be trained in higher education in France and in Austria.

Training materials (books and slides) will be translated into Dutch, German, and French. Moreover, at least 120 trainees will take their exams in order to obtain the ECQA certificate associated with this curriculum. Until October 2016 three multiplier events are planned: in the Netherlands, Austria, and France, the project results will be disseminated during automotive events for students, teachers, and professionals in automotive. In May 2016 the project promoted their outputs at the Dutch Technology Week.

The transition to the exploitation phase of the project will be marked by the opening up of the consortium for interested new partners to join and help disseminating and continually improving the project results.

Acknowledgements. The "Automotive Engineer" project is financially supported by the European Commission in the Erasmus+ Programme under the project number 2014-1-NL01-KA200-001189. This publication reflects the views only of the authors, and the Commission cannot be held responsible for any use which may be made of the information contained therein.

The authors want to thank all the involved industry partners from Austria, Germany, France, Spain, and the Netherlands for their valuable contributions so far.

References

1. Kollenhof, M., Riel, A., Messnarz, R.: Empowering graduates for engineering jobs in the automotive industry. In: Proceedings of the 22nd EuroAsiaSPI^2 Conference 2015, Whitebox, pp. 9.3–9.12. ISBN 978-87-998116-5-6
2. http://www.automotiveengineer.eu. Accessed 26 June 2016
3. Kreiner, C., Messnarz, R., Riel, A., Ekert, D., Langgner, M., Theisens, D., Reiner, M.: Automotive knowledge alliance AQUA – integrating automotive SPICE, six sigma, and functional safety. In: McCaffery, F., O'Connor, R.V., Messnarz, R. (eds.) EuroSPI 2013. CCIS, vol. 364, pp. 333–344. Springer, Heidelberg (2013)
4. The European Qualification and Certification Association (ECQA). www.ecqa.org. Accessed 28 April 2016. The European Qualifications Framework (EQF). http://ec.europa.eu/ploteus/search/site?f%5B0%5D=im_field_entity_type%3A97. Accessed 25 Nov 2014

A GSN Approach to SEooC for an Automotive Hall Sensor

Xabier Larrucea[1(✉)], Silvana Mergen[2(✉)], and Alastair Walker[3(✉)]

[1] Tecnalia, Bizkaia, Spain
xabier.larrucea@tecnalia.com
[2] TDK-EPC AG & Co. KG, Stahnsdorf, Germany
silvana.mergen@epcos.com
[3] Lorit Consultancy, Edinburgh, Scotland, UK
alastair.walker@lorit-consultancy.com

Abstract. One of the key challenges for manufacturers of automotive systems, hardware components and software products is not only the process of defining explicit and implicit requirements but also the ability to satisfy safety requirements such as those specified in ISO 26262. From an element point of view, the Safety Element out of Context (SEooC) defined in ISO26262 is becoming a reference for developing systems, elements and components in the automotive sector. Integration teams have limited prior knowledge of how these third party devices have been defined, the assumed requirements used during the validation and verification phases. Goal Structuring Notation (GSN) can be used to define and document the assumed SEooC requirements in a graphical manner. However, development teams are facing several challenges for example how different requirements are implemented in SEooC, or how far GSN is able to represent SEooC definitions. This paper provides a GSN based approach to represent SEooC requirements in a practical example of an automotive hall sensor.

Keywords: Argument · Assurance case · Claim · Safety element out of context

1 Introduction

Hall sensors are used in the automotive sector in a variety of applications [1], including control systems [2], and control of position/velocity [3]. These devices must operate reliably in both wide-ranging and harsh environment conditions [4]. A hall sensor provides a useful industry implementation, integrating hardware and software components [7]. Hall sensors are becoming increasingly more complex elements [6]. In fact, vehicles are becoming increasingly more complex and the demands placed upon elements such as halls sensors equally so. Since 2011 with the emergence of the ISO26262 standard [7] this type of element is typically developed using the SEooC process. Examples of how to implement a SEooC process are documented in part 10 of ISO26262 [8]. SEooC development is based upon assumed requirements. One of the key exercises for a team that has to integrate the SEooC element into an item, is to check the validity of the assumptions. This requires not only clearly defined and documented assumptions, but also clearly documented solutions.

Goal Structuring Notation (GSN) [9] allows a clear graphical representation of the assumptions, strategies, justifications and solutions. This notation allows both teams – developers of the SEooC element and the integrators of it - to review, discuss and challenge the assumptions [10]. GSN has been used as a notation for justifying sufficient confidence in software safety arguments [11]. In the automotive sector, requirements engineering is a central discipline [12]. Assumed requirements can be easily listed using a requirements capture tool such as DOORS. However, the process of capturing the justification of these assumed requirements is far more difficult. Ultimately the team integrating the SEooC element must clearly understand the reasoning behind the assumptions made by the development team. This paper reports an industrial case study using GSN as an indicative tool for defining ISO26262 requirements and also the process used in deriving the assumed requirements. The key component of this approach is the intuitive representation of the assumptions. GSN allows the strategies, assumptions and justifications to be clearly represented and understood. The addition of context descriptions provides additional supporting information.

This context implies, at least, the following set of research questions:

- How are the hall sensors requirements (hardware and software) defined in a GSN notation?
- What coverage does GSN provide in the context of ISO26262 SEooC activities?

This paper is structured as follows. First the background description, followed by the method of defining the SEooC hall sensor requirements using GSN. Subsequently the integration process for the SEooC into the item and finally, the conclusion of the process and recommendations.

2 Background

2.1 The SEooC Challenge

In accordance with ISO 26262-10 [8] SEooC follows the process illustrated in Fig. 1. Two parties are involved in the SEooC implementation, the developers who define the assumed requirements and the integrators who implement the SEooC element in the item.

The SEooC process then has two distinct phases, the development phase and the integration phase. The development phase consists of two different assumption processes, as indicated in Table 1. As many different products can be developed according to the SEooC process, a system, an array of systems, a subsystem, a software component, a hardware component or a part, then System SEooC element development can be a complex and multi-faceted process.

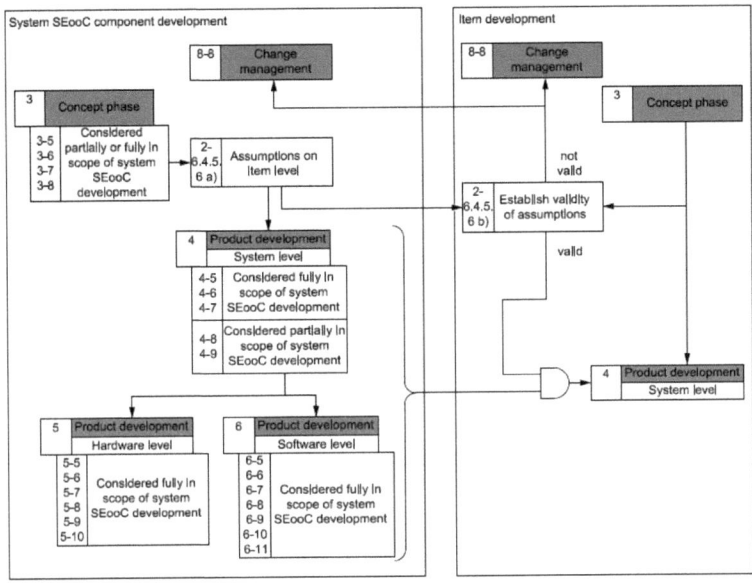

Fig. 1. Assumed requirement relationship component and item development [8]

Table 1. SEooC development and item integration processes

SEooC Phase	Process	Activities
System SEooC component development	Assumptions on the functional safety requirements allocated to the SEooC	Manufacturer defines the safety assumptions on the component
	Assumptions on the context of the SEooC	The manufacturer lists the assumptions that will impact safety when the component is integrated in the item
Item development	Match the functional safety requirements of the item with the functional safety requirements assumed for the SEooC to establish the validity	The integrator validates the assumed requirements see Fig. 1
	In the case of an SEooC assumption mismatch, a change management activity beginning with an impact analysis	The integrator initiates a change in either the item or the component based on the nature of the mismatch

2.2 The SEooC Challenge

The object of the GSN exercise is to build up an Assurance Case that clearly indicates the assumed requirements of the SEooC element. The definition of the Assurance Case is:

A reasoned and compelling argument, supported by a body of evidence that a system, service or organisation will operate as intended for a defined application in a defined environment [13].

In order that Assurance Cases can be developed, discussed, challenged, presented and reviewed amongst the stakeholders and maintained throughout the product lifecycle, it is necessary for them to be documented concisely. The documented argument of the Assurance Case should be structured to be comprehensible to all safety-case stakeholders. It should also be clear how the evidence is being asserted to support this argument. By appealing to core concepts of argumentation, GSN helps address these objectives.

The principle elements of GSN are as follows; however for further information refer to [9].

- Goals – the claims of an argument
- Solutions – items of evidence
- Strategies – document how claims are said to be supported by sub-claims
- Contexts – document goal or strategy context in which the claim or reasoning step should be interpreted
- Assumptions – some claims and argument strategies rely on assumptions to hold valid
- Justifications – provide a claim or argument strategy, with some explanation as to why it is acceptable

GSN provides two types of linkage between elements:

- SupportedBy relationships – represented by lines with solid arrowheads – indicate inferential or evidential relationships between elements.
- InContextOf relationships – represented as lines with hollow arrowheads – declare contextual relationships.

There are two distinct approaches to devising a goal structure top-down or bottom-up. As bottom-up tends to lend itself to construction of a goal structure when evidence already exists, it is not the subject of this paper. The 6 steps for a top down approach [13] are listed below:

- Step 1: Identify goals – identify top goal(s) and principle claim
- Step 2: Definition of the basis on which goals are stated – ensure adequate and correct understanding of the context surrounding the claim
- Step 3: Identification of strategy – how the claim can be substantiated
- Step 4: Definition of the basis on which the strategy is stated
- Step 5: Elaborate strategy
- Step 6: Identify solutions – claims are at a sufficient level they can be supported by evidence.

2.3 Hall Sensor Architectural Overview

As stated previously hall sensors fulfil different applications [1] in the automotive sector, including control systems [2], and control of position/velocity [3]. For example, hall sensors are usually utilised in anti-locked brake, throttle control and valve position applications.

A typical architecture could be as indicated in Fig. 2. The reading from the actual hall sensor interface along with the temperature is digitised and processed in the microcontroller (MCU). The MCU transmits the hall sensor reading digitally via a Single Edge Nibble Transition (SENT) interface. Configuration of the unit is possible using an external control interface CNRTx. To provide the redundancy in the design the hall sensor has two channels and each has a separate power supply Vccx. Calibration settings are stored in non-volatile memory.

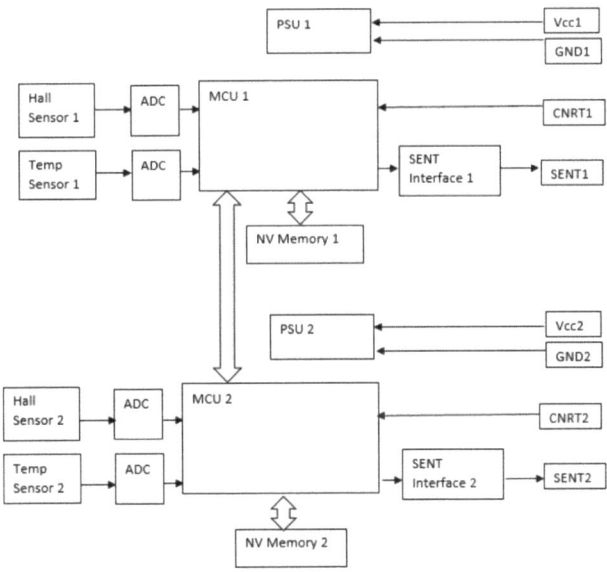

Fig. 2. Hall sensor block diagram

3 SEooC Hall Sensor Requirement Capture Utilising GSN

This paper only refers to the functional safety requirements of the hall sensor as defined in ISO 26262, other requirements are not the focus of this paper.

3.1 Hall Sensor Functional Safety Requirement Assumptions

Typical functional safety requirements that would be relevant to a hall sensor may include:

- ASIL requirement to ASIL D
- Maximum magnetic field strength ± 250 mT
- Sensitivity shall be minimum of 10 LSB/mT
- Non-linearity ± 0.1 % of the maximum magnetic field strength
- Magnetic drift shall be a maximum of ± 5 µT
- On board diagnostics to ensure single fault and latent faults detected within the allocated time
- Calibration to ensure the sensor remains accurate over time stored in non-volatile memory
- Diversity of the design to minimise common cause failures
- The non-volatile memory shall be single fault tolerant
- Redundant design prevents a single point failure from rendering the component inoperable
- Lifetime – ensure that the product remains safe and operational for the specified duration.

3.2 Hall Sensor Context Assumptions

In addition to the activity of defining assumed functional safety requirements, in order to achieve the assumed safety goals, specific assumptions on the context must also be defined.

In the case of the hall sensor, these may include:

- the external source will ensure there is adequate diversity and freedom from interference between the two power supplies to the hall sensor
- in the case that the hall sensor has detected an internal error and communicated this to the external source, the external source shall take the necessary actions to switch the item to the safe state within the defined fault reaction time
- the external source will ensure that mechanical limits of the magnet position are met
- the external source will maintain the recommended operating conditions.
- the external source will meet the latency requirements for the hall sensor such that the ISO 26262 fault tolerant time interval (FTTI) requirements are met

Certain applications may require such sensors to meet ASIL D requirements, hence making the process of requirements assumption even more critical.

3.3 GSN SEooC Development Implementation

Figure 3 shows the system level development of the hall sensor assurance case starting from the top goal, the hall sensor meets the ASIL D requirements. The subsequent Figs. 4, 5 and 6 illustrate the modules that expand the detail of specific areas of the Assurance Case in Fig. 3.

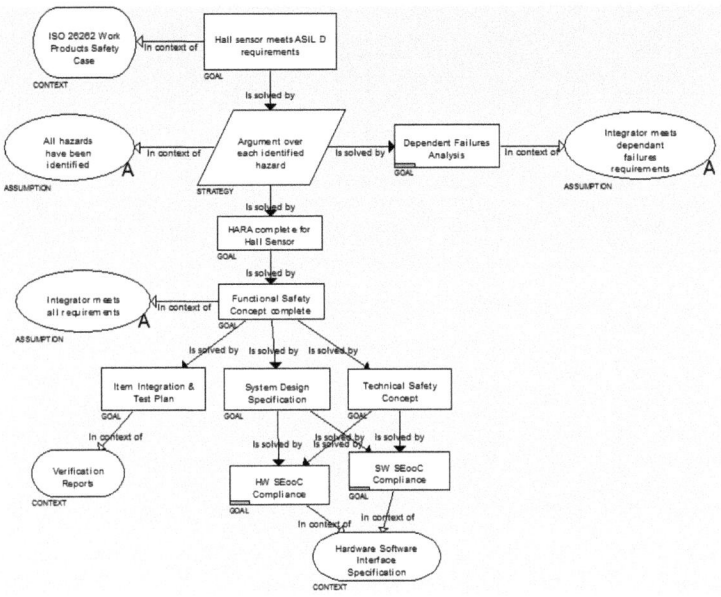

Fig. 3. GSN hall sensor system level assurance case

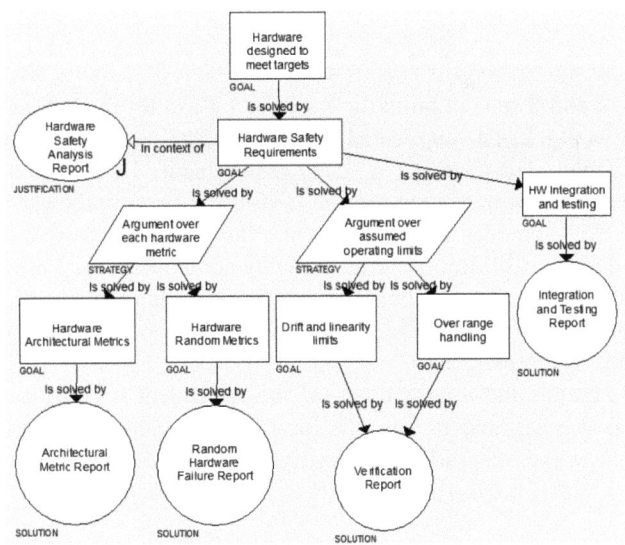

Fig. 4. Module HW SEooC compliance

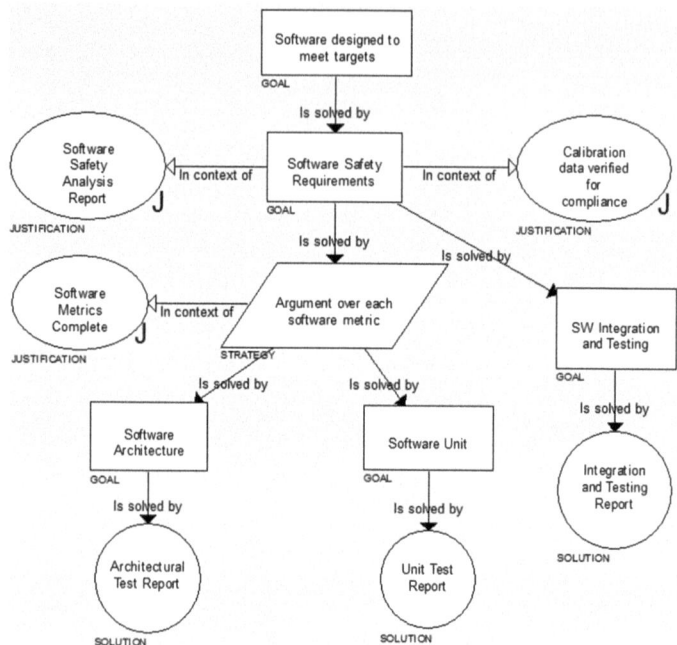

Fig. 5. Module SW SEooC compliance

Figures 3, 4 and 5 start to build the Assurance Case for the hall sensor architecture indicated in Fig. 2. The duplicated hall sensor circuit is being defined to provide adequate redundancy to meet the ASIL D requirement. The detailed definition of diverse software design is beyond the scope of this paper, but the use of two microcontrollers (MCUs) enables the freedom from interference requirements to be met. The fault handling capabilities of the architecture are indicated in a simplistic manner in Fig. 4 i.e. the ±250 mT range being exceeded represented by the goal 'Over range handling'. In practice this would be expanded to fully represent each relevant assumed safety requirement.

Figure 6 expands the assumptions on the dependent failures as the ASIL D requirement is decomposed to lower ASIL ratings. Again, many assumptions are dependent on how the integration team utilise the hall sensor in the Item.

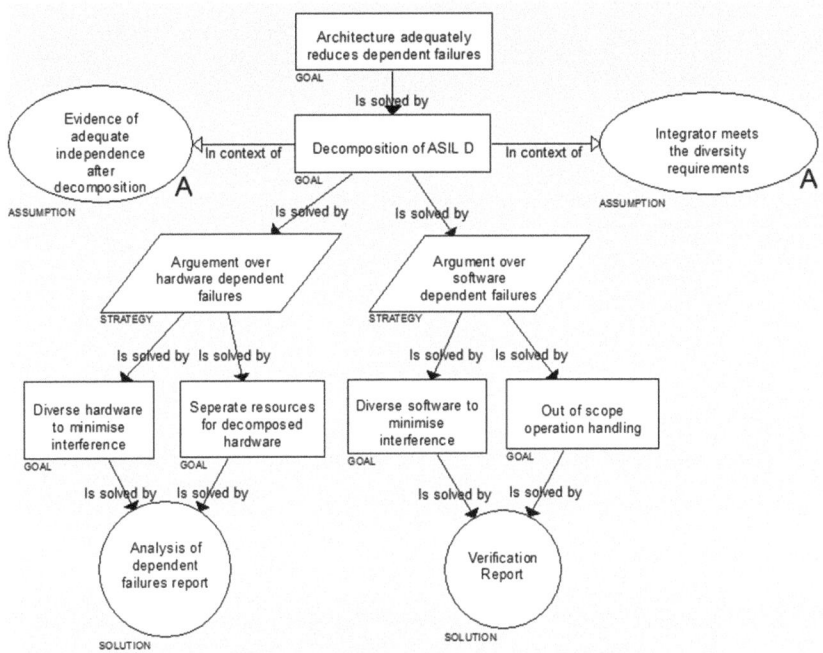

Fig. 6. Module dependant failure analysis

4 Item Development SEooC Integration

Referring to the right-hand side of Fig. 1, the activities applied during the integration of the SEooC into an Item may have an impact on the assumed requirements defined during the element development phase.

4.1 Assumption Validity

One major advantage of generating the assumed requirements using GSN is that the Assurance Case can be supplied to the integrators and they can use this model during the assumption validation phase (right-hand side of Fig. 1). At each stage of the integration the team will validate not only the assumptions, but also the requirements for the item integration. Figure 7 indicates a typical amendment of the system level Assurance Case where certain assumptions indicated in Fig. 3 are converted to justifications in Fig. 7. During the activity illustrated in Fig. 7 the integration team would justify assumptions such as a diversity between the power supplies interfacing with Vcc1 and Vcc2. A software based assumption justified at this point might be that the Item meets the diagnostic error detection requirements of the context based assumptions defined in Sect. 3.2.

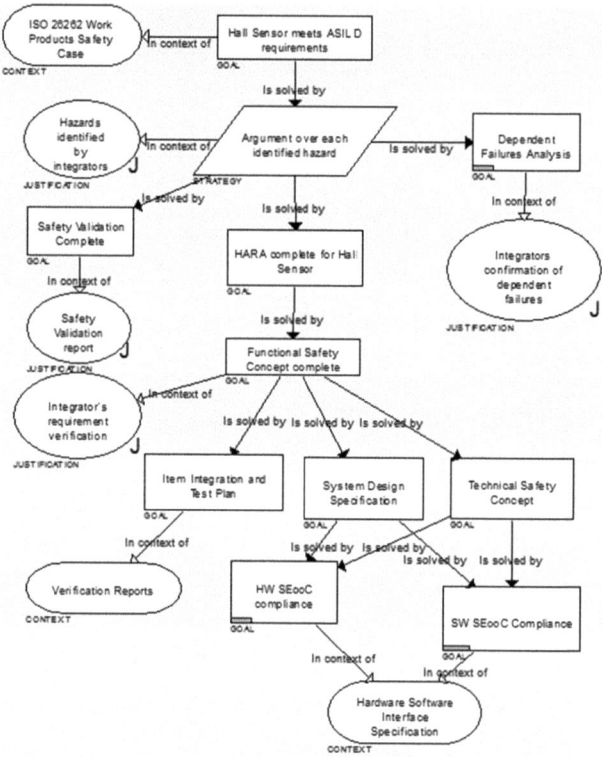

Fig. 7. Integrator validation of assumptions

4.2 Assumption Mismatch

One of the three potential outcomes listed in ISO 26262 for an SEooC during the integration phase is that a change in the SEooC itself is required. A detected difference may not meet the Item Safety Goal(s) and hence initiate a change to the SEooC.

The result of the assumption validity exercise may not necessarily be positive and both the manufacturer of the element and the item integrator need to be prepared to initiate a change management process in the event that there is a mismatch between assumed requirements and item requirements. Again GSN is a powerful graphic tool that enables a clearly defined mismatch to be high-lighted and communicated between the element developer and the item integrator. As the two parties work to resolve the conflict, the GSN assurance case can be amended and exchanged between the teams.

5 GSN and ISO 26262 Coverage

Literature reflects scarce industrial applications of GSN or completed Assurance Case supporting ISO26262 SEooC definitions. As represented by Fig. 1, a system SEooC development consists of system, hardware and software assumptions. This paper presents different figures supporting the whole ISO26262 SEooC definition processes described in Table 1:

- Assumptions on the functional safety requirements allocated to the SEooC
- Assumptions on the context of the SEooC
- The validation of the functional safety requirements of the item with the functional safety requirements assumed for the SEooC
- A change management activity, beginning with an impact analysis

Many SEooC manufactures at present list the assumed requirements in accompanying documents. These can be distributed over many pages and the relationship to other assumed requirements may not be easily identified. GSN representation as indicated in Figs. 3, 4, 5 and 6 assists in increasing the clarity of the ISO 26262 SEooC activity.

6 Conclusion

GSN, as a technique for documenting assumed requirements, lends itself very well to the process defined in ISO 26262 for SEooC. Assumptions and the rationale behind them can be documented and this documentation shared between the team developing the element and the team integrating the element into the item. A graphical representation such as GSN is both concise and clearer to understand. The granularity of the figures used in this paper are not as fine as an actual GSN representation due to the restricted space in the paper. However, the detail of justification and context in the GSN can be greatly expanded to eliminate ambiguity and support the assumptions used.

The ability to share a GSN assurance case between the teams involved in the development enables a more efficient working relationship between the two teams.

GSN cannot improve the quality of the assumed requirements, this is down to the expertise of the personnel involved, but it can assist those working on the project to reach their conclusions in a more efficient and timelier fashion.

GSN as a technique enables a concise overview of requirement assumptions. However, for a complex element such as a hall sensor the assurance case may reach a size where the comprehension is more of a challenge, due to the large number of strategies, assumptions and justifications.

GSN supports the definition of assumptions that may have been incomplete. This is another area that can benefit from a graphical representation, and in the case of sharing between the two teams, the Assurance Case can then be concluded by the Item integration team.

References

1. Chen, C., Sun, W., Zhou, X., Feng, X.: Magnetic induction model of the hall sensor: analysis and simulation of an automotive shift. IEEE Veh. Technol. Mag. **7**(1), 38–43 (2012)
2. Ra, W.-S., Lee, H.-J., Park, J.B., Yoon, T.-S.: Practical pinch de-tection algorithm for smart automotive power window control systems. IEEE Trans. Ind. Electron. **55**(3), 1376–1384 (2008)

3. Romero, L., Concha, A.: Control of position/velocity in a mobile robot using DC brushless motors. In: Electronics, Robotics and Automotive Mechanics Conference (CERMA 2006), vol. 2, pp. 200–205 (2006)
4. Ausserlechner, U., Motz, M., Holliber, M.: Drift of magnetic sensitivity of smart hall sensors due to moisture absorbed by the IC-package. In: Proceedings of IEEE Sensors, pp. 455–458 (2004)
5. Messerschmitt, D.G.: Rethinking components: from hardware and software to systems. Proc. IEEE **95**(7), 1473–1496 (2007)
6. Wells Counter point: Understanding hall effect sensors, Wells Counter point (1999). http://www.wellsve.com/sft503/Counterpoint3_1.pdf. Accessed 31 Mar 2016
7. International Standard Organisation: ISO 26262-1:2011- road vehicles – Functional safety – Part 1: Vocabulary (2011)
8. International Standard Organisation: ISO 26262-10:2012- road vehicles – Functional safety – Part 10: Guideline on ISO 26262 (2012)
9. Spriggs, J.: GSN - The Goal Structuring Notation. Springer, London (2012)
10. Nair, S., de la Vara, J.L., Sabetzadeh, M., Briand, L.: Classification, structuring, and assessment of evidence for safety – a systematic literature review. In: 2013 IEEE Sixth International Conference on Software Testing, Verification Validation, pp. 94–103, March 2013
11. Ayoub, A., Kim, B., Lee, I., Sokolsky, O.: A systematic approach to justifying sufficient confidence in software safety arguments. In: Ortmeier, F., Lipaczewski, M. (eds.) SAFECOMP 2012. LNCS, vol. 7612, pp. 305–316. Springer, Heidelberg (2012)
12. Fabbrini, F., Fusani, M., Lami, G.: One decade of software process assessments in automotive: a retrospective analysis. In: 2009 Fourth International Multi-conference Computing Global Information Technology, pp. 92–97 (2009)
13. Origin Consulting: "GSN Community Standard Version 1," Origin Consulting (2011). http://www.goalstructuringnotation.info/documents/GSN_Standard.pdf. Accessed 06 Apr 2016

Formal Methods and Functional Safety

Micheal Mac an Airchinnigh[(✉)]

ISCN LTD/Gesmbh, Bray, Ireland
mmaa@iscn.com

Abstract. Functional Safety is always a featured topic of the EuroSPI conferences. Hence it seems to be a given to consider all those related technical aspects. In our culture the car seems to reign supreme. The car is now endowed with all sorts of technologies. Perhaps one of the key technologies is the breaking system? Another important aspect of the modern car is the air bag, and the seat belt. Both of these have been designed and tested. There is a cultural aspect to the car, the shape and look. Once cars were basically functional. Now they (all) have a certain well-designed aesthetic. But there is another foundational aspect to this: the formal method of design, of shape.

Keywords: Formal methods · Functional safety

1 Definitive Standards and Up-to-date Definitive Descriptions

Let us imagine that one wishes to introduce the concept of functional safety to a new group of engineers in, for example, a typical automotive or aeromotive industry, such as AirBus? Naturally, today in 2016, one expects to find a reasonably good account of a subject such as functional safety in the Wikipedia. How shall we begin? Personally, I begin my research on Wikipedia (a sort of cloud wisdom that has emerged, grows, and constantly improves with age/time). I know something of how it works in practice. I am a Wikipedia editor. Wikipedia changes over time. It is on an up-spiral. Casual editors come and go. Regular editors have their own "identification page". Many, such as myself are anonymous. In the interest of impartiality I am not going to reveal my "Nom de Plume." When I first came across the article on Functional Safety (2015) I checked the corresponding Talk Page (Fig. 1).

Unfortunately, this nice warning no longer appears. In its place there is another. On the talk page, there is a rating: start-class [bottom of the class, in layperson's language]. There are 5 steps given (a minimum) by which functional safety may be achieved. I kept the sweeping brush icon for colourful effect. It is important to check the Talk page. One notes that today (2016-06-13) the article deals with the history of Functional Safety. There is a comment to the effect that EN 61508 was not addressed in 2009. The latest action is dated January 2013. When one turns to the IEC 61508, Functional Safety of Electrical/Electronic/Programmable Electronic Safety-related Systems (E/E/PE, or E/E/PES), one finds what appears to be a good account. But what is the real standard? On the Talk page there is little to be said (Fig. 2), as there is no indication of the quality of the article.

This article **may require** cleanup to meet **Wikipedia's** quality standards.

The specific problem is: **see talk page**. Please help improve this article if you can.

(January 2014)

Fig. 1. Wikipedia talk page

This article includes a list of references, but its sources remain unclear because it has insufficient inline citations. Please help to improve this article by introducing more precise citations. (February 2015)

Fig. 2. Wikipedia talk page

Let us get back to the (minimum) 5 steps by which functional safety may be achieved:

1. Identification of hazards: there are formal techniques, the HAZIDs, the HAZOPs, and the Accident Re-views [1].

   - The HAZID (Hazard Identification Studies),
   - The HAZOP (Hazard and operability study),
   - The Accident Reviews (e.g. reviews).

2. Assessment of risk-reduction
3. IEC 61508 (Functional Safety of Electrical/Electronic/Programmable Electronic Safety-related Systems (E/E/PE, or E/E/PES))
4. Mean Time Between Between Failures
5. Functional safety.

This is my chosen collection. I do not drive a car; I am often driven in a Skoda Octavia that I own. Consequently, it is now of personal interest in what way a formal standard such as ISO 26262 is applicable. It is "considered a best practice framework for achieving automotive functional safety". There are 10 parts, in the order:

- ISO 26262-10:2012 Road vehicles – Functional safety – Part 10: Guideline on ISO 26262 [yes! Part 10 comes first in the list.]
- ISO 26262-1:2011 Road vehicles – Functional safety – Part 1: Vocabulary
- ISO 26262-1:2011 Road vehicles – Functional safety – Part 2: Management of functional safety
- ISO 26262-3:2011 Road vehicles – Functional safety – Part 3: Concept phase
- ISO 26262-4:2011 Road vehicles – Functional safety – Part 4: Product development at the system level
- ISO 26262-5:2011 Road vehicles – Functional safety – Part 5: Product development at the hardware level

- ISO 26262-Road vehicles – Functional safety – Part 6: Product development at the software level
- ISO 26262-Road vehicles – Functional safety – Part 7: Production and operation
- ISO 26262-Road vehicles – Functional safety – Part 9: Automotive Safety Integrity
- Level (ASIL)-oriented and safety-oriented analyses [yes! Part 9 comes after Part 7 in the list.]
- ISO 26262-Road vehicles – Functional safety – Part 8: Supporting processes
- Software Process Improvement and Capability Determination (SPICE), https://en.wikipedia.org/wiki/ISO/IEC_15504 [2015-07-13][unassessed]
- "ISO 26262 is intended to be applied to safety-related systems that include one or more electrical and/or electronic (E/E) systems and that are installed in series production passenger cars with a maximum gross vehicle mass up to 3 500 kg."
- "ISO 26262 does not address unique E/E systems in special purpose vehicles such as vehicles designed for drivers with disabilities."

It seems to me that the relevant section that applies to the Skoda is Part 7: Production and operation. However, in the development, parts 4, 5 and 6 are crucial. What methods are used? To what extent are Formal Methods used?

2 Formal Methods: From Abstract State Machines (ASMs) to Z Notation

There are many kinds of formal methods. The keyword "formal" implies a certain amount of rigour and precision. In particular, formal logic fits the bill precisely. Hoare & Jifeng state "Scientists and engineers are entirely familiar with the practice of describing systems by predicates with an understood alphabet of free variables... Such practices have been decried by pure mathematicians and logicians who tend to use bound variables and closed mathematical abstractions like sets, functions and (less commonly) relations" [2].

It is important to note that there is an organization entitled Formal Methods Europe (FME) http://www.fmeurope.org. It has a presence on LinkedIn (https://www.linkedin.com/groups/3202098). I am one member of 1,442. The next conference, "The 21st International Symposium on Formal Methods" will be held in Cyprus 7-11 November 2016. To the best of my knowledge, FME has its repository hosted in Graz University of Technology.

2.1 The Vienna Development Method (VDM)

Towards the end of 1972 the Vienna group again turned their attention to the problem of systematically developing a compiler from a language definition. The overall approach adopted has been termed the *"Vienna Development Method"*. Based on the above comments it should be no surprise that a "denotational" approach was adopted for the definition itself. (Using, however, the exit approach rather than "continuations").

"The meta-language actually adopted ("Meta-IV") is used to define major portions of PL/I. There is really not much space here to give a considered account of the use of a formal method, A simple example from 1978 shall suffice:

```
Example 0 — the Grocery Shop
Semantic Domains
1. GROCER :: SHELVES   STORE   CASH   CATALOGUE
2. SHELVES = Wno —> N
3. STORE = Wno —> N
4. CASH = N_0
5. CATALOGUE = Wno —> N
6. Description :: Price Minimum Maximum Size
7. Price = N_1
8. Minimum = N_1
9. Maximum = N_1
10. Size = N_1
```

- Annotations: "The model is concerned with rather self-contained fragments of a grocery: its inventory, cash and catalogue subsystem."
- "A grocery is here selectively abstracted by abstractions of its shelves and store, i.e. inventory, its cash register, and its catalogue."
- "The shelves display a finite, non-zero number of items of a finite variety of merchandise. Merchandise presently being abstracted by ware number codes."
- "In the store-room is similarly kept a finite, non-zero number of boxed quantities of items of a finite se-lection of wares."
- "The cash register is simply abstracted by the cash it contains." (The euro did not exist at that time).
- "The grocers' catalogue lists a description of each sort of merchandise."
- Such a description here consists of the unit (item) sales price; the minimum and maximum (lower– & upper–bound) numbers of items, of the described merchandise, which ought, respectively may be placed on the shelves; and finally the size of the stored box, measured in terms of the number of merchandise items it contains.
- Prices are measured in integer (positive number) units of currency.

Comments. The above description 'read' the formulae as describing a grocery. The formulae (1–10), and (12–15) below, constitute an abstract syntax (abstract syntaxes). Each line (1, 2, … 10) is an abstract syntax rule. The rules all have their left-hand sides being identifiers. The right-hand sides are so-called domain-expressions.

The described domains are said to constitute the semantic domains. Semantic domains are "what the whole thing is about". Syntactic domains, described below in formulae 12–14, are (just the) objects which denote manipulations of semantic objects.

```
Well-Formedness Constraints
is-wf-GROCER(mk-GROCER(shelves, store, cash, catalogue))
  .1 (dom store ≤ dom shelves ≤ dom catalogue)
  .2  ^ (for all wno in dom catalogue)
  .3     (let mk-Description (price, min, max, size) = cat-
alogue (wno) in
  .4      (0 <= size <= max - min)
  .5          ^ (( wno in dom shelves)
  .6       in (let items = shelves(wno) in
  .7        (( wno in dom store) -> (min <= items <= max),
  .8         T          -> items <= max)))
_ _ annotations:
```

The domain descriptions captured the essence of how we abstractly view groceries, but the defined domains contain objects, i.e., groceries, which do not satisfy natural constraints:

- 11.0 For a grocery(…) to be well-formed, the following constraints must be satisfied… and so on.

Comment. From a personal perspective, I noted that my copy is signed by the authors: Dines Bjoerner (Technical University of Denmark) and Cliff B. Jones (IBM International Education Centre, B-1310 La Hulpe). I picked up my copy in Cologne, Germany, whilst on a cycling tour. My memory suggests that this subsequently had a major impact on my Doctor's Degree in Trinity College Dublin.

2.2 Agile Methods

"Agile methodology is an alternative to traditional project management, typically used in software development." http://agilemethodology.org. [23.10.2008]. It has charming words such as "agility" and "scrum." It seems to me that the "scrum" is clearly borrowed from the game of Rugby, https://en.wikipedia.org/wiki/Scrum_(rugby). The picture shown (Fig. 3), exhibits precisely the closeknit grouping of the [actors/players/programmers.] [The picture is courtesy of PierreSelim [own work], taken 13 November 2011, 17.30.08. Heineken Cup, Stade Ernest Wallon. Match between: Stade toulousain—Gloucester Rugby.

To what extent does formality enter into the input or output of the scrum? How are actions (programlets) documented and tested? Clearly, the method is strictly informal? What would it take to formalize it? There is, of course, Agile software development, https://en.wikipedia.org/wiki/Agile_software_development. Wikipedia presents a good account of same.

"Agile methods were initially seen as best suitable for non-critical software projects, thereby excluded from use in regulated domains such as medical devices, pharmaceutical, financial, nuclear systems, automotive, and avionics sectors, etc. However, in the last several years, there have been several initiatives for the adaptation of agile methods for these domains".

Fig. 3. Scrum

Well, although I am a bit late, I have contacted the Graz folks and find: Bernhard K. Aichernig is an associate professor, key researcher and project manager at Graz University of Technology, Austria. He is an expert in formal methods and testing. His research focuses on the foundations of software engineering in order to achieve more reliable computer-based systems. Since 2006, he runs European projects on this topic (CREDO, MOGENTES, MBAT). Bernhard is also a board member of Formal Methods Europe (FME), an international organisation that promotes well-founded techniques in software engineering and organizes the Formal Methods (FM) conferences. From 2002 to 2006 he worked as a Research Fellow at UNU-IIST in Macao S.A.R., China, a research institute of the United Nations on software technology. He holds a habilitation in Practical Computer Science and Formal Methods, a doctorate, and a diploma engineer degree from Graz University of Technology.

2.3 What Does It Mean to Be Formal?

"In Epheseus… when an architect accepts the charge of a public work, he has to promise what the cost will be… when more than one fourth has to be spent in addition on the work, the money required to finish it is taken from his property." Vitruvius https://en.wikipedia.org/wiki/Vitruvius [born c. 80–70 BC, died after c. 15 BC] the development of any large system must be preceded by the construction of a specification of what is required… Computer systems need precise specifications. Unfortunately, the current practice in the software industry is to employ an informal mixture of text and pictures." [3].

Ultimately, one must be practical. One must write the program. An Agile approach suggests that this can be done in piecemeal fashion.

3 Programming Languages Ada to "X Knows Where"?

There are hundreds of programming languages? There are 54 listed in Wikipedia, beginning with the letter A. Naturally, there are a small number of such languages which stand out. I pick out those that I have actually used in the past, [exceptions are marked X].

Under A, one immediately recognizes Ada, ALGOL, APL; under B, there is B, BASIC; Under C there is C, C ++ X, COMAL, CSP; Under D, nothing special; Under E, Eiffel X, Erlang X; under F, Forth, Fortran, Franz Lisp; under G, Go! X; under H, Haskell, HyperTalk; under I, nothing special under J, Java X, Javascript; under K, nothing special; under L, LaTeX; Lisp, [note formally named Lisp – ISO/IEC 13816], Logo; under M, Mathematica, Metafont, Modula X; under N, nothing special; under P, Pascal – ISO 7185, PL/I – ISO 6160, PostScript, Prolog; under Q, nothing special; under R, nothing special; under S, Simula, Smalltalk X, SNOBOL(SPITBOL), SPARK (i.e. SPARKAda) X, Squirrel; under T, TeX; under U, UCSD Pascal, Unix shell; under V, Visual Basic; under W, Wolfram Language; under X, nothing special; under Y, nothing special; under Z, Z notation X.

3.1 MISRA C

"MISRA C is a set of software development guidelines for the C programming language developed by MISRA (Motor Industry Software Reliability Association). Its aims are to facilitate code safety, security, portability and reliability in the context of embedded systems, specifically those systems programmed in ISO C. There is also a set of guidelines for MISRA C ++. MISRA has evolved as a widely accepted model for best practices by leading developers in sectors including aerospace, telecom, medical devices, defence, railway, and others." It is to be noted that "MISRA C is not an open standard; the guideline documents must be bought by users or implementers." https://en.wikipedia.org/wiki/MISRA_C. It was highlighted in the paper, Messnarz, Richard et al., Implementing Functional Safety Standards. Software Quality Professional. Vol. 17, Issue 3, June 2015. The company may be contacted @ http://www.misra.org.uk.

Being a "closed shop" one is not able to give any sort of coherent account of what is involved. However, it is interesting that C is used.

3.2 Ada & SPARKAda

The Ada programming language (1980) was developed for the Department of Defense, USA. Jean Ichbiah was the designer. SPARKAda is currently a stable release: 15.0.1/February 17, 2015. From a European perspective, one focuses on Ada-Europe @ http://www.ada-europe.org/info/board. Curiously, the latter shows only the 2013 Workplan. The next conference is in Pisa, Italy @ http://www.cister.isep.ipp.pt/ae2016/. "This edition of Ada-Europe will feature a focused Special Session on Safe, Predictable Parallel Software Technologies. Following the intensifying trend of usage of Multi-/Many-core systems, it is increasingly important to assess how reliable software technologies need to adapt to these complex platforms, as well as how parallel models need to adapt to domains where safety and predictability is a must."

One of the topics is the "Serious game". Another interesting (old) paper is "Formal Methods: State of the Art and Future Directions", by E.M. Clarke and J.M. Wing, https://www.cs.umd.edu/~mvz/cmsc630/clarke96formal.pdf. [4] Carnegie Mellon University. Thanks to Google? It is still accessible.

4 WrapUp

One likes to have a "Proof of Concept" when embarking on an innovative development path. Yes, we have good systems today. Yes, we have good programs, good software. Where shall we be in 2017? Will it be more of the same? Predictions are fun! Outcomes are highly unpredictable.

"Commercial pressure to produce higher quality software is always increasing. Formal methods have already demonstrated success in specifying commercial and safety-critical software; and in verifying protocol standards and hardware designs." E. W. Clarke and J.M. Wing [5].

E-Cars are on the road/on the way. In Ireland. There are currently "1,200 public charge points across the Island of Ireland, including fast chargers along main inter-urban routes." A map is available online at https://esb.ie/our-businesses/ecars/charge-point-map: CHAdeMO, ComboCCS, FASTAC43, StandardType2, Hotel/Other. A typical example is located at

```
Supervalu, Courthouse Road, Fermoy, County Cork
CHAdeMO DC 45kW Instructional Video CPs:C9PQM
```

See also

```
Combo DC 45kW Instructional Video CPs:C9PQM
Fast AC (Type-2) 43kW Instructional Video CPs:C9PQM
24 hour access
Lat/Long: 52.137660,-8.266641 Google Map
```

4.1 Postscript: Brexit?

Naturally, one now asks what the impact of Brexit will have on "The Global Car Industry".

- http://jalopnik.com/here-s-how-brexit-could-affect-the-global-car-industry-1782568391 posted by Michael Ballaban.
- Ford considers UK job cuts after Brexit vote as carmakers eye future (Financial Times) https://next.ft.com/content/120f17d4-3a17-11e6-a780-b48ed7b6126f.
- NERI Working Paper Series : The Economic Implications of BREXIT for Northern Ireland, Paul Mac Flynn, April 2016 http://www.nerinstitute.net/download/pdf/brexit_wp_250416.pdf.

References

1. Safety & Risk Management Services, GL Plants & Pipelines (Germany). Hazard Identification Studies (HAZID), Germanischer Lloyd — Service/Product Description. http://www.germanlloyd.org/pdf/Hazard_Identification_Studies.pdf. Accessed 06 April 2016

2. Hoare, C.A.R., Jifeng, H.: Unifying Theories of Programming. Oxford University Computing Laboratory, Prentice Hall, London (1998). ISBN 0-13-458761-8
3. Jones, C.B.: Systematic Software Development Using VDM. Prentice-Hall, Upper Saddle River (1990)
4. Clarke, E.M., Wing, J.M.: Formal Methods: State of the Art and Future Directions. Carnegie Mellon University

Supporting Innovation
and Improvement

Forming a European Innovation Cluster as a Think Tank and Knowledge Pool

Richard Messnarz[1,2], Andreas Riel[3(✉)], Gabriele Sauberer[4], and Michael Reiner[5]

[1] ISCN LTD, Bray, Ireland
[2] GesmbH, Graz, Austria
rmess@iscn.com
[3] EMIRAcle and ISCN Group, Grenoble, France
andreas.riel@grenoble-inp.fr
[4] Termnet, Vienna, Austria
gsauberer@termnet.org
[5] University of Applied Sciences Krems, Krems an der Donau, Austria
michael.reiner@fh-krems.ac.at

Abstract. In the ECQA (European Certification and Qualification Association, www.ecqa.org) there are different Job Role Committee consortia which have developed training and certificates related to entrepreneurship and innovation. This paper elaborates an innovation and improvement strategy for Europe where the different consortia join forces to form a Europe wide alliance based on a pool of several modern certified job roles comprising more than 120 knowledge and training modules, 400 performance criteria and learning outcomes, as well as an online campus. The strategy is to bring these different consortia and qualifications together and create an entrepreneurship and innovation portfolio available for universities and businesses across all the European member states. An ECQA certified terminology manager qualification approach will be used to create an ontology linking all these entrepreneurship qualifications to form a European knowledge pool.

Keywords: Innovation · Entrepreneurship · Pool of knowledge · Terminology · ECQA

1 The Need for an Innovation Knowledge Pool Strategy

About 50 % of new businesses fail during their first five years, the so-called 'valley of death' of business development. To achieve the increased economic growth rates targeted by Europe 2020, it is vital to increase the resilience and competitiveness of these firms [1]. Support in the form of dedicated information, professional services and technical advice are fundamental means to achieving this goal. Promoting entrepreneurship in schools and other educational settings is of key importance to encourage more entrepreneurial mind-sets [2]. Education for entrepreneurship makes a difference, as young people who go through entrepreneurial programmes and activities start more companies. The percentage of alumni who become entrepreneurs 3 to 5 years after leaving school is 3–5 %, whereas for those who participated in any entrepreneurship education this percentage rises to 15–20 % [3]. They also start companies earlier. Studies show that university students who had received entrepreneurship education founded businesses 0.7 years before graduation, while those without an education in entrepreneurship founded enterprises 2.8 years after graduation [3].

There is a need to stimulate the entrepreneurial mind-sets of young people and to create a more favourable societal climate for entrepreneurship, as the EU is not fully exploiting its entrepreneurial potential. In the European reference framework, 'Entrepreneurship and a sense of initiative' is one of eight key competences for lifelong learning which citizens require for their personal fulfilment, social inclusion, active citizenship and employability in a knowledge-based society [4]. Education has an important role to play for improving this situation.

In an EU report about New Skills for New Jobs, one of the recommended key actions is to: "Develop the integration of the key enabling competences such as creativity, innovation, entrepreneurship, and citizenship, in schools, in higher education and initial and continuous vocational education and training. Develop and provide tools for individual self-assessment" [5].

Innovation and entrepreneurship competences represent key skills to leverage industry growth in Europe and to increase the job opportunities for people entering the labour market [4]. So far innovation management, entrepreneurship and innovation training and education programs are offered in different member states with different certificates and different content. Recent unemployment and economic growth figures clearly illustrate that there is a high demand for such programs. There is an especially high demand for the combination of innovation and entrepreneurship skills, because innovative approaches and solutions are a solid ground for successful and sustainable entrepreneurship. So far, many entrepreneurship programs fail to include the dimension of innovation and innovation management in an adequate manner [6].

2 Approach to Forming the Pool of Innovation Knowledge

In the ECQA (European Certification and Qualification Association, www.ecqa.org) there are different Job Role Committee consortia which have developed training and certificates related to entrepreneurship and innovation. The entrepreneurship and innovation learning strategy for Europe presented in this paper is based joining forces of industry-academia consortia to form a Europe wide alliance with a pool of currently 8 job roles and certificates, more than 120 knowledge and training modules, as well as 400 performance criteria and learning outcomes. All of them are part of an EU online campus which facilitates on-line and distance learning.

DEUCERT (a former EU project aiming at disseminating the ECQA on a broad European scale) has been awarded as LLP Best Practice in 2014. Members of this project are founding members of this ECQA. ECQA standardized how skills are described in Europe, set up skills and exam portals and standardized the way how exams for specific job roles are performed, and built clusters of job roles (currently more than 30 job roles). Inside the ECQA job role communities and consortia (JRC) a cluster of different Entrepreneurship and innovation related qualifications have been set up since 2005:

- ECQA Certified Innovation Manager – improve and excel in innovation processes in industry (origins in EU LLP project ORGANIC, 2003–2005, rework and extension in 2013) [7].
- ECQA Certified Diversity Manager – leverage diversity in organizations for creativity, innovation and sustainable business [8].
- ECQA Certified Researcher Entrepreneur – prepare students at universities for entrepreneurship (EU LLP project ResEUr, 2009–2011).
- ECQA Certified Idea to Enterprise Expert – prepare students aged 14-18 for either a university study in innovation or entrepreneurship in their work life. (EU LLP project I2E in 2013–2014.
- ECQA Certified Corporate Social Responsibility Manager – social responsibility and ethics based on ISO 26000 (EU LLP project SOCIRES in 2011–2012).
- ECQA Certified Valorization Expert – exploitation and valorization of results of innovation. (EU LLP project VALO, 2013–2014).
- ECQA Certified Social Media Networker – networking skills (EU LLP Project SIMS, 2013–2014).
- ECQA Certified Terminology Manager – master terminology as a practical and strategic means to foster collaboration and communication among experts (EU LLP project EU Cert, 2007–2009).

The plan is to create a JRC cluster into which all innovation related JRCs are merged. This approach will bring these different consortia and qualifications together and create an entrepreneurship and innovation education and training portfolio available for universities and businesses in the European member states. In order to neatly link the knowledge made explicit by the different JRCs, a terminology model will be created. Terminology experts from the ECQA Certified Terminology Manager JRC will facilitate this task, and therefore be invited to join the cluster for innovation qualification.

3 Architecture of an Integrated Knowledge Pool for Qualification

The ECQA has standardized how skills are described in Europe (see skills set structure in Fig. 1), has set up skills and exam portals and standardized the way how exams for specific job roles are per-formed, and built clusters of job roles (total 30 job roles). The innovation cluster concept brings these different entrepreneurship and innovation consortia and qualifications together and creates an entrepreneurship and innovation portfolio strategy for the European member states.

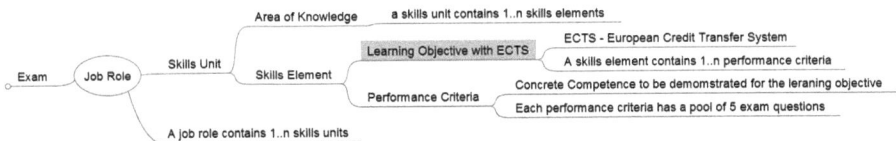

Fig. 1. The skills set for a job role (with ECTS mapping)

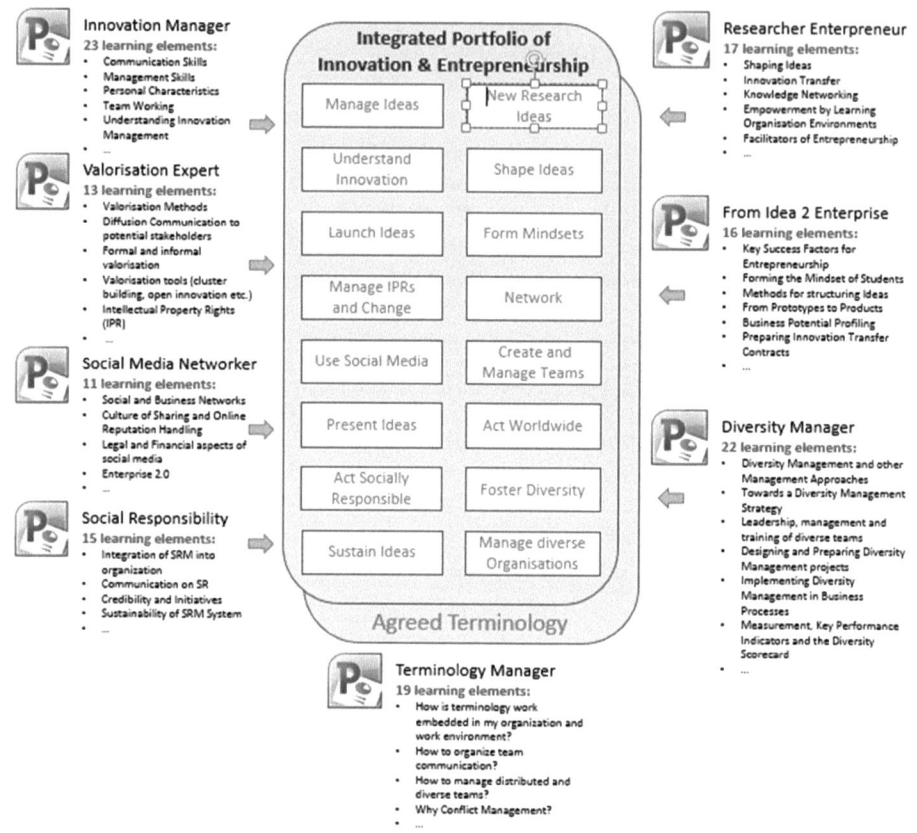

Fig. 2. The integrated pool architecture

The cluster strategy also integrates innovation methods from different viewpoints (see Fig. 2) [9].

In this innovation cluster the ECQA JRCs share the pool of more than 120 knowledge elements and each knowledge element has training material, exam questions, skill card with learning objectives and a multimedia online lecture. Based on this pool a new ontology and learning path can be elaborated based on identified links between the elements and a clustering of elements by content across the different job roles.

4 Different Integration Methods

To create the portfolio strategy a number of mapping strategies need to be implemented (see Fig. 3).

A. The Portfolio Approach. The industry can access a pool of 120 learning elements which each represents a unique 1–2 h lecture with training materials and exercises. This way, trainers from industry, academia and government can pick the interesting and

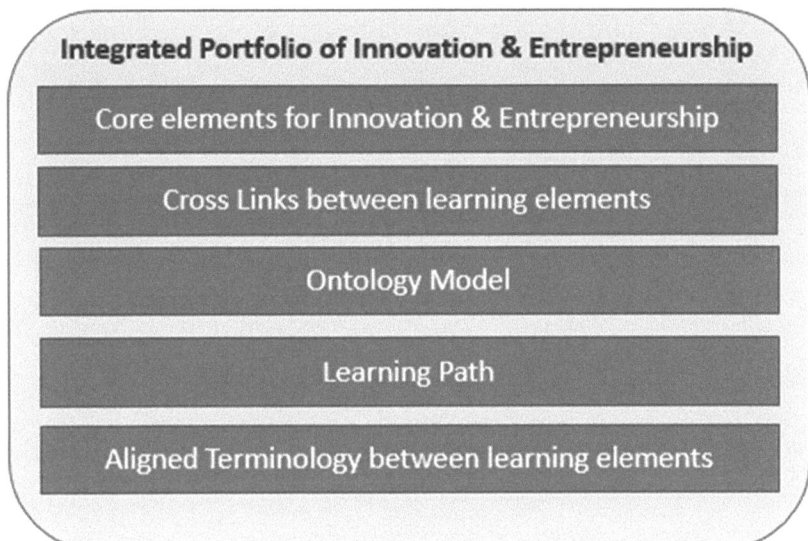

Fig. 3. Integration methods

relevant elements and configure their innovation strategy trainings adapted to the specific needs of their target groups.

This requires the following functions and services to be provided by the ECQA:

- The user can browse all the 120 elements in a pool with a guidance about the content of the elements.
- A configurator allows to select the elements and configure a new job role specific to the needs of the user.
- The exam software in ECQA creates the exam based on the selected elements across all job roles.
- The ECQA certificate is based on the selected elements and displays the agreed ECTS and the passed level.

B. The Core Elements for Innovation and Entrepreneurship Approach. The cluster (integrating different ECQA job roles, see Fig. 2) defines an innovation manager basic level and different options to continue on an advanced level (see Figs. 4 and 5). There are two options to define an advanced level. In Fig. 4 the advanced level is defined as the field in which a person wants to specialise. In Fig. 5 the advanced levels are just defined by more elements to cover and a master level is achieved when all elements are covered.

C. The Cross Links Between Elements Approach. The cluster (integrating different ECQA job roles, see Fig. 2) collaborates with ECQA certified terminology managers to define and structure relationships between elements. For the entity relationship diagrams different types of relationships can be defined.

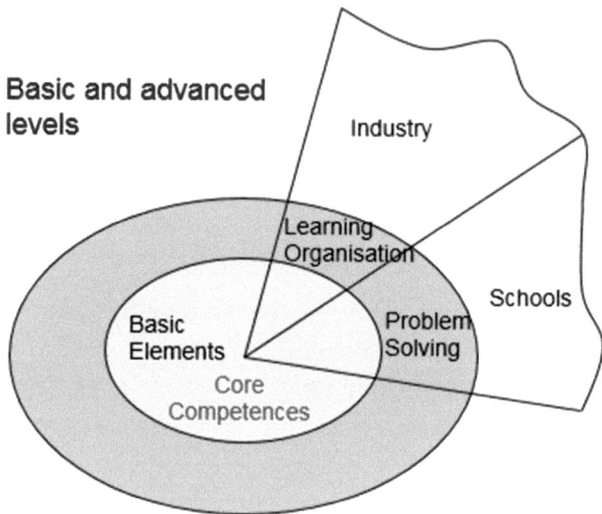

Fig. 4. Core elements and advanced level based on the specialisation area

1. Content Link – overlapping content
2. Content Link – complementary content
3. Content Link – contradictions

Type 3 "contradictions" must be solved. The inputs from type 1 "overlapping" and type 2 "complementary" can be used to classify the slides in related elements into a base level, advanced level and strategy level of slides. This classification will then support the approach described in Fig. 5 above.

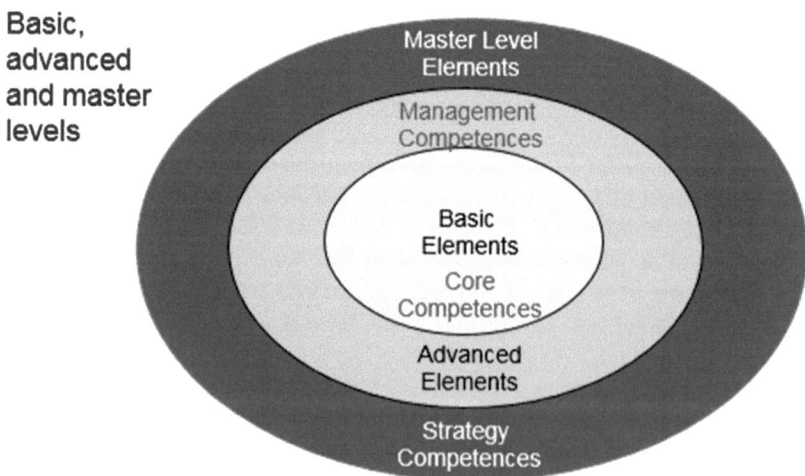

Fig. 5. Core elements and advanced level based on number of elements covered

Another way to use these content links type 1 and type 2 is to classify the slides in related elements into a base level and a specific theme based advanced level. This classification will then support the approach described in Fig. 4 above.

D. The Ontology Model. The cluster (integrating different ECQA job roles, see Fig. 2) defines different views to display the relationships between elements which allow to offer an ontology based view to the innovation users (Fig. 6).

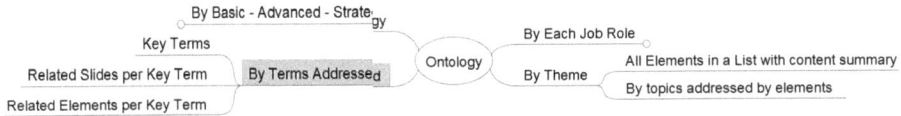

Fig. 6. Creating links between elements and slides by ontology

This requires

- that key terms can be selected;
- a view allowing to browse key terms and see the related elements;
- within each element the slides addressing a specific term to be highlighted (including high-lighting the location of the search term on each slide).

E. The Learning Path Approach. The cluster (integrating different ECQA job roles, see Fig. 2) defines a relationship "<" between the elements. Element A < Element B means that to understand B the users need to attend A first. This allows to create a directed graph which guides the users through the pool of 120 elements. An example is shown in Fig. 7.

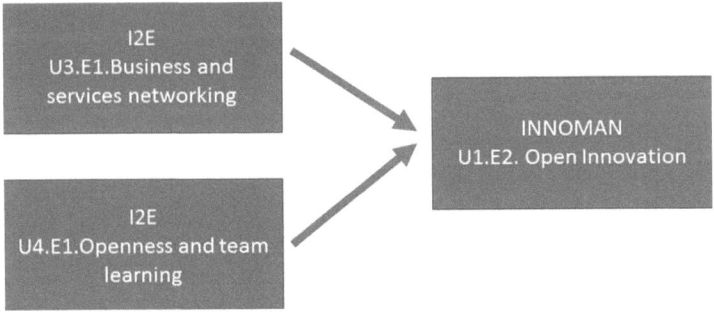

Fig. 7. Creating a learning path

F. The Terminology Approach. A team of ECQA certified terminology managers scans all 120 elements (approx. 4000 slides) and establishes a list of concepts and terms which are used in all elements. The list shall focus on key concepts and terms comprising approx. 300 terms. For each term related elements and slides are assigned. This allows to create a view in ECQA where based on a selected term a set of elements is proposed to innovation users. For these terms a list of definitions (glossary) is made available.

5 Acknowledgement and Disclaimer

This paper presents the core ideas of the ECQA's strategy leading to the implementation of an EU-wide agreed portfolio of certified learning elements supporting the teaching and learning of modern skills in innovation and entrepreneurship. Such a portfolio is needed in order to forge innovation and entrepreneurship attitudes and skills consistently across all levels of education and professional training. An ontology-driven approach will be used in order to provide guidance through the innovation knowledge pool, and modular certification will be a driver for the international recognition of acquired competences. This implies the creation of a formally networked thesaurus of innovation-related terms signifying the knowledge space related to modern innovation and innovation management paradigms.

In order to implement the vision of the European Think Tank and Knowledge Pool around innovation and entrepreneurship skills, the ECQA has defined a strategy based on pillars representing key success factors of modern, innovative organisations. The objective is to create expert clusters around each of these pillars, based on the JRCs of existing certified program associated with them. Within these clusters, work groups will be formed in order to elaborate the outlined approaches.

The ECQA also plans to continue their long and successful of EU projects in order to help scale up initiatives of work groups to the European level and beyond. They are also working on extending the pedagogic approaches to teaching and learning innovation and entrepreneurship skills. One of the most prominent trends actively pursued by key cluster members is gamification, i.e., ludic approaches to teaching and learning.

References

1. Gaynor, J., Mackiewicz, A., Ramaswami, R.: Entrepreneurship and innovation. Editorial. The keys to global economic recovery. Ernst & Young (2009)
2. Fostering entrepreneurial mindsets through education and learning. Commission Communication COM, 33 final (2006)
3. Final Report: Report on the results of public consultation on The Entrepreneurship 2020 Action Plan. http://eur-lex.europa.eu/legal-content/EN/TXT/?uri=celex%3A52012DC0795. Accessed 02 May 2016
4. The Green Paper on Entrepreneurship in Europe. http://europa.eu.int/comm/enterprise/entrepreneurship/green_paper/index.htm. Accessed 22 Feb 2011
5. New Skills for New Jobs: Action Now: A report by the Expert Group on New Skills for New Jobs prepared for the European Commission European Union (2010)
6. Entrepreneurship in higher education, especially within non-business studies. Final Report of the Expert Group. European Commission, Enterprise and Industry Directorate-General. Promotion of SMEs competitiveness Entrereneurship (2008)
7. Riel, A.: Innovation managers 2.0: which competencies? In: O'Connor, R.V., Pries-Heje, J., Messnarz, R. (eds.) EuroSPI 2011. CCIS, vol. 172, pp. 278–289. Springer, Heidelberg (2011)

8. Sauberer, G.: Masterthesis 2014: Der Europäische Diversity Führerschein: Neue Fähigkeiten und Strategien für Diversitäts- und Innovations management in Europa und weltweit, Masterarbeit zur Erlangung des akademischen Grades Master of Business Administration an der Fachhochschule Burgenland, Austrian Institute of Management (2014)
9. Riel, A., Messnarz, R., Sauberer, G.: Towards an integrated learning and certification strategy for global innovation. In: Proceedings of the 23rd EuroAsiaSPI² Conference, Ankara, pp. 8.15–8.20 (2015)

Innovative Marketing in Low-Tech Micro Companies - Lessons Learned from Study Projects

Michael Reiner[1(✉)], Christian Reimann[2], and Elena Vitkauskaite[3]

[1] University of Applied Sciences Krems, Krems an der Donau, Austria
Michael.reiner@fh-krems.ac.at
[2] University of Applied Sciences and Arts Dortmund, Dortmund, Germany
christian.reimann@fh-dortmund.de
[3] Kaunas University of Technology, Kaunas, Lithuania
elena.vitkauskaite@ktu.edu

Abstract. In current markets, there is a strong need for innovation (products, marketing, etc.) to set yourself apart from competitors. However, innovation is usually labour and capital intensive, and requires qualified employees with freedom for creative endeavours. Large or medium sized companies in most cases do have resources for that. High-tech micro companies (such as start-ups) appear in the market by creating innovation and therefore lack the pressure of existing companies. Low tech-micro companies on the other hand, work in established industries, have many competitors, and do not have time to do little else besides routine core activities of running their business. Therefore, these companies have a need for innovation but this need is practically impossible to fulfil, because of lack of capital, access to the required innovative technologies, the necessary experts (qualification) and general lack of time. The study project presented was aiming to develop virtual reality marketing game prototypes for low-tech micro companies. Participants of the project were marketing students from Lithuania, business administration students from Austria and computer science students from Germany. Oculus Rift game prototypes were successfully developed because of this project to two Lithuanian micro companies, one veterinarian practice and a tree nursery. Both micro companies now are having the opportunity to use these marketing innovations in cooperation with the universities. Project results were supported by feedback from the companies. Experts of the field as well as participating companies rated the transfer of innovation as good practice and a transferable model for innovation within low-tech micro companies.

Keywords: Innovation · Virtual reality · Lessons learned · International project team · Communication · Innovative marketing

1 Introduction

A study of S&P 500 index of Innosight (2012) shows that the average lifespan of a company in 1958 was 60 years, while it is today only 18 years. It is expected that until 2027 approx. 75 % of all the most valuable companies will be replaced by (mostly) young companies. While most of these companies will be high tech start-ups, there is a chance for low tech companies if they know about the potential of Industry 4.0 and Internet of Things. It seems that basically Start-ups and innovative small companies will profit from the digitalization of the world market more that established companies due to low barriers at the generation of new products (Blank, 2013). More and more it will be important for small and micro companies to cooperate with established companies or universities to increase innovative power, as seen by the European Commission. According to Eckstein (2009) the success of a global scale project depends on the success of an established and cultivated communication channel amongst distributed and diverse groups. But author also points out that agile programming here is much harder due to the great amount of communication that is necessary.

In this contribution we are going to identify the lessons learned from running an interdisciplinary inter-national study project and to highlight the potential synergies of micro companies cooperating with universities to create marketing innovations.

2 Background

According to OECD (2005), marketing innovation is "the implementation of a new marketing method involving significant changes in product design or packaging, product placement, product promotion or pricing". In current markets there is a strong need for innovation (products, marketing, etc.) in order to gain a competitive advantage and to make a company, brand or product stand out of mass of competitors. The positive relation between innovation and performance is proved by available wealth of evidence (Love, and Roper, 2015). However, innovation process is usually labour and capital intensive, and requires qualified staff with freedom for creative endeavours. Large or medium sized companies in most cases can invest in new technologies, equipment, and qualified staff (Laforet, 2008). High-tech companies appear in the market by investing "in rapidly emerging or evolving technology as a key part of its product development, production or marketing strategy" (Park, 2005), namely by innovating. Therefore, high-tech micro companies (such as start-ups) lack the pressure of existing companies and appear because they innovate and obtain competitive advantage already. Small low-tech companies can hardly afford investment required for innovation, though (Laforet, 2008). Low-tech micro companies often operate in established industries, have a lot of competitors, and do not have time to do little else besides routine core activities of running their business. Hirsch-Kreinsen, Jacobson, Laestadius and Smith (2005), stress the importance of low-tech industries to the market by emphasizing their benefits to the economies, such as employment, growth, and knowledge formation. These authors claim, that low-tech industries have critical innovative capabilities that support technological advance elsewhere. Low-tech companies have a need for innovation but this need is practically impossible to fulfil, because of lack of capital, access to the required innovative technologies, the necessary experts (qualification) and general lack of time. Research on innovations in small and medium sized companies, not to speak of low-tech micro companies specifically, is still fragmented, based on small sample sizes, and lack scientific rigour (Laforet, 2008; Heidenreich, 2009; Love, and Roper, 2015). Research presented in this paper does not presume to apply high level of scientific rigour, and is based on single study project, however, taking into account the lack of research in general, attempts to push the knowledge about marketing innovation in low-tech micro companies forward.

Universities are recognized important stakeholders in innovation ecosystems (Charles, 2006). Universities, along with other public research organizations, produce technical personnel and cutting-edge scientific knowledge, both of which are crucial for innovation (Whittington, Owen-Smith, and Powell, 2009). However, researchers mostly focus on role of universities for innovation in knowledge-intensive industries. In this paper we consider a role of university for innovations in low-tech micro companies too, by considering them as locations educating prospective qualified staff and therefore constantly looking for hands-on projects for students, preferring real life business problems.

3 Method and Approach

Although most low-tech micro companies usually spend most of their effort simply operating their business successfully, being innovative or at least applying innovative methods is becoming more and more crucial for them to gain or keep their competitiveness in their respective field of business. This creates a significant challenge for those companies due to many reasons, especially when it comes to areas which are out of the focus of their usually narrow field of core competencies. Without external support, they can at best apply best practices within areas they already work in. We apply this cooperative approach for low-tech Micro companies with universities or research Institutes, which offers mutual benefits for both parties and allows the involved companies to overcome the barriers keeping them from using innovative methods.

4 Cooperative Fugle Innovation Process

The range of cooperation with regard to the Fugle Innovation Process can be seen in the Fig. 1. While the micro company continues to mainly concentrate on its core competence of running the exploitation of their current products and services, all other parts of the process will be done in cooperation with the respective research partner. The intensity of involvement of both parties shift from left to the right from a strong involvement of the research partner on the very left to a growing influence of the micro company to the very right. However the whole cooperation is coordinated and mainly driven by the research partner to allow the micro company to continue focusing on its core business.

5 Roles and Responsibilities

This leads to the roles within the cooperation as shown in Table 1. The role of the coordinator of the cooperation is filled by a person from the university or research partner and takes over the tasks typically assigned to a project manager. Besides the overall coordination, this includes managing the involved stakeholders, possible risks, controlling the budget and other resources and so on. In general, this role could be taken over

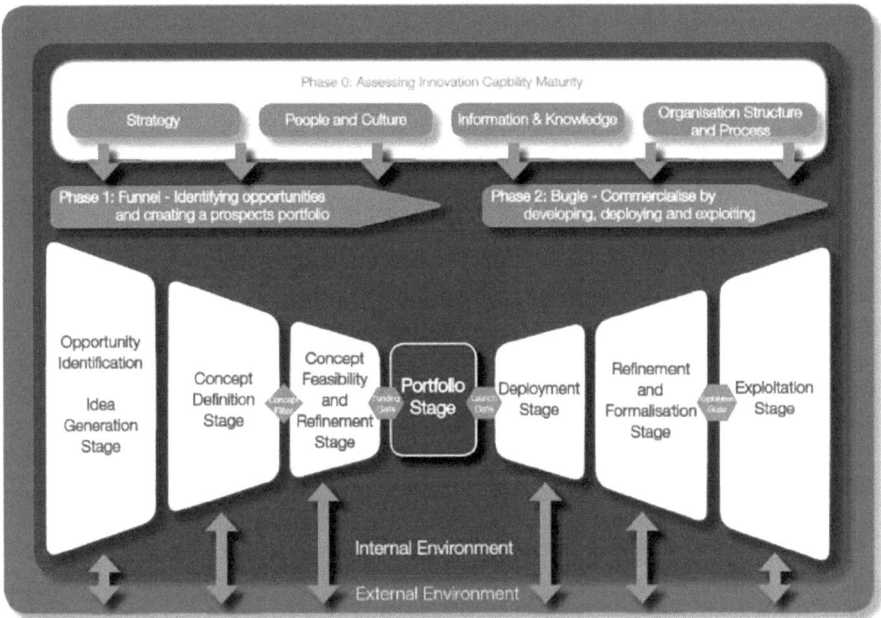

Fig. 1. Diagram of Fugle Innovation Process Model (Du Preez, N.D., Louw, L., Essmann, H, 2006)

by a representative of the company as well, but usually micro companies do not have the necessary resources to do so.

Table 1. Roles and responsibilities of university-company cooperation in innovation process

Role	Partner	Responsibilities
Coordinator	University	Project Manager: coordinating the cooperation, managing stakeholders, etc.
Expert	Company	Consultant: Expert in new methods and technologies, Advising about usage
Business operator	University	Supervisor & Consultant: supervising the whole cooperation and consulting about business details
Operational staff	University	Project Staff: execution of the project, divers qualification

The role of the expert is to advise and consult concerning new methods and/or technologies that should or might be used. Usually micro companies are lacking a person who would qualify for this role, as they do not have employees specialized in these technology or fields of business. On the other hand this role is easily filled by someone working at a university, as this usually matches his or her qualification profile very well.

The only role, which definitely requires the involvement of a company representative, is that of the business operator. The tasks of the business operator here are first to act as a supervisor to the whole project thus making sure it is aligned with the business interests of the company and second offer detailed information, wherever it is required, about the business, processes, target markets, and so son.

Finally yet importantly the operational staff is in general contributed by the university partner as well, as this allows access to a wide variety of qualification and areas of expertise. Nevertheless it is possible to integrate employees of the company as well, if that should be beneficial.

6 Operational Setup

The operational setup and staffing of those roles of course depends on the tasks that are set, but in general can be done as follows. The basic idea is to embed this cooperation on the university side into an interdisciplinary and international teaching project. The role of coordinator then is usually taken by a senior employee of the involved university, e.g. a professor. The role of the experts, of which usually more than one is used, can be taken by any employee of the university. As micro companies do not have high hierarchies, the role of the business operator is often the owner him/herself or someone close to that person. The embedding of the cooperation into a teaching unit allows staffing the operational activities with students. The goal of those student teams is to provide and execute the knowhow that is not available within the micro company, while also having a fresh and unbiased view from many different viewpoints. To ensure this necessary diversity it is beneficial or even necessary to involve students from different disciplines as well as from different countries.

On a timescale, the typical teaching of only a few hours per week might be a feasible solution, but the intensive interaction within a block-teaching unit promises better results.

7 Benefits for the Partners

Cooperation can only be initiated and then work in a sustainable way, if both partners are offered and then delivered some kind of benefits.

For the micro company the cooperation offers access to state of the art knowledge and the possibility to try out innovations, while keeping own investments and involvement to a level, which can be handled even during every day operational business.

For the involved university or universities this cooperation is also beneficial on many levels. To the researchers it offers the possibility to validate new technologies and methods in practise and helps to ensure a link to "normal business" and an exchange of practical experience, which can be essential to (re-)focus research activities and ensure their applicability in "real life". For the involved students this setup creates the possibility to use newly acquired knowledge in a real example and furthermore helps them to apply and improve their soft skills. While working in interdisciplinary (and often also international) teams is typical for working in a company, most degree programs at universities put a lot of emphasize on in-depth specialized knowhow in the respective field of study, with the result, that students often do not interact with other disciplines at all or very little during their studies. The teaching unit in cooperation with a company offers this "real-world-experience".

8 Application of the Approach

To validate the approach described in the paragraph before, it was applied during a teaching unit, starting with one week of block teaching.

8.1 Cases

Two companies, a nursery garden and a veterinary practice, both located in Kaunas County, Lithuania, were chosen and introduced to the idea of the project. Both companies are in need of innovative approach to marketing activities due to large competition but lack money and workforce to invest more. Both companies are looking for solutions in this and other parts of their daily work. Both companies can be classified as micro companies with few employees or even only family members. These companies do feel a lot of pressure by having a lot of competitors, mostly medium or large companies. Either the small companies do concentrate on niches where the competition is smaller or even competition does not exist, or these companies have to calculate with very low profit which makes it hard to survive.

8.2 Teaching Unit

During a one week block teaching units students from Kaunas University of Technology (KTU), from FH Dortmund and IMC University of Applied Sciences were asked to work together in interdisciplinary, international teams. The main task here focused on an innovative solution for micro companies by using a technical tool like to Oculus Rift to create a new kind of marketing instrument for the company. The main idea here was to have students from diverse degrees working together and to communicate with participants from different countries and different viewpoints on solving problems. While students from FH Dortmund were mainly from computer science related study programs, students from IMC and KTU were business students. The outcome should be usable by the participating companies with the help of the university and their students, as they themselves lack knowledge and investment needed for these solutions.

8.3 Teams and Roles

For the whole project, the role of the coordinator was taken by a team of lecturers, who served as well as experts in their respective field of expertise. The business operator was one of the owners of the veterinarian clinic and the daughter of the owner of the nursery school, who is responsible for marketing. As planned, the students were contributing as the operational staff.

Based on the total number of students in the course, they were asked to form three groups. In the first iteration, each group had to come up with different first ideas for both companies. Based on these 6 ideas, the lecturers (in their role as coordinator) decided which group should concentrate on what company. The next step was for each group to create five different concepts for "their" company. Students then had to present those ideas in front of all others and then the students and lecturers had the option to vote for their favourites. Additionally the companies were informed about those ideas so they also could give the groups their feedback and impressions. Groups now had a feed-back which of their ideas was the "best" voted one. Then each group had to decide what idea they want to concentrate on and then start working on the idea. Programming made good progress with different feedback rounds by the lecturers, who were as coordinators also in contact with the business operator to give feedback without the need for many in person meetings.

8.4 Results

On the last day of the workshops, the students had to show and pitch their outcome. All three groups presented demos that could be run and used with the oculus rift and the critical questions by the lecturers were answered very well. The generated prototypes were redesigned throughout various steps and have some clearly formulated ideas for the "customers". Pictures shown here are screenshots of the prototypes.

The veterinary clinic was given a prototype with a virtual walkthrough the clinic. As the real clinic also sells products (dog food, pet care,…) those products and recognisable items were integrated in the game and people trying this will have the task to search for products according to a given list under time pressure. As well as this adds to the overall understanding of a vet clinic (as you normally can´t walk into the surgery part) it also shows the products to be sold and makes people familiar with certain brands and products. The nursery garden company asked in their talks for game to be played while waiting at their company, so the decision was made (and agreed with the company) that it should be some casual game but still add to the flavour of the company. The students decided to go for a "tower defence" kind of leisure game. Here (in the final version depending on the season) different task need to be solved. The programmed version demonstrates the summer time, where you have to protect your planted tree of pests (rabbits and fungi). Those pests need to be battled by "shooting" with sleeping pills at them (as the students decided not to kill any virtual animal). The idea was to change the settings in different seasons as for example to run for water and fertilizer in the spring time as well as to collect falling apples in the fall. The next task will be to work until the very end of the different semesters in distributed teams and to coordinate work and results by using video conferencing tools as well as shared documents (Google Docs, SharePoint,…). At the very end there was an additional presentation at the universities where the students present the final outcome of this semester's project.

Innovative Marketing in Low-Tech Micro Companies - Lessons Learned 309

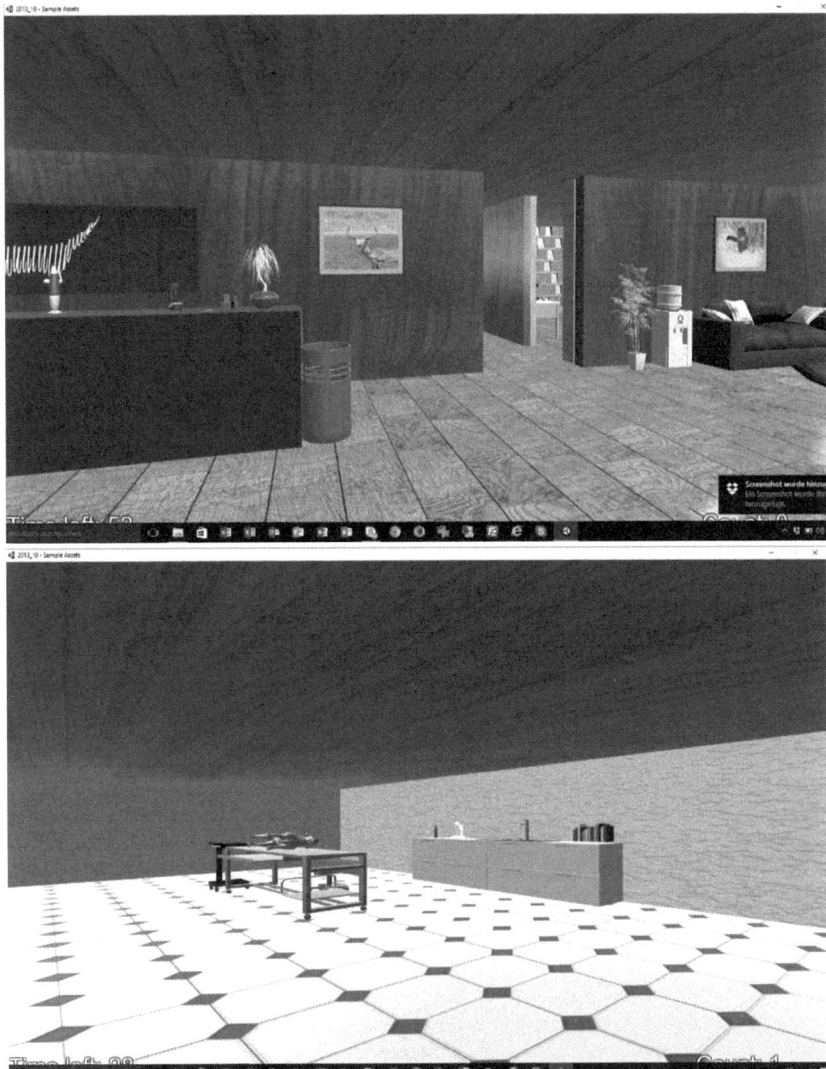

8.5 Validation

To validate whether the used approach could achieve to expected results, the participants were inter-viewed after the block-teaching unit. The students pointed out, that the possibility to work in a new environment, with a new team was challenging for them, but that at the end of the week, they had learned to overcome most initial problems, like communication with students from other disciplines. Those students who already had work experience as software developers in a company pointed out, that the experience of the project was not perfectly realistic, although much more realistic than other methods that they used during their studies.

During their interview both companies pointed out they were amazed by the outcome of the short timeframe for this first part of the project. Veterinary clinic owner was very happy with the look of the virtual clinic as well as with the promised outlook to the future improvements (list to be displayed in the beginning of the game and then to present the products, sold in the clinic). The tree nursery company also was happy with the outcome, as the agreed idea should be a good way for customers to relax within the waiting time. Both are looking forward to continue the project and found it interesting to have the opportunity to try out new technologies for their marketing activities. Although both do not plan to use a game with the oculus for marketing in the near future, the project inspired many new ideas and technologically simpler variations of the proposed solutions.

9 Lessons Learned

The chosen cooperative fugle innovation process, can be used to work in a distributed environment like this project. The process is applicable to students and participating companies as well, the main aspect to take care of is the role of the business operator, which the lecturers have to take over! Here the coordination of the process as well as their knowledge about processes, innovation, project management and business administration are needed to successfully run this project. The benefit for the companies are clearly innovative applications and the use of new technical tools that they normally would have the chance nor the knowledge to use. The advantage for the universities is to improve their network of contacts to work with as well as to have "hands on experience" for their students on real cases and real life problems, but also real life constraints of companies. The theoretical approach combines with the practical try-out phases to a deeper understanding and thus better learning outcome of the students. The cooperation with different degrees and by this adding to the diversity of the project, is not only a very good learning enhancement, but proves also to improve the outcome of the given tasks. All the companies were happy with their prototypes and stated that this was a very good idea and learning for them, additionally they would recommend this to other companies and by this add to the repeating aspect of learning within communities.

References

Blank, S.: Why the lean start-up changes everything. Harvard Bus. Rev. **91**(5), 63–72 (2013)

Charles, D.: Universities as key knowledge infrastructures in regional innovation systems. Innov. Eur. J. Soc. Sci. Res. **19**(1), 117–130 (2006)

Eckstein, J.: Agile Softwareentwicklung mit verteilten Teams. dpunkt-Verlag, Heidelberg (2009)

Du Preez, N.D., Louw, L.: A framework for managing the innovation process. In: 2008 Portland International Conference on Management of Engineering & Technology, PICMET 2008, pp. 546–558. IEEE (2008)

Hirsch-Kreinsen, H., Jacobson, D., Laestadius, S., Smith, K.H.: Low and medium technology industries in the knowledge economy: the analytical issues (Doctoral dissertation, Peter Lang) (2005)

Innosight. Creative Destruction Whips through Corporate America: An Innosight Executive Briefing on Corporate Strategy (2012). http://www.innosight.com/innovation-resources/strategy-innovation/creative-destruction-whips-through-corporate-america.cfm. Accessed 9th May 2016

Laforet, S.: Size, strategic, and market orientation affects on innovation. J. Bus. Res. **61**(7), 753–764 (2008)

Love, J.H., Roper, S.: SME innovation, exporting and growth: a review of existing evidence. Int. Small Bus. J. **33**(1), 28–48 (2015)

Du Preez, N.D., Louw, L., Essmann, H.: An innovation process model for improving innovation capability. J. High Technol. Manag. Res. **2006**, 1–24 (2006)

OECD: The Measurement of Scientific and Technological Activities: Guidelines for Collecting and Interpreting Innovation Data: Oslo Manual, 3rd edn. Working Party of National Experts on Scientific and Technology Indicators, OECD, Paris (2005). para 169

Park, J.S.: Opportunity recognition and product innovation in entrepreneurial hi-tech start-ups: a new perspective and supporting case study. Technovation **25**(7), 739–752 (2005)

Whittington, K.B., Owen-Smith, J., Powell, W.W.: Networks, propinquity, and innovation in knowledge-intensive industries. Adm. Sci. Q. **54**(1), 90–122 (2009)

http://www.innosight.com/innovation-resources/strategy-innovation/creative-destruction-whips-through-corporate-america.cfm

https://www.researchgate.net/publication/4363117_A_framework_for_managing_the_innovation_process

Method to Establish Strategies for Implementing Process Improvement According to the Organization's Context

Mirna Muñoz[1(✉)], Jezreel Mejia[1], Gloria P. Gasca Hurtado[2], Maria C. Gómez-Álvarez[2], and Brenda Durón[1]

[1] Centro de Investigación En Matemáticas, Av. Universidad no 222, 98068 Guanajuato, Zacatecas, Mexico
{mirna.munoz,jmejia,brenda.duron}@cimat.mx
[2] Facultad de Ingeniería, Universidad de Medellín, Cra. 87 No. 30-65, Medellín, Antioquia, Colombia
{gpgasca,megomez}@udem.edu.co

Abstract. Software process improvement has become a logical way to address the growing need of increasing the competitiveness in software development organizations. Unfortunately, not all process improvement implementations have the desired results, because the existing models and standards focus their attention on "which activities to implement" without addressing "how to implement them". However, identifying which are the activities to implement is not enough; the knowledge of how to implement them is required for a successful implementation of software process improvement initiatives. This paper shows a method that provides strategies for the implementation of software process improvements based on the contextual aspects in which the software is developed, so that, the strategy is provided according to the organization needs and their work culture regarding project management.

Keywords: Software process improvement · Strategies for implementing improvements · Software development organizations · Organizational work culture

1 Introduction

In recent years the growth in the importance of the software as the core of many organizations provides the opportunity for small and medium enterprises (SMEs) to produce quality software products and services. Therefore, it is important to guarantee the quality of their software products. Then, SMEs have a continuous need for improving their development processes in order to stay in the market and to achieve a steady growth.

Introducing improvements in SMEs aim to help them in the implementation of a set of best practices in order to get benefits such as increasing their product quality, reducing their delivering time, and reducing their costs of production, among others [1].

In this context, models or standards such as CMMI [2], Moprosoft [2], ISO 15504 [3] and ISO 29110 [4] have been developed to help SMEs in the implementation of software process improvements (SPI). However, these models are focused on providing a set of best practices that covers "what practices to do" without covering "how to implement them".

Nevertheless, the knowledge of how to implement a set of practices is needed in order to achieve success in the implementation of SPI initiatives. A current problem in the implementation of process improvements is not the lack of models and standards, but the lack of effective strategies for implementing the practices provided by those models and standards. Taking into account this problem, this paper presents a method which aims to help SMEs in the implementation of improvements within their processes, providing an adequate strategy according to their project management work culture and having into account the factors that can inhibit or promote the success in the implementation of SPI, "the human factor" [5, 6].

This paper is structured as follows: Sect. 2 presents the method background; Sect. 3 describes the method; Sect. 3 shows how the method was validated; and finally, Sect. 5 presents the conclusions.

2 Method Background

Software process improvement aims to increment the efficiency and effectiveness of software development as well as the quality of software products [7]. SPI is based on the implementation of best practices within the organization's processes, so that it allows the organization to focus on preventing errors instead of implementing corrective actions [8].

Therefore, SPI allows any kind of organizations, to solve key issues to reduce or eliminate quality problems, and to examine in an objective way their processes to determine in which level the processes are tying with their specific needs.

However, the effort in the file of SPI has been addressed to provide models and standards focused on "what practices to do" without covering "how to implement them". As a result, the success in the implementation of improvements is limited because it is necessary not only to identify what the organization need to improve, also, it should be identified what are the factors that influence the success of the implementation and should be provided the guidelines of how to implement the improvements.

According to Cuevas et al. [10], the needs of the software industry regarding SPI are, among others: (a) guidance on how to apply process improvements with equal effectiveness in different contexts; (b) how to implement the change management within a software process improvement context, and (c) more automatization in activities related to the process.

This research work arises from two premises that highlight the importance of human factor: (1) the processes entirely depend on the organization work culture and the motivation of people to evolve processes, and (2) the main source of commitment and responsibility to achieve effective, efficient and quality processes is the human factor.

The method presented in this paper arises from the idea presented in [9] named as *"proposal two: Selection of strategies for implementing the process improvements"*.

The method consists on providing a correct strategy to implement SPI in an appropriate way according to the specific organizational context and project management work culture (that means the way the organization perform its project management).

To achieve that, the method starts using a checklist that analyzes the organization context such as its project management work culture, its business goals, and its process improvement goal. Then, the organization identifies its context according to a set of categories. Finally, the strategy that best ties with the organization's needs is provided.

3 Strategy Selection Method

According to Niazi, et al. [11] to implement SPI programs, it is required real experiences to learn from errors in order to achieve a continuous process improvement implementation. Therefore, the method was developed based on the next aspects: *(a) it takes into account the organizational context; (b) it manages the process improvement as a project; (c) it manages the process improvement as an a iterative and gradual process according to the organization's project management work culture; (d) it reuses the lessons learned reported by the industry and literature; and (e) it reduces the resistance to change of the organization's employees.*

Based on the above mentioned, the method is composed of three phases: (1) a set of developed strategies; (2) method to select the developed strategies; and (3) a tool for using of the method. Next, each activity is briefly described.

3.1 A Set of Developed Strategies

To define the set of strategies, three activities were performed:

Analyze the models, methods, guides and frameworks to implement software improvements: around 21 process improvement models, methods, guides and frameworks from the literature were analyzed in order to obtain a generic structure with the minimum activities that should be performed to implement a process improvement. Table 1 shows a summary of the analyzed models. The analyzed features were: (A) It targets the implementation of a software process improvement; (B) It performs an analysis of the context; (C) It defines SPI goals aligned with the organization; (D) It has a support tool; (E) It includes activities related to change resistance; (F) It is focused on SMEs; (G) It provides a framework; and (H) It has been validated.

Select the Strategy Elements: After analyzing the generic structure, the elements of the strategy are three: (a) strategy elements: they include a set of activities containing communication channels, support and related measures; a sequence for performing the activities, roles and their responsibilities; (b) risks and barriers: provide activities regarding the mitigation of risks and barriers identified; (c) success factors: suggest activities that promote the process improvement success.

Table 1. Analysis of SPI models, methods, guides and frameworks

Improvement Method	A	B	C	D	E	F	G	H
KDMK[12]	x	x		x				x
OWPL[13]	x	x	x	x	x	x	x	x
Empirical evaluation of BP in SPI[14]	x	x	x		x			x
SPI implementation maturity model[15]	x							x
Applying grounded theory to understand SPI [16]	x	x			x			
Business strategy & SPI[17]	x	x	x		x			x
SPI-IF[11]	x	x					x	x
Agreeing viewpoints for strategic SPI[18]		x	x					x
Iflap[19]		x					x	x
Competisoft[20]	x	x	x	x		x	x	x
Approach to SPI in SMEs[21]		x	x		x			x
MIGME-RRC methodology[22]	x	x	x		x			x
ASPEI/MSC[23]	x	x	x	x		x		x
P4SPI[24]	x	x		x				x
MEDEPRO[25]	x	x		x	x			x
IDIEF[26]	x	x			x	x	x	
Toshiba SPI-framework[27]	x	x					x	x
ProPAM[28]	x	x						x
BG-SPI[29]	x		x		x			x
O-SPI[30]	x		x					x
Tutelkan[31]	x			x		x	x	x

In this way the strategies are reinforced, taking into account the success factors, barriers and best practices of literature, as well as those practices identified as triggers to achieve a successful process improvement.

Define the Strategy Elements: Based on the strategy elements the strategy elements were defined taking into account the two most common project management work cultures in organizations (agile and traditional). Then, there were selected two methodologies that allow us to reflect the identified project management work culture, TSP for traditional and Scrum for agile.

On the one hand, TSP provides a methodology to perform projects in a formal way under a defined process scheme that for many organizations is perceived as "traditional way". On the other hand, Scrum provides a methodology to perform projects in a more informal way under an agile scheme that for many organizations is perceived as "agile way".

3.2 Method to Select the Developed Strategies

The method is focused on helping organizations to select an adequate strategy to implement a SPI according to the context and the organizational project management work culture. It is composed of three phases as follows:

The first phase named as *"initial analysis"* aims to identify the organizational project management work culture, business goals, improvement objectives, and expected performance.

The second phase named as *"context assessment"* aims to perform a characterization of the organizational context by mapping the organization's context information with those of the stored strategies. The mapping is done using categories with assigned weights that allow us to address the selection of an adequate strategy according with the organization needs. Finally, the third phase named as *"strategy selection"* aims to provide an adequate strategy by analyzing the categories and their assigned weights.

It is important to mention that this method is focused on helping organizations in the implementation of improvements according to their project management work culture. Therefore, the method assumes that the organization has identified what practices should improve. Next, each phase is briefly described.

3.2.1 Initial Analysis

This phase performs an analysis to ensure that the organization has a solid base to start an improvement. Then, it provides a set of requirements that an organization must take

Table 2. Requirements, requirement's category and their related questions

Requirements	Category	Related questions
Business goals	Desired	Do you have clearly identified: (1) the organizational business goals; (2) the organizational vision, and (3) the strategic plan of the organization.
Organization's vision	Desired	
Business strategic plan	Desired	
SPI goals	Needed	Before starting the improve implementation, Do you perform the next activities: (1) identify the improvement goals; (2) identify the improvement target; (3) identify and communicate the goals to the stakeholders; (4) get support and commitment of the top level management; and (5) perform the processes assessment.
Communicate the organization about the intention to implement a SPI	Desired	
Have support and commitment regarding the SPI	Needed	
SPI target	Desired	What are the main goals for implementing a software process improvement: (1) improve software quality; (2) reduce development cost; (3) reduce development time; (3) increment productivity; (4) met the customer requirements; (5) get an standard or model certification; (6) measure the process effectiveness
Assess the organizational context	Needed	Have you had experience in SPI?
		According your experience: Have you defined the improvement goals? Have you met the planned goals? Are the improvements still working?

into account to start a process improvement implementation. In this way it is ensured that the organization has a real awareness of what they want to achieve and which are its priorities. The requirements, requirement's category and their associated questions used in the initial analysis are showed in Table 2.

3.2.2 Context Assessment

This phase performs an assessment of a set of contextual aspects, which aims to characterize the organization by assigning weights to the contextual aspects. Figure 1 shows the contextual aspect covered by the method that adds information to characterize the real context of an organization.

Fig. 1. Contextual aspects

3.2.3 Strategy Selection

This phase analyzes the weights assigned to each contextual aspect. This analysis allows selecting and providing an adequate strategy (traditional or agile). Figure 2 provides an

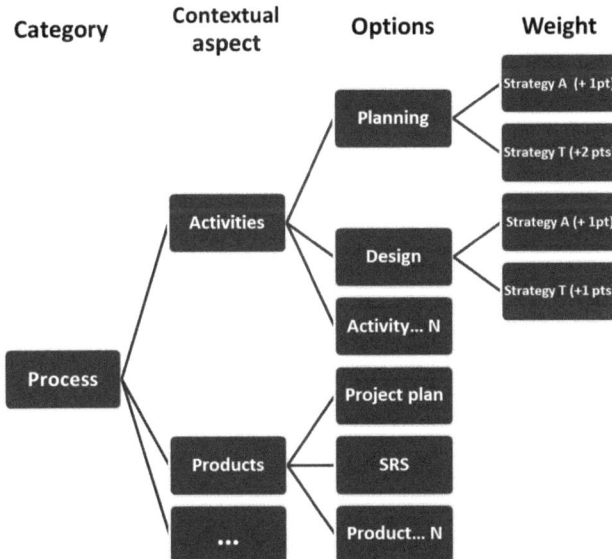

Fig. 2. Example of the assignment of weights of the contextual aspect "process" to select the an adequate strategy

example of how has been set the structure to assign weights to the contextual aspects "process". As the figure shows, each contextual aspect has a set of options and each one has an assigned weight according to the strategy it belongs. Therefore, all weights should be added, so that, at the end of the analysis the value resulting from the addition of all weights help us to know which strategy should be selected "the agile implementation strategy based on SCRUM" or "the traditional implementation strategy based on TSP".

3.3 A Tool for Using the Method

This section provides an overview of the web tool, which support the use of the strategy selection method. The tool functionality allows supporting the three method phases. Next, the Fig. 3 shows the initial analysis and its obtained results; Fig. 4 shows the context assessment and its obtained results; and Fig. 5 shows the strategy provided. Actually, the tool is in Spanish language; for this reason the figures contain notes of the information contained in them.

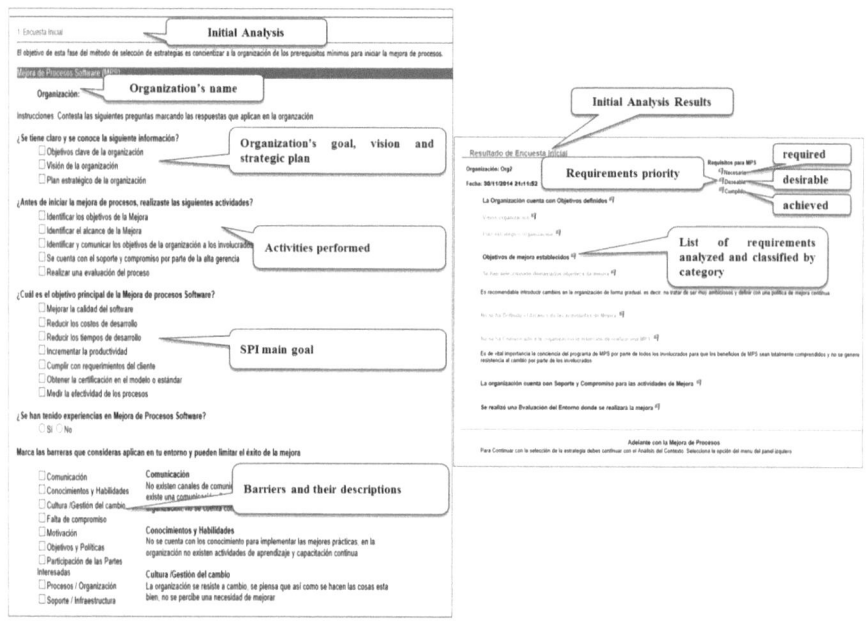

Fig. 3. Screen for performing the "initial analysis" and the obtained results

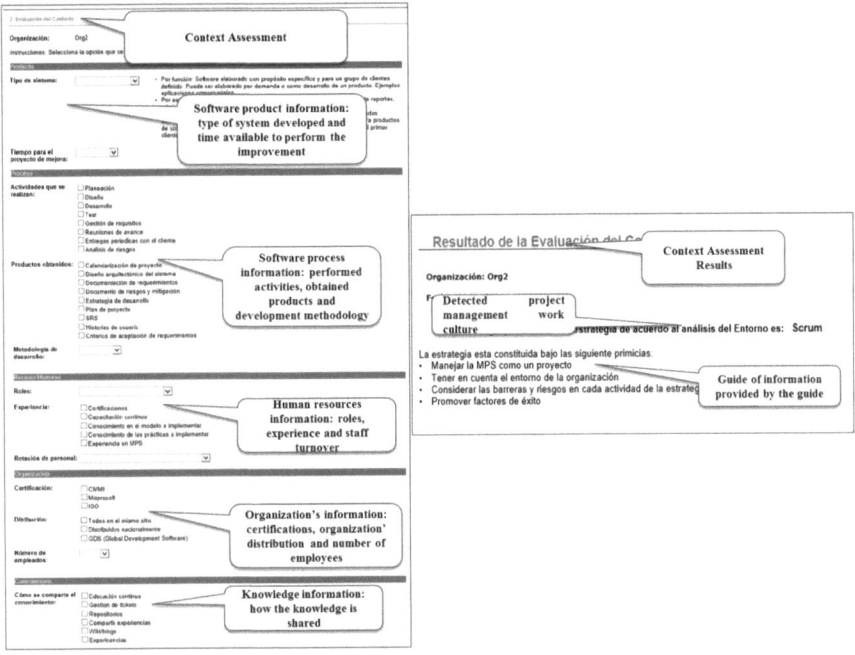

Fig. 4. Screen for performing the "context analysis" and the obtained results

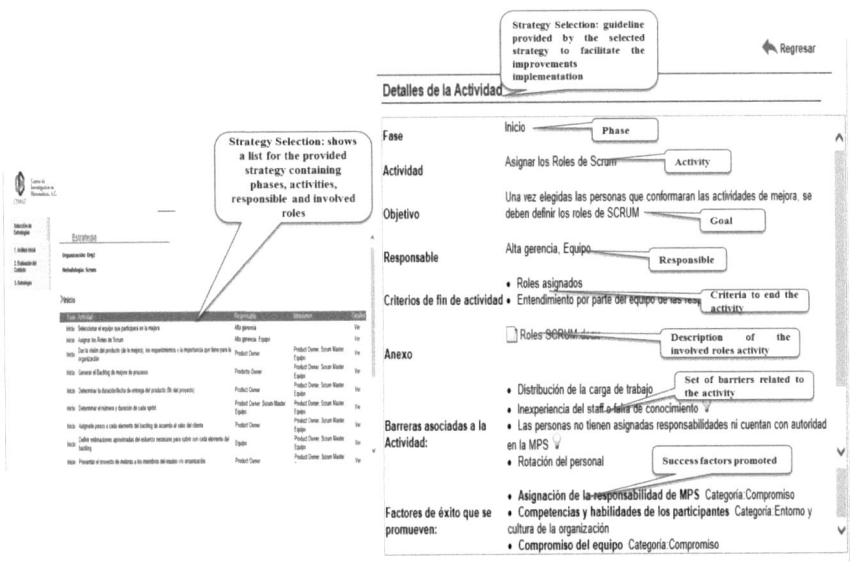

Fig. 5. Screen of the strategy provided and the guideline detail

4 Case Study

To validate the viability of the method a case study was performed. Next the case study design and the results are presented.

4.1 Case Study Design

Following the case study guideline provided by Wieringa in [32] the case study design was established as follows:

1. *Knowledge goal*: the goal of this case study was to validate the viability of both the method and the generated strategies.
2. *Current Knowledge*: Even when SPI offers a way to launch the competitiveness in software development organizations, not all process improvement implementations have the desired results. This is because the existing models and standards used as reference in the implementation of SPI focus their attention on what activities are implemented without addressing on how to implement them. This highlight that a current problem in the implementation of process improvements is not the lack of models and standards, but the lack of effective strategies for implementing the practices provided by those models and standards.
3. *Knowledge questions*: Table 3 shows a set of the knowledge questions and its related assessed goal.
4. *Population*: The case study was focused on managers of software development SMEs both with and without experience in SPI. This way allows evaluating the viability of the method in different environments regarding the SPI engineers' experience.
5. *Measurement Design:* (1) variables: requirement identified, strategy provided, and environment characterized; (2) data source: managers; (3) measurement instruments: via web survey using google documents; (4) measurement schedule: the survey should be answered after using the method's tool.

Table 3. Knowledge questions and their assessed goal

#KQ	Knowledge questions	Assessed goal
1	Do the obtained results help the organization in the identification of the minimal requirements to implement an improvement?	This question aims to validate if the method allows the organization to identify the requirements to implement an improvement
2	Do the obtained results allow characterizing the organizational environment?	This question aims to validate if the method allows the organization to characterize its current environment
3	Is it possible to provide a strategy according to the organization's needs and current context?	This question aims to validate the viability of the method regarding the strategy provided

4.2 Case Study Execution

To execute the case study, the method's tool was implemented in two different environments, the academy and the industry with a total of 13 participants of 9 organizations. Table 4 shows the organizations' information.

Besides, the case study started introducing the participants to the case study goal. Then, each participant used the web tool and validated the results. Finally, each participant answered a survey via web, defined to assess the method viability as well as the generated strategies.

Table 4. Population of engineers participating in the case study

ID	Description	Participants	SPI experience
Org-A	Custom software development	2	Without experience
Org-B	Educative organization with a software development department	3	With experience
Org-C	Educative organization with a software development and maintenance department	1	Without experience
Org-D	Software and web development and payrolls support	1	With experience
Org-E	Quality software development with the use of international standards; consulting and training	1	With experience
Org-F	Custom software development	1	Without experience
Org-G	Bank software development	1	Without experience
Org-H	Academic researcher	2	Without experience
Org-I	Custom software development	1	Without experience

4.3 Case Study Results

This section shows the results of the case study. The results are shown in Fig. 4 focusing on the three main variables.

Analysis of the main variables:

- *Requirements Identified.* This variable allows us to get information to answer the KQ1. Do the obtained results help the organization in the identification of the minimal requirements to implement an improvement? As Fig. 6 shows, all engineers answered "yes", which means they considered the initial analysis allowed them to identify the minimum requirements to start a process improvement.
- *Environment characterized.* This variable allows us to get information to answer the KQ2. Do the obtained results allow characterizing the organizational environment?

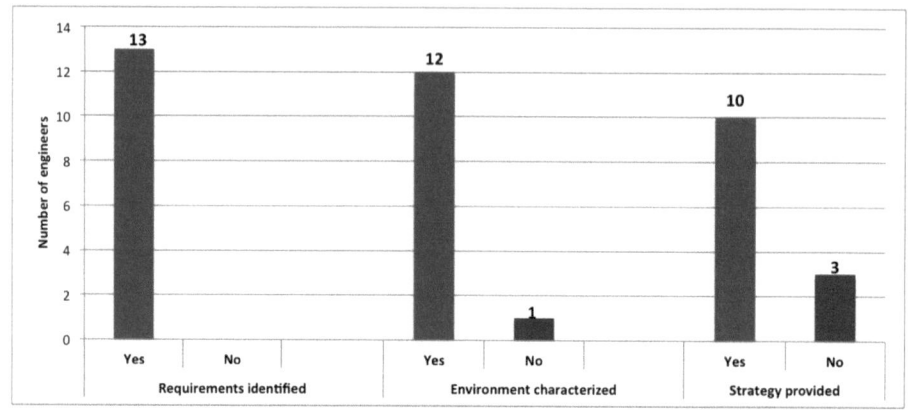

Fig. 6. Data collected from three main variables through the web survey

As Fig. 6 shows, 12 engineers answered "yes", which means they considered that the contextual aspects covered by the method allowed characterizing their organizational context.

Strategy provided. This variable allows us to get information to answer the KQ3. Is it possible to provide a strategy according to the organization's needs and current context? As Fig. 6 shows, 10 engineers answered "yes", which means they considered that the strategy provided was adequate according to their organization's needs and context.

5 Discussion and Conclusions

This paper presents a method that aims to provide implementation strategies for SPI according to the organization's needs and real context. According to the results of the case study, we concluded that: (1) the method tool allows performing a quick analysis and provides information that helps the organization to know the minimal requirements that are required to implement an improvement; (2) the method allows characterizing the current organizational context; and (3) the method provides an adequate strategy containing a detailed guide that allows the organization to manage the improvement as a project. It is important to mention that the importance of this research work arises because it takes into account the organization's context characterizing the environment in which the improvement will be implemented. Besides, the validation of the method with 13 engineers of 9 SMEs organizations demonstrates that the method and its tools have a good acceptance for the participants; in both cases, with experience and without experience in SPI. As future work, we are refining the method according to the suggestions collected from the case study. Also, we are translating the tool to the English language.

References

1. Chrissis, M.B., Konrad, M., Shrum, S.: CMMI for Development: Guidelines for Process Integration and Product Improvement. Pearson Education Inc., Boston (2011)
2. International Organization for Standardization ISO/IEC 15504: 2004 Information technology – Process assessment (2004)
3. Oktaba H., Vázquez A.: MoProSoft: a software process model for small enterprises. In: Software Process Improvement for Small and Medium Enterprises, Techniques and cases studies, (Information Science Reference), p. 170 (2008)
4. Laporte, C.Y., Alexandre, S., O'Connor, R.V.: A software engineering lifecycle standard for very small enterprises. In: O'Connor, R.V., Baddoo, N., Smolander, K., Messnarz, R. (eds.) EuroSPI 2008. CCIS, vol. 16, pp. 129–141. Springer, Heidelberg (2008)
5. Korsaa, M., Johansen, J., Schweiger, T., Vohwinke, D., Messnarz, R., Nevalainen, R., Biro, M.: The people aspects in modern process improvement management approaches. J. Softw. Evol. Process **25**, 381–391 (2013)
6. O'Connor, R., Basri, S.: The effect of team dynamics on software development process improvement. Int. J. Hum. Cap. Inf. Technol. Prof. **3**, 13–26 (2012)
7. Pressman, R.: Ingenieria del Software Un enfoque práctico. Mc Graw Hill, Madrid (2010)
8. O'Regan, G.: Introduction to Software Process Improvement. Undergraduate Topics in Computer Science. Springer, London (2011)
9. Muñoz, M., Mejia, J., Gasca-Hurtado, G.P., Valtierra, C., Duron, B.: Covering the human perspective in software process improvement. In: Barafort, B., O'Connor, R.V., Poth, A., Messnarz, R. (eds.) EuroSPI 2014. CCIS, vol. 425, pp. 123–134. Springer, Heidelberg (2014)
10. Cuevas A., Calvo-Manzano, J.A., García, I.: Some key topics to be considered in agile estimation techniques and innovative approach to software process improvement. In: Colomo-Palacios, R., et al. (eds.) IGI Global, pp. 119–142 (2014)
11. Niazi, M., et al.: A framework for assisting the design of effective software process improvement implementation strategies. J. Syst. Softw. **78**(2), 204–222 (2005)
12. Alagarsamy, K., et al.: Implementation specification for software process improvement supportive knowledge management tool. Softw. IET **2**(2), 123–133 (2008)
13. Alexandre, S., et al.: OWPL: A gradual approach for software process improvement in SMEs. In: 32nd Conference on EUROMICRO, Software Engineering and Advanced Applications, SEAA 2006 (2006)
14. Galinac, T.: Empirical evaluation of selected best practices in implementation of software process improvement. Inf. Softw. Technol. **51**(9), 1351–1364 (2009)
15. Niazi, M., et al.: A maturity model for the implementation of software process improvement: an empirical study. J. Syst. Softw. **74**(2), 155–172 (2005)
16. Montoni, M.A., Rocha, A.R.: Applying grounded theory to understand software process improvement implementation. In: 2010 Seventh International Conference on the Quality of Information and Communications Technology (QUATIC) (2010)
17. Asato, R., et al.: Alignment between the business strategy and the software processes improvement: a roadmap for the implementation. In: Portland International Conference on Management of Engineering & Technology, PICMET 2009 (2009)
18. Karlstrom, D., et al.: Aggregating viewpoints for strategic software process improvement-a method and a case study. IEE Proc. Softw. **149**(5), 143–152 (2002)
19. Pettersson, F., et al.: A practitione's guide to light weight software process assessment and improvement planning. J. Syst. Softw. **81**(6), 972–995 (2008)

20. Pino, F.J., García, F., Piattini, M.: An sintegrated framework to guide software process improvement in small organization. In: O'Connor, R.V., Baddoo, N., Cuadrago Gallego, J., Rejas Muslera, R., Smolander, K., Messnarz, R. (eds.) EuroSPI 2009. CCIS, vol. 42, pp. 213–224. Springer, Heidelberg (2009)
21. Diana, K., M. Stephen, A.: Systems approach to software process improvement in small organizations. In: Industrial Proceedings of EuroSPI 2009 (2009)
22. Calvo-Manzano, J.A., Cuevas, G., Gómez, G., Mejia, J., Muñoz, M., San Feliu, T.: Methodology for process improvement through basic components and focusing on the resistance to change. J. Softw. Evol. Process **24**(5), 511–523 (2010)
23. Hauck, J., et al.: Process reference guides– support for improving software processes in alignment with reference models and standards. In: O'Connor, R.V., Baddoo, N., Smolander, K., Messnarz, R. (eds.) EuroSPI 2008. CCIS, vol. 16, pp. 70–81. Springer, Heidelberg (2008)
24. Landaeta, J., et al.: Practical SPI planning. In: O'Connor, R.V., Baddoo, N., Smolander, K., Messnarz, R. (eds.) EuroSPI 2008. CCIS, vol. 16, pp. 82–93. Springer, Heidelberg (2008)
25. Bayona, S., Calvo-Manzano, J.A., Cuevas, G., San Feliu, T.: MEDEPRO: a method to deploy processes focused on people. In: Winkler, D., O'Connor, R.V., Messnarz, R. (eds.) EuroSPI 2012. CCIS, vol. 301, pp. 13–24. Springer, Heidelberg (2012)
26. Ayanwale, A.M., Georgiadou, E.: IDIEF - an integrated framework for software process and product improvement in SMEs. In: EuroSPI 2012 Industrial Proceedings (2012)
27. Ogasawara, H., et al.: Proposal and practice of SPI framework - Toshiba´s SPI history since 2000. In: EuroSPI 2012 Industrial Proceedings (2012)
28. Martins, P.V., da Silva, A.R.: ProPAMet: a Metric for process and project alignment. In: O'Connor, R., Baddoo, N., Smolander, K., Messnarz, R. (eds.) EuroSPI 2008. CCIS, vol. 16, pp. 201–212. Springer, Heidelberg (2008)
29. Aysolmaz, B., Demirörs, O.: A detailed software process improvement methodology: BG-SPI. In: O`Connor, R.V., Pries-Heje, J., Messnarz, R. (eds.) EuroSPI 2011. CCIS, vol. 172, pp. 97–108. Springer, Heidelberg (2011)
30. Yan, X., et al.: Research on organizational-level software process improvement model and its implementation. In: International Symposium on Computer Science and Computational Technology, ISCSCT 2008 (2008)
31. Valdés, G., Visconti, M., Astudillo, H.: The tutelkan reference process: a reusable process model for enabling SPI in small settings. In: O`Connor, R.V., Pries-Heje, J., Messnarz, R. (eds.) EuroSPI 2011. CCIS, vol. 172, pp. 179–190. Springer, Heidelberg (2011)
32. Wieringa, R.J.: "Observational Case Studies" in Desing Science Methodology for information Systems and Software Engineering, pp. 225–245. Springer, Berlin Heidelberg (2014). (eBook). ISBN 978-3-662-43839-8

User Orientation through Open Innovation and Customer Integration

Dimitrios Siakas[1] and Kerstin Siakas[2]

[1] Citec, Vaasa, Finland
dimitrios.siakas@citec.fi
[2] Department of Informatics, Alexander Technological Educational Institute of Thessaloniki,
P.O. Box, 141 57400 Thessaloniki, Greece
siaka@it.teithe.gr

Abstract. The concepts of market orientation in innovation practices and its interrelationship with business success has been explored from a number of perspectives for establishing deeper understanding of the role of the customer/user in the innovation process. User oriented design offers a significant role in the success of innovation of products and services and is found to be an effective way for value creation and competitive advantage. Value of any service is created, comprehended and defined by the customer/user in the situation of service use, also called value-in-use.

This study aims to make explicit the process of integrating/involving the customer/user in the innovation process and of conceptualising customer value creation, by identifying different perspectives of customer value creation. Subsequently open innovation is investigated as a tool for integrating customers/users in the innovation process, in particularly in the ideation stage of innovation. Open innovation, is a paradigm that assumes that companies can and should use external ideas in addition to internal ideas in order to create value. Open innovations also assume that internal ideas can be taken to market by external channels, outside the current business of the company. Online social networks are in particular suitable channels for creating value in the light of open innovation. Potential ways for gaining added business value through the use of social networking practices are investigated.

Keywords: Open Innovation · Crowdsourcing · Customer Integration · User Participation · Value Creation

1 Introduction

Recent trends in the world economy push organisation to produce innovative products and services for survival, sustainability and growth. Innovation is about finding new ways of doing things and of obtaining strategic advantage. In order to keep costs down and to improve productivity processes also need to be innovative. The degree of unique offering and novelty in products or services, faster, cheaper, customised processes create the strategic advantage of innovation. Offering something unique, doing something in different ways, designing through robust platforms others can build on, reconfiguring of parts and how systems work together can also be considered innovations providing strategic advantage (Tidd et al. 2001). Chesbrough (2003) argues that innovation is an invention implemented and taken to market. Disruptive innovation changes social practices by changing consumer behaviour and causing disruption in the way business is done. Christensen and Raynor (2003) argues that disruption innovations can initially be rejected by mainstream customers because they are not ready to use the new product or service.

In service and product innovation the concept of market orientation has been explored from a number of perspectives and its interrelation with customer value and business success has been found to be fundamental. Lewrick et al. (2011) found that competitor orientation, which is an imperative key component of market orientation, has positive relationship to incremental innovation (innovations that do not cause a significant deviance from status-quo) for start-up companies. Incremental innovations include improvements of existing products, services, processes, technical or administrative conditions. In mature organisations, on the contrary, a strong customer/user orientation was found to be related to radical innovations (breakthroughs that fundamentally change a product, service or process among others). The findings of Lukas and Ferrell (2000) also show that organisations that concentrate on their competitors are less likely to come up with radical innovations. In this paper we concentrate on the second component of market orientation, namely customer/user participation in the innovation process.

Important innovations may decline because the company developing the innovation failed to concentrate on new customers/users for the products or the services of the future. More players are brought into the game as innovation develops over time (Van de Ven et al. 2008). Customers, partnerships, company acquisitions, sponsors and others create a complex network that engages in diverse transactions necessary in order to launch the innovation to the market. The incorporation of desires and needs of customers/users in the design process has increasingly been established in recent years (Veryzer and de Mozota 2005). Especially in the early stages of the design process customers/users are consulted in order to participate in the design (Kujala 2003; Sanders 2005). The literature has suggested that higher customer involvement results in higher quality, especially in terms of meeting requirements (Berki et al. 1997). The agile development approach, for example, entails the user in the entire development process in order to ensure conformance to requirements, user satisfaction and competitive advantage. On-site customers/future users providing real life scope, setting priorities, resolving ambiguities and providing test scenarios are fundamental inputs not only in the early stages but throughout the development process (Siakas and Siakas 2006). User involvement and frequent iterations increases domain knowledge in the development process, which in turn increases developer motivation, commitment and satisfaction, key elements for success (Abrahamsson 2005; Siakas and Georgiadou 2003).

In this paper we explore the significance of customer/user involvement in the innovation process for increasing innovation and realising improved value as a result, either this happens by crowd-sourcing, co-working agreements, acquisition of start-ups with appealing technologies, or extending new developments into external companies.

2 Open Innovation

Open innovation is increasingly being introduced in international and national organisations for the creation of value (Aranha et al. 2015). Chesbrough (2003), who coined the term open innovation, describes how organisations have shifted from so called closed innovation processes towards a more open way of innovating. Closed innovation, in which companies use only ideas generated within the organisational boundaries, are characterised by big corporate Research and Development (R&D) departments and closely managed networks of vertically integrated partners. Open innovation is a paradigm that assumes that companies can and should use external ideas in addition to internal ideas to create value (Chesbrough 2003; 2011).

2.1 Value Creation Through Open Innovation

The ultimate object of innovation is to create and sustain value, preferably across various cultures. The quest to innovate drives the company to capture knowledge outside its boundaries. This can be considered as a dynamic capability of the company. The supply of information and knowledge captured externally is transferred to the company and contributes to the creation and delivery of value, thus increasing performance, profits and growth of the organisation, as well as, contributing to the reach out to new domestic and international markets. This movement to capture knowledge from outside the company is one of the driving elements in the creation of value for the company. This happens due to the fact that openness makes the operation of multifaceted dynamic capabilities (through diverse stakeholder commitment) visible. Simultaneously openness facilitates understanding and mapping of opportunities and threats. Competitiveness is increased through the increase in new ideas, combination of different viewpoints, protection and reinvention of the business model (Teece 2007).

A central concern in an open innovation strategy is how the generated value can be captured and how potential risks can be managed and minimised. Companies need to develop business models that realise the value potential of novel technologies in uncertain contexts (Gay 2014). Customer satisfaction and value is exclusively perceived by the customer and usually involves trade-offs between what is received (e.g. quality and benefits) and what is given up to acquire this (e.g. money and time) (Overvik-Olsen and Welo 2011; Spiteri and Dion 2004). Increased customer value implies increased loyalty and for the company expanding the innovation potential to new ways of working with external partners and customers/users, thus a reciprocal value expansion.

Value of any service is created, comprehended and defined by the customer in the situation of service use. This is called value-in-use (Grönroos 2008; Vargo and Lusch 2004; 2006). The main approaches/perspectives of customer value creation in the literature were identified:

(i) *Interaction perspective*: the use of the service by the customer is considered as mutual co-creation of value with the company that practice open innovation (e.g., Grönroos 2008; Michel et al. 2008; Prahalad and Ramaswamy 2002).

(ii) *The service function perspective*: The emphasis is on the way the customer/user utilises the service (Wynstra et al. 2006; Christensen and Raynor 2003; Ulwick 2002).
(iii) *Process perspective*: The processes the customer/user applies regarding the service use (Shostack 1992).
(iv) *Customer goals perspective*: The emphasis is on the activities, experiences and goals of the customer (Heinonen et al. 2010).

Increased customer value enable companies to optimise revenue. A by-product of open innovation approach is the identification of partners for the whole open innovation value chain.

2.2 Challenges of Open Innovation

The concept of open innovation suggests that firms can boost their innovative performance by acquiring knowledge from outside the company and by deploying external channels, outside the current business of the company for commercialisation of non-core technologies (Savitskaya et al. 2010). As innovations emerge increasingly from inter-organisational cooperation, the background for such cooperation can also have an impact on the involvement of companies into open innovation processes.

There are three issues that the company interested in applying open innovation practices should take a closer look at, namely:

i. The understanding of the importance of open innovation (Siakas et al. 2014b).
ii. Investigation of practices for implementing open innovation (Chiaroni et al. 2011; Ebersberger, et al. 2012).
iii. Investigation of practices of the open business model that result in creation of value (Saebi and Foss 2014; Gay 2014; Frankenberger et al. 2014; Weiblen 2014).

The literature on open innovation concentrated in the early days on Information and Communication Technology (ICT) innovations, where companies such as IBM, Intel and Lucent were used to illustrate their 'open' practices to create and capture value (Chesbrough 2003). Since then the concept of open innovation, as a business practice, has received much attention, and it has been diffused to other sectors besides ICT (Gassman et al. 2010; Huizingh, 2011).

The existing literature on open innovation has focused more extensively on the benefits than on the costs, disadvantages, limitations and risks that need to be emphasised so that companies can prepare accordingly. The following challenges were identified:

i. *Lack of Control:* Openness implies an inherent lack of control both regarding the processes and the potential results (Mahr et al. 2010).
ii. *Difficulties to manage incoming innovations*: Integrating ideas, insights, concepts, and solutions from open innovation initiatives into established new product development processes is a significant challenge. Also cost cuttings in R&D departments of the companies can make it more difficult to manage incoming innovations from customers/potential customers and thus decreasing the effectiveness of the open innovation (de Wit et al. 2007).

iii. *Misappropriation of ideas*: Competitors and others may misappropriate the openly exposed business idea (Gould 2012; Wadhaw et al. 2011; Dahlander and Gann 2010).
iv. *Protection of Intellectual Property Rights (IPRs)*: Many open innovation mechanisms assume disclosure of information, for example by freely revealing experimental result to the public. The complexity of IPR and fear of infringements may be a barrier for companies to engage in open innovations (Savitskaya et al. 2010).
v. *Reduction of openness:* At some point returns of openness may be diminishing due to poor maintenance of an open attitude (Laursen and Salter 2006).
vi. *Human resource challenges*: How to improve employee engagement (Siakas et al. 2014b).
vii. *Culture of sharing*: Sharing information without and trusting stakeholders (Siakas et al. 2012).
viii. *Information and Communication Technology (ICT) literacy*: Not all people are confident users of ICTs (Georgiadou et al. 2016).

Involvement within the open innovation process requires interaction and disclosure (Gould 2012). Relationship building and engagement stimulates the organisation to access information from its stakeholders (Sharma 2005). This information creates a knowledge transfer that can be used to create tactics that successfully impact operations, profitability and the creation of value. Considering organisational, social and ethical benefits of engagement with relevant stakeholders enhances the concept of open innovation to levels beyond pure practical issues.

2.3 Social Networking as a Tool for Open Innovation

Online social networks are particularly suitable channels for creating value in the light of open innovation (Siakas et al. 2014a). One form of innovation can be reflection in practice by launching prototypes for user tests before the product is launched on the market (Siakas et al. 2012). An emergent opportunity is tapping collective explicit and tacit knowledge and intelligence of users (customers and consumers) by social media networks and thus reaching beyond the conventional boundaries of the organisation (Siakas et al. 2012). The advantage is the leverage of disparate assets of people from different cultures, different disciplines and different organisation. However little research is done so far to clearly indicate how valuable the delivered service is in the end.

Another term used in social networking context is 'crowdsourcing', the act of outsourcing tasks, traditionally performed by an employee or contractor, to a large group of people or community (a crowd), through an open call (Siakas et al. 2014a). Crowdsourcing can be seen as a tool to bring external input into the organisation. Another contemporary word is 'user-driven innovation', which can be considered as a technique in which companies gain insights from users, which can then be used in the innovation process.

The movement of online social networks, which generally refers to communities and hosted services facilitating collaboration and sharing between users, promote the interaction among members by providing a dynamic platform which enables versatile services such as discussions, sharing of multimedia content, organisation of social events and information sharing to name a few. These networks can comprise millions of active members from all continents and from all age groups. Social media is a media for co-creation. When social media is used for social product development, an active, creative and social collaboration process between producers and customers/users takes place, facilitated by a company, in the context of new product or service development. It is important to make a differentiation between customer co-creation and conventional market research in new product development. In market research, companies ask a representative sample of customers for input to their innovation process. In the early stages of an innovation project, customer preferences or unmet needs are identified via surveys, qualitative interviews, or focus groups. In the later stages of an innovation project, different solutions or concepts are presented to customers so they can react to proposed design solutions.

A recent form of market research, without active co-creation, is to analyse existing customer information from diverse input channels, such as feedback from sales people, internet log files, or research reports by third parties (Dahan and Hauser 2002). In this area social media applications have created an enormous additional input cannel. In this context, particularly the method of netnography is noteworthy; "*a new qualitative research methodology that adapts ethnographic research techniques to study cultures and communities that are emerging through computer mediated communications*" (Kozinets 2002).

3 Customer Integration for Obtaining Stakeholder Requirements and Expectations

The literature suggests customer integration (customer involvement) as an important factor for success of innovation (Straub et al. 2013). In particularly service companies, which inherently build on customer interaction, need to appreciate this approach.

Three main factors are considered to have a positive influence by customer involvement, namely:

(i) *Decreased costs* (Boyer et al. 2002; Xue and Harker 2002; Lovelock and Young 1979);
(ii) *Increased customer satisfaction* (Auh et al. 2007);
(iii) *Increased market shares* (Herstatt and von Hippel 1992).

3.1 Customer Job-Roles

There are different job-roles that a customer can adopt when involved in the innovation process of a company. Straub et al. (2013) identified five customer roles that are the most relevant for the industry.

(i) *Service-Specifier:* The customer, who has a precise expectation of what the service should do, specifies the requirements of the service before the service delivery

(Berki et al. 1997). In addition to defining the service, the customer triggers the actual service delivery through his/her actions (Lengnick-Hall 1996).
(ii) *Co-Designer:* The customer assists as an *'organisational consultant'* during decision-making and design processes (Schneider and Bowen 1995). The customer contributes to the creation of new products and services in this role, and the company obtains an early insight into the opinions and preferences of the customer.
(iii) *Co-Producer:* The customer provides input in the form of production factors, such as work, know-how, information, money, etc. The customer acts in a way comparable to a part-time employee of the company during his involvement in the processes (Schneider and Bowen 1995). In the agile approach of software development, for example, the customer is part of the software development team taking actively part in the specification and creation of the service (software in this case) throughout the life-cycle (Siakas and Siakas 2007).
(iv) *Co-Marketer:* The customer supports the marketing of a product or service, particularly through Word-Of-Mouth (WOM) actions. The commercial effect of this can be positive or negative, depending on the satisfaction and experience of the customer with the product or service (Siakas et al. 2014b; Swan and Oliver 1989).
(v) *Quality-Controller:* The customer assists in assuring the quality of production and delivery. This can be achieved e.g. through involvement in testing phases, or through timely and correct feedback for improvements (Zeithaml and Bitner 2003).

The Service-Specifier and Co-Designer are mentioned as two of the most important customer roles in customer integration, particularly in the early phases of service and solution development (Olsen and Welo 2011). In the co-producers job-role the customers/users are partners in the design process. In the agile approach on-site customers, provide scope, set priorities, resolve ambiguities and provide test scenarios. The success of agile practices lies in their flexibility to volatile end-user requirements through intensive informal developer and customer interaction (Siakas and Siakas 2009).

3.2 Customer Value Through Customer Integration

It is generally accepted that the main object of innovation is to create value. However, value manifestations are often complex, temporal and highly context dependent. To create and sustain value, the innovators must not only appreciate the complexity of value, they must also cater for the time-variant and context dependent user conceptions of value (Sheriff et al. 2013). Straub et al. (2013) noticed that the main value derived for the customer in the customer integration process is increased customer satisfaction that subsequently leads to customer loyalty. They conclude that the potential of customer integration in the early phases of the innovation process, also called the ideation process (Siakas et al. 2012), clearly correlate with the level of specialisation and individualisation of the solution. The key features of value from the various conceptualisations can be summarised as follows (Sheriff et al. 2013):

i. Value is a complex and multi-dimensional phenomenon;
ii. Value can be instrumental and/or terminal;
iii. Value is often temporal or time variant;

iv. The sources of value include: the objective characteristics of an object, the subjective disposition or opinion of a subject (perceiver) and the interaction between a subject and an object;
v. Value manifestations are largely context dependent;
vi. Value manifestation at individual user level is often in the form of Conceived value (the user's projection of the potential benefit they might derive from an object), Operative value (the extent to which a user likes or dislikes the content or process of use of an object or service), Object value (approximates to the quality of the object or service, or what it affords the user by virtue of its characteristics) or a combination of these forms of value.

The more involved the customer/user is in the innovation process the more customer value and satisfaction is created (Berki et al. 1997, Siakas et al. 2012). Three customer groups that the organisation needs to deal with have been observed (Straub et al. 2013), namely:

i. Customers that are happy their suggestion was implemented and for whom the new solution offers an actual improvement.
ii. The group of customers that have not been involved in the solution development, but could potentially also benefit from the results.
iii. The group of customers whose suggestions were not integrated into the new developments, or who do not benefit from the new solution, because their needs diverge to a high degree from the needs of the first group of customers.

Customer value is a dynamic concept as it may change over time depending on the situation. Customer value also has to be defined at different abstraction levels. Consequently, it is important to selecting appropriate target customers when designing customer integration programmes.

3.3 Challenges in Customer Integration

From the available literature, we have identified three main challenges that can arise in customer integration:

i. Lack of customer motivation (Siakas and Siakas 2007);
ii. Coordination and control of overhead costs (Straub et al. 2013);
iii. Loss of know-how (Enkel et al. 2005a; 2005b).

To obtain satisfied customers and repeat orders customers/users are usually put first recognising that user satisfaction and fitness for purpose is the ultimate measurement for high quality (Siakas and Siakas 2006). Quality attributes considering the end product is for the user of greatest interest. Thus it is inevitable that the more customer/user involvement in the development and innovation process the higher the possibility for conformance to requirements, fit for purpose and user satisfaction and ultimately quality of end product. However, customer identification can be difficult and may require the identification of suitable internal customer representative(s) providing a single point of contact both for the team and senior management on a daily basis. In this case Social Networking has offered new opportunities to reach out to potential customers.

In development of information systems, customer/user involvement has been identified to improve software quality (Siakas and Siakas 2006; 2007; 2009). In agile development participation is a main key issues. Co-This is due to the intangible nature of software and the difficulties of software professionals to capture and understand the business domain/system requirements. The cyclic and incremental development with high iteration frequency in agile development also provides opportunities for product feedback (Karlström and Runeson 2005). Collective code ownership, pair programming, user involvement and team rotation are examples of participation. The reason for the enthusiastic software developers in agile development seems to be that they have high levels of job satisfaction because of broadened participation and their enthusiasm is an expression of their job satisfaction (Siakas and Siakas 2006).

4 The Connected Customer/User

The model of the customer/user/consumer that is connected is a shift for the company, creating an enterprise that will draw strength by its stakeholders in general and its customers/users in particular. In this approach social networking tools and cooperating technologies are the driving factors of the next generation of productivity and creates a completely different model of leadership (Marks 2009). *"The companies that will manage to use the incredible power of social networking are those who will design an IT architecture capable of supporting the use of these technologies and mitigate the risks that they pose"*.

4.1 The Increased Use of Social Networking Tools

In the CISCO survey (Marks 2009), carried out in 2009 by 105 extensive interviews of 97 organisation in 20 countries around the globe, it was found that social networking tools are being used in mainly core business areas including marketing and communications, human relations, and customer service departments. Within marketing and communications, these tools have already become an integral part of the initiatives of the organisation. It was found that a shift from *"broadcast"* to *"conversational"* communications and rich interactions are taking place.

4.2 Need for Better Management and Involvement of IT in Social Networks

However, only one in seven companies taking part in the CISCO survey (Marks 2009) presented a typical process related to the adoption of social networking tools for the purposes of the business, indicating that potential risks related to social media tools in a business are either neglected or are insufficiently understood.

Only one in five participants identified what tactics are used in the social networking technologies in business. By these results we understand that the control and management of the social media initiatives is difficult; a specific person responsible within the company is needed. Due to the unstructured nature of social networking, companies are still fighting over the creation and the adoption of tactics, as the compliance with a standard governance process by more structured areas (IT for example) often does not work in social networking. Businesses find it difficult to find the appropriate balance between social and personal nature of these tools, while maintaining the business supervision.

Only one in 10 surveyed stated direct involvement of IT in social networking initiatives. Although, the IT department is not typically involved in the decisions regarding use of social media in business, the surveyed acknowledged the need for these tools to be upgraded and properly integrated with existing business processes, to yield the best results and added value.

4.3 The Future of Social Networking and Collaboration Tools in the Business

The online social networking and collaborations tools are here to stay and to evolve to more and more complex social business software; web-based applications for creating online communities that incorporate a broad range of features found in social networking software, community software, and collaboration software. Social business software applications are designed for use in a business context, mainly to supplement or substitute for company intranets in internal instances and, in external instances, to supplement the web properties that companies use to organise their outbound communications. These tools will continue to influence the way that people work and businesses operate. The key for businesses is to adopt and integrate these tools in a controlled manner (Siakas et al. 2014a).

5 Potential Ways of Using Social Media in Business

With regard to business strategy, the social media are used as means for creating corporate image, information, communication and development of relationships with clients (Haythornthwaite 2005). Recently, social networking is increasingly used for reaching out to potential customers in the ideation process of innovation and for valorisation (dissemination and exploitation) of innovative results (Siakas et al. 2012).

Companies that are able make proper use of the social networks can shape their image, develop public relations and create and/or positively influence the discussions taking place around the brand increasing significantly their readability and reliability (Yamada et al. 2012).

Regular users of social media, consider it a great place to find others working in the field, to share and build on information, rather than multiple users reinventing the wheel. Trust and relationships are built with an increased focus on authenticity through regular interaction, whether that is with new external contacts, or for internal communications. Users become adept at adapting to each new system.

5.1 Social Media for Understanding Customer/User Needs

Efficiency of social media lies in the details. The social media platform is a source of information and knowledge; it has a clear identity and gives the user multiple options of interaction. In order to be effective it should be updated frequently.

The social networking applications create a significant number of opportunities and challenges in the business world. In recent years, there is a rapid growth of technological applications based on the logic of social networking on the World Wide Web, affecting the business. New technologies, such as weblogs (blogs), wikis, social labelling (tagging), social networking websites, create opportunities for new ways of intragroup cooperation and knowledge creation, knowledge sharing and knowledge transfer. They change the landscape of providing services but also influence inter-company exchanges, while reshaping existing business applications.

5.2 Social Media for Valorisation

Effective innovation should not only facilitate the creation of value but should also ensure that such value is sustained and shared to its optimum potential. In particular projects consisting of purely research oriented and/or technically oriented partners seem to lack knowledge of the importance of dissemination, exploitation and valorisation for sustainable development (Siakas et al. 2012). Social media in business can also be used for valorisation. Potential outcomes of valorisation include (Siakas et al. 2014b; Georgiadou et al. 2013):

i. Direct interaction and communication with members inside and outside the group;
ii. Horizontal and vertical flow of information;
iii. Strengthened relations and exchange of views;
iv. Development of creativity and openness;
v. Tools for project management and team organisation.

All innovation projects need to valorise their results for maximising achievements and increasing sustainability after their lifetime. This includes transfer of results and best practices to different and broader contexts. Social media is a tool in particular useful for reaching out to different and broader contexts. In order to maximise value of valorisation a meta-framework, called INCUVA was developed by Sheriff et al. (2013) including the following components:

i. Defining and understanding value;
ii. Determining the potential value manifestations;
iii. Understanding the diverse cultural settings in which the innovation would be used;
iv. Developing and adopting effective dissemination strategies and tools (including social media) to optimise the value of the innovation.

The INCUVA meta-framework will help organisations to formulate strategies, policies and actions for maximising the probability of successful innovations and valorisation.

5.3 Practical Issues Regarding Social Media in Business

In the preparation for adopting a suitable social media platform it is important to try to answer the following questions:

i. Vision, aims: What are the objectives and goals of the company - want does it want to achieve?
ii. Target group: What audience will the company focus on?
iii. Resources: What is the capacity of the company? How will technologies be managed and how will they be used by the employees?
iv. Competitors: Who are the main competitors and what do they do?
v. Plan: Which tools and tactics does the company aim to use? When, how and what initiatives should be taken (or not taken)?
vi. Metrics: How will success be measured?

Some practical steps will help answering the questions:

i. Identify the reasons why the company/project is interested/aims to start using social media;
ii. Browse through diverse social media platforms to find their advantages and disadvantages;
iii. Select a suitable platform;
iv. Ensure that adequate technology is available for fast and secure access to cyberspace;
v. Appoint a specific person within the company for daily checking the posts, replying when needed and informing the company about movements on the social media.

In short companies need to investigate different concerns before creating a social media strategy and a content plan. There are several issues that need to be solved, regarding the adoption, development and governance of social networking in business.

5.4 Advantages and Disadvantages of Using Social Media in Business

The main advantages offered by social media in a business are various. Some of them are listed below:

i. Market segmentation based on various criteria such as social, geographical, demographic, ethnic, religious becomes much easier, while the "information" conveys easily and rapidly';
ii. The opportunity offered to the company to approach and appeal to a huge market size, without geographical limitations;
iii. The social networking applications enable a company to constantly offer incentives to consumers, which increases their loyalty to products and services (Kim 2000);
iv. Continuous and easy feedback on the behaviour and consumer satisfaction, which facilitates the research and contributes to the development of business (Kim 2000);
v. The use of social networking tools such as Facebook and Twitter, as collaboration platform brings technology together with businesses, connects people with

information, establishes potential new routes to market and improves customer communication and dissemination of the trademark (Boyd and Ellison 2007);

vi. Company presentation 24 hours circadian throughout the year (Siakas et al. 2014a);
vii. Reduced operating costs (Siakas et al. 2014b);
viii. It is relatively easy to find new staff (Gross and Acquisti 2005).

The business world is in the early stages of adopting these tools and in the process to adopt major challenges, such as the need to manage these tools and the participation of Information and Communication Technology (ICT) that may affect the completion and adoption of new platforms and technologies (Haythornthwaite 2005).

On the other hand social media can act also have a negatively impact on a company (Gross and Acquisti 2005), such as:

i. Consuming of time and subsequent cost involved in the process of informing clients, creating and processing information;
ii. Failure to accept the new application from the company staff as a result of lack of knowledge and skills;
iii. Unsafe environment when publishing information on the Internet;
iv. Negative reviews/publication by customers and competitors;
v. The use of social networking at work can lead to inefficiency of staff.

6 Discussions

The use of social networks by customers/users in the course of their work has the potential to transform the whole world of work. Many well-known companies leverage the connectivity options offered by social media to enhance innovation, productivity, reputation, cooperation, as well as commitment of customers/users (Reffay and Chanier 2003).

More and more companies are discovering the benefits and usefulness of social networks for their innovation practices. Developing new approaches to innovation is no longer just an option for organisations that want to grow and thrive; it is a 21st century imperative. The process of ideation is a key element to any innovation portfolio strategy. Open innovation is about expanding the innovation potential extending the innovation process into new ways of working with external partners. Whether this manifests itself as new collaboration agreements, acquisition of start-ups with contemporary ideas and technologies, or spinning out new developments into external companies the ultimate goal is the same, namely to increase innovation and realise increased value as a result.

As innovations emerge increasingly from inter-organisational cooperation, the background for such cooperation can also have an impact on the involvement of companies into open innovation processes. Open innovation is facilitated by a company with an active innovation strategy in the context of new product or service development. Customers/users are invited to co-creation thus denoting an active, creative and social collaboration process between the company and customers/users. Crowd-sourcing is a contemporary tool for reaching out to potential customers/users for social networking.

The number of companies implementing open innovation and co-creation is steadily growing. However, there is a potential that innovative customers could become a scarce resource in the future, for which companies have to compete in order to get them on-board, thus adding a new side to competition among customers.

7 Conclusion and Further Work

This paper was concentrating on an extensive conceptual literature review through regarding customer/user integration/involvement in the innovation process and its relationship with potential value creation. The open innovation approach was investigated and in particularly different ways of using social media for involving potential user/customers in the innovation process was examined. Further work will concentrate on collecting data from the industry regarding their practical experiences and success stories.

References

Abrahamsson, P.: Project manager's greetings - agile greetings. Agile Newsl. **1**, 1 (2005)

Aranha, E.A., Garcia, N.A.P., Correa, G.: Open innovation and business model: a Brazilian company case study. J. Technol. Manag. Innov. **10**(4), 91–98 (2015)

Auh, S., Bell, S.J., McLeod, C.S., Shih, E.: Co-production and customer loyalty in financial services. J. Retail. **83**(3), 359–370 (2007)

Berki, E., Georgiadou, E., Siakas K.: A methodology is as strong as the user involvement it supports. In: International Symposium on Software Engineering in Universities - ISSEU, 7–9 March 1997, Rovaniemi, pp. 36–51 (1997)

Boyd, D., Ellison, N.B.: Social network sites: definition, history, and scholarship. J. Comput. Mediated Commun. **13**(2), 210–230 (2007)

Boyer, K.K., Hallowell, R., Roth, A.V.: E-services: operating strategy – a case study. J. Oper. Manag. **20**(2), 175–188 (2002)

Sheriff, M., Georgiadou, E., Abeysinghe, G., Siakas, K.: INCUVA: a meta-framework for sustaining the value of innovation in multi-cultural settings. In: McCaffery, F., O'Connor, R.V., Messnarz, R. (eds.) EuroSPI 2013. CCIS, vol. 364, pp. 270–281. Springer, Heidelberg (2013)

Chesbrough, H.W.: Open innovation: the new imperative for creating and profiting from technology. Boston, MA (2003)

Chesbrough, H.W.: Open Services Innovation: Rethinking Your Business to Grow and Compete in a New Era. Jossey-Bass, San Francisco (2011)

Christensen, C.M., Raynor, M.E.: The Innovator's Solution. Harvard Business School Press, Boston (2003)

Chiaroni, D., Chiesa, V., Frattini, F.: The open innovation journal: how firms dynamically implement emerging innovation management paradigm. Technovation **31**(1), 34–43 (2011)

Dahan, E., Hauser, J.R.: The virtual customer. J. Prod. Innov. Manag. **19**(5), 332–353 (2002)

Dahlander, L., Gann, D.M.: How open is innovation? Res. Policy **39**(6), 699–709 (2010)

de Wit, J., Dankbaar, B., Vissers, G.: Open innovation: the new way of knowledge transfer? J. Bus. Chem. **4**(1), 11–19 (2007)

Ebersberger, B., Bloch, C., Herstad, S., Van de Velde, E.: Open innovation practices and their effect on innovation performance. Int. J. Innov. Technol. Manag. **9**(6), 125–140 (2012)

Enkel, E., Perez-Freije, J., Gassmann, O.: Minimizing market risks through customer integration in new product development: learning from bad practice. Authors J. Compilation **14**(4), 425-437 (2005a)

Enkel, E., Kausch, C., Gassmann, O.: Managing the risk of customer integration. Eur. Manag. J. **23**(2), 203–213 (2005b)

Frankenberger, K., Wiblen, T., Gassman, O.: The antecedents of open business models: an exploratory study of incumbents firms. R&D Manag. **44**(2), 173–188 (2014)

Gassman, O., Enkel, E., Chesbrough, H.: The future of open innovation. R&D Manag. **40**(3), 213–221 (2010)

Gay, B.: Open innovation, networking, and business model dynamics: the two sides. J. Innov. Entrepreneurship **3**(2), 1–20 (2014)

Georgiadou, E., McGuinness, C., Siakas, K., Koukourakis, M., Repanovici, A., Khan, N., Rahanu, H.: A framework for quality management of information literacy projects and the role of ICTS. International Journal of Human Capital and Information Technology Professionals (IJHCITP) (2016, in press)

Georgiadou, E., Siakas, K.: VALO^5 – innovation, maturity growth, quality and valorisation. In: McCaffery, F., O'Connor, R.V., Messnarz, R. (eds.) EuroSPI 2013. CCIS, vol. 364, pp. 294–299. Springer, Heidelberg (2013)

Gould, R.W.: Open innovation and stakeholder engagement. J. Technol. Manag. Innov. **7**(3), 1–11 (2012)

Gross, R., Acquisti, A.: Information revelation and privacy in online social networks. In: Proceedings of WPES 2005, pp. 71–80 (2005)

Grönroos, C.: Adopting a service business logic in relational business-to-business marketing: value creation, interaction and joint value co-creation. Otago Forum 2, Academic Papers No. 15, 8–12 December 2008, University of Otago, Dunedin, New Zealand (2008)

Haythornthwaite, C.: Social networks and internet connectivity effects. Inf. Commun. Soc. **8**(2), 125–147 (2005)

Heinonen, K., Strandvik, T., Mickelsson, K.-J., Edvardsson, B., Sundström, E., Andersson, P.: A customer-dominant logic of service. J. Serv. Manag. **21**(4), 531–548 (2010)

Herstatt, C., von Hippel, E.: From experience: developing new product concepts via the lead user method: a case study in a "low-tech" field. J. Prod. Innov. Manag. **9**(3), 213–221 (1992)

Huizingh, E.K.R.E.: Open innovation: state of the art and future perspectives. Technovation **31**(1), 2–9 (2011)

Karlström, D., Runeson, P.: Combining agile methods with stage-gate project management. IEEE Softw. **22**(3), 43–49 (2005)

Kim, A.J.: Community Building on the Web. Peachpit Press, Berkeley (2000)

Kozinets, R.V.: On Netnography: initial reflections on consumer research investigations of cyberculture. In: Alba, J.W., Hutchinson, J.W. (eds.) Advances in Consumer Research, vol. 25, pp. 366–371, Provo (2002)

Kujala, S.: User involvement: a review of the benefits and challenges. Behav. Inf. Technol. **22**, 1–17 (2003)

Laursen, K., Salter, A.: Open for innovation: the role of openness in explaining innovation performance among UK manufacturing firms. Strat. Manag. J. **27**(2), 131–150 (2006)

Lengnick-Hall, C.A.: Customer contributions to quality: a different View of the customer-oriented firm. Acad. Manag. Rev. **21**(3), 791–824 (1996)

Lewrick, M., Omar, M., Williams Jr., R.L.: Market orientation and innovators' success: an exploration of the influence of customer and competitor orientation. J. Technol. Manag. Innov. **6**(3), 49–61 (2011)

Lovelock, C.H., Young, R.F.: Look to customers to increase productivity. Harv. Bus. Rev. **57**(3), 168–178 (1979)

Lukas, B., Ferrell, O.: The effect of market orientation on product innovation. J. Acad. Mark. Sci. **28**(2), 239–247 (2000)

Mahr, D., Rindfleisch, A., Slotegraaf, R.J.: Innovation beyond firm boundaries: the routines and resource investment of successful external problem solvers. In: American Marketing Association Winter Educators' Conference, 19–22 February 2010, New Orleans, LA (2010). http://ebookbrowse.com/rindfleisch-background-paper-march-2010-pdf-d138594519. Accessed 2 Mar 2016

Marks, O.: 3rd party external social media research findings article published by Cisco (2009). http://www.zdnet.com/blog/collaboration/cisco-2009-3rd-party-external-social-media-research-findings/1289. (visited 19 Mar 2015)

Michel, S., Brown, S.W., Gallan, A.S.: Service-logic innovations: how to innovate customers, not products. Calif. Manag. Rev. **50**(3), 49–65 (2008)

Overvik Olsen, T., Welo, T.: Maximizing product innovation through adaptive application of user-centered methods for defining customer value. J. Technol. Manag. Innov. **6**(4), 172–191 (2011)

Prahalad, C.K., Ramaswamy, V.: The co-creation connection. Strat. Bus. 114–127 (2002)

Reffay, C., Chanier, T.: How social network analysis can help to measure cohesion in collaborative distance learning, designing for change in networked learning environments. In: Proceeding of the International Support for Collaborative Learning, vol. 3, pp. 343–352 (2003)

Saebi, T., Foss, N.: Business models for open innovation: matching heterogeneous open innovation strategies with business model dimensions. Eur. Manag. J. **33**(3), 201–213 (2014)

Sanders, E.: Information, inspiration and co-creation. In: 6th International Conference of the European Academy of Design, University of the Arts, Bremen, Germany (2005)

Savitskaya, I., Salmi, P., Torkkeli, M.: Barriers to open innovation: case China. J. Technol. Manag. Innov. **5**(4), 10–21 (2010)

Schneider, B., Bowen, D.E.: Winning the Service Game. Harvard Business School Press, Boston (1995)

Sharma, S.: Through the lens of managerial interpretations: stakeholder engagement, organisation knowledge and innovation. In: Sharma, S., Aragón-Correa, J.A. (eds.) Environmental Strategy and Competitive Advantage, pp. 49–70. Edward Elgar Academic Publishing, Northampton (2005)

Shostack, G.L.: Understanding services through blueprinting. Adv. Serv. Mark. Manag. **1**(1), 75–90 (1992)

Siakas, K., Kermizidis R., Kontos K.: Using social media in business as a tool for open innovations. In: Business-Related Scientific Research Conference 2014 (ABSRC 2014), 10–12 December 2014, Milan, Italy (2014a)

Siakas, K.V., Belidis, A., Siakas, E.: Social media marketing for improved branding and valorisation in small family businesses. In: International Conference on Contemporary Marketing Issues (ICCMI 2014), 18–20 June 2014, Athens, Greece, pp. 764–772 (2014b). ISBN:978-960-287-145-4

Siakas, K., Messnarz, R., Georgiadou, E., Naaranoja, M.: Launching innovation in the market requires competences in dissemination and exploitation. In: Winkler, D., O'Connor, R.V., Messnarz, R. (eds.) EuroSPI 2012. CCIS, vol. 301, pp. 241–252. Springer, Heidelberg (2012)

Siakas, K., Siakas, E.: Agile software development in distributed environments. In: Industrial Stream of the 16th European Software Process Improvement (EuroSPI 2009), 2–4 September 2009, Alcala, Madrid, Spain, pp. 8.19–8.31 (2009)

Siakas, K., Siakas, E.: The agile professional culture: a source of agile quality. Softw. Process Improv. Pract. (SPIP) J. **12**(6), 597–610 (2007). Wiley

Siakas, K., Siakas, E.: The human factor deployment for improved agile quality. In: Tukianen, M., Messnards, R., Nevalaninen, R., Koining, S. (eds) European Software Process Improvement and Innovation (EuroSPI 2006). International Proceedings Series 6, 11–13 October 2006, Joensuu, Finland, pp. 4.11–4.23, University of Joensuu (2006)

Siakas K.V., Georgiadou E.: The role of commitment for successful software process improvement and software quality management. In: The 11th Software Quality Management Conference, SQM2003, 23–25 April 2013, Glasgow, UK, pp. 101–113 (2003)

Spiteri, J.M., Dion, P.A.: Customer value, overall satisfaction, end-user loyalty, and market performance in detail intensive industries. Ind. Mark. Manag. **33**(2004), 657–687 (2004)

Straub, T., Kohler, M., Hottum, P., Arrass, V., Welter, D.: Customer integration in service innovation: an exploratory study. J. Technol. Manag. Innov. **8**(3), 25–33 (2013)

Swan, J.E., Oliver, R.L.: Postpurchase communications by consumers. J. Retail. **65**(4), 516–533 (1989)

Teece, D.: Explicating dynamic capabilities: the nature and microfoundations of (sustainable) enterprise performance. Strat. Manag. J. **28**(13), 1319–1350 (2007)

Tidd, J., Bessant, J., Pavitt, K.: Managing Innovation, Integrating Technological, Market and Organisational Change, 2nd edn. Wiley, West Sussex (2001)

Ulwick, A.W.: Turn customer input into innovation. Harv. Bus. Rev. **80**(1), 91–97 (2002)

Van de Ven, A.H., Polley, D.E., Garud, R., Venkataraman, S.: The Innovation Journey. Oxford University Press, New York (2008)

Vargo, S.L., Lusch, R.F.: Evolving to a new dominant logic for marketing. J. Mark. **68**, 1–17 (2004)

Vargo, S.L., Lusch, R.F.: Service-dominant logic: what it is, what it is not, what it might be. In: Lusch, R.F., Vargo, S.L. (eds.) The Service Dominant Logic of Marketing – Dialog, Debate, and Directions, pp. 3–28. M.E. Sharpe, Armonk (2006)

Veryzer, R.W., de Mozota, B.B.: The impact of user-oriented design on new product development: an examination of fundamental relationships. J. Prod. Innov. Manag. **22**, 128–143 (2005)

Wadhaw, A., Bodas-Fritas, I.M., Sarkar, M.B.: The paradox of being open: external technology sourcing and knowledge protection. In: The Dynamics of Institutions and Markets (DIME) Final Conference, 6–8 April 2011, Maastricht, Netherlands (2011). http://final.dime-eu.org/files/BodasFreitas_etal_E3.pdf. Accessed 2 Mar 2016

Weiblen, T.: The open business model: understanding an emergent concept. J. Multi Bus. Model Innov. Technol. **2**(1), 35–66 (2014)

Wynstra, F., Axelsson, B., van der Valk, W.: An application-based classification to understand buyer-supplier interaction in business services. Int. J. Serv. Ind. Manag. **17**(5), 474–496 (2006)

Xue, M., Harker, P.T.: Customer efficiency – concept and its impact on e-business management. J. Serv. Res. **4**(4), 253–267 (2002)

Yamada, A., Kim, T.H.-J., Perrig, A.: Exploiting privacy policy conflicts in online social networks, pp. 1–9, CMU CYlab 12-005 (2012). https://www.cylab.cmu.edu/files/pdfs/tech_reports/CMUCyLab12005.pdf. Visited 20 Mar 2015

Zeuthaml, V.A., Bitner, M.J.: Service Marketing: Integrating Customer Focus across the Firm, 3rd edn. McGrawHill College, Boston (2003)

Author Index

Atasoy, Berke 203

Barafort, Béatrix 83, 106
Biffl, Stefan 163
Biró, Miklós 94
Boersma, Sebastiaan 259
Brenner, Eugen 148

Calafat, Antoni Lluís Mesquida 47
Clarke, Paul M. 47, 132, 203
Colomo-Palacios, Ricardo 3, 234
Cortina, Stéphane 83, 106

Durón, Brenda 312

Ekert, Damjan 47, 259
Ekstrom, J.J. 47

Gaisch, Monika 176
Gasca-Hurtado, Gloria Piedad 212, 312
Gmeiner, Johannes 94
Gómez-Alvarez, María Clara 212, 312
Gommans, Ron 259
Gornostaja, Tatjana 47

Herranz, Eduardo 3, 234
Höller, Andrea 119

Iber, Johannes 119
Illibauer, Christa 94
Ito, Masao 58

Johansen, Jørn 47
Jovanovic, Milos 47, 225

Klespitz, József 94
Kollenhof, Monique 259
Kosa, Mehmet 242
Kovács, Levente 94
Kreiner, Christian 119, 148, 176

Laporte, Claude Y. 15, 30
Larrucea, Xabier 269

Mac an Airchinnigh, Micheal 281
Macher, Georg 148
Martens, Jean-Bernard 203
Mas, Antònia 47, 225
McCaffery, Fergal 132
Mejía, Jezreel 70, 212, 312
Menaceur, Jamil 15
Mergen, Silvana 269
Mesquida, Antoni-Lluís 225
Messnarz, Richard 47, 176, 251, 259, 293
Muñoz, Mirna 70, 212, 312
Musil, Angelika 163
Musil, Juergen 163

Nevalainen, Risto 132

O'Connor, Alexander 47
O'Connor, Rory V. 3, 30, 47, 132, 203

Pekki, Jaana 188
Peña, Adriana 70
Picard, Michel 83, 106
Poliquin, Denis 15

Rangel, Nora 70
Rauter, Tobias 119
Reimann, Christian 302
Reiner, Michael 47, 293, 302
Renault, Alain 83, 106
Riel, Andreas 176, 251, 259, 293
Rodic, Miran 176, 251

Sanchez-Gordón, Mary-Luz 3, 234
Sauberer, Gabriele 47, 293
Schmitz, Klaus-Dirk 47
Siakas, Dimitrios 325

Siakas, Kerstin   325
Sporer, Harald   148
Stolfa, Jakub   176, 251
Stolfa, Svatopluk   176, 251

Tichkiewitch, Serge   176
Tremblay, Nicolas   15

Varkoi, Timo   132
Villar, Blanca Nájera   47
Vitkauskaite, Elena   302

Walker, Alastair   269
Winkler, Dietmar   163

Yilmaz, Murat   47, 203, 242

MIX
Papier aus verantwortungsvollen Quellen
Paper from responsible sources
FSC® C105338

If you have any concerns about our products,
you can contact us on
ProductSafety@springernature.com

In case Publisher is established outside the EU,
the EU authorized representative is:
**Springer Nature Customer Service Center GmbH
Europaplatz 3, 69115 Heidelberg, Germany**

Printed by Libri Plureos GmbH
in Hamburg, Germany